The Novel and the New Ethics

Post•45 Florence Dore, Loren Glass, and Kate Marshall, Editors
Post•45 Group, Editorial Committee

The Novel and the New Ethics

Dorothy J. Hale

Stanford University Press
Stanford, California

STANFORD UNIVERSITY PRESS
Stanford, California

©2020 by the Board of Trustees of the Leland Stanford Junior University. All rights reserved.

Parts of Chapter 3 were original published as "*On Beauty* as Beautiful? The Problem of Novelistic Aesthetics by Way of Zadie Smith," *Contemporary Literature* 53.4 (2012): 814–844. © 2012 by the Board of Regents of the University of Wisconsin System. Reprinted courtesy of the University of Wisconsin Press.

Parts of Chapter 5 were originally published as "Aesthetics and the New Ethics: Theorizing the Novel in the Twenty-First Century," *PMLA* 124.3 (March 2009): 896–905. Reprinted by permission of the copyright owner, the Modern Language Association of America (www.mla.org).

No part of this book may be reproduced or transmitted in any form or by any means, electronic or mechanical, including photocopying and recording, or in any information storage or retrieval system without the prior written permission of Stanford University Press.

Printed in the United States of America on acid-free, archival-quality paper

Library of Congress Cataloging-in-Publication Data
Names: Hale, Dorothy J., author.
Title: The novel and the new ethics / Dorothy J. Hale.
Other titles: Post 45.
Description: Stanford, California : Stanford University Press, 2020. | Series: Post 45 | Includes bibliographical references and index.
Identifiers: LCCN 2020013816 (print) | LCCN 2020013817 (ebook) | ISBN 9780804794053 (cloth) | ISBN 9781503614062 (paperback) | ISBN 9781503614079 (epub)
Subjects: LCSH: Fiction—Moral and ethical aspects. | Fiction—20th century—History and criticism. | Fiction—21st century—History and criticism. | Other (Philosophy) in literature.
Classification: LCC PN3347 .H26 2020 (print) | LCC PN3347 (ebook) | DDC 808.3—dc23
LC record available at https://lccn.loc.gov/2020013816
LC ebook record available at https://lccn.loc.gov/2020013817

Cover design: Kevin Barrett Kane

Typeset by Kevin Barrett Kane in 10/15 Minion Pro

For Jeffrey and Madeline

Contents

Preface ix

Acknowledgments xix

1	The New Ethics and Contemporary Fiction	1
2	Henry James and the Development of the Novelistic Aesthetics of Alterity	47
3	Zadie Smith's *On Beauty*: An Ethical Aesthetic as the Problem of Perspectivalism	96
4	J. M. Coetzee's *Elizabeth Costello*: The Tradition as the Sum of Its Parts	135
5	The New Ethics in the Academy: The Lesson of the Master, the Master as the Lesson	173
	Coda: Henry James in the Clinician's Office	218

Notes 231

Bibliography 285

Index 309

Preface

This book argues that over the course of the twentieth century writers and readers have increasingly understood the art of the novel as an ethics of otherness. The chapters that follow investigate the literary history that helps consolidate this Anglo-American conception of the novel's generic nature. Key to this literary history is the link between the century's end and its beginning: the contemporary novelist's explicit appreciation for and engagement with modernist modes of narration fortify the contemporary novelist's equally explicit ethical project. While the current investment in ethics establishes a new and significant period in the novel's history through the break it stages with postmodernism, the turn to the new is performed as an attempt to return, recapture, restore literature's lost (or at a minimum, its floundering) cultural prestige. *The Novel and the New Ethics* seeks to illuminate how the felt need in the present moment to revivify the social relevance of literature sparks a new ethical description of the novel's particular social value that is rooted in the modernist notion of narrative form.

My use of the term "new ethics" thus emphasizes the relation between two different historical moments in the Anglo-American novel's cultural re-newal. There is first of all the modern novelists' sense that they had discovered a new truth about the novel as genre: that the novel had narrative modes particular to it that could be the basis of an aesthetics, that could win it cultural prestige as an art form. But as this book seeks to show, in a way that modern novelists point to but do not fully theorize, the modernist understanding of novel form also assumes that novelistic narrative entails a necessary ethics. This is the first "new" ethical moment for the art of the novel. The second moment comes at century's end with the contemporary novelist's desire to re-new the age-old conversation about literature's ethical value. An engagement with phenomenological and poststructuralist philosophies of the self is the sign of the new in contemporary ethical inquiry. While the philosophical language of contemporary ethical thought does indeed offer late-twentieth-century novelists a new vocabulary for describing the novel's art of otherness, I argue that the modernist notion of the novel's narrative ethics so powerfully structures the representational strategies of new ethical novels that contemporary philosophical notions about ethical value intensify and complexify rather than supersede or significantly depart from the modern novelist's ethical project. The work of this book is to analyze the relation between these two "new" ethical moments in the Anglo-American novel's literary history, and the chapters that follow explore the relation between the implied ethical value that modernists attributed to novelistic narrative and the explicit pursuit of a new ethical defense of literary value undertaken by contemporary novelists.

I can't state too often that this is not a book that seeks to prove that reading fiction makes us better people. My resistance to such monolithic accounts of literary effects in fact spurred my inquiry into novelistic ethics. I also remain skeptical about the recent findings of sociological and neurological studies that seem to me weak on empirical evidence and overly generalizing in their proclamations about the ethical value of novel reading.[1] In their desire to assert the unambiguous ethical good of novel reading—the usual finding is that fiction makes its readers more empathetic or altruistic—social scientists reproduce and thereby reinforce the sidelining of literary history practiced by many contemporary academic theorists and literary critics. As I show in Chapter 5, new ethical philosophers and theorists make the case for the absolute ethical value of literature by editing out the novel's own critical and creative investigation of that idea.[2]

By drawing together work by modern and contemporary fiction writers, as I do in this book, I lay out the novelistic terms in which the contemporary cultural desire for a literary ethics of otherness has been cast. But to say that these creative writers make the case for ethical value is not also to say that novelists prove the case for ethics in a way that academic theorists and researchers do not. In other words, I am not arguing that we should critique the academic claims for the novel's ethical value—whether espoused by sociologists, psychologists, philosophers, or literary critics—and embrace the truth that only novelists know. The novelists with whom I engage offer their nonfictional ideas about ethics as philosophical propositions, theoretical claims, or personal testimonials. These are exhortative, sometimes anecdotal, meant to be logically or rhetorically persuasive rather than factually verifiable. *The Novel and the New Ethics* does not attempt to adjudicate among the ethical defenses of literary value, philosophical or literary, with the goal of settling the debate by putting forward the "right" theory of novelistic ethics. What concerns this book more specifically is the fact that the exceptionalist claims made for the ethical value of the novel, claims that were for two centuries the primary justification in the Anglo-American tradition for the writing and reading of novels, have developed through the twentieth century and now into our own moment into a popular assumption about the novel's superior social value as a literary form. By calling attention to the connection between contemporary and modernist notions of novelistic ethics, this book helps to explain the dawning awareness in our own cultural moment, to which this book contributes, that the genre that was thought for two centuries to be distinguished by its lack of form is now not only fully admired for the complexity of its narrative resources but has gained cultural preeminence as a literary form precisely to the degree that its aesthetic richness is believed to entail ethical enrichment.[3] It is this long twentieth-century literary tradition that I call attention to with the descriptor "the novelistic aesthetics of alterity."

The novel's protean nature has always posed unique problems for developing a theory of the art of the novel. Whereas a haiku or even an epic can be defined in formal terms (e.g., as having so many syllables, as beginning in medias res), and whereas a genre such as lyric has been equated with an epitomizing rhetorical practice (e.g., apostrophe), I argue that the novel became recognizable and appreciable as a literary form only when that form was understood as laden with ethical meaning.[4] In other words, modern novelists could describe the novel's defining formal qualities when the signature feature of novel content—the ethical drama enacted in the novel's storyworld—became the distinguishing feature of its narrative form.[5] The modernists, in pursuit of transforming the novel into high art, do not simply "discover" the elements of novelistic form; they stabilize the genre by making normative its narrative nature. When ethical content can be allied with an ethics of form, the novel emerges as an appreciable aesthetic creation. What the novel's literary history can show us is how the novelist's ongoing engagement not just with ethics but with the problem of ethics propels the tradition forward, intensifying and complicating the storyworld investigation of ethical meaning as well as the possible values ascribable to narrative. My aim is to describe why otherness emerges as the key ethical stake for novelistic representation and how the task of representing otherness is worked out as a formal problem by strong novels in the tradition. Literary history thus brings to light both the aesthetic intensity that is derived by freighting narrative with complex and often competing ethical stakes, as well as the contingency of novelistic ethics regarded as a formal project.

Of course, the modern novelists who are most devoted to the aesthetic project of elevating the novel to a high art form—writers such as Henry James, James Joyce, Virginia Woolf, and William Faulkner—strongly reject the notion that any aspect of their artistic practice should be regulated by prevailing social arbiters of the *moral* good.[6] These fiction writers associate morality with the didactic use of literature, which they believe instills hegemonic social values under the cover of care for the general public good.[7] Thus it is certainly true that the twentieth century positions its notion of the art of the novel against the nineteenth century's view of the novel as valuable for the social good it can accomplish, and that, so it was judged at the time of their publication, some novels—by Stowe, Dickens, Eliot, but also countless others—did accomplish. But while it is a commonplace that the twentieth century newly imagined the art of the novel as a matter of form, *The Novel and the New Ethics* seeks to demonstrate that twentieth-century novelists break with an older view of novelistic ethics precisely by installing ethics as an aspect of novelistic narrative. The twentieth-century discovery of novel form ushers in the realization that the lives of characters are bound to the narrative techniques used to represent them, and thus the ethics of otherness begins with debates about beneficial or deleterious storyworld action and exemplars becoming increasingly intertwined with assumptions about the success or failure of narrative technique to do justice to the personhood of characters.

The Anglo-American novelistic aesthetics of alterity can be exemplified by the difference between George Eliot and Henry James—the difference between two novelists, both supremely concerned with ethical behavior, both masters of narrative composition, but only one concerned with developing a theory of novelistic form. As I have argued in *Social Formalism*, James inaugurates the novelistic ethics of alterity through his theory of point of view. The Jamesian notion of point of view subjectifies novel form by equating the representation of characterological personhood with a particular narrative resource.[8] The novelistic ethics that develops out the subjectification of novel form situates the author's act of composition as an ethical encounter with the fictional life that is their task to bring into being. The success or failure of the author's endeavor sets the possibilities for the encounter with other lives that is available to the novel reader. For the

Jamesian literary tradition, the novel's social value need not be measured by the stance it takes on world historical events such as the American Civil War (*Uncle Tom's Cabin*) or civic goods such as prison reform (*Oliver Twist*): the ethics of alterity that is believed to inhere in novel form means that the social value that the novel as a genre is equipped to accomplish can be obtained through what are regarded as the ethical acts of novel reading and writing. The encounter with fictional modes of otherness that takes place in and through novels counts in this tradition as real ethical experience.

The argument of *The Novel and the New Ethics* thus builds on my earlier study of the development of Anglo-American novel theory in the twentieth century while also extending the reach of that argument by showing how an ethics of narrative guides the creative practice of novel writing in the Anglo-American tradition. In *Social Formalism* I develop the notion of the Jamesian art of the novel as an ethical project and explore the way that view persists within the theoretical account of novel form that grows up in the twentieth century. Uncovering the implied ethics of alterity that unite, on the one hand, political thinkers such as Roland Barthes and Henry Louis Gates, and, on the other hand, narratologists such as Gerard Genette with theorists of the novel who explicitly argued for the novel's ethical nature (Henry James and M. M. Bakhtin), I argue that this comparative approach to theories of the novel allows us to attend to the pseudomaterial properties (language, text, figuration) that the social formalist tradition credits with the power to fix and instantiate social relations as aspects of narrative form.[9]

The Novel and the New Ethics takes on board the findings of this earlier project to explore how the Jamesian notion of the art of the novel drives James's own novelistic practice—which in turn influences the Anglo-American understanding of novelistic aesthetics as a narrative ethics of alterity. As I focus on twentieth- and twenty-first-century novelists and theorists who explicitly advocate for the ethical value of literature, I am once again interested in drawing out untheorized assumptions about novel form. Because the literary tradition I am investigating here is temporally coordinate with the tradition of novel theory mapped in *Social Formalism*, the privileging of materiality remains at issue, especially when I turn in Chapter 5 to the academic theorists who take up the banner of the new ethical defense of literature. But in my current focus on the literary development of the Jamesian ethical aesthetic, I am most interested in the congruence between the narrative effects prized by modernists and those embraced by contemporary novelists. In this regard, I find that novel theory often helps me articulate ethical issues that claim the attention of modernist and contemporary novelists alike. What effect does the story/discourse model have in projecting characters—and the social world of the novel more generally—as an ontological autonomy? Why should contemporary theorists be interested in discerning how narratorial mediation and omniscience operate on a granular level of narrative representation, and what might be the modernist source for that view? What is the ethical value of working with a theory that calibrates the degrees and distribution of characterological opacity or knowability? How for different authors does narrative seem to function as an instrument of characterological oppression? How does novelistic realism work to establish spatial autonomies? Why are narrative and novel theory not interested in the problem of stylistic beauty? These are the kinds of questions that build out from the notion of novel form undertaken in *Social Formalism*.

To propose that the aesthetics of alterity names a significant literary tradition that has coherence and force is not to imply that all twentieth-century novels contribute to this tradition, nor is it to suggest that all novels that belong to the tradition make an equally powerful contribution to the theory and practice of the aesthetics of alterity. In limning the tradition, I focus on novelists for whom the ethical representation of the personhood of fictional characters is a grounding narrative task. In this regard, there are certainly lines of affinity between the Jamesian tradition and the twentieth-century tradition of metafiction. For example, when the narrator of *The French Lieutenant's Woman* (1969) interrupts his realist enterprise to offer a disquisition on the ontology of fiction, and even more particularly when he writes that "It is only when our characters and events begin to disobey us that they begin to live," John Fowles is positioning the novel's art of "world making" as an ethics of otherness.[10] But in their metafictional projects modernists such as Flann O'Brien and Samuel Beckett and postmodernists such as Thomas Pynchon and Ishmael Reed are either less explicitly concerned with the ethics of novel form or actively dismissive of ethics as a category of literary value. The oeuvre of J. M. Coetzee serves as a particularly exciting example of how the priority given to narrative ethics in the contemporary moment forges a strong connection between the antirealist novel tradition and the Jamesian novel of character. In my analysis of *Elizabeth Costello* (2003), I show not only how the aesthetics of alterity expands into a self-conscious and all-encompassing theme for the contemporary novel, but also how a writer who absorbs so much from Russian and European antirealist traditions (especially Dostoevsky and Kafka) comes to see the metafictional inquiry into the other state of being that fiction might represent as a facet of the novel's generic capacity for the ethical representation of states of being different from the author's own.

Without question, there are plenty of twentieth-century novels of character that do not approach novelistic narrative as an ethical task. A writer such as Philip Roth, for example, although profoundly influenced by Henry James (as evidenced by the protagonist of *Letting Go* whose dissertation is on *The Portrait of a Lady*), carries forward the nineteenth-century practice of reportage to which Virginia Woolf so strongly objected. Alternatively, a strong example of a counteraesthetic to the ethics of alterity can be located in the Proustian tradition. Proust's use of first-person narration signals his diminished investment in a narrative ethics of alterity, which is bolstered by the epistemology articulated in *À la recherche du temps perdu*, a philosophy of personhood significantly different from the phenomenology of ethics I describe. Marcel relates his idea of novelistic character to a more general philosophical conception of what might be called an emotional epistemology:

> None of the feelings which the joys or misfortunes of a "real" person arouse in us can be awakened except through a mental picture of those joys or misfortunes; and the ingenuity of the first novelist lay in his understanding that, as the image was the one essential element in the complicated structure of our emotions, so that simplification of it which consisted in the suppression, pure and simple, of "real" people would be a decided improvement. A "real" person, profoundly as we may sympathise with him, is in a great measure perceptible only through our senses, that is to say, remains opaque, presents a dead weight which our sensibilities have not the strength to lift. If some misfortune comes to him, it is only in one small section of the complete idea we have of him that we are capable of feeling any emotion; indeed it is only in one small section of the complete idea he has of himself that he is capable of feeling any emotion either. The novelist's happy discovery was to think of substituting for those opaque sections, impenetrable to the human soul, their equivalent in immaterial sections, things, that is, which one's soul can assimilate.[11]

Marcel's aesthetics of substitution steers the novelistic theory of character away from ethical phenomenology and toward affective assimilation. And even though, as Gérard Genette has discussed, Proust's handling of free indirect discourse (which he keeps to a minimum) and characterological speech (which he objectivizes) are on a continuum with the Jamesian project, the notion that fiction represents the complexity of persons best when they are rendered by "equivalent immaterial sections" is a step in the direction of abstraction that significantly moves Proust's idea of novel reading and writing away from the realm of ethics and into a psychological theory of apprehension, the "purely mental state" of emotional intensity that allows fictional characters to "appear to us in the guise of truth."[12] For Proust, the novel is not about degrees of autonomy or singularity to which characters have a right but about the shareability of highly specific literary emotions that seem other only because they have not been experienced before by a particular reader.

But whereas Proust's epistemology has always been discussed in terms of an aesthetic sensibility, my aim in offering an intensive analysis of a few strong novels is to describe the aesthetic intensity that the pursuit of ethics confers on the novel in the Anglo-American Jamesian tradition. Chapters 1 and 2 strive to balance this intensive focus with a synthetic overview of the lines of connection between the modern and the contemporary ethical project. While this procedure seems the right one for a book that strives to identify and analyze the primary features of a literary tradition, I also hope it creates interest in future work that might expand and deepen my account of the novelistic aesthetics of alterity. On the one hand, there is opportunity for more intensive engagement with the full oeuvre of the novelists I discuss. On the other hand, there are modern and contemporary writers whom I don't discuss but who might be good candidates for inclusion. For example, my account in Chapter 2 of the tradition's development through the British line might be matched by attention to an American line that would focus on *Winesburg, Ohio* (1919); *Cane* (1923); and *Their Eyes Were Watching God* (1937). Certainly, Toni Morrison has Toomer in mind as much as she has James, Woolf, and William Faulkner—and in *On Beauty* Zadie Smith pays homage not only to E. M. Forster and Iris Murdoch but also, in naming the Beasley daughter Zora, to Zora Neale Hurston. Smith's rapturous essay on Hurston gets pride of place in *Changing My Mind* (2009), and the story Smith tells in that essay (about how, at the age of fourteen, reading *Their Eyes Were Watching God* transformed her notion of what novelistic style might and should be) has been linked to her own name change—from Sadie to Zadie—also at the age of fourteen.[13] The narrative ethics that inform the representation of social otherness as a domestic condition of US life might be investigated through the formal experiments of Jennifer Egan's *A Visit from the Goon Squad* (2010) and Tommy Orange's *There There* (2018), while the global dimensions of social otherness are addressed in the narrative management of a host of novels, including Nadine Gordimer's *July's People* (1981), Jessica Hagedorn's *Dogeaters* (1990), David Mitchell's *Ghostwritten* (1999), Junot Díaz's *The Brief Wondrous Life of Oscar Wao* (2007), and Phil Klay's *Redeployment* (2015). My working sense is that some of these novels more successfully engage the problematic nature of ethical otherness as a narrative mode, but even those that take for granted the novel's narrative power to do justice to states of being different from the author's own help consolidate the cultural view of the novel's superior social value as a literary form.

By concluding my study with the new ethical defenses of literary value mounted from within the academy, I aim to show how contemporary assumptions about the novel's ethics of alterity have established a pedagogic norm—that readers/students of literature should be trained to read for the ethical experience they provide—as well as an impassable disagreement among critics about which narrative modes best deliver the experience of ethical otherness to the reader. Through the influence of the new ethical theorists whom I discuss in Chapter 5, reading for narrative ethics regrounds literary study as an academic discipline, a discipline tied to readerly self-discipline. It is now generally assumed that to read a novel rightly—*any* novel—is to decode the ethical values that are taken for granted to inhere in novelistic narrative. Although anyone reading a novel can appreciate the difficulty the genre takes up when it seeks to represent a variety of social types, especially types different from the author's social identity, in the classroom reading for ethics becomes a specialized skill that requires training in the decoding of narrative form. As I have stated, I describe this ethics as an aesthetics because I take seriously the disconnect between, on the one hand, the unprovable claims made by academic philosophers, theorists, critics, and the novelists themselves for the ethical power of literature in general and the novel in particular, and, on the other, the verifiable cultural practice that novels are read for and judged in regard to the ethics that are believed to inhere in their narrative practices. In other words, even if readers remain ethically untouched by the act of reading a novel, they have come to regard the act of novel reading to be one of detecting the ethical values that inhere in novelistic narrative.

Again, I want to emphasize that, in an affinity for the novels I study, my aim is not to attempt to refute, correct, or refine new ethical arguments by approaching them with a commitment to a particular philosophical tradition. I do not, for example, recommend that Wayne Booth and Martha Nussbaum, self-described Aristotelians, become Kantians or deconstructionists—or that J. Hillis Miller and Gayatri Spivak become Aristotelians. Instead, in my concluding chapter I am interested to show how theorists who disagree philosophically about the meaning and nature of ethics all agree that certain features of novelistic narrative offer the reader an ethical encounter with otherness, an encounter that begins with a writerly or readerly act of self-restriction. And for an overwhelming number of these new ethical theorists, the novelist who provides the master lesson in the narrative art of otherness is Henry James.

Acknowledgments

The argument of this book has come to fruition through the ongoing support and intellectual contribution of many dear friends and colleagues, some close at hand and others far flung. Victoria Kahn, Jeffrey Knapp, Samuel Otter, Nancy Ruttenburg, and Cindy Weinstein all have been constant companions and sources of inspiration, meeting my ideas with enabling care and scholarly expertise. I owe to Nancy the path of inquiry that followed her question, now many years ago, "Have you read J. M. Coetzee?" And to Vicky, the door that opened when at a key moment she asked, "Have you thought of changing the order of your chapters?" Jeff, Cindy, and Sam have heard about or read every word. Their generous responses and unflagging faith have made the whole project possible. To say more would still not be to say enough to express all my gratitude.

To Florence Dore, I also am happily indebted. She has believed in this project from the first, offered her tremendous critical powers in service of its completion, and also lent her practical powers as past series editor at Stanford University Press to help bring the book to fruition. I can't thank the press enough for its ongoing support. Christine Gever, Jessica Ling, Faith Wilson Stein, and Erica Wetter have been an author's dream team. I am also especially grateful to the press for finding anonymous readers who so generously and substantively engaged with the book manuscript.

At Berkeley, I have benefited profoundly from the opportunities to share work in progress, particularly through events sponsored by the Doreen Townsend Center for the Humanities and the Berkeley Consortium for the Study of the Novel. I am especially grateful to Charles Altieri and Susan Maslan, organizers of The Experience of Value, a Townsend Center Strategic Working Group that enabled me to develop my thinking about J. M. Coetzee in conversation with Dan

Blanton, Whitney Davis, Robert Kaufman, Niko Kolodny, and Kate Van Orden. Through the Townsend Center's fellowship group and works-in-progress faculty group, I received enormously helpful insights from Whitney's continued engagement with the project and from Alan Tansman, Paula Versano, and Sophie Volpp. The writing group of two that Sophie and I formed fueled the last lap of the manuscript's completion.

I have been fortunate to have a team of dedicated and talented research assistants over the years. I hope they will be happy to see how their excellent work has made all the difference for the project. Deep thanks to Joseph Jeon and Erin Edwards (for research at the earliest stage), Alex Catchings, Jason De Stefano, Marta Figlerowicz, Taylor Johnston, Max Sala, and Adeline Tran—and much gratitude to Maia Rodriguez for seeing the manuscript through production. I'm also grateful to the Berkeley English Department for course assignments that have allowed me to bring my research into the classroom, where I could think through ideas in lively conversation with my undergraduate and graduate students. All my dissertation students have made me smarter. I am indebted to their published work, which advances so many of our shared research interests, and for the ongoing dialogue we share.

Throughout my career, my work has been greatly inspired by my involvement with members of the International Society for the Study of Narrative. I have benefited especially from the society's openness to new ideas and modes of inquiry, which has generated leading-edge work in the field. For the opportunity to think through arguments specifically related to this project, particular thanks are due to Paul Dawson, Susan Snaider Lanser, and James Phelan. Robert Caserio, David James, Henrik Skov Nielsen, James Phelan, and Changcai Wang, all colleagues from the society, generously helped to bring into print early versions of some of the material included in this book. Special thanks also to Christopher Looby and Cindy Weinstein for publishing early work related to Chapter 2, and to Ana Carolina Mesquita and Marcelo Pen Parreira for their translation into Portuguese of work related to Chapter 2.

Incorporating previously published material into the book manuscript has meant substantially revising two early publications: "Fiction as Restriction" (*Narrative* [2007]) and "Aesthetics and the New Ethics" (first published in *PMLA* [2009] and then reprinted in *Why Study Literature?* [2011] and *American Literature's Aesthetic Dimensions* [2012]). Chapter 5 incorporates my reworked thinking about the arguments advanced in these two essays. I am grateful to Cambridge University Press for allowing "The Art of English Fiction in the Twentieth Century" (*The Cambridge Companion to the Twentieth-Century English Novel* [2009]) to appear here as part of Chapter 2. The first part of Chapter 3 includes a revised version of "*On Beauty* as Beautiful? The Problem of Novelistic Aesthetics by Way of Zadie Smith" (*Contemporary Literature* [2012]).

I am deeply indebted to the many colleagues who made it possible for me to present my work at their home institutions. Warm thanks to Reyna Cowan at the Psychoanalytic Institute of Northern California; Deirdre D'Albertis at Bard College; Amy Elias at the University of Tennessee, Knoxville; John Ronan at the University of Memphis; Alex Woloch and Nancy Ruttenburg at the Stanford Center for the Study of the Novel; and my hosts at Johns Hopkins University and Princeton University, respectively. I am especially grateful to Lynda Zwinger for inviting me to participate in the *Arizona Quarterly* Symposium (hosted by the University of Arizona), for the benefit of her own work on Henry James and for the delight of our conversations about the novels we both have read or want each other to read. I can't thank enough the colleagues further afield who generously took time out of their demanding schedules to host me: Ronald Bush at the Rothermere Institute for Americanist Studies and St. John's College, Oxford; Lingmei Fan at Capital Normal University, Beijing, China; Gwendolyn Haevens and David Watson at Uppsala University, Sweden; Per Krogh Hansen at the University of Southern Denmark; Lorna Hutson at St. Andrews University, Scotland; Emilee Moran at the University of York, England; Henrik Svok Nielsen, Stefan Iverson, and Stefan Kirkegaard at Aarhus University, Denmark; Marcelo Pen Parreira at the University of São Paulo, Brazil; my Berkeley colleague Karin Sanders, who with Lasse Horne Kjaeldgaard and Martin Hansen hosted me at the University of Copenhagen, Denmark (where we waited out the volcano together); Pram Sounsamut at Chulalongkorn University, Bangkok, Thailand; Nan Wang at Beijing Normal University, Beijing, China; and my hosts at the University of Sydney, Australia.

Warm thanks also go to those who asked and listened, out of love and friendship: Oliver Arnold, Caverlee Cary, Laurie Doyle, Milena Edwards, Abigail Franklin, Walter Greenblatt, John Hale, Raluca Iuster, Doreen Klein, Jesse Knapp, Steven Knapp, Greg Lowry, Susan Rieder, and Henry Wigglesworth.

Jeff Knapp and Maddie Hale shoulder the burden and make the joy. Jeff remains my first, last, and best reader. And now Maddie will know a time when this book can finally be read rather than always still to be written. I can't begin to thank both of them for our shared life together, which has entwined us all with the making of this book.

D.J.H.

The Novel and the New Ethics

The New Ethics and Contemporary Fiction

When I am writing fiction, I'm . . . interested by the fact that somehow or other I can have the feeling of actually seeing things through someone else's eyes. I know I'm concocting them, I know that—but the sensation is still there. You say, given this, given that, given another thing, how would the world look. And you can kind of re-conceive the world around that. You can make the effort. I think maybe that's why people write fiction, and why people read it, is because you don't know who you are unless you can imagine being otherwise.

Marilynne Robinson

"Marilynne Robinson on Democracy, Reading, and Religion in America"[1]

"It's the greatest of mysteries, I think . . . What it's like to be another person, to be William . . . What it feels like, I mean. Literature. Life. They give us little glimpses, leaving us hungry for more."

Richard Russo

"Horseman"

Full disclosure: what insults my soul is the idea—popular in the culture just now, and presented in widely variant degrees of complexity—that we can and should write only about people who are fundamentally "like" us: racially, sexually, genetically, nationally, politically, personally. That only an intimate authorial autobiographical connection with a character can be the rightful basis of a fiction.

Zadie Smith

"Fascinated to Presume: In Defense of Fiction"

WHAT IS THE VALUE OF LITERATURE in the contemporary moment? A popular new answer to this age-old question revives the most ancient defense of literature: its ethical power. Among contemporary fiction writers, J. M. Coetzee, Jonathan Franzen, Gish Jen, Ian McEwan, Toni Morrison, Marilynne

Robinson, and Zadie Smith have, in their fiction and in their writing about fiction, influentially expounded the ethical capacities of literary reading and writing. For many of these authors, the return to ethics is framed as a turn away from the parody, pastiche, and play of postmodernism. These fiction writers share David Foster Wallace's sense that the relevance of postmodernism's "gasp and squeal" has run its course, that a new cultural power lies, as Foster Wallace puts it, in the hands of those "who dare somehow to back away from ironic watching, who have the childish gall actually to endorse and substantiate single-entendre principles."[2] The always-ironic attitude, the implied position of superiority in constant critique, the complicity in commodification that attends pastiche, the endlessness of deconstructive play—these postmodernist stances of the 1970s and 1980s have given way to a new regard for an old cultural claim: that literature offers its readers a serious, perhaps even uniquely powerful engagement with ethical values.[3]

The return to ethics for these contemporary writers is explicitly formulated as a renewed appreciation for novelists such as Henry James, Virginia Woolf, E. M. Forster, and William Faulkner, modernists for whom the "discovery" of the form of the novel—the fact that the novel could be thought to have a form—made the representation of fictional characters an artistic task that required an ethical duty on the part of their author. The belief ushered in at the beginning of the twentieth century that the Anglo-American novel might be more than a "cannibal art," to use Woolf's phrase, tasked the author with making the best use of the narrative resources particular to the novel to bring to life a character's individuality.[4] For Woolf, James, Faulkner, and a host of other modernists, the art of the novel is indistinguishable from the ethical task of representing characters as autonomous individuals, defined by an identity distinct and different from their author's. The new ethical enterprise thus has ushered in, perhaps not surprisingly, a renewed concern in fiction writing with the representation of character.[5]

Of course, poststructuralism had predicted a very different future for the novel. By midcentury, this modernist theory of novelistic ethics seemed to have been exploded. Poststructuralism challenged the philosophical assumptions that defined, on the one hand, persons as liberal individuals, and, on the other hand, ethics as a matter of individual responsibility and agency. Writing in 1957, Alain Robbe-Grillet could call for a new novel that would accurately reflect what he regarded as the new political reality of the social subject at midcentury. Under the institutional administration of high capitalism, he argues, the agency of the individual has ceased to matter. How could novels of character continue to be written, he goes on to ask, when individuals no longer direct the operation of social power? Thus he proclaims in his essay "On Several Obsolete Notions" that "the novel of characters belongs entirely to the past, it describes a period: that which marked the apogee of the individual."[6] About a decade later, in S/Z Roland Barthes elegantly elaborates the difference between the old novel of character and the new novel of the deconstructed subject. Looking back to the realist novel, Barthes theorizes the narrative features that create the ideological illusion of characterological individuality in Balzac's work. Looking forward to the future of the novel, Barthes argues that novelistic narrative should perform the absolute textuality of all subjectivity. He declares: "What is obsolescent in today's novel is not the novelistic, it is the character; what can no longer be written is the Proper Name."[7]

But what postmodernist theorists couldn't have recognized is how their critique of the liberal subject actually supported the modernist notion of ethical value as inhering in literary form—and even more particularly, as inhering in novelistic narrative. To begin with, theorists such as Robbe-Grillet and Barthes, with their acute, critical attention to the properties of narrative per se and the politics of realist narration in particular, end up expanding and variegating the understanding of novelistic form. Read for the ideological assumptions about personhood expressed through narrative structure, a novel written by Dickens or Eliot could be revealed as having a formal complexity and aesthetic integrity unappreciated in its own historical moment.[8] Crucially, this ideological understanding of narrative form—the idea that the novel's narrative structure could reveal true values that were hidden even from the authors themselves—connects the postmodern theory of the novel with the modernist ethics of form.[9] Poststructuralist theories of the novel do not dismantle the modernist understanding of the novel as the art of ethical form but add to the notion of ethical agency by conceiving of the otherness of narrative as an impersonal location for the communication of ethical value. As against authors who represent through their depiction of character the ideological lie of individuality and humanist ethics (as seen from the poststructuralist perspective), elements of novelistic form (plot design, description, point of view) and even more abstractly, properties of language, textuality, and narrative structure (causality, contingency, positionality) could tell the political truth, an ethical task.[10] The cultural idea of the art of the novel thus develops at midcentury to include a more particularized understanding of its formal qualities and a more extended sense of the ethical modes of otherness at stake in its form.

Seen in retrospect, the intensity of the postmodern mission to deconstruct character is itself a sign of the novel's particular generic resources for representing persons and their social worlds, the death of character a hopeful protestation rather than an accomplished execution. John Barth's work, for example, frequently entertains the idea that the nineteenth-century novel's ethical investment in character may be so fundamental to the novel's generic makeup that poststructuralist attempts to deconstruct the mimetic representation of social worlds and decenter characters will be short-lived. The conflict between mimetic effects and linguistic play is explicitly addressed by the first-person protagonist-writer of Barth's "Life-Story," who describes himself as caught between the love of traditional novels, with "heroes I can admire, heroines I can love," and the obligation he feels in the mid-twentieth century to write in the Beckettian tradition of "avant-garde preciousness" (119). The end result is that Barth and his fictional fiction writer can write of nothing other than this state of philosophical suspension between the metafictional self-consciousness of the new novel and the human appeal of the old, even as he worries that the entire debate may prove to be culturally ephemeral: "How will such nonsense sound thirty-six years from now?" (119). In keeping with his sense that the significance of aesthetic criteria can only be judged by the long view of their cultural endurance, Barth's narrator jokingly invites his aesthetic meditation to be situated in literary history (exactly as I am now doing) by precisely dating it "10:00 A.M., Monday, June 20, 1966" (119).[11]

The Novel and the New Ethics undertakes this long view of twentieth-century novelistic aesthetics. I contend that what poststructuralist theorists such as Barthes and Robbe-Grillet and postmodern fiction writers like Barth couldn't have anticipated at midcentury is that by 2002 (to take Barth's projected date) their intense scrutiny of the genre's realist conventions would not upend the notion of the novel's ethical value but, on the contrary, become a basis for attributing ethical value to novel form, down to the molecular level. *The Novel and the New Ethics* argues that the Anglo-American art of the novel, defined and developed at the beginning of the twentieth century as a celebration of the novel's narrative resources for representing fictional characters as autonomous individuals, develops over the course of the century into a novelistic aesthetics grounded in the assumption that the social value of literature lies in the ethical encounter made possible through the reader's phenomenological experience of modes of ontological otherness that is credited to narrative form.[12] As I will show, the idea of ethical otherness that is foundational for this defense of literary value derives from the notion that fictional characters possess a personhood that imbues their narrative representation with ethical value. No matter how deconstructed or politicized the notion of the individual has become, in our contemporary moment the novel is regarded as offering a privileged ethical engagement with social difference through the reader's affective experience of characterological personhood as mediated by the novelistic narrative art. The poststructuralist critique of liberal individualism (that propels the rejection of novelistic character conceived as a unique personality, an autonomous individual, a responsible agent, a deep plenitude, a centered consciousness) does not do away with the ethical defense of literature but has made more philosophically complex both how social otherness might be defined and how literary texts might be regarded as embodying otherness in their own right. I want to show how even as the literary ethics of alterity has become more abstract in recent decades, the cultural notion of the art of the novel has become more focused: contemporary novelists and academic theorists increasingly define the social value of literature more and more exclusively as the ethical encounter with otherness made available through novelistic form.

I use the contemporary term "ethics of alterity" to describe this literary tradition, because alterity can capture three major features of the tradition's ethical logic at once: the tradition's investment in representing fictional characters as particular individuals distinct and different from the authors who invented them; the politicized understanding of subaltern subjects as radically other—and thus ethically unrepresentable—from the point of view of social hegemony; and the ontological notion of narrative as an ethical other, resistant to and capable of exposing a specific author's ideological investments. As adapted by contemporary novelists, the defining premise of the novelistic ethics of alterity is that novel form establishes a relation among ethical agents, understood as authors, readers, fictional characters, and (in a way not self-consciously formulated by the modernists) narrative itself. Within the literary historical tradition I am mapping, alterity derives from the phenomenological notion of the self's encounter with states of being outside of and different from the self. This can include, of course, otherness within—the conscious apprehension of an unconscious force within or the felt struggle between rational modes of knowledge and affective states of being. It can also include the human encounter with nonhuman states of being: the lives of animals, states of divinity, or even the nature of fiction. The novel's investigation of otherness is also invested in exploring the states of difference that obtain within the human condition. On the one hand, some novels subscribe to a radical individualism that asserts, with William James, that the "breaches" between personal consciousness "are the most absolute breaches in nature."[13] On the other hand, there is the ideological view of alterity that begins with the critique of radical individualism that we find, for example, voiced by Fredric Jameson, who credits/blames William's brother, Henry, for contributing, through the latter's use of point of view, to the late capitalist projection of the self as a socially alienated monad.[14] While for William James the otherness of persons is a natural condition, for Jameson a transformation in the material conditions of society would reduce or eliminate reification and alienation.

Although deriving from phenomenology, alterity as a term now encompasses a wide variety of philosophical understandings of otherness. The Levinasian phenomenological view of ethical singularity and "face to face" intersubjective relation, for example, has a different philosophical basis than Ian Watt's influential articulation of the highly particularized individualism offered by the novel, but for both thinkers the singularity/particularity that defines personhood is the condition of otherness that is the foundation from which social and ethical understanding must proceed. Thus when Marilynne Robinson states that her goal as a fiction writer is to pursue the good of "being otherwise" (qtd. in the epigraph to this chapter), the phrase may come from Levinas but has more to do with the novelist's task of character creation than with Levinas's idea of ethical transcendence. As this book will demonstrate more generally, for the contemporary Anglo-American novelist the idea of otherness signifies a family of ideas that not only goes beyond a single philosophical tradition but is derived as much from the novel's literary history as from philosophy. For example, Elizabeth Strout and Barbara Kingsolver share Robinson's view that the contemporary novelist can and should accomplish the ethical task of striving to be otherwise, but they hold very different assumptions about the way fiction delivers the experience of alterity, as well as how the good of alterity should be defined. For Robinson "seeing things through someone else's eyes" yields self-knowledge ("you don't know who you are unless you can imagine being otherwise"). Strout, by contrast, describes otherness as a merging of identities so profound that it feels organismic, a bodily, molecular reconstitution. Ariel Levy gives this account of views expressed by Strout in their 2017 interview:

> [Elizabeth] Strout recalls having almost mystical experiences of temporarily inhabiting other people. The first time it happened, [Strout] was twelve years old. . . . "This woman came in—she seemed old to me, but she was probably like fifty-five—and she started to talk to me about how her husband had had a stroke, and it had left him depressed," she recalled. "And I remember so clearly almost feeling her molecules move into me—or my molecules move into her. I understood there was some sort of merging."[15]

While the views of Robinson and Strout establish a set of philosophical poles for the ethical understanding of otherness—otherness as reflective self-knowledge versus otherness as the embodied merging of identities—Kingsolver adds a political dimension to the ethical stakes. On her view, the value of "inhabiting otherness" is that it brings into visibility the socially disenfranchised, the ignored, the abject. In praising the work of Dave Eggers, Kingsolver arguably credits him with achieving the ethical project that she herself undertakes in *The Poisonwood Bible*:

> The phenomenally productive Eggers has talent to spare, applying it beyond writing to editing and active engagement with traumatized and at-risk communities. In his books he has revealed a remarkable aptitude for inhabiting otherness and illuminating the world's darker corners, from post-Katrina New Orleans (in "Zeitoun") to southern Sudan (in "What Is the What").[16]

Kingsolver implies that Eggers brings a novelist's narrative ability, defined by an ethical sensibility, to all his writing, including his nonfiction. His "aptitude for inhabiting otherness" illuminates "the world's darker corners" not through reportage or perspectival appropriation but through a narrative ethics of alterity that travels to and into the social bodies (places and persons) whose existence is defined by material disenfranchisement as well as by individual and collective trauma. Richard Russo's short story "Horseman" (the second epigraph to this chapter) is a testament to the fiction writer's awareness that the ethical philosophy of otherness emerges from and is cultivated in the university setting, circulating from and back to the campus as professors, students, and writers export aspects of academic thought to formulate an ethics of fiction. "Horseman" portrays Marcus Bellamy, a celebrity literature professor, espousing the view that fiction gives readers access to the "mystery" of "another person," "little glimpses," that do not solve the problem of otherness but leave "us hungry for more" (31). In the chapters that follow, I explore the family of ideas about fiction's ethical capacity that is advanced under the sign of "otherness." I describe the ethics of alterity from the fiction writer's point of view as well as from the academic's perspective in order to offer a synthetic and thoroughgoing analysis of the assumptions, influence, and legacy of this literary tradition.[17]

The fact that so many contemporary novelists have rewritten modernist novels makes a prima facie case for the connection between century's beginning and century's end. Ian McEwan stylistically alludes to Woolf in *Atonement* (2001)[18] Michael Cunningham explicitly honors Woolf's influence: he not only re-creates *Mrs. Dalloway* (1925) through *The Hours* (1998) but uses modernist techniques to bring Woolf to life as a fictional character. Zadie Smith pays homage to E. M. Forster in a series of critical essays and by rewriting *Howards End* (1910) as *On Beauty* (2005). Jeffrey Eugenides has Edith Wharton's *The Age of Innocence* (1920) in mind as he updates *The Marriage Plot* (2011) for the twenty-first century. Toni Morrison writes her master's thesis (1955) on Virginia Woolf and William Faulkner, revives modernist techniques of interior monologue in *Sula* (1973) and *A Mercy* (2008), and reworks characters and events from Faulkner's *Absalom, Absalom!* (1936) for her novel *Jazz* (1992). And Joyce Carol Oates ("The Accursed Inhabitants of House Bly" [1994]), Alan Hollinghurst (*The Line of Beauty* [2005]), Cynthia Ozick (*Foreign Bodies* [2010]), and John Banville (*Mrs. Osmond* [2017]) join a legion of refashioners of Henry James's works. Along with their modernist precursors, the contemporary novelist asks how novelistic narrative should best do justice to the life of a character as other to the author. In this regard, the return to character is also a return to the modernist notion that the novel is best defined as a genre by the narrative modes particular to it. The novelist's choice and handling of narrative modes reflects the author's ethical sensitivity to the degree and kind of otherness characters represent within the social world of a particular novel.

Driving the novelistic aesthetics of alterity is the question of how best to honor otherness through and as narrative representation. If otherness becomes knowable through "positive" narrative representation, has it been domesticated, translated into the same? Does otherness require nonnarrative modes of knowing? Emotional responses that disrupt one's cognitive modes of certainty? Can one know the other through identification (that stranger is I)? If emotion is an ethical mode for honoring otherness, are all emotions equally ethical? Is identification better or worse than sympathy? Is perplexity more ethical than love? These are the kinds of questions explored within the social world of the modernist and contemporary novels that make up this literary tradition and that drive attitudes about the narrative modes best suited to portray characterological otherness. As I will show, over the course of the century the formal properties of the novel come into critical visibility to the degree that they are valued as participating in the narrative representation of alterity, complexly understood: characterological point of view, narratorial stance, the teleology of plot, the role of minor characters, the distribution and register of dialogue—these qualities of narrative and many more acquire genre-defining importance as they become integrated into a strong critical and creative paradigm that takes as its governing assumption not only the novel's inherent capacity for doing justice to states of otherness but its ability to offer an encounter with otherness that is ethically valuable. Staged through the unfolding narrative choices, the degree and kind of the author's ethical capacity for otherness thus finds its objective correlative in novel form.

In their critical understanding and their artistic practice, contemporary novelists develop the political dimension of modernist narrative ethics into a phenomenological paradigm. The encounter with alterity staged in and through narrative is posited as giving the apprehending self (author, character, narrator, and/or reader) the opportunity to bring to self-consciousness the sociopolitical conditions of normativity that mark the limits of their interpretive horizon as a culturally constructed subject. The experience of otherness is defined as the experience of self-limit, a self-consciousness about the self's implication in the operation of social power that opens up the possibility of ethical action—ethical action defined by its difference from political domination. In the family of ideas that this book will be exploring, the possibility of the self's ethical self-transformation might be realized through new knowledge or rational understanding, as an affective experience that opposes itself to rational modes of thought, as an act of imagination, or as a new kind of social action (the act of taking care of another, for example, or of separation from a familiar community to enter a community of others). Contemporary novelists and academic theorists build out from this phenomenological notion of narrative to include the experience of alterity made available to novel readers through the narrative positioning of the reader in relation to characterological and authorial personhood.

As affiliates to major universities, Toni Morrison (Princeton University), Zadie Smith (New York University), and J. M. Coetzee (University of Adelaide, Australia), the contemporary novelists whom I take as my main case studies for the return to ethics, are especially well positioned to bring academic thought about alterity home to their novelistic practice. But as I will show, the notions of otherness that drive their narrative practice are highly generalized, inflected by philosophical work on alterity but not attempting to contribute to that discipline in the same way that Jean-Paul Sartre or Thomas Mann, for example, wrote novels of ideas. *The Novel and the New Ethics* argues that the philosophically heterogeneous notion of alterity that informs the Anglo-American literary tradition generates the aesthetic program of these works. Over the course of the twentieth century, novelists and novel readers increasingly assume that the novel has a privileged responsibility to the depiction and deployment of otherness—and this cultural assumption freights novel form with an array of ideas, more or less philosophically developed, more or less demonstrated or contradicted, about how alterity might best be understood and how it might also best be encountered. This is to say that the works of fiction that form the core of my study hold in tension conflicting or underdeveloped ideas about ethical alterity, and this failure in philosophical coherence fosters a family of ideas that makes novelistic aesthetics seem more than a list of compositional dos and don'ts, more than a craft to be mastered. The ethics of alterity at once restricts the novel by defining it as a particular generic endeavor and makes its aesthetic protocols seem more than formal play or art for art's sake through the social good imputed to preferred narrative practices.

Indeed, it is a register of the strength of this tradition in our current cultural moment that it is controversial for me to argue, as I do, that no absolute or necessary ethics of narrative develops from this tradition—despite the fact that it is this necessary ethics that novelists seek as a guide to their artistic practice and, as

I will show in Chapter 5, that literary critics believe they find there. As I hope to prove, understanding the literary context for recent claims about narrative ethics per se enables us to see how the power for alterity accorded to the novel as a genre is in fact artistically contingent, linked to the defining ethical problematic developed in the storyworld and influenced by the nonprogrammatic nature of authorial thinking about ethical otherness. In the tradition's strong artworks, the complex and frequently contradictory notion of otherness generated through storyworld action (including dialogue) resists consolidation into a single philosophical system or a confident truth claim—an irresolvability that can become its own source of ethical value for a particular novel's narrative practices. But so thoroughly do these novelists devote themselves to exploring the value of otherness as an ethical good that in their work the value of otherness is determinative for plot and characterization as well as theme. The ethics of otherness becomes, in other words, a basis of aesthetic unity: all the narrative choices and procedures of their novels are infused via their artistic task with the ethical pursuit of otherness. By linking the problem of narrative form to the ethical good of otherness, novels in this tradition offer themselves as highly accomplished artworks that match form to content in a complex and variegated way. They thereby also set a standard for readerly interpretive competence that is linked to the reader's ability to recognize the ethical values at play in narrative management.

While my focus is not on the institutional formation of novelistic aesthetics, we can see from the attention given to the topic of novelistic ethics in the pages of the *New York Times*, the *New Yorker*, *The Atlantic*, and other journals that the subject is currently regarded as one of general social importance.[19] One of the benefits of taking the long view of the aesthetics of alterity, of linking century's end to century's beginning, is that it allows us to see that the accusations of cultural appropriation that are being leveled at fiction writers in the contemporary moment are informed by a long literary history. A 2017 *New York Times* article provides a powerful example of exactly how politicized the ethical stakes of novelistic representation have become. As reported by the *Times*, in an on-line editorial published in *Write*, a magazine of the Writers Union of Canada, Hal Niedzviecki describes contemporary Canadian literature as "exhaustingly white and middle-class." But the solution he proposed lit a firestorm: "In my opinion anyone, anywhere, should be encouraged to imagine other peoples, other cultures, other identities.... I'd go so far as to say there should even be an award for doing so—the Appropriation Prize for best book by an author who writes about people who aren't even remotely like her or him."[20] Niedzviecki's statement powerfully indicates the persistence of George Eliot's view that the art of the novel can and should perform the social good of representing social others. Eliot's explicit goal in writing a novel like *Middlemarch* is to create readers who, like herself as novelist, "should be better able to *imagine* and to *feel* the pains and joys of those who differ from themselves in everything but the broad fact of being struggling, erring human creatures."[21] Eliot famously thematizes the difficulty of this ethical project when the narrator of *Middlemarch* interrupts her "study of provincial life" to ask:

> But why always Dorothea? Was her point of view the only possible one with regard to this marriage? I protest against all our interest, all our effort at understanding being given to the young skins that look blooming in spite of trouble; for these too will get faded, and will know the older and more eating griefs which we are helping to neglect. In spite of the blinking eyes and white moles... Mr. Casaubon had an intense consciousness within him, and was spiritually a-hungered like the rest of us.[22]

Rather than getting readers to identify with people who only *seem* different from themselves, Niedzviecki's ethical imperative ties the author's ethical attempt to bring to life "other peoples, other cultures, other identities" to the difficulty of *speaking for* "people who aren't even remotely like him or her." The novel in our own cultural moment can be regarded by writers such as Niedzviecki as powerfully equipped to engage authors and readers in the ethical task of knowing characters as others, but gone is Eliot's belief in the grounding universality of human experience. As we see in the "why always Dorothea?" passage, Eliot's deeply perspectival approach to novel character already helped to problematize that universal ground by demonstrating the subjective limits to understanding other people, including the narrator's limits in distributing her own sympathetic apprehension.[23] Within our contemporary moment, because social others are now regarded within a new political framework as radically other, as defined by identities whose difference and particularity is the constitutive feature of their cultural identity, Niedzviecki has no standing, no authority, to speak for others, and his attempt to do so turns Eliot's positive claim about the novel as an art for social betterment into a negative political critique of the novel as the art of cultural "appropriation."²⁴ In the wake of Niedzviecki's statement, *Write* received so much criticism that Niedzviecki resigned from his editorial position. We may not be able to prove whether or not novels have the power to make their readers more ethical, but we can certify that in our contemporary moment the fictional status of characters makes no difference for their status as social others: the novelist is tasked with the ethically responsible representation of social others, even though the "people who aren't even remotely like him or her" are imaginary beings, derived from authorial imagination. Thus an aesthetic program—beliefs about the narrative conditions proper to the treatment of fictional characters—has become of such cultural importance as to factor directly into the material conditions of publication and employment in the world of publication.

The contribution of secondary schools to establishing the novelistic ethics of alterity as a cultural norm cannot be overestimated, and a sociological study of secondary-school and even elementary-school teaching of the novel is a much-needed research project in its own right. The pedagogic mission to educate students in the ethical good of social diversity has contributed to a more positive conception of how novel form works to avoid the bad politics of appropriation. Novels are the preferred genre for giving students not just knowledge about cultures different from their own (which can be covered in history class) but, even more important, an affective investment in the lives of social others. Thus we find appearing in one high school curriculum a young-adult best-seller, David Levithan's *Every Day* (2012; Orion Pictures feature film, 2018), whose plot tells the story of a soul/mind that wakes up each morning as a new and distinct social type (male, female; Asian American, Latinx, African American; fat, athletic, beautiful, homely; rich, poor) and whose narrative structure performs its conception of the novel's generic ability to honor the fact of social difference while bringing each social type to life as a particularized individual.²⁵ In stark contrast to the postmodernist writer who strove to represent individuals as textual effects or cultural clichés (think Pynchon's Oedipa Maas in *The Crying of Lot 49*), Levithan's protagonist is nothing but character, the protagonist's life nothing but the intimate experience of other people—people who are defined as other to the protagonist. Through the novel's narrative resources, a diversity of social subjects can be represented not just as complex, individualized interiorities but also in and through the protagonist's sense of their social difference. Thus the premise of Levithan's novel (that the protagonist is simultaneously themselves and a social other) serves as a self-conscious description of its aesthetic project: the novel reader is invited to think that, through the ethical structure that inheres in the novel's narrative technique, novel readers can experience the lives of social others while remaining themselves.

The very first page of *Every Day* establishes the ethical terms of the narrative project, inviting the reader to consider how the novel makes possible a double social experience: "I know I am myself," the narrator explains, "but I am also someone else."[26] This account of the novel's narrative power—that it possesses technical resources for representing the value of social diversity as the noncolonizing inhabitation of other people (i.e., that it allows readers to stay themselves even as they are also someone else)—is a strong claim to make for the positive social value of novelistic ethics. But is it true? Has the novel really succeeded in giving the reader an ethical encounter with otherness, or has it instead performed its allegiance to this value through the form and content of its artistic practice? Does Levithan as a novelist possess high powers of ethicality that enable him to know and represent social others as others? Or is Levithan's conception of social alterity underwritten by a stereotypical view of social difference? To my mind, such questions raised from within the novel about the nature and pursuit of ethical alterity are precisely what invests a particular novel's narrative procedures with value—a value that refuses any prefabricated or formulaic notion of what right narrative ethics might be or whether right narrative ethics can in fact be self-consciously achieved.

To begin to understand how the contemporary view of the novel that informs popular works such as Levithan's and public debates about the authorial limits to the fictional depiction of social identities connects to the modern novelist's ethical concern with characterological autonomy, we can start with Gish Jen's recent championing of character in *Tiger Writing*, the published version of the Massey Lectures she delivered at Harvard in 2012. I turn to Jen first precisely because her investment in characterological autonomy could not be more explicit:

> Every fiction writer worth her salt knows how a character will up and walk off with a piece. You know that to write is as much to give your character their freedom as it is anything else; and you know that in the end, nothing matters more than that they should breath and stretch and laugh in your face.[27]

Jen is not simply concerned with the ethical dilemmas confronted by her characters in the storyworld but the art of fiction as an ethical practice. For Jen, the successful depiction of fictional characters is the achieved narrative representation of a certain kind of personhood: the novelist's task is to bring to life an individual with free will who then enjoys the condition of ontological freedom as a fictional being. While the felt power to create persons with free will makes the novelist godlike, the fact that these creations are fictional, their lives the product of the novelist's imagination, burdens the author with aesthetic responsibilities that are decidedly human. For Jen the gauge of a novel's aesthetic success lies in the quality of the ethical relation she has established with her fictional characters. She has met her goals as an artist when she feels she has developed a narrative form that successfully empowers her characters, and the measure of this achievement is, for Jen, the authorial experience of disempowerment in relation to the fictional world. On her view, narrative art does not just bring characters to life (gives them breath and free movement), but, when fully brought to life through narrative, characters are installed in a power relation with their author. The sign of aesthetic success for Jen, then, is when she feels that her characters display their autonomy as an antagonism directed back to their author, which is to say, when they treat her as a risible social presence in a world that she has brought to life but cannot control.

Jen's statement not only shows the contemporary novelist's investment in character but, importantly for my argument, frames that investment in terms that echo the modernist project ushered in a hundred years before. Jen's description of the art of the novel so closely repeats that of William Faulkner that she might be alluding to him. In an interview that has been widely quoted, Faulkner defines his artistic goal as first and foremost the creation of "flesh-and-blood, living, suffering, anguishing human beings" (*Faulkner in the University*, 47). A testament to Faulkner's success in the execution of this task can be found in the philosophical question an interviewer put to him during a different class conference held at the University of Virginia: "Do you believe in free will for your characters?" (38). Faulkner's immediate answer casts "the right to free will" in terms of a general philosophical "conception of man" that does not explicitly address the problem of fictional characters having independent agency (38). But in answer to another interviewer's question that same year, Faulkner extends this philosophical conception to the free will of imaginary persons. Faulkner declares that his characters "exist" beyond any story he tells of them: "They are still in motion in my mind. I can laugh at the things they're doing that I haven't got around to writing yet.... The characters themselves are walking out of that book still in motion, still talking, and still acting" (197–198).

The closeness of Jen's language to Faulkner's—the repeated trope of laughter as well as the figure of the characters walking off—calls attention to the way modernist proclamations about characterological freedom have helped to generate a durable notion of Anglo-American novelistic aesthetics that has survived postmodernism. But to hear Jen's echo of Faulkner is also to be able to see an interesting difference in the way each author formulates the power relations between author and character—and this begins to make the case for the usefulness of understanding novelistic aesthetics of alterity as a family of ideas. While Jen's author is laughed at, Faulkner's does the laughing.[28] In Faulkner's formulation, the achievement of characterological independence comes at no cost to the author; on the contrary, the characters' freedom creates aesthetic value for the author himself. When the characters walk out of Faulkner's books, they don't desert their creator but provide him with the gift of entertainment, continuing to perform their lives for his inspection and amusement on the stage of his imagination. The author's felt disempowerment becomes for Faulkner the fruitful condition of future artistic enterprise. The implication is that the aesthetic pleasure he takes in watching his "people" exercise their own agency yields the creative benefit of having more to write about for his next novel.

To understand how Jen's and Faulkner's authorial views contribute to the novelistic aesthetics of alterity is not just to hear the echo of Faulkner in Jen but to be sensitive to the different attitudes toward authorial power implied in their respective descriptions of the commonly held artistic goal of characterological freedom. The problematic that is the novelistic aesthetics of alterity gains its specifying attributes through the kinds of interpretive questions generated through a comparison of authorial attitudes. Why is Faulkner's sense of authorship unthreatened by the independence of his characters, while Jen feels that her characters not only mock their author but also take over her creative agency, "up and walk[ing] off with the piece"? Should the difference in understanding the achieved relation between author and character be explained merely as a matter of personal temperament: Faulkner's ability to laugh versus Jen's willingness to be laughed at? Or is the difference ideological, a register of the difference in gender and ethnicity that defines their subject positions? Or does the source of their difference lie in the way each understands novelistic narrative as a power structure that establishes inherent possibilities of relation between author and character? In Jen's case, when a character successfully comes to life as a life through narrative, that character in turn defines herself against the agent who made her, reducing that creator to an individual no greater than herself. For Faulkner, the author cedes authority to the character, but this is because the character's independence ultimately accrues to the author's advantage, making writing a novel no more than the writing down of his characters' doings.

Of course, long before the twentieth century authors routinely described novel writing as an encounter with other persons. And these descriptions also formulated this encounter as a power struggle between the author and the autonomous characters he strives to create. Anthony Trollope, for example, famously equates the project of fiction writing with the author's success in bringing the creations "of his brain" to life as "speaking, moving, living human creatures" (*Autobiography*, 192). He goes so far as to assert that novelistic success depends upon the author's capacity, in the act of creation, to establish real, interpersonal relations with his fictional characters, living with them "in the full reality of established intimacy. He must learn to hate them and to love them. He must argue with them, quarrel with them, forgive them, and even submit to them. . . . The depth, breadth, narrowness, and shallowness of each should be clear to him" (192–193). William Makepeace Thackeray, happy to assume in his novelistic practice the role of puppet master, describes the creative process in a reversal of power relations as the characters' control over their author. He states that after finishing a book, he felt like a deserted inn and missed the people "who have been boarding and lodging with me for twenty months! They have interrupted my rest: they have plagued me at all sorts of minutes: they have thrust themselves upon me when I was ill, or wished to be idle" (*Early and Late Papers*, 397). Here it is the author who is at the beck and call of his imaginary people. And they are described by Thackeray as possessing a presence no different from his own, to such an extent that he can feel that they also possess a social status superior to his own: he is the innkeeper, they the demanding guests he is there to serve. Indeed, as social beings the characters are so vivacious and so successful in their mastery over him that, in Thackeray's figurative logic, their humanity reduces his to a hollow shell: in Thackeray's description, the author descends first to innkeeper and then to the status of the inn itself, an empty dwelling made lively through the vitality of the characters while they occupy the premises.

By 1871, the power struggle between novelists and their characters had become such a defining feature of the novel as a genre that a playwright could poke fun at it. W. S. Gilbert wrote in this year *A Sensation Novel in Three Volumes*, a comic operetta that might have been called "Four Characters in Confrontation with Their Author."[29] Gilbert depicts the novelist as a weak-willed hack whom the characters bully and bribe. These fictional characters possess an ontological existence prior to their appearance in the writer's mind. Reading the pages of the in-progress novel and appalled by the fates assigned to them, they decide to "summon the Author and have it out with him," to "insist that the novel shall end as *we* like."[30] On stage, their autonomy is not only embodied literally but also expressed through actual physical conflict: the stage direction stipulates, "Author enters and they attack him vociferously."[31] A bargain is struck: the hack agrees to shape a story that will allow the characters to live happily ever after in accordance with their preexisting social lives, especially their love relations. In turn, they will bestow aesthetic power on the hack's writing by making available the complexity and depth of their characters.

In Gilbert's play we can see how the stage is set, as it were, for the notion of the novelistic aesthetics of alterity that is ushered in with the twentieth century. From the dramatist's point of view, the signal difference between the representation of character in the novel and the drama is narration. Tellingly for this generic difference, Luigi Pirandello's *Six Characters in Search of an Author* (1921) will later frame the representational problem of drama as the problem of *too much* characterological autonomy, of the longing of fictional beings to meet their author.[32] From this perspective on the generic difference between the art of the novel and the art of the drama, it is drama, not the novel, that bears the burden of Lukácsian transcendental homelessness.[33] As a narrative art, the novel holds author and character in relation, even though that relation may be fraught with struggle or seemingly one-sided. As aptly diagnosed by *A Sensation Novel in Three Volumes*, a defining feature of the twentieth-century art of the novel becomes the ethical management of the social relation that novelistic narrative forges between authors and their fictional people. Unlike a play that is performed, the novel can only create the effect of characterological autonomy through the medium of a narrator. Narrative effects of characterological autonomy—such as the illusion of physical embodiment, deep interiority, or agential power—structurally refer back to a narrating agent.

Thus a creative disposition that is as old as the novel itself—the novelist's testimony to the felt autonomy of his imagined characters—is taken in the twentieth century to be an ethical basis for theorizing the structure of novelistic narration.

And as the aesthetics of alterity is launched at the beginning of the twentieth century, authorial statements that might have earlier seemed more or less interesting as providing biographical information about the creative temperament of particular fiction writers or psychologically significant for the light they shed on the novelistic imagination become newly suggestive for the directions they seem to give for decoding the ethical values at work in the form of the novel as a genre. That Trollope wrestled with his characters and Thackeray waited on them might have been items of interest to their readers, but it is only when an author's relation to his characters becomes an issue of narrative form that the reasons for the difference in conceptualizing power relations become crucial for literary critical interpretation. Readers like Henry Fielding could long ago laugh at Samuel Richardson for the dissonance that results when Richardson makes a serving girl the mouthpiece of his bourgeois ethical program (and satirize that program first in *An Apology for the Life of Mrs. Shamela Andrews* [1741] and then through the gender reversal of *Joseph Andrews* [1742]), but at issue was only Richardson's failure of imagination, not his social right as an author to speak for a serving maid. By the time of George Eliot, the artistic project of the novel is linked more tightly to a narrative ethics of character, and the representation of character is defined precisely as the author's responsibility to the lives of social others.[34]

But it would be an oversimplification of the aesthetics of alterity to think that it develops neatly over the century from a liberal humanist politics to a cultural politics. More typically, notions of characterological individuality that derive from liberal humanism accompany (sometimes uneasily) a notion of social otherness suggestive of a more radical politics. The following chapters will investigate this convergence in more detail, but I can introduce the idea here by returning to Jen's *Tiger Writing* (and the comparison with Faulkner) and then situating her understanding about the novelistic aesthetics of alterity in relation to Henry James, Virginia Woolf, Zadie Smith, and Ian McEwan. To read across the Massey Lectures is to find that the paradigm of ethical personhood that underwrites Jen's notion of characterological autonomy—the free agent who operates according to her own free will—stands in tension with her decentered view of her own ethnic identity. In *Tiger Writing* Jen claims that her artistic ability—the ability to create autonomous characters—is a direct result of her Chinese upbringing. She believes that Asians and Asian Americans are raised to be "other focused."[35]

Jen thus works out a position whereby her novels can seem protected against the charge of cultural appropriation. First of all, she is not attempting to speak for others but is instead speaking for herself in representing through fiction the value of social otherness. But second, her position also implies that because Asian Americans are other focused, they in fact do have a superior ethical capacity to appreciate otherness as an ethical and social good. By extension of this logic, her narrative solution to the problem of social alterity offers itself as ethically responsible, which is to say, as a nonappropriative representation of social others. Her project of representing in fiction people who are unlike herself seeks to be true both to what she considers the distinguishing quality of her own particular social identity and to the different identity of the other through whom her own identity is constituted as and in a defining narrative revelation.

Note that in the family of ideas that I am bringing to light, Jen's position chimes with Levithan's but is not identical to his notion of narrative ethics. For Levithan, the novel both represents in its storyworld and takes as the ethical imperative of its form the human experience of understanding others as a double social experience: one stays oneself even as one experiences life as another person. By contrast, for Jen, the Asian American novelist potentially serves as an ethical mentor for any novel reader: her culturally derived capacity for otherness, her essentially mediated identity, allows her to present the value of social diversity as an ethical good for her readers, no matter their cultural background. Thus Jen's own notion of her decentered subjectivity—the idea that to be oneself as an Asian American is to be constituted by others—does not prevent her from aiming to communicate the universal ethical good of other-orientation to readers raised with a different notion of personal identity. In other words, even the Western reader, whose own identity (Jen believes) derives from a Western notion of individualism, can, through reading Jen's novels, come to appreciate the ethical good of seeing, as she puts it, "the world through the eyes of others"—even if they, as Westerners, must try to cultivate that ability individually, as an ethical task.[36]

In *Tiger Writing* Jen credits her own novel reading for bringing her to self-consciousness about the constitutive capacity for otherness that she believes defines her Asian American identity. It is the Western novels that she read in her youth, she believes, that provide her with an early introduction to and education in the Western notion of individualism. Tristram Shandy, Jane Eyre, David Copperfield—Jen does not name these characters but they certainly fit her description of the Western novel's devotion to individuals who "tell long narratives about themselves that help illuminate, explain and celebrate what is special about them."[37] By contrast, in her novels Jen deploys narrative techniques that honor and equalize the experiences of a wide variety of social types within a shared community. In *The Love Wife*, for example, Jen experiments with new modes of multiperspectivalism. Her goal is not to bring one social other to life but many and to situate otherness as a degree and kind of social identity.[38]

But I would argue that while Jen may be right that her idea of the novel is very different from that of pre-twentieth-century English novels, it is not so different either in its form or in its ethical goals from that of Henry James or Virginia Woolf or Faulkner. In a novel such as *The Love Wife*, Jen's narrative techniques are clearly on a continuum with the great experimental novels of high modernism: her multiperspectivalism is akin to *As I Lay Dying*; her breaks out of narrative and into dramatic dialogue are reminiscent of James Joyce's *Ulysses*; and the homogeneity of idiom used by all the characters recalls Virginia Woolf's *The Waves*. To read with a full view of the novelistic aesthetics of alterity is to see this similarity and also to note that Jen mobilizes specific aspects of narrative in service of a late-twentieth-century idea of multiculturalism as an ideal for the ethical conceptualization of social otherness. Unlike Woolf's all-encompassing lyrical mode in *The Waves*, *The Love Wife*'s homogenized narrative voice is slightly inflected by each character's idiolect.[39] In her pursuit of the ethically good narrative, Jen employs this method in order to highlight the importance of her characters' social difference from each other—to establish, that is to say, that social difference is a constitutive feature of personal identity, and to show also that differences in the command of English do not affect the equality and legitimacy of each character's subjective perspective. For example, interpreted in the light of this understanding of narrative ethics, the immigrant Lan is not stigmatized by her less sophisticated self-expression in English.[40] Jen's representation of character in *The Love Wife* is also in this regard on a continuum with *As I Lay Dying*, which combines lyric language and dialect to register a character's capacity for deep consciousness along with his or her social position.[41]

The comparison of Jen and Faulkner also allows us to note finer-grained commonalities and divergences in modernist and contemporary narrative ethics. In contrast to Jen, Faulkner's handling of narrative in *As I Lay Dying* hierarchizes social subjectivity by depicting some individuals as possessing a deep private consciousness and others as with no depth at all. The ontological autonomy that Faulkner ascribes to his fictional characters, in other words, plays out in his narrative practice as the differential quality of complex consciousness. At the same time, Jen's view of the ethical good of other-oriented subjectivity suggests a new way to understand Faulkner's narrative depiction of his protagonist, Darl Bundren. Darl's ability to see his social world through the eyes of others, to represent events that he did not witness, was understood through the early 1980s to be a technical awkwardness, the remnant of a pre-aesthetic notion of how omniscient narration should be formally rendered.[42] But interpreted through the contemporary novelist's new ethical understanding of the positive good of the other-oriented self, Darl's ability to see the world through the eyes of others can be understood as a deliberate narrative technique that sets the terms of Darl's protagonicity.

And we have only to remember Woolf's paean to that interesting other, Mrs. Brown, to understand as well that a politics of identity is already at work in the modern novelist's understanding of narrative ethics, which can in turn alert us to the variety of ways in which socially mediated identity can be philosophically understood, not just for the contemporary novelist but for the modern novelist as well. In "Mr. Bennett and Mrs. Brown," Woolf argues that the novel's narrative conventions recirculate and entrench politically conservative attitudes. Relying on formulaic plots and social stereotypes, the traditional novel does an injustice to the ethical singularity of personhood as defined within Woolf's philosophical framework. Woolf's story of Mrs. Brown is first of all the story of novelistic inspiration as grounded in the ethical encounter with social strangers. "Late for the train" and "jump[ing] into the first carriage" she comes to, Woolf discovers the compartment is already occupied by a woman and then finds that her imagination is irresistibly drawn to the stranger: "Here is a character imposing itself upon another person. Here is Mrs. Brown making someone begin almost automatically to write a novel about her. I believe that all novels begin with an old lady in the corner opposite" (199).

For Mrs. Brown to impress her character upon her is for Woolf, on her view, to be called to the task of knowing and representing the unfamiliarity that is Mrs. Brown's defining attribute. To respond to the call of Mrs. Brown's otherness is for the novelist to attempt to do justice to the unfamiliarity of Mrs. Brown as a life. Stereotypes must be resisted. The hot water bottle and umbrella must be forgone, the daughter who predictably would work as a milliner left out (207). To see Mrs. Brown as she is and not as patriarchal, bourgeois society would have her be is to understand the value of the stranger as an ethical call. For Woolf the ethical value of unfamiliarity applies not just to the way that Mrs. Brown should be regarded by other persons in her social world but to a philosophy of personhood that credits any self with the ethical capacity for endless self-invention, unpredictability, limitless potential. Mrs. Brown is "an old lady of unlimited capacity and infinite variety; capable of appearing in any place; wearing any dress; saying anything and doing heaven knows what" (212).

Jen and Woolf thus both define themselves as novelists by their constitutive interest in people different from themselves (for Woolf the compelling stranger, for Jen the cultural other), and both believe that their project as novelists is to bring their characters to life as autonomous beings. Woolf's famous claim in "Mr. Bennett and Mrs. Brown" serves as a foundational statement for the tradition I am tracing: "I believe that all novels, that is to say, deal with character, and that it is to express character—not to preach doctrines, sing songs, or celebrate the glories of the British Empire, that the form of the novel, so clumsy, verbose, and undramatic, so rich, elastic, and alive, has been evolved" (199). But it is the goal of Woolf's narrative ethics to present her characters' capacity for unpredictability and self-difference that on her view defines the ethical singularity of being human. To express this better ethical understanding of Mrs. Brown means doing violence to ("smashing and crashing") the formulaic plots and stereotypical assumptions that are the English novel's standard narrative attributes and inventing new narrative protocols that will launch the art of the novel as an aesthetics of alterity (209). *The Waves*, for example, depicts Bernard's enlivening self-difference through its narrative suggestion that the other characters in the novel are both individuals in their own right but also aspects of Bernard's multifaceted and unpredictable personhood.

In other essays, Woolf extends the logic of her defense of Mrs. Brown's alterity to encompass the novel itself as the genre of alterity. She rails specifically against the view that the novel's concern with character marks it as woman's work. As she explains in "Women and Fiction," the sexist assumption that women are inherently more invested in the quotidian doings of the social world is culturally linked to the power structures that keep middle- and upper-class women employed in care-taking activities.[43] Not only do these duties prevent women from traveling, but, according to Woolf, they created the conditions of labor under which a woman who wanted to be literary artist would choose the novel as her genre: "George Eliot left her work to nurse her father. Charlotte Brontë put down her pen to pick the eyes out of the potatoes. And living as she did in the common sitting room, surrounded by people, a woman was trained to use her mind in observation and upon the analysis of character. She was trained to be a novelist and not to be a poet" ("Women and Fiction," 581). Importantly, Woolf does not rebut the view that "fiction was, as fiction still is, the easiest thing for a woman to write" (581). On the contrary, by equating the novel's artistic enterprise with the representation of characterological lives, she both establishes a ground for a novelistic aesthetics and links that aesthetics to the social conditions—then and now—that position women as especially qualified to write novels of character. The ethical art of the novel that Woolf develops (and which I will discuss further in Chapter 2), an art based in the discovery of the narrative resources that can best do justice to Mrs. Brown or Mrs. Dalloway in all their unfamiliarity, thus serves as a defense of the aesthetic competence of woman writers. While George Eliot despaired that the novel's lack of form "constitutes the fatal seduction of novel-writing to incompetent women," Woolf links the subaltern status of women to her own ability to see—in ways that more socially secure writers need not—that what distinguishes the novel as an art form are the narrative resources that it possesses for representing social otherness.[44]

A comparison of Jen's and Woolf's notions of identity politics can contribute to the interpretive framework for reading with the novelistic aesthetics of alterity that I am interested in formulating. On the one hand, Woolf's ideological analysis of the view that women are naturally overinterested in the everyday doings of other people suggests political grounds for critiquing Jen's belief that Asian Americans have been culturally conditioned to be more other-oriented than Westerners. On the other hand, the views of both novelists raise shared questions about the author's ethical relation to the characters she represents. What makes a particular authorial subject position entitled to depict or prohibited from depicting particular social lives? Can two narrative methods be more or less the same formally and yet hold different ethical value because their authors write from different subject positions? Is the novelist's refusal to represent certain kinds of social others ethically superior to the narrativization of the power relations that create their subject positions? The point I want to make is that the novelistic aesthetics of alterity does not offer a systematic or programmatic way of reading narrative that results in a unanimous view of either the defining properties of the novel understood as a narrative form or the ethical values inherent to in specific novels, but instead positions the ethical value of alterity as the end point of novel reading, however ethics is defined and whatever narrative features are credited with conveying that ethics. This is to say that although the ethical attitudes at stake in a given novel are conflicted or even contradictory, the questions circulated about knowing and representing others make narrative legible and bestow a unifying aesthetic value upon the genre.

To see this strong connection between contemporary and modern novelists' understanding of narrative ethics thus explains why Jen earns the praise of a *Western* editor, who tells her that the "quality of secondary characters" is the register of "the author's awareness of others besides him or herself."[45] As I have been arguing, it is my contention that the ethics of alterity—of seeing the world through the eyes of others—is central to the Anglo-American novel as it develops into a high art form at the turn of the twentieth century and comes into visibility as a Western aesthetic through the contemporary novelist's explicit engagement with—to the point of rewriting—the modernist novel. I want to argue more particularly that the novelist who most inspires and authorizes this tradition within the Anglo-American context is Henry James. As Jen declares in *Tiger Writing*, "You need to know that the great god of writing is, of course, Henry James, whose book, *The Art of the Novel*, was when I was in graduate school, and still is, the Bible."[46] In the Bible that James has given modern and contemporary fiction writers, the art of the novel is first and foremost the expression of character—and the aesthetic success or failure of a particular novel can be referred back to the author's ethical capacity for representing characters different from himself.

To locate James as the fountainhead for the aesthetics of alterity may at first seem counterintuitive. After all, in "The Art of Fiction," delivered as a lecture in 1884, James emphatically declares that "questions of art are questions (in the widest sense) of execution; questions of morality are quite another affair" (24–25). But James immediately complicates this view by also asserting that "no good novel will ever proceed from a superficial mind; that seems to me an axiom which, for the artist in fiction, will cover all needful moral ground" (26). James thus not only reinstalls the morality of novelistic aesthetics as an aspect of the novel, he tellingly redefines it as a single attribute: the depth of the author's mind. By depth he means not simply intelligence but what he terms "immense sensibility" (12). An "immense sensibility" is that which "converts the very pulses of the air into revelations." And to James's mind the capacity of the fiction writer to "guess the unseen from the seen" (13) is what enables him to imagine the experience of people different from oneself. To illustrate this point, James offers the anecdote of

> an English novelist, a woman of genius, telling me that she was much commended for the impression she had managed to give in one of her tales of the nature and way of life of the French Protestant youth. She had been asked where she learned so much about this recondite being, she had been congratulated on her peculiar opportunities. These opportunities consisted in her having once, in Paris, as she ascended a staircase, passed an open door where, in the household of a *pasteur*, some of the young Protestants were seated at table round a finished meal. The glimpse made a picture; it lasted only a moment, but that moment was experience. (13)

The person with immense sensibility is not only interested in social others but has the ability to turn the novel over to her characters. The artistic "genius" (12) is also the virtuous ethical agent who can through the narrative art bring to life social identities other to her own.

Importantly, James does not lay down rules about how novelistic narrative should best be managed to convey the author's impression of "the nature and way" of other social lives. Objecting to the treatment of novel form "as if it were a work of mechanics," James explicitly rejects the supposed "laws" of narrative composition advanced by his contemporary, Walter Besant (8). James instead views the novel's narrative capacity as generically open-ended. Aesthetic success is not defined by a narrative formula—good novels do this and not this—but by the way narrative expresses the author's capacity to know and bring to life, from her point of view, other social lives. In other words, the novel can accomplish its aesthetic goals through a plurality of narrative modes because the success or failure of those narrative strategies refers back to the unique subjectivity that constitutes the author's "impression" of life, out which others are known and rendered.

It might seem as though James's career-long project of describing the types of narrative deployed in his own novelistic practice works against his stated belief in the pluralist narrative aesthetics of the novel. But for James the classificatory endeavor—the distinction he makes, for example, between picture and scene, or between the advantages of limited omniscience and the detriments of first-person narration—is driven by his desire to bring to self-consciousness the values that drive his own narrative treatment of character. Writing a novel is thus for James "not of an author's plotting and planning and calculating, but just of his feeling and seeing, of his conceiving, in a word, and of his thereby inevitably expressing himself, under the influence of one value or the other" (preface to *The American*, 31). What is more, James does not undertake the work of narrative classification in order to break the novel into its constitutive formal parts so as to suggest that the art of the novel is something along the lines of an airplane model, easily assembled from prefabricated narrative components. On the contrary, over the prefaces taken as a whole, James distinguishes among narrative modes to better recognize how each of his published works strives to project the form of the novel as an organic unity by achieving an irreducible intertwining of narrative modes:

> I cannot imagine composition existing in a series of blocks, nor conceive, in any novel worth discussing at all, of a passage of description that is not in its intention narrative, a passage of dialogue that is not in its intention descriptive. . . . What is character but the determination of incident? What is incident but the illustration of character? What is either a picture or a novel that is *not* of character? ("Art of Fiction," 15–16)[47]

Thus, although the novel is for James an inherently plural genre whose proper narrative form cannot be legislated in advance, it is also a genre that can achieve aesthetic unity to the degree that a particular work mobilizes its narrative resources on behalf of the otherness of character.

James inaugurates the Anglo-American theory of the novel by linking the art of the novel to the representation of character—and through his understanding of the novel as an organic form (as "a living thing, all one and continuous, like any other organism" [15]), whose every narrative element is potentially expressive of character, James thus also launches the aesthetics of alterity. The value of a more differentiated account of the novel's formal properties is for James simply to be able to describe better how an author does or does not succeed in the novel's ultimate aesthetic task of integrating these elements so the novel as a whole brings its fictional characters to life and as lives different from the author's own. Crucially for the tradition I am tracing, James views novelistic narrative as establishing a necessary ethical connection between the life that the novel is (as an artistic creation) and has (in the lives of characters) and the quality of the author's sensibility: "There is one point at which the moral sense and the artistic sense lie very near together; that is in the light of the very obvious truth that the deepest quality of a work of art will always be the quality of the mind of the producer" (26). The subjectification of novelistic narrative that James installs into his account of the art of the novel thus is conceptualized not simply as the representation of the personhood of a particular fictional character but more specifically as the ethical relationship between fictional character and the ethical character of the author.

To show how James's notion of narrative ethics drives the contemporary novel's return to character is one of the central endeavors of *The Novel and the New Ethics*. Let me introduce this idea by demonstrating how the very figures that James uses to express his own ethical relation to his characters equally inform the notion of narrative ethics held by two contemporary novelists with very different narrative styles: the "hysterical realist," Zadie Smith, and the self-described ironist, Ian McEwan.[48]

In Chapter 3, I offer a reading of *On Beauty* (2005) that locates Smith's creative practice within the tradition of the novelistic aesthetics of alterity. As I will discuss further in Chapter 3, Smith has throughout her career actively defended the ethical value of fiction. Here I want to establish her connection with James through her nonfictional statements about the novel's capacity for otherness. Her most recent essay, "Fascinated to Presume: In Defense of Fiction" (qtd. as the third epigraph to this chapter and also discussed in Chapter 3), emphatically restates her enduring opposition to the notion, "popular in the culture just now," that "we can and should write only about people who are fundamentally 'like' us" (6). Ethical otherness is so central to her notion of fiction as an ethical task that shortly after *On Beauty*, she published *The Book of Other People* (2007), a collection of short stories written by a range of contemporary fiction writers who responded to Smith's editorial invitation to imagine someone other than themselves. Although she claims in her introduction that "the book has no particular thesis or argument to convey about fictional character" (vii), in other nonfiction writing Smith does make these arguments. For example, in "Fail Better," also published in 2007, Smith explicitly links the art of the novel to the author's ethical attempt to know and represent people different from herself. To illustrate this thesis, she offers an anecdote about a fictional novelist whom she calls Clive. Clive finds himself stalled when it comes to representing "the character of the corrupt Hispanic government economist, Maria Gomez.... He found it hard to get into her silk blouse, her pencil skirt—even harder to get under her skin" (par. 2). Smith explains Clive's failure (in free indirect style) as lying "not simply in flaws of language or design, but rather flaws of . . . what? Him" (par. 2). In other words, Clive's failure to represent Maria as an individualized social subject, knowable through her particular consciousness, is indicative of Clive's own failure of character. In Smith's words, "what appear to be bad aesthetic choices very often have an ethical dimension" (par. 7). But Smith thus makes clear that it is also impossible for her not to think of the art of the novel, even when it fails, as successfully expressing authentic ethical value. The narrative that does not bring Maria to life brings the author all too clearly into view as authentically lacking the depth of sensibility prized by James. Because Smith so thoroughly regards novelistic narrative as expressive of the author's capacity to know and represent social others, because the novelist is first and foremost defined as a social being responsible for the lives of other social beings, she can read not just aesthetically successful novels but all novels as revelatory (to use James's phrase) "of the quality of the mind of the producer."[49]

Smith's 2007 account of Clive's failure has been prepared for by James's 1907 account of his own artistic success: "A beautiful infatuation this, always, I think, the intensity of the creative effort to get into the skin of the creature; the act of personal possession of one being by another at its completest" (preface to *The American*, 37).[50] Thus we find Smith's notion of the novelist's ethical goal—to get under the skin of a person different from oneself—already at work in James's understanding of the art of the novel. In this well-known passage from the preface to the New York Edition of *The American*, James, looking back on this early novel at the end of a long career, favorably appraises the narrative techniques that he uses to bring to life the novel's protagonist, Christopher Newman. James believes he has in fact succeeded "in getting under the skin" of Christopher Newman to sit "at the window of his wide, quite sufficiently wide, consciousness." The value for James of taking this seat is emphatically the attainment of otherness: seeing with Newman "the interest of everything is all that it is *his* vision, *his* conception, *his* interpretation" (37; emphasis in the original).[51] Discovering that Smith conceptualizes her own artistic project in the same terms as James—as getting under the skin of fictional characters to represent them not just as persons but as persons defined by their difference from the author—shows how the Jamesian imperative to understand form as ethically freighted remains a governing assumption of the novelistic aesthetics of alterity even as what constitutes the difference between people becomes more explicitly theorized as ideological difference. As I have already discussed in relation to Jen, what Smith as a contemporary writer adds to the novelistic aesthetics of alterity is an emphasis given to political determinants in the definition of fictional characters as social others. In the example of Clive and Maria, Smith's description emphasizes the differences in gender, sexuality, ethnicity, class, and professional occupation that Clive must somehow overcome in accomplishing the ethical task of bringing to life, in Smith's words, "people who aren't even remotely like" the author.

To hear the echo of James in Smith is, as it is to hear the echo of Faulkner in Jen, not just evidence of how the Jamesian subjectification of novel form gets carried forward into the contemporary moment, but also an invitation to read the beginning of the tradition in light of its future development. Taking Smith's view of Clive's artistic difficulty, we can ask of James: What after all is the social distance between novelist and character? Is James's self-described success at getting under Newman's skin driven by the fact that his character's skin is not so different from his own? We can also note that the eroticized description of Clive's relation to his character's body—the imaginative act of embodiment starts off as the groping gesture of getting underneath Maria's silk blouse and pencil skirt—is active in James's description as well. As Eve Sedgwick has argued, James's language of possession bears an erotic charge, even when it is applied to his fictional characters.[52] If we read with James, if we follow his idea of narrative ethics in the terms he has laid out, then the "personal possession of one being by another at its completest" can be understood to be in keeping with his notion of the ethical author's deep sensibility, the novelist-genius who personally possesses people different from himself through his deep sensibility and the intensity of his impressions. Also reading with James, we can register the ethicality implied (as it was for Jen) in an author who so completely regards his fictional characters as autonomous agents that he apprehends them as fully embodied socially beings, strangers whose personhood can only be known by penetrating their bodily façades to reach the hidden interiorities that define them as individualized persons. But for James to describe this act of knowing as a possession not only complicates the purity of the author's ethical achievement by suggesting that the "infatuation" satisfies the author alone, but in so doing also draws attention to the power relation installed in James's notion of narrative ethics. James may regard his character's "being" as equal to his own ("personal possession of one being by another as its completest"), but possession always only goes in one direction. James looks with his character, but Christopher Newman does not look back at his author.

Thus we see that locating James's notion of the art of the novel in relation to Smith's or Jen's ideologically politicized understanding of narrative ethics doesn't change the conception of novelistic narrative but adds a politics of power to the notion of the author's personal responsibility to characterological autonomy. As I will develop further in the chapters to come, many of the key literary questions posed from within this tradition are extrapolations about the nature and operation of authorial power. In using Newman as a center of consciousness for the aesthetic design of the novel as a whole, is James instrumentalizing the characterological subjectivity he imputes to narrative? Does his narrative technique give life to a character in order to be better ruled by the author? Do Clive and James share the same problem because, unlike Woolf, they believe that individuals are defined by their self-consistency? If so, is it the notion of self-consistency, construed either as the uniqueness of individual identity or as the ideological barrier of subject position that makes it impossible for the novelist to get under the skin of a person different from himself—which is why, applying Smith to James, all James can do is to try to "fail better" in making his novels books of other people?

A chapter of *The Novel and the New Ethics* might have been devoted to Ian McEwan, since his statements about the novel and his novelistic practice so clearly locate themselves within the tradition I am tracing.[53] But to further my case for the foundational influence of James for contemporary novelistic ethics, I want to at least establish here how James's idea of narrative ethics is key to McEwan's thinking about the art of the novel. On the occasion of his acceptance of the 2011 Jerusalem Prize, an honor awarded biennially to "writers whose work deals with themes of individual freedom in society," McEwan put forward his idea of the progressive evolution of novelistic form: "Throughout the nineteenth and twentieth centuries, in the works of masters like Charles Dickens, George Eliot, James Joyce and Virginia Woolf, the literary illusion of character and the representation of consciousness were refined, with the result that the novel has become our best, most sensitive means of exploring the freedom of the individual—and such explorations often depict what happens when that freedom is denied."[54] Important for my argument, in this statement McEwan credits the novel generally with the power to represent character, but he attributes to the modernists' "refinement" of technique the full ethical power of the genre, its qualification as the "most sensitive means of exploring the freedom of the individual."

In this speech we find McEwan not only reproducing James's emphasis on consciousness as a defining feature of individual personhood but also his notion that there is not a single formula for how narrative can best be managed to achieve the ethical task of representing characters as "free." Echoing James's view in "The Art of Fiction" that it seems a "mistake" to attempt to say "beforehand what sort of an affair the good novel will be," McEwan defines the art of the novel as essentially "plural." And as we saw in James, the plurality of possible narrative methods for representing the individual freedom of characters is for McEwan balanced by the singleness of the ethical task that defines the novel as a genre: to register the freedom of fictional characters through their difference from their author.[55] But whereas a contemporary writer such as Smith sees this ethical task as impeded by ideological barriers and thus develops an aesthetics that derives from the way narrative registers the degree and kind of ethical capacity that make one novelist's effort a noble failure and another a register of his own flawed character, McEwan credits the novelist with an ethical imagination that is stronger than ideological differences: "The novel as a literary form was born out of curiosity about and respect for the individual. Its traditions impel it towards pluralism, openness, a sympathetic desire to inhabit the minds of others. There is no man, woman or child, Israeli or Palestinian, or from any other background, whose mind the novel cannot lovingly reconstruct."[56] Respect, sympathy, love— these are precisely the virtues that liberal humanist interpreters of James such as Lionel Trilling and Martha Nussbaum believe to be the basis of James's novelistic ethics.[57] I will discuss these interpretations of James in more detail in Chapter 5, but I want to emphasize here that the humanist virtues are valuable to McEwan strictly because they fulfill the novel's ethico-literary capacity to bring other people to life as knowable fictional characters. Respect, sympathy, love are, in other words, qualities that promote the higher ethical good of otherness; they are what, in McEwan's words, direct curiosity to a specific ethical end: to be "curious about other minds, about what it is to be someone else." The novelist's capacity to know and represent others through what Nussbaum calls love's knowledge is understood by McEwan as a narrative effect: "a sort of divine authorial attention" that confers "respect on the individual," whatever that individual's social identity ("high or low, rich or wretched").

McEwan's strong interest in novelistic ethics is reflected in his many novels that self-consciously draw attention to the ethical crises caused by unscrupulous fiction writers. There is of course the much-discussed example of Briony in *Atonement* (2001), but we can see the strong link to James most easily by turning briefly to *Sweet Tooth* (2012).[58] *Sweet Tooth* tells the story of Tom Hayley, a novelist of some renown who sets himself the task of representing a particular other: his girlfriend, Serena Frome. Addressing Serena in a letter, Tom echoes both James and Smith as he explains his imaginative attempt "to get out of my skin and into yours" (291). Through Tom, McEwan puts to the test his stated belief that "there is no man, woman or child, Israeli or Palestinian, or from any other background, whose mind the novel cannot lovingly reconstruct." Tom's description of what it might mean to be imaginatively embodied as Serena, to gain access to the window of her consciousness, to look at the world with her, shares Smith's sense of the ideological barriers that impede him: "I needed to be translated, to be a transvestite, to shoehorn myself into your skirts and high heels, into your knickers, and carry your white glossy handbag on its shoulder strap. On my shoulder. Then start talking, as you. Did I know you well enough? Clearly not. Was I a good enough ventriloquist? Only one way to find out" (291).[59] But although Tom's description of Serena clearly registers the power of social determinates to set limits to the novelist's imaginative capacity for alterity, Tom interprets the pinched fit of othered embodiment, as Smith puts it about Clive, only as a flaw of "him." As Tom sees it, if he only had a deeper mind, a more responding imagination, more sympathy, better love, he would have more knowledge, would be less a man in woman's clothing and be more fully a woman, less a mimic and more completely the other that is Serena.[60]

The metafictional surprise of McEwan's novel is that its first-person narrator, Tom's girlfriend, Serena Frome, is revealed about two-thirds of the way through to be the fictional creation of Tom Hayley. In other words, first-time readers believe for most of the novel that they are reading a fictional story written by

Ian McEwan and narrated in the first person by his fictional protagonist, Serena Frome. It turns out, though, that the story we are reading, told by Serena in the first person, is authored by Tom. When this fact is revealed by Tom, through the letter I have just quoted that interrupts and takes over from her first-person narration, we are invited to go back to page one and reread in light of an additional ethical dimension. The novel's narrative structure invites the rereader to search Serena's first-person narration for signs of Tom's identity, to interpret the narrative techniques that have projected Serena as an autonomous person, "consistent with herself" (to use James's term), as Tom's mimicry. Instead of thinking that's how Serena sees the world, we now think that's how Tom imagines that Serena sees the world, that's how a man tries to sound like a woman, that's how a wronged lover enacts his revenge, that's how a wronged lover forgives the woman he still loves. The narrative twist ultimately directs us back, of course, to McEwan and the ethics that attend his own authorial position. *Sweet Tooth* encourages us to ask the same questions of McEwan that we ask of Tom: What does this representation of Serena say about McEwan's ability to know people different from himself? Are Tom's worries about his representation of Serena's gendered identity also McEwan's? Does McEwan in fact introduce the metafictional twist in order to relieve himself from final responsibility for the ethical task of making Serena seem consistent with herself rather than a reflection of his own identity?

Notably, *Sweet Tooth* further contributes to the problematic of the novelistic aesthetics of alterity by posing the problem of real people's lives to the ethics of fiction writing. The bringing to life and the conferring of independence upon fictional characters is one ethical task, the overcoming (or attempt to overcome) the obstacles of ideology another; but now we are asked to consider as well whether the novelist also has a responsibility to the people in his own life whom he treats as referents for his fictional characters. The ethics of Tom Hayley's narrative practice thus expands to include the problem of the aesthetic use he makes of the woman he loves. On the one hand, as an artist he has met the Jamesian standard of ethical characterological representation: he has successfully handed over his novel to his character. But the autonomy he succeeds in bestowing upon the fictional Serena has been won through the instrumentalization of the real-life Serena. The ethical curiosity that as a novelist has led him to try to know "what it is to be someone else" results in the violation of the privacy of the novelist's intimates (their personal lives made public).

But lest we rest with such a clear-cut, negative judgment of Tom's narrative ethics, McEwan wittily provides his fictional novelist with an ethical justification for the aesthetic use to which he puts Serena. The plot of *Sweet Tooth* turns on a discovery that Tom makes about Serena, after they have become lovers. Serena Frome is a spy for M15 and Tom is the object of her professional mission.[61] When Tom turns the tables and spies on Serena spying on him, his counterespionage seems a way of knowing Serena that, unlike embodiment, he can experience. To know a spy, be a spy.

Spying on Serena spying on him, Tom concludes that persons may not be defined by their self-consistency, or if they are, that that self-consistency can be defined as a consistent capacity for emotional doubleness. In his letter, Tom tells Serena that he can simultaneously "want you and watch you. The two weren't mutually exclusive. In fact, they fed each other" (292). Tom then develops this psychological understanding of personhood into a new version of the ethics of novelistic alterity. On this view, the spy's capacity for leading a double life best analogizes the novelist's ethical stance: the novelist who can best bring others to life in his fictional worlds is he who can in his own life occupy simultaneously two different emotional positions: to both be in life and outside of it, to enjoy emotional intimacy and simultaneously achieve observational distance, to be the real-life lover who sleeps with his beloved while taking notes on the experience. Tom's idea of the novelist thus suggests that the socially impossible position of godlike, infinite love toward others—a position that the human novelist must necessarily fail to achieve fully—might be usefully improved upon by the socially achievable covert agent.

But to see how McEwan contributes to the problematic that is the novelistic aesthetics of alterity through his depiction of Tom's views about novelistic ethics is not, of course, to argue that McEwan endorses his character's position. On the contrary, McEwan as a master of irony suggests through the language that Tom uses that the novelist's felt capacity to lead a double emotional life is nonetheless a betrayal of other people in his life. (As I will show in Chapter 5, this same view of narrative as surveillance informs J. Hillis Miller's view of novelistic ethics in general and more particularly his understanding of the ethics of narration in Henry James.) Being and seeing may, according to Tom, exist within the novelist as "sealed compartments side by side," but this relation of separation is not a neutral one: the seal quarantines the turpitude of watching from the good of loving, "never letting the dank stench of one invade the sweetness of the other" (292). Despite Tom's assertions to the contrary, the doubleness of the novel's emotional stance is an ethical double-dealing, a failure to be truly intimate and an exploitation of other persons for aesthetic ends.

The ethical critique that McEwan brings to Tom's position ostensibly upholds the liberal humanist view of the novel he presents in his prize-acceptance speech. But the destabilization of Tom's view of the novelist as a participant-observer throws into question the visual epistemology that is the philosophical ground for Jamesian narrative ethics—and in so doing also throws into question the Jamesian negative capability that McEwan echoes in his speech. As has been well explored in James studies, James's thoroughgoing reliance on visual terms and figures to describe both the experience of life and the production of art situates him squarely within what Elizabeth Deeds Ermarth calls the realist "perspective system":

> The litmus test of realism . . . is whether or not a text, a painting, an architectural order, or a political structure encodes the value of neutrality through the use of a perspective system that creates universal common denominations, especially the media of modernity, time and space. . . . The media of modernity, especially in narrative, give a certain privilege to a particular notion of consciousness as something that transcends particulars and assembles them.[62]

Faith in the novel's perspective system is what allows James to believe that as a novelist he can transcend the particulars of his own consciousness in order to assemble the consciousness of a fictional other, that he can represent the personhood of Christopher Newman as a point of view, as a position of watching, and also, from his own point of view as Henry James, watch the watcher.

To throw into question the Jamesian mode of point of view that makes narratorial transcendence seem possible is to throw back into the personal realm the question of novelistic ethics. As the prefaces to the New York Edition of his work amply demonstrate, the Jamesian novelist is precisely the person who believes he can both live life and watch it, be the person whose immense sensibility gets more from life and the novelist who "reports back" about his experience. But like McEwan, James is also well aware of the difficulty of sustaining this compartmentalization: we have only to remember Strether's worry in *The Ambassadors* that he may have failed to "live all you can" by watching others live. And as has been often remarked upon by readers of James, the theme of lives wasted in watching extends over James's whole career, from "Daisy Miller" to the "The Beast in the Jungle" and the "Altar of the Dead." At the end of his life, writing his autobiography, James channels his anxiety about being a watcher of his own life into an origin story for the novelistic ethics of otherness. Of his boyhood companions he writes, "They were so *other*—that was what I felt; and to *be* other, other almost anyhow, seemed as good as the probable taste of the bright compound wistfully watched in the confectioner's window" (*Small Boy*, 101; emphasis in the original). The condition of felt difference—James's sense that what distinguishes him from other boys is that he is a watcher and they are doers—is represented as a basis for novelistic ethics. Positioned at the window of "the confectioner's hard glass" (101), the ethical good of knowing persons as others is analogized through the gustatory good of a pastry to a child. To follow out McEwan's suggestion in *Sweet Tooth* and refer James's aesthetics of alterity back to the ethics of his own real-life character—either critically, to the cold-bloodedness of his observational stance toward people in his own life, or more sympathetically, to his boyhood dream of being other, almost anyhow—does not do away with the tradition but, on the contrary, intensifies the understanding of narrative as a debate about the right way to define ethical value rather than about whether or not narrative is given value through ethics.

Before I develop the Jamesian trajectory of the novelistic ethics of alterity through the close readings of *What Maisie Knew*, *On Beauty*, and *Elizabeth Costello* that are the basis for Chapters 2–4, and before I make the case in Chapter 5 for James's influence on new ethical theory as developed within the Anglo-American academy, I want more generally to consider how a contemporary belief in the power of novelistic narrative to make otherness available for readerly inspection promotes an ethical view of novel form by comparing the liberal humanist ethical defense of novel reading advanced by Jonathan Franzen with the Foucauldian political critique of novel reading mounted by D. A. Miller. I hope this seems like an unlikely comparison—and that by demonstrating the role the novel plays in the constitution of the otherness that is the value at issue for both thinkers, I can begin to make good on the claim I proposed at the outset of this chapter: that the postmodern critique of the liberal subject does not do away with the ethical value ascribed to novelistic narrative but, on the contrary, credits narrative—in a way that is compatible with new ethical thought—with the ontological power to make visible ideological modes of social domination. In staging this comparison, I am anticipating some of the points that *Elizabeth Costello* makes about the ubiquitous but various modes of alterity credited to the novel in the contemporary moment. I will return to Miller's Foucauldian account of the novel in Chapter 5 in order to show how the turn to ethics in the academy is inspired by a desire to refute the discrediting of individual agency endemic to what Eve Sedgwick, in her own turn to ethics, calls Miller's "paranoid" view of the novel.[63] And in Chapter 2, I will show that we can begin to see the retheorization of novelistic narrative's power to "other" ideological hegemony through Toni Morrison's notion of "Africanist presence" as that which operates through narrative to upset ideological mastery. That Morrison both praises and blames James for the ethics of alterity expressed in *What Maisie Knew* further consolidates James's position as a master thinker for this tradition. But a more general comparison of Franzen and Miller usefully establishes the way the alterity effects credited to the novel reform the "cannibal art" by theorizing it not as a devourer of an infinite variety of other discourses but as a complex, aesthetic unity due to the single task that the novel performs: the task of engaging the novel reader in an encounter with alterity.

Putting Franzen and Miller in relation first of all allows us to see how they both interestingly take as their starting point that the novel's greatness as an art form was established through its liberal social mission. Charles Dickens, Harriet Beecher Stowe, George Eliot—these are all writers who wrote, as Franzen says, with the "dream of changing the world" ("Perchance to Dream," 18). Franzen believes that with the rise of photography, film, and the web, other media have taken over from the novel the task of social critique. Although Franzen wrings his hands over the commodification of the novel in our own moment, calling "the blockbuster novel" a "mass-marketable commodity" that is a "portable substitute for TV" (18), and although he admits to bouts of despair in which the decline of reading generally encourages writer's block—"You ask yourself, why am I bothering to write these books?" (44)—he holds to the notion that literature can and should be a saving remnant, imbued with its own power to better the world through its modes of ethical value and aesthetic complexity. Franzen credits the research of Shirley Brice Heath (who at the time of his interview with her was professor of linguistic anthropology at Stanford and who now as professor emerita holds the Marjorie Bailey Professorship in English and Dramatic Literature) for rescuing him from the slough of despair. According to Franzen, Heath's research helped him to understand that he had been wrong to project the reading public as a monolith of commodity consumers. According to Franzen, Heath's interviews with individuals who self-identify as serious readers convinced him that an audience did in fact still exist for social-purpose fiction. Significant for the argument I am building about the novelistic ethics of alterity, Franzen links the project of bettering the real world to the phenomenology of otherness that structures the novel reader's experience of fictional worlds. Franzen makes this link through a finding he attributes to Heath's research: the discovery that many readers identify with the "social isolate" (46), "the stranger, who takes this sense of being different into an imaginary world. But the world, then, is a world you can't share with the people around you—because it is imaginary. And so the important dialogue in your life is with the *authors* of the books you read. Though they aren't present, they become your community" (46; emphasis in the original). From this sociological description of one type of reader, the reader whose engagement with fiction becomes a real social experience, a dialogue with the author as a social subject conducted through the materializing power of literary form, Franzen develops a phenomenology of reading more generally that is tied to an ethics.[64] Working through Franzen's idea of ethics, we can see how the power to change the world that he attributes to the great social novels of the past now becomes the power to engage the reader in an ethical reading experience that can be found in any novel that situates readers in an affective relation to its characters—and through its characters—with the author as an ethical agent.

Franzen's ethical phenomenology rests on the notion that the task of projecting the seen from the unseen, of making visible the invisible, is a project of co-creation that installs the reader not just in a dialogue of ideas with the author but in an "interior collaboration of writer and reader in building and peopling an imaginative world."[65] In other words, the great social novel can still do its work, if we understand this work not as pointed outward to the dream of ending slavery or encouraging prison reform but as a significant kind of social experience for the reader: the experience that fiction allows of communal co-creation with the author to bring into being an autonomous social world that is also a specific cultural world belonging to particular persons. The reader of fiction thus voluntarily takes on a double social responsibility: she binds herself first to the author through the responsible work of collaboration and, through that ethical act, to the fictional world that she projects as its own social autonomy. A private act of cognition thus is understood as the valuable and serious activity of social commitment. As an act of co-creation, fiction reading thus engages the reader in an ethics of alterity. The reader is made better by literary reading because while she is reading she is working ethically on behalf of author and characters, putting her freedom in the service of the act of othering. In this readerly model of the novelistic ethics of alterity, Franzen interestingly takes for granted that the fictional status of characters is not an obstacle to ethical work but a condition for its production. The imaginary nature of the fictional world is what creates the need for the reader to work with the author on its behalf: the shared ethical task is to build and people an imagined social world by bringing it to life. The act of reading is thus also an act of alterity-making: it is the work of creating an autonomous world.

Franzen believes that the reader's ethical collaboration—with both author and character—is a particular function of the linguistic nature of literary representation. Co-creation takes place between reader and author as they work together to "see" something that is not there, to instantiate an imaginary world as a social reality, to project, in James's terms, the unseen from the seen. Thus, although the explosion of new media may have taken over the novel's documentary function, the old technology of the novel—the material form as codex—is for Franzen the key to its ethical value. Franzen explicitly contrasts the ethical work demanded by the material modality of literature with the material mode of film. Film as a visual medium does not, he believes, call upon the viewer to do the same kind of collaborative imaginative work, to bring a world to life with the author, to do the creative work of "seeing" something that is not in fact there. In film, the social world is simply set before the viewer; it is what cannot not be seen. And even more important, Franzen believes that film's visual language fails to enlist the reader in the ethical project of characterological care: there is no need to lend one's own feelings to the cinematic character because interior states are less cultivated by film—hence Franzen's dismissive judgment of the "inevitable superficiality of film" (42).

When Franzen describes in more detail the way characters are constituted by the reader as social others through the ethical work of imagination, we find that the fictional world's capacity to seem other, to be constituted through the work of imagination as autonomous, as something to be made in order to be viewed, powerfully informs his account of the reader's emotional response to those imagined people who have been brought to life through the reader's coproduction with the author. Rather than describing readerly affect in terms of identification or projection, psychoanalytic terms that cast the reader's social relation to fictional characters in terms of a psychic compulsion or personal lack, Franzen instead figures the reader's relationship to character as a practice of gift-giving.⁶⁶ He supports this generalized description of the novel reader by offering the example of his own reading experience of the novel *Desperate Characters* by Paula Fox.⁶⁷ Franzen states that he brings the protagonist of this novel to life by meeting the representation of her emotional states with his own emotional equivalences, pouring "my own feeling of fear and estrangement into my [readerly] construction" of her. In the novelistic ethics of alterity assumed by Franzen, readerly emotion is not gendered, not threatening, not colonizing, not solipsistic or egotistical. On the contrary, readerly emotion is responsibly and generously summoned on behalf of an imaginary being in order to help "construct" her as a person, in her own right, consistent with herself. "My own" feeling thus bestowed on the character operates like the Kantian model of beauty: the fear and estrangement that each reader cedes to the character will be particular to that reader, but the act of ceding emotion is itself, as Franzen's phenomenology of fiction would have it, a universal condition of the ethicality of fiction. For Franzen, the measure of good fiction, of fiction that can be called literary, is the degree to which it successfully enlists readers in bestowing their emotion upon characters, bringing them to life as independent persons. This is why, for Franzen, to begin to read a literary work is to open oneself to an ethical task: "When you hold a book, the power and the responsibility are entirely yours" (40). As a free ethical agent, the reader must decide whether or not to undertake acts of imagination conducted on behalf of realizing the autonomy of this particular author's vision, the autonomy of this work's social world, and the autonomy of complex individuals defined by their deep interiority.

It would be easy to quarrel with Franzen, to argue to begin with that "great literature can come to grips with the ethical, philosophical, and sociopolitical dimensions of life" in a way that has nothing to do with literary form. Or one could make the case for the ethical value of other types of literary form—allegory, for example, or drama, as Walter Benjamin and Bertolt Brecht have done. Just about any film theorist might be invoked to challenge Franzen's notion of film viewing as an inferior form of imaginative endeavor. But what interests me most is how Franzen doesn't feel obliged to defend his views. He feels them to be true—and he is glad and hopeful when Heath's work proves to him that other readers exist who read in the same way. By writing an essay for *Harper's* about the value of literature, his purpose seems less to persuade than to affirm—or rather perhaps to persuade by affirming. Rhetoric, not logic, is his most potent resource: his use of the second-person pronoun describes his own experience as a reader *for* his readers. In an extension of the relationship of gift giving, he provides a description of his reading experience for readers to recognize themselves in or perhaps (in the same way that Tom Hayley comes to believe that Serena's identity as a spy is the key to the novelistic ethics of alterity) to learn to imitate. The power and responsibility are yours, but only if we first share the idea that literary reading is an act of power and responsibility.

We can see how the findings of a very different kind of sociologist provide the interpretive grounding for D. A. Miller's tour de force study of the alterity made available through the form of the Victorian novel, a theory of the novel set forth in his *The Novel and the Police* (1988). Whereas Heath's empirical work reassures Franzen that serious readers not only exist as distinctive social types (and thus variegate the monolithic notion of a general public that no longer cares to read literature), and whereas the descriptions she offers of these social types inspire Franzen to develop a phenomenology of novel ethics based on one type of reader in particular ("the stranger who takes this sense of being different into an imaginary world," the social isolate who approaches the task of fiction as an ethical task of co-creation), Miller draws his idea of novelistic ethics from the post-Marxist ideological vision of society theorized by Michel Foucault. Miller's interest in the Victorian novel starts where Franzen's starts. The "great social novel" that is written with, in Franzen's words, "the dream of changing the world" (18) is described by Miller as "the primary spiritual exercise of an entire age" (x). "No openly fictional form has ever sought to 'make a difference,' in the world," Miller declares, "more than the Victorian novel" (x). But while Franzen bemoans the fact that the novel has ceded to other new media its power to make a difference in the social world, Miller, through Foucault, views the Victorian novel's ethical mission from a position of political critique. And here we see how character continues to matter for the new ethical understanding of the novel, even for critics who share Robbe-Grillet's belief that under the institutional administration of high capitalism individuals no longer direct the operation of social power. It is precisely Miller's endeavor—through Foucauldian theory—to show how the ideological condition of individual disempowerment is prepared for in the Victorian period and how the great social novels of the period promote the illusion of continued individual power through the narrative techniques deployed in the service of binding the individual within the institutional administration of social control. Thus Miller argues that in a novel such as *Oliver Twist*, Dickens's cultivation of readerly outrage, the "moral shock" he seeks to inspire through his depiction of prisons and other corrupt social institutions, is part of a complex affective solicitation that ultimately deploys ethical "'scandal'" as "a systematic function" of the "routine self-maintenance" of "modern social organization" (xii). On the Foucauldian view, the "liberal subject forgets or disavows his functional implication in a system of carceral restraint or disciplinary injunctions" (10).

Miller would presumably view Franzen's notion of the freedom that attends the ethical reader as a neoliberal expression of ideological disavowal. But Miller's sense of how the novel as a literary form fosters the ideological production of the liberal subject is anchored in an aesthetics of alterity that is available to Miller as a twentieth-century critic who assumes, in a way that Dickens himself would not have assumed, that the management of narrative holds necessary social value. Thus, while for Miller narrative does not structure a social relation between individuals—reader and author, author and character, reader and character, reader and author—it does produce the reader as a general social type (the liberal individual) whose affective responses are not a matter (as they were for Franzen) of free ethical choice but are instead a necessary component of institutional functioning, installed in novelistic narrative as a technology of power. In keeping with the argument I have been developing about the novelistic aesthetics of alterity, the Foucauldian model of power as a circulatory network that inhabits even the "tiniest practices of everyday social life" (17) encourages Miller's assumption that the novel's narrative strategies are microtechnologies for the "fluidity and density" of social regulation—which thus bestows upon the novel as an art form a dense and multiform aesthetic intensity.

But it is not just that Miller freights narrative technique with necessary and objective social value that makes his ideological critique of ethics compatible with the novelistic ethics of alterity that I have been describing. Miller's ideological description of those narrative techniques is especially concerned with the novel's particularly formal ability to project an autonomous social world. This is of course what Franzen was interested in as well. But whereas Franzen describes the production of this social world as an ethical act of co-creation between the reader and author, "the building and peopling of an imaginative world," for Miller ideology works through narrative to project an autonomy that is insidiously imaginary because falsely autonomous. In the nineteenth-century novel, the projection of the storyworld as an independent reality that exists prior to its narration, as a referent of narration, creates "an apparent gap in the novel's system of knowledge" in order to better veil the technologies of power that work to make social value seem necessary and objective. In other words, through its narrative effects of seeming to describe, or to use McEwan's term, to report back about events and people in a real social world, the novel instantiates the ideological illusion that the social world exists as a material state prior to and free from any necessary value—that its "reality" is simply in the neutral materiality of its objective being. But because novelistic narrative projects the illusion of this factual real through a narrator's discursive act, the storyworld is made visible as a social world precisely through the categories of value that the narrator brings to the task of world making, and that, as discursive technologies, bring that social world into visibility. The ability of the Victorian novel to mask the narrator's control over the social construction of the seemingly objective world-defining qualities of "character, space, and time" (26) is for Miller confirmation of the genre's more extended ability to promote in the reader the imaginary, private interiority that the novel reader like Franzen takes to be the ground of his engagement with the fictional social world represented by the novel and the real social world in which the novel is produced.

Miller's understanding of the bad ethics to be found in novelistic form yields one of the most exciting accounts we have of how narrative modes can be understood as objectifying the operation of social power. For example, interpreting *Oliver Twist*, Miller attends to the novel's narrative protocols for describing characters. He discovers that the novel's narrative intention to give a "full account" of Oliver produces him as social subject who can "be traced against his will": "to constitute Oliver as an object of knowledge is thus to assume power over him as well" (9). Novelistic description is thus revealed to be not a neutral element of fictional form but an act of narrative that is powerfully invested with necessary social value. Miller's analysis extends past the general category of narrative description to the molecular structures of novelistic alterity. He argues that even when the novel is not performing explicit acts of character description, it is entrapping its seemingly free individuals in the nets of ideological incarceration. The tonal modulation that the novel expresses as an aspect of narrative—the fluctuation of irony, sympathy, and wisdom that is read as "voice"—projects the narrator as a liberal subject, whose affective response expresses the ethical care that he brings to the social world that he watches and records. But this use of narrative voice also functions as a strategy of ideological power. "Disciplinary power constitutively mobilizes a tactic of tact: it is the policing power that never passes for such, but is either invisible or visible only under cover of other, nobler or simply blander intentionalities (to educate, to cure, to produce, to defend)" (17).

Miller's analysis further molecularizes narrative voice by attending to the role of free indirect discourse in the creation of ideological personhood. Free indirect discourse creates the effect of reporting character by "respeaking a character's thoughts or speeches," and in doing so, "the narration simultaneously subverts [the character's] authority and secures its own" (26). Miller thus makes a formal distinction between the vocal effects of narratorial personhood (understood as the tones of care and judgment) and the systematic operation of narrative through free indirect discourse as an agent of impersonal institutional authority. For Miller, novelistic form is so thoroughly saturated with necessary social value that even the most basic narrative convention, the representation of character speech as quoted dialogue, becomes a significant aspect of the novelistic aesthetics of alterity. It is perhaps the essence of disciplinary power that novelistic characters come alive as free individuals by seeming to speak for themselves words given to them by their narrator.

The chapter design of *The Novel and the New Ethics* takes us from the consolidation of the aesthetics of alterity as an aesthetic program for Anglo-American novelists that implies a reading practice (Chapters 1–4) through to new ethics as a recommended academic program for the professionalized training of readers. The book thus shows how authorial statements about the ethics of fiction that may at first seem casual or nonconsequential gain philosophical force as an aesthetic tradition when synthesized; and it also shows how contemporary academics who seek to move beyond the gasp and squeal of postmodern critical styles have attempted to put the case for the ethical value of literature on a more objective footing by turning to philosophers, sociologists, and neurobiologists for ways to prove that literature possesses an ethical value that goes beyond a particular culture's construction of that value, or the say-so of however many practicing novelists, or a particular reader's testimony to the ethical improvement brought about through reading a work of fiction. By putting authorial statements on the same plane as scholarly work, I want to show how the cultural construction of the novel as the literary genre most defined by the ethics of alterity it makes available to its readers fulfills the Jamesian project of elevating the novel to an art by bestowing a unifying value on its form. As James declares in his preface to *The Ambassadors*, "the Novel remains still, under the right persuasion, the most independent, most elastic, most prodigious of literary forms" (36). The "right persuasion," we will find, comprises the strategies of ethical confinement, of composition, that each author individually projects for the form. James tells us in the same preface that his choice of narrative technique, his representation of Strether's consciousness through third-person focalized narration, was arrived at by his sense that novels written in the first person "are foredoomed to looseness" (320). Throughout the prefaces he theorizes his narrative choices as bringing the novel into being as a limit, as projectable as a distinct genre through the laws of composition that each novelist—and I would add each new ethical theorist—honors and invents, honors by self-subjection to their invention. The novel is produced as the most independent, the most elastic, the most prodigious of literary forms precisely because it does not solve in advance the problem of its own regulation. Novels instantiate the value of variety, since there is no limit to the way this regulation can be imagined. Each novelist who projects the law of a particular novel affirms the genre's prodigiousness, its endless potentiality to be different, to incite the imagination of its future possibility.[68] For James, the ethical virtue inherent in the novel as a form is what Judith Butler calls the "evanescence" (a notion I explore more thoroughly in Chapter 5) that gives it not just life but "a life": the alterity that derives from its endless variety positions the man of imagination "by the very law of his genius, [to believe] . . . in a possible right issue from the rightly-conceived tight place" (preface to *The Ambassadors*, 311). It is precisely the tension between such absolute claims made for the novel's capacity for alterity and the endless variety of ways in which novelistic alterity has been culturally formulated that constitute the ethics of alterity as its own literary historical tradition.

Henry James and the Development of the Novelistic Aesthetics of Alterity

IN *PLAYING IN THE DARK* (1992), Toni Morrison introduces her study of "whiteness and the literary imagination" in America by way of a provocative claim about the difference she believes becoming a writer of fiction made to her reading experience:

> As a reader (before becoming a writer) I read as I had been taught to do. But books revealed themselves rather differently to me as a writer. In that capacity I have to place enormous trust in my ability to imagine others and my willingness to project consciously into the danger zones such others may represent for me.¹

The provocation in this statement lies in Morrison's contention that the novelist has an ethical relationship with her fictional characters—that persons who don't exist, who are products of her imagination, call upon her to do justice to their personhood. Her assumption raises any number of intriguing questions. Is an ethics of imagined alterity an imaginary ethics? A pseudo-ethics? Can a person be responsible to invented characters? To characters that she herself has invented? Can the imagination know and depict real otherness? Or is the imagination of the other always only a self-reflection? But significantly, in *Playing in the Dark* Morrison herself does not raise these philosophical questions. In fact, what makes Morrison's claim so interesting is that she simply takes for granted that novels can and should engage their authors in an ethical act. In this chapter, I want to establish that Morrison holds this view because she is the inheritor of a novelistic aesthetics of alterity that in the Anglo-American literary tradition develops out of the work of Henry James. Morrison's description of the ethical engagement with characterological otherness that attends "reading as a writer" is, I want to argue, particularly indebted to Henry James's narrative theory and practice.

As I have discussed in my opening chapter and want to develop here with a more sustained attention to Morrison's position, the contemporary novelist conceives of the aesthetics of alterity as a rich problematic that interprets a particular novel's narrative technique in terms of a complex—and conflictual—notion of the ethical value of personhood. I want to show how Morrison's notion of the novelistic aesthetics of alterity uneasily combines a liberal humanist idea of ethics as originating in personal responsibility and individual action with an ideological understanding of subject position. As a writer, Morrison deliberately sets herself the ethical task of creating characters whom she regards as moral strangers; but this agential view of novelistic ethics as a felt relation to alterity is complicated by her belief that racism works indirectly—unconsciously—as an ideological force that limits and determines the writer's view of the other. Morrison's certainty that novelistic narrative holds an ethics of alterity and yet her lack of clarity as to how this ethics should be described provides the strong link between her view of the novel as a genre and James's. Her conflicted view of the novelistic ethics of alterity is itself Jamesian. In this chapter, I want to explain how Morrison's engagement in *Playing in the Dark* with *What Maisie Knew* (1897; rev., 1908) not only helps situate Morrison and James in the same literary tradition—the tradition of novelistic aesthetics that defines the novel's value as a capacity for alterity—but also leads to a new appreciation of the key position *What Maisie Knew* holds in James's development of the theory and practice of novelistic aesthetics. Morrison does not misread *What Maisie Knew* but interprets that novel through the very paradigm that James establishes for defining the art of the novel as a narrative ethics.

The novel writer's felt experience of his characters' freedom (as old as fiction itself) becomes for James the foundation for this early Anglo-American "theory" of the novel. George Eliot and Charles Dickens could create the illusion of a social world teeming with a variety of living characters, and they could achieve this mimetic effect with little or no concern for systematizing their methods of representation. William Makepeace Thackeray and Anthony Trollope could link the success of the novel to the "full reality of established intimacy" that the author establishes with his characters—but they did not have a theory of narrative form by which that achieved intimacy could be estimated. James strives to raise the novel to a high art form by identifying formal elements and capacities particular to the genre. Scene and summary, the handling of point of view, the balance and symmetry of the story's "treatment"—these are some of the narrative techniques that allow James to theorize the novel as held together by principles of design and composition, as capable of an achieved aesthetic unity. But if James is to be credited for helping to define the art of the novel as an aesthetic endeavor, he still shares the realist view that the novel's generic raison d'être is to represent "living" characters. Almost all of the elements of fiction that James identifies are resources for intensifying the projected autonomy of characterological identity. James simultaneously increased the subjectification of novel form by infusing it with characterological point of view and then sought to ground a novelistic aesthetics in the novel's capacity for alterity.[2] The techniques that James develops for the subjectification of novelistic form help to install the representation of character as an ethical task inseparable from the novel's artistic project. James's theory and practice of the art of the novel thus introduces the notion not only that there are better and worse narrative techniques for depicting characterological autonomy, but that these compositional methods put the author in an ethical relation to his characters. For James, the art of the novel is inseparable from an aesthetics of alterity that is grounded as much in the implied interpersonal relation between author and character established by the novel's form as in the representation of characters themselves as "living" others. After showing how Morrison helps illuminate the narrative ethics at work in James's novelistic practice through my own sustained analysis of *What Maisie Knew*, I will turn to the larger literary history that connects James and Morrison. I want particularly to chart the ways the notion of alterity is developed by other novelists working in this tradition to include not just the ethical relation between author and character but a more abstract definition of narrative as the vehicle of ethical alterity. As the notion of novelistic otherness develops over the course of the century, it expands to include the reifying power of structural forces such as language and the unconscious as well as politically transformative acts of creative imagination manifested by the disruption of realist narrative through allegorical modes (symbolist, magical realist, etc.).[3]

What Maisie Knew is initially invoked by Morrison in passing, as one example among many of works she admires for their successful representation of characterological otherness. And as we can see from Morrison's list, on her view the encounter with alterity provided through fiction is linked to characters who are not simply strangers to the author (in the sense of people not previously known to her) but strange: unconventional, odd, aberrant—even violent, criminal. As a reader, she values "the way Homer renders a heart-eating Cyclops so that our hearts are wrenched with pity; the way Dostoevsky compels intimacy with Svidrigailov and Prince Myshkin. I am in awe of the authority of Faulkner's Benjy, James's Maisie, Flaubert's Emma, Melville's Pip, Mary Shelley's Frankenstein" (*Playing in the Dark*, 3–4). For Morrison, the art of the novel is directly related to an author's willingness to risk "intimacy" (her word as well as Trollope's) with an other whose difference is not simply or perhaps not even a matter of the number and variety of characters she can imagine but is located precisely in the "danger zones" that ethical difference represents (3). The confrontation with characterological autonomy that Trollope and Thackeray figure as an embodied, social encounter between novelist and character (Trollope's "the author must argue with them, quarrel with them, forgive them, and even submit to them") becomes for Morrison a risky psychological event, threatening not the body but the soul.[4] The "full relation of established intimacy" (Trollope) with novelistic characters is envisioned by Morrison not as a boisterous, temporary takeover of authorial consciousness by a demanding band of clamoring guests whom the author waits upon (Thackeray), but as the extension of the self into the being of subjects whose difference represents a "quarrel" so profound that to know these others is to risk the violation of one's own identity.

Although Morrison has said that it is her ability to read as a writer that allows her also to admire the way these fiction writers engage the reader in the project of ethical alterity, her use of the pronoun "we" to describe a consensus of readerly response suggests that her writerly view is in fact available to readers who are attuned to narrative technique. As we are made to engage the lives of these strangers, we are "wrenched with pity," compelled to "intimacy," and held in "awe." The writer has, in other words, made these autonomous others available to the reader for her own felt encounter with the stranger, her own ethical risk. By the 1990s, Thackeray's view of the novel as a hospitality service, with the innkeeper entertaining his demanding, fictional guests, has been complicated by the ethical stakes attributed to the encounter with alterity. How to accommodate, let alone welcome, beings whose values are incommensurate with one's own? The ethical difficulty of the task is worth pursuing, as Morrison sees it, because the personal reward is so great. To authors and readers alike, fiction offers a real opportunity for profound self-transformation: "Imagining," Morrison states, "is not merely looking or looking at; nor is it taking oneself intact into the other. It is, for the purposes of the work, *becoming*" (4; emphasis in the original).

What are the novel's narrative resources for staging this encounter with alterity? As Morrison develops her idea of becoming, we can see that it requires both a positive and a negative imaginative accomplishment. On the one hand, author and reader must take up the imaginative challenge of seeing the stranger from the stranger's point of view, of knowing from the inside what it is like to be a criminal, a murderer, or a madman. But, on the other hand, the experience of otherness demands an encounter with the limits of intelligibility, experienced as the resistance of the stranger to becoming a familiar. The value of estrangement is multivalent in Morrison's conception. We can know a fictional character as a person different from ourselves through a positive account of their defining attributes, and even through the access to their private interiority that fiction can seem to provide—but novelistic alterity, for Morrison, also is successfully represented through narrative by what seems missing from the novelist's depiction of the characterological other: "I am interested in what prompts and makes possible this process of entering what one is estranged from—and in what disables the foray, for purposes of fiction, into corners of the consciousness held off and away from the reach of the writer's imagination" (4).

For Morrison, then, a novel is most successful aesthetically when it deploys narrative techniques that depict its failure to make all its characters fully present as autonomous individuals. A character who is not fully drawn, who resists full representation, who keeps private "corners of consciousness," is the narrative realization of what Morrison views as a superior ethical position. The ostensible failure of narrative to represent the characterological other as fully present marks the limit to the authorial imagination even as it enhances the novelistic effect that characters exist prior to and beyond their creator's control or knowledge. To judge that the author has failed to make the other fully present is both to credit the character with a personhood (in Morrison's example here, a complex consciousness) that exceeds the author's imagination of alterity and to call attention to the authorial values by which the depiction of "strangeness" is always measured as the relation between character and author or character and reader established through narrative positioning. Narrative stages an encounter first of all with an other who is projected as specifiably strange—as murderer, as madman—but also with the more abstract conditions of unknowability, inherent in personal identity, what remains "held off and away from" imagination. The person-to-person ethical encounter between real and fictional persons is thus structured by a different order of the unknowable, the limiting and delimiting power of the unconscious, which for Morrison is first and foremost a political unconsciousness, the subject positions created within a racist society.

The primary goal of *Playing in the Dark* is to track the estranging power of a culturally specific notion of black identity on "the mind, imagination, and behavior of [white] masters" (12). Morrison calls this ideological force "Africanist presence" (6). Like the characters who occupy Thackeray's inn (the characters who "have been boarding and lodging with me for twenty months! They have interrupted my rest: they have plagued me at all sorts of minutes: they have thrust themselves upon me when I was ill, or wished to be idle" [327]), Africanist presence is the guest who cannot be refused. But unlike the felt experience of the author's encounter with a characterological other, racial ideology performs its othering power indirectly. This time the corner of consciousness that is "held off and away from" the writer's imagination is the writer's own.

Morrison points to James's description of the American "countess" in *What Maisie Knew* as a prime example of the way racial formation can disable the narrative mastery of even the master of narrative. She argues that for James to have chosen a London life (both for Maisie and for himself) is not for him to have escaped his ideological formation as an American. And it is precisely the oddity of the countess as a presence in James's storyworld—manifested in the combination of the gratuitous nature of her racial identity and the lack of specification given to that identity in the storyworld (she is described in the novel from Maisie's point of view as being "brown")—that for Morrison signals her symbolic function as an ideological formation. As Morrison points out, Maisie's encounter with the countess comes at a moment of crucial decision-making for Maisie. But when Morrison states that she "lubricates the turn of the plot and becomes the agency of moral choice and meaning in *What Maisie Knew*" (13), this can be true only when agency is understood on the highly symbolic level of a racial politics that in fact compromises the novel's explicit representation of moral choice and ethical action defined as interpersonal relationships—a point that Morrison implies but does not develop.[5]

What particularly interests me about Morrison's analysis of *What Maisie Knew* is how it derives a standard for the novel's aesthetic accomplishment through a theory of James's ethical failure. The novel succeeds, on her view, precisely because its representation of racial otherness eludes the author's authority.

By failing to do justice to the personhood of the countess, James succeeds in representing her as an estranging agent in the narrative representation of the social norms of the novel.[6] Morrison's reading of *Maisie* thus illuminates, in effect, how the novel narratively represents not just the conflict between the operation of social power and the ethos of liberal humanist ethics, but the way the invisible operation of ideology enables a liberal humanist ethics. If Morrison is right that Maisie's decision to renounce her father is driven by unconscious racism, then the liberal humanist view of ethics (so crucial to characters' explicit discussion of right and wrong, necessity and freedom, that develops the plot of the novel) is deeply ironized. As both an expression of James's own socially limited understanding of racial otherness as well as a metarepresentation of the unconscious/invisible work performed by ideology, the countess's role in the novel is to throw the mystification of her estranged presence over the actions of others: the agency of Africanist presence is registered through the illegibility it introduces into the novel's positive representation of ethical choice and decision-making. Africanist otherness thus is known not just by the barrier it poses to the full realization of the countess's identity as a person in the storyworld (in Morrison's words, the "nodding mention" James gives her), but also by its power to master the master of fiction by causing the "breakdown in the logic and machinery of [James's] plot construction" (25). The novel succeeds, according to this view of ethical alterity, because its author fails: the limits to authorial control mark the novelistic presence of achieved alterity, alterity understood both as a marker of difference between author and character (James and the countess) and as the invisible conditions that limit authorial knowing.

But what of Maisie herself? Why does Morrison include her in her list of achieved strangers? On what basis does Maisie keep company with Svidrigailov, Prince Myshkin, Faulkner's Benjy, Flaubert's Emma, Melville's Pip, and Mary Shelley's Frankenstein? If the countess represents the narrative manifestation of alterity as a limit, a failure of representation, then does Maisie by contrast represent an achieved and "authoritative" depiction of otherness? And if so, what kind of alterity does Maisie represent? Does her otherness lie, like Prince Myshkin's, in a moral purity so radical as to earn her the appellation of "a little idiot" (*Maisie*, 23) from the corrupt adults who surround her? Or is Maisie really a moral "monster" (as the adults in the novel also call her [95]), on par with the Cyclops and Svidrigailov? Is it Morrison's point that James gives us a stranger who, although just a girl of six, has an affinity for "wantonness" (210) and an acceptance of "depravity" (200)? Whose otherness lies in "the evil" that has been "poured into her little gravely-gazing soul as into a boundless receptacle" (22)? Is Maisie a heart-eater who opens our heart? Morrison's discussion of James's unconscious racism directs us to think about the qualities of Maisie's "strangeness" as inseparable from her narrative representation. Is it Maisie as well as her author whose views are informed by racist ideology? Or does the operation of novelistic narrative sequester authorial ideology from characterological identity?

From *Playing in the Dark* one can't determine which view of Maisie's otherness Morrison herself holds, but her analysis of *What Maisie Knew* as an achievement of alterity that establishes an economy of power between representer and represented is central to James's own conception of his relation to Maisie Farange. As James describes it, the novel is grounded in an act of alterity: he sets himself the task of giving the whole narrative over to Maisie's point of view, "to make and to keep her so limited consciousness the very field of my picture" (preface to *What Maisie Knew*, 6). As we turn to James, it is important to note that his working out of a novelistic aesthetics of alterity is not grounded in a systematic ethical philosophy that establishes a priori a particular emotional connection or type of interpersonal relation as a requirement for the achievement of alterity. As I discuss in Chapter 5, his approach to novelistic otherness differs from that of recent critics who have claimed on an abstract, philosophical basis that certain emotions—sympathy, for example—inherently deny or co-opt the alterity of the person to whom the emotion is directed.[7] As his oeuvre attests, Jamesian narrative mobilizes a dynamic complexity of narrative stances toward its characters. These include emotions of altruism, love, and identification but also the negative relations of irony, alienation, mediation, instrumentalization, corruption, contamination, seduction, sacrifice, and even a kind of narrative murder. What is more, the representation of character is not something that happens once and for all in a James novel: it establishes a relation between representer and represented that infuses the length and breadth of the novel itself, creating its own narrative dimension.[8] The Jamesian aesthetics of alterity asks us to register the modulations and deviations in narrative stance—why this view of this character now?—and to refer these renderings of alterity back to an author who is responsible for their success or failure in doing justice to the other, in his imagination of what otherness should be and how it can be most effectively rendered.

The intensive discussion in James's storyworlds about the right way to treat others—especially what one can, might, and should do for others—provides, as Morrison and most other readers of James have observed, an ethical discourse that sets a standard for judging character motivation and action.[9] But perhaps because so many readers of James also use this ethical discourse as a norm by which to judge the narrative's techniques for representing characters as ethical beings, fewer critics have investigated what it means for the novel as a genre that James's project of raising the novel to a high art form through its formal properties of composition is attended by a belief in narrative representation as more or less ethical, more or less successful in doing justice to the personhood of characters.[10] Usually the debate is fought out on a localized ethical level: Is James the apostle of love's knowledge, rendering character with unprecedented depth and detail?[11] Or is James an Alfred Hitchcock of prose, treating his fictional persons as living props or "stupid children" for aesthetic effects?[12]

What Maisie Knew has from the time of its first publication prompted strong readerly condemnation of James.[13] Some more recent critics suggest that James's narrative exploitation of his young girl is akin to Humbert Humbert's molestation of young Lolita.[14] I will return to this indictment of James because I think readers and critics who accuse James of ethical transgression—even to the point of sadism and destruction—are not naïve but in fact are responding sensitively to the ethics of alterity that James himself is incorporating into his formal effects. As I will discuss, for an author to seem to corrupt his character is a powerful way to project the autonomy and independence of the character who seems to be the author's victim. And as *Maisie* shows, James can encourage this interpretation of his representation of Maisie because the characters in the storyworld give voice to an ethical standard that puts a premium on personal freedom and autonomy even as they themselves instrumentalize Maisie for their own selfish ends.[15]

But it is worth noting before we turn to an examination of James's narrative strategies for depicting Maisie that the ethical discourse of the storyworld places in contention competing models of ethicality. If all of these are not explicitly engaged by James's own handling of narrative form, they do help theorize the different philosophical frameworks that his critics have brought to bear on the novel—and James—in the ongoing controversy that this novel still stimulates. On the one hand, the idea that Maisie has a right to her own life can be understood as a claim about the value of singularity that attends the life of any person, a view associated with the philosophy of Emmanuel Levinas. But the novel also manifestly upholds a liberal humanist view of ethical relations as enacted by and toward a community of persons defined by their right to choose, an expectation of individual decision-making that defines ethics as action.[16] The novel offers a third alternative through its representation of the possibility of an innate disposition toward good or evil. If Maisie is born into the storyworld as an ethical stranger (either extraordinarily good or bad), can she be blamed or take credit for her actions? Should her freedom be curtailed or maximized? Do her qualities trump her singularity? The fourth model that the novel represents is one of ethical development. On this view, Maisie enters into ethicality when she ceases to be a child. In the developmental model, the question of social influence becomes paramount. Is the child's ethical task to steer the proper course among good and bad ethical influences, learning from experience? Or is the burden of the child's development an ethical responsibility of the adult, who should provide the proper moral instruction and emotional care to nurture her growth into ethicality?

Most readers of the novel respond to one or another of these options, making it the key to their interpretation of Maisie's character. But I want to argue that the novel circulates these competing ethical models because James himself is uncertain which best applies to his own treatment of Maisie. Should he regard his character as a singular being, whose personhood is best represented by its exceedance of his view of her? Is his task instead to depict her as a developing liberal subject, whose specific steps to maturity he must imagine and depict? Or does he think of Maisie as he would all fictional characters, as a dependent who relies on her author's representational power to bring her into novelistic life? Alternatively, he may regard her, as Morrison does, as a moral stranger, whose extraordinary corruption or goodness challenges the quotidian view of life that is generally considered to be the proper subject matter of realist fiction. Before I turn to an analysis of the aesthetics of alterity as it manifests itself as a component of James's narrative technique, I want to look briefly at the way James mobilizes these competing models of ethicality in the storyworld discourse and in the formal structure of *What Maisie Knew*.

Without question the ethical problem posed most explicitly in the storyworld of *What Maisie Knew*, the problem that drives all the action, is one that is incessantly articulated by the characters themselves: Is there anyone in the storyworld qualified to take good care of Maisie? But the value of care is in the novel no monolithic ethical condition. In the developmental model of ethicality, Maisie needs to be cared for so that and until she achieves the condition of adult independence. Indeed, most of the criticism on *What Maisie Knew* is divided over the issue of whether this care is ever provided, and if so, which character in the novel uses his or her own condition of independent agency to voluntarily take up the responsibility of Maisie's life, sacrificing his or her own freedom on her behalf. Readers tend either to argue for a single adult as the ultimate moral center (Sir Claude and Mrs. Wix are the usual candidates) or else to conclude that all adults in the novel are guilty of attempting to instrumentalize Maisie for their own selfish purposes, that the care offered for her is always only a strategy for obtaining selfish ends, that James's purpose is to depict—with pathos set off by wit and comedy—the world of adults as a world of scoundrels.[17] Although each of these two options may be hard to definitely evaluate in any particular instance, and although this ambiguity may imply the inextricability of selfish and generous motives, in this version the ethics of care is driven by a liberal humanist notion of personhood that prioritizes the autonomy of personhood and defines care as a voluntary, generous act of restricted adult independence.[18]

Of course, much of the novel's wit comes from James's depiction of how easily within the liberal humanist framework the ethics of care can be co-opted as a strategy to validate adult irresponsibility. The novel shows that the characters who successfully divest themselves of their position as caretaker routinely claim that their state of independence has been achieved by noble self-sacrifice.[19] For example, when Ida tracks down Maisie and Sir Claude at Folkstone, she announces to Maisie that "I came to sacrifice myself" (172), "to let you off" (173), "to spare you everything" (172). The implication is that by giving in to a decision that Maisie has made as a mature ethical agent, the decision to be with Sir Claude, Ida has spared herself everything: she is free to live as she pleases. The ethical language of self-sacrifice thus becomes a hypocritical means for abandoning persons to whom care is owed, what the characters in the novel call "chucking" a person. As Sir Claude vividly figures Ida's desertion of her daughter: "It's the most abominable thing ever done. She has chucked our friend here overboard not a bit less than if she had shoved her, shrieking and pleading, out of that window and down two floors to the paving stones" (190). The continuum that James establishes between the comically hypocritical and the potentially noble ethical action of self-sacrifice engages the reader in difficult ethical judgments that require the parsing of generous and self-interested motives as well as a judgment about the triviality or profundity of an individual case of hypocrisy (e.g., is lying to protect Maisie a small act of real self-sacrifice, a willingness to sacrifice one's ethical purity to achieve a good for another?).

Often these comic scenes are worked out with a poignancy that is the result of the pressure put on Maisie to choose through her own free will a course of action beneficial to the adult who proposes the decision. In the scene with the countess that interests Morrison, for example, Maisie is asked by her father to choose her future parental guardian: "'I don't want to bully you—I never bullied you in my life; but I make you the offer, and it's to take or to leave'" (147). Beale's rhetoric positions Maisie as a free agent—and by insisting that he is not using his parental power to bully Maisie to decide one way or another, he is, of course, in fact bullying her to be a free agent before her time, precisely so he can relinquish his position of power over her, his parental responsibility to care for her, and hold her responsible for his abandonment by attributing it to her freely willed decision. Mrs. Wix later in the novel similarly presses Maisie in an emotionally charged scene to make a reasoned judgment that will prove that Maisie has gained mature moral comprehension. Alone together in their hotel at Boulogne, Mrs. Wix wants to know if Maisie "condemns" the recent actions taken by Sir Claude and Mrs. Beale, specifically their sharing of a bedroom (218). As we move progressively to the final climactic scene of decision, the demands for Maisie to choose multiply and intensify. Maisie fears that Sir Claude has taken her out to breakfast to tell her that he has decided to abandon her. But instead, the scene conforms to the ethical structure: Maisie is asked to decide, to take responsibility. Now it is Mrs. Wix for whom Maisie is asked to take responsibility: "'Should you see your way to sacrifice her? Of course I know what I am asking'" (254).

If Maisie is not yet the responsible agent that the adults take her to be—if her father's ultimatum seems unfairly put to his young child, if we note that Mrs. Wix repositions Maisie as a child when she gives up on her request that Maisie condemn and instead advises Maisie to "'Just *trust* me, dear; that's all!'" (219; emphasis in the original)—these scenes are arguably part of Maisie's ethical education, experiences that educate her into an ethical standard and that also, through their emotional difficulty, help her develop her independence.[20] And certainly the narrator enhances this view by providing commentary that insists not only on Maisie's growth but even on the increasing rate of her maturation. For example, when Maisie is ready to leave with Sir Claude for France, the narrator remarks upon the difficulty he is having doing justice to the detail and complexity of her experience:

> It was granted her at this time to arrive at divinations so ample that I shall have no room for the goal if I attempt to trace the stages; as to which therefore I must be content to say that the fullest expression we may give to Sir Claude's conduct is a poor and pale copy of the picture it represented to his young friend. (159)

The narrator, in his self-described role as the historian who tracks the linear progress of Maisie's developing consciousness, thus suggests that although the adults in the novel may prematurely ascribe full maturity to Maisie, the ethical model of development, rightly applied, remains the standard for judgment. Indeed, most readers respond to the narrative as a bildungsroman. For many who accept the liberal humanist framework, who take the narrator as historian at his word, Maisie's isolation at the end of the novel (she is standing with Mrs. Wix but emotionally removed from her) is a figure for the independence that attends the condition of full adult knowledge.[21] The assumption is that Maisie has outgrown the need for care, that the value of achieved autonomy, of the independence that comes from mature ethical judgment, is represented by her solitariness.[22] The philosopher Robert Pippin, for example, interprets the climactic final scene of the novel as Maisie's "difficult achievement" ("On Maisie," 122): the moment when Maisie makes the passage into ethical responsibility by taking responsibility for independent judgment, acting on that judgment, and abiding by her decision. Thus Pippin reads the emotional violence of the scene as necessary to the ethical condition: "the resistance to the exercise of power over one and the achievement of an inner realm of one's own as well as a link between a first-person avowal of expression or assertion of such a view of one's own and a stand taken in the social world that affects what others would otherwise be able to do" (127). Developing these qualities, Maisie becomes equal to the adults in her world, having successfully learned, as Pippin puts it, "how to play the game" (125).[23]

But to read the novel only as a bildungsroman is also to refuse to read the ways that James persistently undermines a liberal humanist model of ethical agency by problematizing the view of Maisie's growth into adulthood. On this counterview, Maisie is from the very start of the novel possessed of a character that remains completely consistent, whose experience is an occasion for the demonstration of an identity that never changes.[24] Maisie is alternately viewed by the adults in her world as possessing an innocence so pure that no amount of exposure to corruption can harm it, or being from the start so inherently open to corruption that nothing can make her worse.[25] Already by chapter 9, Mrs. Wix can remark to Maisie: "'It isn't as if you didn't already know everything, is it, love?'" and "'I can't make you any worse than you *are*, can I, darling?'" (66). A little while later, Sir Claude also describes Maisie as always only what she intrinsically is, which in his opposing view is "the gentlest spirit on earth" (96), made ethically beautiful by the "charm of character" (107).

And although the narrator represents Maisie herself as ascribing to the developmental view of her own character—in one meditation, after they've moved to France, Maisie reasons that if she "was condemned to know more and more," at some point she "should know Most" (216)—there is no positive evidence of this knowledge in the novel's representation of her behavior, speech, or manner of thought. Unlike Flora in *The Turn of the Screw*, Maisie doesn't have a breakdown brought on by the moral burden of knowing "most" or by the false imputation that she already knows all there is to know.[26] In short, the claims the novel makes on behalf of the developmental ethical model are difficult to credit because Maisie's difficult ethical achievement is so little shown (to use a Jamesian name for dramatization) as having a positive content. Maisie's divinations may be many—but they arguably make no significant difference to who she has been from the start (either bad or good).

If we interpret the final scene of the novel with a model of ethical intrinsicality in mind, we notice how remarkably consistent Maisie remains and how her consistency drives an alternative view of the ethical meaning and social manifestation of care. The turning point for Maisie comes not from any action that she has undertaken and not even from any position that she feels she must stick to, but from a change in Sir Claude that decisively closes her options. This emotional cataclysm is registered by her perception of a tiny physical movement made by Sir Claude: "Maisie, with Sir Claude's hands still on her shoulders, felt, just as she felt the fine surrender in them, that over her head he looked in a certain way at Mrs. Wix" (272). Claude's surrender, his acceptance of the impossibility of continuing with Maisie, is what determines Maisie's fate. Claude's movement gives Mrs. Wix her opportunity: "The next thing the child knew she was at [Mrs. Wix's] side with an arm firmly grasped" (273). Maisie, surrendered and grasped, has very little room for choice. The decision about her future that she voices in the final scene simply repeats what she has declared all along, what she has felt, for good or bad, since she first met Sir Claude: "I love Sir Claude—I love *him*" (272). She has no desire, in other words, to be "free," as the other characters describe her position of ethical choice. And her choice tellingly is worded as a request for others to act: to "give him up," so her position can remain the same.

The adults in the final scene similarly persist in seeing Maisie only as they always have. For Mrs. Beale, Maisie is still the moral monster, the "abominable little horror" (272) to whom one can say anything. Mrs. Wix forms a similar conclusion, once again, and always as if for the first time establishing its definitiveness: "'But now your eyes are open, and I take you!'" (271). Sir Claude persists in seeing in Maisie "the fatal gift of beauty," which is the "charm of character." Defending himself against Mrs. Wix's accusation that he is responsible for killing off Maisie's budding moral sense, he replies:

> "I've not killed anything . . . on the contrary I think I've produced life. I don't know what to call it—I haven't even known how decently to deal with it, to approach it; but, whatever it is, it's the most beautiful thing I've ever met—it's exquisite, it's sacred." (268)

The intrinsic model of ethical identity thus posits adult care as either so powerful an influence as to have determined Maisie's identity by age six (the age by which her parents have "poured into her little gravely-gazing soul as into a boundless receptacle . . . the evil they had the gift of thinking or pretending to think of each other" [22])—or such a nurturing force that it is crucial not just to the maturation of Maisie but to her spiritual life.[27] By this latter measure, the model of intrinsicality can foster ethical relations between persons that thrive on the condition of dependence. Rather than positing dependence as a temporary condition, a condition of immaturity that poses a barrier to ethicality, Claude's ongoing care for Maisie enables "life" to flourish. By this measure, Maisie's isolation brings no offsetting ethical compensation. It is rather the loneness of the abandoned, the giving up of vivifying dependence for unwanted freedom. Left with "nobody," as Maisie terms Mrs. Wix (236), Maisie's "achievement" of adulthood is defined by the loss of being cared for, of the emotional sustenance that Maisie has experienced as being oneself by being for another.[28]

After the good-bye with Sir Claude, Maisie's point of view is no longer portrayed. The narrator describes Maisie and Mrs. Wix as both being "breathless" and "scared," but the intimate access to Maisie's consciousness that has been the modality of the novel is suddenly closed off (274). It is here that we can begin to appreciate how James's narrative management suggests the condition of an aesthetics of alterity. This narrative change in James's representation of Maisie is routinely understood by readers as freighted with ethical significance. Some readers may interpret the narrative removal from Maisie's point of view as figuring the happy culmination of Maisie's self-sufficiency. Others may read it in terms of her freedom from corrupting adult influences: she is now outside and beyond the sordid doings of her social world.[29] Or it may be read as the figure for her depraved spirit, bereft of the scoundrels who have been and should be her proper company. Other readers may interpret the disappearance of her point of view as the final extinguishment of her spirit, understood either as the withdrawal of care or as the right end for an empty soul,[30] or as the plight of those moral paragons who, born with the "fatal gift" of a beautiful character (98), are too good for the social world altogether. The aesthetics of alterity emerges more specifically when the aesthetic success of the novel is linked to the rightness or wrongness of abrogating Maisie's point of view in this final page. The aesthetics of alterity begins, in other words, with the preface that James writes to the New York Edition of *What Maisie Knew* that theorizes the representation of Maisie as a narrative act of othering.[31] Turning to the preface we can see how the competing models of ethicality that I have described are at play for James as he alternately describes his authorial relation to Maisie as one of equal ethical agents; as a nurturer whose care on her behalf realizes her ethical condition as a living subject; as the beholder of her intrinsic nature; as the necessary interpreter of her full subjectivity; and as her violator through the instrumentalization of her personhood. James is utterly clear in the preface that, in writing *What Maisie Knew*, he strives to accomplish an ethical act, but in his attempt to clearly describe the ethical power of art generally and of novelistic aesthetics more particularly, he risks becoming unwittingly implicated as an unethical master of his own house of fiction.

Morrison's ideological critique of James relies, as we have seen, on just such an interpretation of *What Maisie Knew*: on her view, the master of narrative is disabled by the ideological blindness that leads him to the unethical treatment of the American countess. But whether we agree with James that the novel he has written enacts a positive ethical good or whether we agree with Morrison that forces beyond James's control reveal his unethical treatment of his characters, the conversation that James has started and that Morrison continues links the art of the novel to the right representation of characterological otherness.

In the preface to *Maisie*, James develops an aesthetics of alterity first and foremost by setting himself the task of telling the novel completely from the point of view of a single character. James states that his whole motive is to achieve a vivid performance of Maisie's acts of apprehension, "the play of the child's confused and obscure notation" (7) of the adult "misbehavior" (5) that surrounds her. By choosing to make his story the story of a single character's identity, and then by choosing to make this identity that of a child, James raises the stakes of a fictional character's otherness. How can he enter into the subjectivity of a character whose subject position is so different from his own? His first idea for solving this problem is by responsibly imposing self-limits: he seeks to "restrict myself in this case to the terms as well as to the experience" (8) of Maisie's subjectivity. At the heart of his novelistic project would be the ethical value of bringing Maisie into novelistic being as a person different from himself who both possesses her own intrinsic identity (her own terms) and her own autonomous understanding (she sees for herself).

But James also states that, upon further reflection, he finds self-restriction and a strategy of citation to be inadequate to the task of representing Maisie's full identity. Adhering to a strict standard of intrinsicality would represent Maisie's autonomy at the price of situating her in the world of social relations. The world seen through her eyes in her own terms would "at the best leave great gaps and voids"; the result, James declares, would be a "systematic surface possibly beyond reproach [which] should nevertheless fail of clearness of sense" (7). To be systematically true to Maisie's point of view would, in other words, fail to make her experience comprehensible to the reader. This method of representation might have the virtue of purity (using only the other's terms), but the very premise of purity would result in a radical autonomy that would make her experience accessible to no one else. To see the world wholly and only through her eyes would be to gain the authenticity of her identity, her identity as a social other to James and as a particular kind of social other, but would sacrifice the social connections and dependencies that make sense of her as a life and make her life legible to others. She would be constituted as an autonomous subject at the expense of being depicted as member of anyone's social world. She would, in effect, stand alone for the whole novel as she stands alone at the end of the novel that James ultimately writes.

James reports in the preface that he finds a solution to this representational difficulty—and it is one that encourages him as author to take on the role of caretaker toward Maisie. He states that upon deeper consideration of the nature of children, it in fact does not do them justice to represent them strictly through their plausible language use. Because "small children have many more perceptions than they have terms to translate them; their vision is at any moment much richer, their apprehension even constantly stronger, than their prompt, their at all producible, vocabulary" (8).[32] How then best to represent with fidelity both the linguistic and the intuitive nature of Maisie's perception? In addition to using her terms, "since her simpler conclusions quite depend on them" (8), James determines that he as author can help Maisie out, can act on her behalf and for her representational good: he will translate her intuitive perceptions into language, finding for her a vocabulary and mode of expression that will do justice to the richness and complexity of Maisie's vision of life:

> It is her relation, her activity of spirit, that determines all our own concern—we simply take advantage of these things better than she herself. Only, even though it is her interest that mainly makes matters interesting for us, we inevitably note this in figures that are not yet at her command and that are nevertheless required whenever those aspects about her and those parts of her experience that she understands darken off into others that she rather tormentedly misses. (8)

In this revised notion of how best to represent Maisie's alterity, James assumes Sir Claude's ethical view. He in effect imagines that he produces Maisie as a "life" through his enabling and sustained care for her, through his capacity to appreciate the activity of her spirit. James believes that his language is, as the adults might say in the novel, all for Maisie. His vocabulary brings the rich complexity of Maisie's point of view into legibility for the reader: he "attends and amplifies" Maisie's perceptions by employing "figures that are not yet at her command" (8). James thus believes that by entering into a caretaking relation with Maisie, he has also solved the problem of situating her experience in relation to the social others of the storyworld: he can represent fully all that she perceives and also demarcate the limit to that understanding, the realities of the social world that she does not directly comprehend.

But can Maisie's vision be made larger and more powerful without also being transformed? Can Maisie's spirit remain her own when it speaks so much in the language of Henry James? Is the author yet another adult who claims, as Sir Claude and Mrs. Beale do, to "make her your duty—make her your life" (90), yet whose benevolence becomes difficult to distinguish from molestation? These are precisely the questions that become aspects of the narrative representation of Maisie and that make this novel so formative in the consolidation of an aesthetics of alterity for the genre as a whole. The novel's project of representing nothing but Maisie's subjectivity in a language that is at times her creator's and at times her own—and at other times is both simultaneously—establishes within the text an intensely intricate social relationship between author and character, one that invests almost every word in the novel with ethical stakes.[33] In *What Maisie Knew*, a whole new dimension of novelistic form thus opens up for aesthetic value, as the reader is invited to gauge the enabling or diminishing effects on Maisie's personhood that occur when James speaks for/as Maisie.

The whole point of this aesthetics is that the dynamic it creates complexly inhabits particular instances of author/character relation as well as developing relationally over the narrative as a whole.[34] I can begin to characterize some of the rich variety of effects that James elicits through the aesthetics of alterity mobilized by *What Maisie Knew* by focusing on a selection of passages that show the range of the economy of give-and-take between character and author that James establishes. These examples include James's attempt to do justice to Maisie's otherness by using "her" terms; his instrumentalization of Maisie, as James uses her language as a medium for the expression of his own wit; his conferral upon Maisie the language of adulthood; and the erotic implication that attends this sophistication of Maisie: that James has narratively tampered with Maisie's childhood innocence by the adult words he makes her say.

James's narrative procedure upholds his claim in the preface that he uses Maisie's terms for expressing the perceptions that she is able to bring into language. These are especially notable at the outset of the novel, when James employs figures that are palpably derived from experiences that might loom large for a small child. Sir Claude's promise is "as bright as a Christmas tree" (55). A friend of her mother's has "eyebrows arched like skipping-ropes and thick black stitching, like ruled lines for musical notes, on beautiful white gloves" (31). But as soon as the descriptive project becomes more complex, the ownership of these childish figures becomes more difficult to determine. For example, when her mother's eyes are described as resembling "Japanese lanterns swung under festal arches" (117), the terms that are signaled as Maisie's (she plausibly would have seen Japanese lanterns) are sophisticated by the narrator's amplification of the figure ("swung under festal arches"). Similarly, Mr. Perriam's face appears to Maisie as having "moustaches over his eyes" and eyes that roll "round the room as if they had been billiard-balls impelled by Ida's celebrated stroke" (79). In this sentence, the characterization of her mother as Ida shifts the point of view, allowing the narrator to turn the phrase, as it were, of Maisie's terms to fill out the figure through the addition of a joke at the expense of Maisie's mother.

The longer the passage, the more dynamism is given to the working of narratorial quotation and amplification and the ethical relation it establishes between James and his character. For example, when Maisie must part from Mrs. Wix for the first time, the narrator states that a recent visit to the dentist provides Maisie with "a term of comparison for the screwed-up intensity of the scene" (33). But it turns out that in this instance the "term" does not equate with a simple figurative comparison but unfurls as the narrator's lengthy narrative rendering of the visit to the dentist. To represent the intrinsicality of Maisie's experience, to use her terms, the whole event of the dentist visit must be described. But the term of comparison thus becomes an occasion for Jamesian amplification by appropriation. Not only is the figure of going to the dentist unfolded as an elegantly constructed anecdote, but it is also infused with a comedy that substitutes for the narrator's representation of Maisie's actual experience of physical pain. The punchline of this anecdote is the humorous revelation that when Maisie's tooth is removed, Mrs. Wix screams in sympathetic substitution for Maisie's stoic silence. By contrast, the narrator positions his relation as a stance that emphasizes the gap between his own sensibility and Maisie's, a stance different from the subjective merging that happens through parental care and psychological identification. But although Maisie's terms in this passage have been instrumentalized by the narrator (albeit in a relatively mild co-optation) for the expression of his own sensibility, the economy of the relationship, the degree to which the narrator harms or helps Maisie through such a substitution, keeps him "embedded" in an ethical relation with Maisie "as her tooth had been socketed in her gum" (33).

It is important to see that what is at issue here is not the narrator's refusal of sympathy but James's cultivation of maximum range and dynamism in narrative stances. The narrator performs a complicated feat of identification, for example, when he uses her terms to represent her purely intuitive emotional states. In this case, the narrator is not representing Maisie's otherness by quoting the language that she has for her experience but complexly imagining what that language might be if she were to bring intuition into language. In other words, in these cases the narrator is also performing his own capacity for otherness as an act of hypothetical mimicry. For example, the narrator describes Maisie's mind as a closet, filled with the experiences that as a young child she does not yet understand but are stored there: "images and echoes kept for her in the childish dusk, the dim closet, the high drawers, like games she wasn't yet big enough to play" (20). The narrator is explicitly telling us something about Maisie that she does not herself know—which makes the figure of the game the narrator's simile on her behalf rather than an actual term he is quoting. The narrator thus amplifies the expressional power of the terms of Maisie's experience, imbuing the objects of her known world—closets, games—with the meaning of what she feels without her knowing.

In another example of the variety of stances available to the narrator, this ethical economy is reversed: the narrator attributes to Maisie herself all the fine analytic distinctions for which James is famous. In the scene with the Captain, a scene that James in the preface singles out as a prime example of the transformative power of Maisie's "good faith," the narrator emphasizes the clear distinction between Maisie's thought process and the feelings that trigger these thoughts (preface, 5). The focus on this distinction places the narrator in the role of reporter of Maisie's explicit thoughts and feelings, the latter of which necessarily demand his linguistic representation. After the Captain's words of praise for Ida,

> Maisie ... found herself, in the intensity of her response, throbbing with a joy still less utterable than the essence of the Captain's admiration. She was fairly hushed with the sense that he spoke of her mother as she had never heard any one speak. It came over her as she sat silent that, after all, this admiration and this respect were quite new words, which took a distinction from the fact that nothing in the least resembling them in quality had on any occasion dropped

from the lips of her father, of Mrs Beale, of Sir Claude or even of Mrs Wix. What it appeared to her to come to was that on the subject of her ladyship it was the first real kindness that she had heard, so that at the touch of it something strange and deep and pitying surged up within her—a revelation that, practically and so far as she knew, her mother, apart from this, had only been disliked. (122–123)

Maisie's thought process is clearly delineated by such cues as she "found herself" and the "new sense" she is given of her mother. Her deliberate act of comparison also expresses the literal progress of her thought, a progress that results in a final "revelation." While Maisie thus takes on the narrator's analytic capacity for fine distinctions, the narrator puts into words the emotions that prompt these thoughts but would not necessarily be part of the thoughts: the throb of joy, her feeling of being hushed, the "something strange and deep and pitying" that surges up in accompaniment to the linguistically formed conclusion of her thought.

The interest of such passages is that, while they are all for Maisie, while they hew formally to the difference between her emotions and thoughts, the combined effect is both so analytically nuanced and so emotionally complex that the sensibility seems hard to credit to a child, not just because it defies stereotypes about the quality of children's perceptions but because it defies expectations about the sensibilities that anyone might have, other than Henry James himself. One can only conclude at such moments in the narration that Maisie is such a rare breed of child that she possesses all the remarkable capacities of her author, or that James has failed in the rendering of otherness by imagining Maisie in his own image.[35]

More troubling on the spectrum of ethical relation established by the novel's aesthetics of alterity are the passages in which James invests Maisie with his adult wit. In these passages, he is not so much co-opting her terms with his comic meaning (as he did in the dentist example), but more complicatedly associating an adult sophistication and urbanity with Maisie herself. When after a separation Maisie sees the newly married Mrs. Beale, the narrator tells us: "The child knew one of her father's wives was a woman of fashion, but she had always dimly made a distinction, not applying that epithet without reserve to the other" (102). The vocabulary is all the narrator's, even as he uses it ostensibly in service of a new thought that Maisie has just come to. But the *mot* seems more appropriate to cocktail party chatter than to a little girl's reflection on her mother's and stepmother's dress. In this example, the aesthetics of alterity works not to give positive evidence of either Maisie's corruption or the narrator's inappropriate bestowal of his own sensibility upon little Maisie but to circulate both these possibilities, which intensifies the ethical freight carried by narration, upping the need for readers to look for more evidence in other passages to conclude whether Maisie is good or bad, a victim of the narrator's wit or as grown up as he, capable in her own mind of matching his social sophistication.

James makes it a feature of Maisie's character that she precociously parrots the language of the adults—but this, too, plays a part in the aesthetics of alterity. There are times when the language of mature and witty reflection seems to happily elevate her by implying that she in some way, linguistically or intuitively, understands the words that she is repeating. For example, Sir Claude's words color Maisie's charming explanation for why it might not be so bad to live in a bare nursery:

> He [Sir Claude] had said as well that there were all sorts of things they ought to have; yet governess and pupil, it had to be admitted, were still divided between discussing the places where any sort of thing would look best if any sort of thing should ever come and acknowledging that mutability in the child's career which was naturally unfavourable to accumulation. (69)

But a final example shows that Maisie's parroting can equally work to suggest her ethical corruption, the embedding of other adult values besides charm along with the adult language that she has picked up. Maisie's insistence that she knows what she is saying (for example, that she will "kill" Mrs. Beale under certain conditions) is one of the reasons why Mrs. Wix declares, over and over again, that she has definitively discovered that Maisie in fact possesses no moral sense. It is also why Mrs. Beale is convinced that there is nothing that Maisie does not know, that there is no need for the adults to protect her from their adult doings, that she in effect is an adult among adults. When Sir Claude admits to having lied to Maisie in order to shield her from the fact that Mrs. Beale and he had shared a bedroom in their suite in Boulogne,

> Mrs. Beale could but vaguely pity it. "Why did you do anything so silly?"
> "To protect your reputation."
> "From Maisie?" Mrs. Beale was much amused. "My reputation with Maisie is too good to suffer."

> "But you believed me, you rascal, didn't you?" Sir Claude asked of the child.
>
> She looked at him; she smiled. "Her reputation did suffer. I discovered you had been here."
>
> He was not too chagrined to laugh. "The way, my dear, you talk of that sort of thing!" (103)

Maisie may have a different meaning in mind as to what it means for Mrs. Beale's reputation to suffer, but even Sir Claude, the champion of Maisie's ethical beauty, is for the moment at least a little chagrined, given pause by the possibility that Maisie certainly sounds more jaded than innocent.

The question of James's relation to Maisie becomes all the more pressing owing to the larger claims James makes in the preface about the artist's imagination not only as that which provides for his character but more generally as an agent of social improvement, even transformation. James tells us that he first got the idea for *What Maisie Knew* from "an accidental mention" that had been made to him of "some luckless child of a divorced couple" whose fate it was to first be fought over for possession and then fought over for rejection (3). The task that James sets himself is to take the "ugly facts" of the situation and, "through the light of imagination," see beyond what actually happened in social life to what might have happened: to see beyond, in his words, the predictable "degraded state" of modern social life to bring into being through his novel "the chance of happiness and of an improved state" for the child (4). The artist's aesthetic project is thus allied with his ethical imagination, defined as the capacity to see beyond the normative operation of self-interested behavior to posit the possibility of and conditions for human flourishing. For the "ugly facts" to "turn to fineness, to richness" is, for James, for the "small creature to be steeped in security and ease" (4) provided by James's ethical intervention. And as James conceives of it, the transformational effect of the artist's ethical imagination undertaken on behalf of the child is supported by the ethical value inherent in his artistic handling of the novel's composition and formal design. The values of "fineness and richness" (4) are what James also attributes to achieved formal beauty: art transmogrifies life to the degree that it replaces the ugly facts of life with the "high firm logic" of integrated design, of the "definite and measurable application" that creates the "controlling grace" of the artwork's formal integrity (8).

But although the correspondence between ethical value and aesthetic value is what drives the representational project of *What Maisie Knew*, we find the attempt in the preface to keep their functions compatible to be a source of constant strain for James. When he describes his idea for how he might develop the plot of Maisie, for example, he appeals to the formal value of a "proper symmetry" rather than to the ethical values proper to Maisie's subjective capacity for security and happiness (3). And as he contemplates the best way to represent Maisie as a character, he betrays the worry that too much "high firm logic" in terms of narrative technique might result in "my subject strangled in that extreme of rigour" (7). In his weighing of the effects that might lead to the most successful design of the novel, James waffles between his description of what would be best for Maisie—what would ensure her security and ease in the world of his novel—and what would be best for his artistic design, what would ensure its formal beauty and grace. The result is that often the production of the aesthetic effect seems to drive the representation of Maisie, as in this discussion of James's justification for limiting Maisie's experience to nothing but the sordid activities of selfish adults:

> The child . . . weaving about, with the best faith in the world, the close web of sophistication; the child becoming a centre and pretext for a fresh system of misbehavior, a system moreover of a nature to spread and ramify: *there* would be the "full" irony, there the promising theme into which the hint I had originally picked up would logically flower. (5; emphasis in the original)

James's justification for placing Maisie in a degraded social world is so that he can depict her intrinsic ethical superiority to this world, which lies not just, according to James, in her incorruptibility but also in her own capacity to imagine and perform positive social transformation. This is to say that in his preface James credits Maisie with an ethical capacity similar to that which he has ascribed to the artist's imagination. Just as James seeks to transmogrify the ugly facts of real social life into the fineness and richness of social possibility in real life, so too does he attribute to Maisie a "wonder working" imagination, the capacity to create positive futures through her inviolable "freshness," the undiminished expectation that no matter how predictably selfish the adults in her world may be, they might prove at any given moment to have a capacity for generosity and love that would enable her to encounter them as "more" than (in excess of) their known ethical capacities. As James describes it, Maisie thus does for the people in her social world what James attempts to do for Maisie herself through his representation of her subjective possibility: "Instead of simply submitting to the inherited tie and the imposed complication, of suffering from them, our little wonder-working agent would create, without design, quite fresh elements of this order" (5). (We can think of Maisie's exchange with the Captain as a representative moment of this.) Maisie's ethical flourishing, as James conceives of it, thus is linked to the social risk she incurs: it comes "at the cost of many conventions and proprieties, even decencies" as she keeps "the torch of virtue alive in an air tending infinitely to smother it; really in short making confusion worse confounded by drawing some stray fragrance of the ideal across the scent of selfishness, by sowing on barren strands, through the mere fact of presence, the seed of the moral life" (6).

In James's description of her, Maisie's capacity to be without "design" ethically distinguishes her from the manipulative adults around her. And it is the mixing of Maisie with James's own artistic design that is precisely what makes his attempt to provide her "with security and ease" structurally resemble the hypocritical rationalizations of the adults who exploit Maisie for their own selfish ends under the cover of working for her benefit. The "torch of virtue" that James implicitly claims as the source of his own capacity for the wonder-working social transformations he conducts through the art of the novel is compromised by his instrumental treatment of Maisie as a functional component of novelistic form. The preface to *Maisie* stresses the analogy between James and Maisie and also emphasizes the way James's aesthetic project corrupts the ethical project through its redeployment of the torch metaphor. James's attempt to cast the ethical depiction of Maisie's subjectivity in an aesthetic form that will contribute to the transformative power of the ethical project results instead in the projection of the artist as the exploiter of life for his own aesthetic ends. The torch of virtue is recast as "the torch of rapture and victory, as the artist's firm hand grasps and plays it" (4).

This pattern of logical tension in James's preface to *What Maisie Knew* is the strong basis of comparison with Toni Morrison—and not just with Morrison's understanding of *What Maisie Knew* but with her own account of why she writes novels. For both James and Morrison, novel writing is ethical first and foremost as a creative act of transmutation: the other is produced from the self; the novelist strives to bring into being a fictional character who seems so autonomous as to be ontologically independent from his creator. The fictional character thus takes on the qualities and rights of personhood: the creator feels installed in a phenomenological relation to her creation. To know this other, the right ethical emotion must be cultivated. For Morrison this means entering into an affective danger zone. For James, it is a nurturing act of care and service. Both affective states are types of self-negation or diminishment: the author who has created the character cultivates an emotional openness or vulnerability that will allow the character's otherness to act in turn upon the author. But for both James and Morrison, this emphasis on the ethical good that can be had through the one-on-one encounter with characters as others is at odds with a view of narrative representation as a structure of power: for Morrison, it is narrative, and not James's ethical intentions, that represents the ideological otherness of the countess; and within James's preface to *Maisie*, it is narrative, and not James's ethical intentions, that instrumentalizes Maisie's personhood in making it a formal element of design.

If we return to the scenes in which Maisie encounters the countess, we can see now how Morrison's ideological understanding of James's narrative enriches rather than disrupts this novel's aesthetics of alterity. The narrative ethics put in play by the novel frames the interpretation of the kind and degree of othering to which the countess is subjected. Who or what is responsible for this othering? Is it Maisie's perception that others the countess? If so, is the basis of Maisie's othering an unconscious racism? And if Maisie's reaction to the countess is structured by unconscious racism, does James represent that attitude as specifically and particularly Maisie's? If the racism is personal to Maisie, does James mean to portray it as the ignorant mistake of a child, a basis for an ethical bildungsroman? Or should Maisie's attitudes about race and ethnicity be understood in absolute terms as ethical or ideological detriments? James's aesthetics of alterity invites the same kinds of questions to be asked of Maisie's author. Is this another example where James speaks for Maisie—and in this case contaminates her by attributing his unconscious racism to her? Or is this an example of when he speaks "through" her, torquing "her" terms for stylistic effect? Is he instrumentalizing Maisie's racist attitudes for his artistic design? And, if he is, is this cavalier attitude toward racism a more heinous ethical position than Maisie's childish emotion? Adding in Morrison's view, the countess's agency invests narrative with another layer of ethical value. Has James failed to render the countess as a realistic character because her "Africanist presence" escapes his knowing? Does the power of her uncontrollable personhood thus disable his artistic design? Or should the ethical disruption of James's artistic control be credited to narrative itself, as the agent and expression of the unconscious racism that on Morrison's view structures white American writing?

Again, my point is not to determine the best answer to these questions but to show how the ethics of othering intensifies the stakes of narrative representation. The Jamesian aesthetics of alterity installs ethical value on a granular level, making every word count. The obviousness of a racialized unconscious expressed through the narrative is complicated by the way the aesthetics of alterity works to ambiguate to whom that unconscious belongs. For example, Maisie first glimpses the countess from afar at the exhibition that she attends with Mrs. Beale. The very first physical description of the countess registers Maisie's sense of her skin color: "the lady was so brown that Maisie at first took her for one of the Flowers" (137). Whether ascribed to Maisie or to James, the register of the countess's skin color indexes a hegemonic attitude that takes whiteness as the norm. What is more, on the basis of skin color Maisie connects the countess with the theatricalized and exoticized racial bodies that Maisie, wandering with Mrs. Beale through the exhibition, has (coincidentally) just observed at the "Flowers of the Forest" entertainment:

> But the upshot of this [a lack of money] was but to deepen her yearning: if Sir Claude would only at last come the shillings would begin to ring. The companions paused, for want of one, before the Flowers of the Forest, a large presentment of bright brown ladies—they were brown all over—in a medium suggestive of tropical luxuriance, and there Maisie dolorously expressed her belief that he would never come at all. (136)

In the storyworld, the normative social space for "brown ladies" is established as the "side show"; and this description seems to depict Maisie's recruitment into a hegemonic position that makes her first exposure to racial ghettoization also an act of participation in the normalization of racial othering. But as we have already seen in other key passages from the novel, determining Maisie's ethical responsibility is complicated by the power dynamic that is staged narratively between James and his character. Although the first sentence seems to lead into a thought quotation that establishes Maisie's point of view as presiding over the passage ("if Sir Claude would only at last come the shillings would begin to ring"), when the narrative shifts to description ("The companions paused"),

James's comic tone mediates the representation of Maisie's point of view to the degree that it becomes uncertain not only whether Maisie herself is registering the exoticizing association of the performers with "tropical luxuriance" (and James is lending her his vocabulary to assist with this comparison) but also whether she rather than the narrator notes that the women were "brown all over." The dashes give the feeling that this is Maisie's observation, a more specifically observed follow-up to a general impression. But the passage has become so dominated by the operation of James's comic tone that it is hard to know. Thus the issue of Maisie's racial perception—Are the performers brown because they are in makeup? Or have they been chosen to play flowers because of their brown skin?—becomes blurred with James's act of style, the way his elevated vocabulary and wry tone deliberately highlight the social distance between his sophistication and Maisie's naïveté and also between his own high art project and the commodified spectacle offered through the "Flowers of the Forest" (not to mention a popular entertainment like the exhibition more generally). Without question the passage represents Maisie's inauguration into the hegemonic operation of racialized othering, but to the degree that the storyworld scene of Maisie's exposure to socially constructed racial difference becomes an occasion for the display of authorial wit, Maisie herself seems a victim not just of James's sense of humor (the fun he is having by using elevated vocabulary to describe her feelings and perceptions) but also an offhand acceptance of racial abjection through the fun he is making of the "Flowers of the Forest."

To develop an interpretation about the degree and kind of racial othering that the narrative performs in relation to the countess is thus to follow out dynamics initiated in this scene, attending to the way James's fluctuating representation of the terms of Maisie's personhood informs the kinds of judgment that can be made about her complicity in racialized othering. Arguably, the crux passage in this regard comes when Maisie finally encounters the countess at close range. In contrast with the low-affect encounter with the "bright brown" flower performers, Maisie's first, "astonished" impression of the countess is that she is ugly. This feeling immediately and absolutely alienates Maisie from the countess and becomes the efficient cause, as Morrison notes, for Maisie's separation from her father. Morrison's interesting observation about the anomalous nature of the countess's characterological depiction (she seems to defy the realist world of this novel by escaping its realist notation; her skin color seems unmotivated in terms of the story's plotline; the narrator offers no information about her, gives no inside view; and the few details about her life that are offered by other characters are conjectural, vague, or implausible) needs to be balanced against what is abundantly—hyperbolically, traumatically—present about the countess, seen through Maisie's point of view: the racist stereotypes that describe her.

> She literally struck the child more as an animal than as a "real" lady; she might have been a clever frizzled poodle in a frill or a dreadful human monkey in a spangled petticoat. She had a nose that was far too big and eyes that were far too small and a moustache that was, well, not so happy a feature as Sir Claude's. (152)

Although in the next description of the countess from Maisie's point of view, color is not referenced (she is described as a "short fat wheedling whiskered person" [153]), this first portrait is completely dominated by the comparison of the countess to an animal. Should we think that this racist stereotype comes spontaneously to Maisie? When we further note that the animals that Maisie invokes—the poodle and the monkey—carry an association with circus and carnival performance, the comparison seems located in her terms, a plausible register of her own childhood experience. If she hadn't actually encountered these animals at the exhibition, she might have (or might have in an age-appropriate way been otherwise exposed to the idea of animal performers). To the degree that these figures seem to belong to Maisie, they don't seem to be quoted or parroted by her. Is James thus unconsciously representing Maisie as a spontaneous racist? Or was her introduction to racial difference through the exhibition a sufficient social recruitment, perhaps providing her with one of those Jamesian glimpses of otherness that becomes a lasting impression for certain acute observers? Is the danger zone that Maisie represents for readers the danger of "becoming," for the time of the reading, a child inducted into racism? Yet even if this passage seems informed by Maisie's terms, James's mediating presence is also clearly detectable in syntactical formulations such as the balanced phrases "clever frizzled poodle in a frill" and "dreadful human monkey in a spangled petticoat"). As in the "Flowers" passage, the style and diction suggest a point of view from which Maisie's othering of the countess might be regarded as droll. To the degree that this clash of values is detected by readers through close reading, the ethical task of becoming the stranger will be exchanged for the virtuous estrangement from the author who at this moment seems to be "grasping and playing" with both Maisie's and the countess's respective personhoods for the sake of style. With every new description of the countess the narrative plot thickens. Ultimately which is more ethically significant: James's ethical responsibility to his characters; the potentially positive estranging force of the countess; Maisie as an ethical danger zone for the reader; or narrative as expressive of the white, racist unconsciousness?

I hope we can now better see the significance of the aporia in Morrison's account of *Maisie*. On her view, as expressed in *Playing in the Dark*, the ethical value of becoming Maisie—or Benjy, or Emma, or Pip, or Frankenstein—is grounded, like James's good intentions in speaking for Maisie, in a view of ethics as a personal task and effort, taken on for the self, the success or failure of which is judgeable by no external rule or authority. But in the same way that Morrison's ideological interpretation of the function of the countess not only is at odds with but also challenges the liberal humanist ethics that authorize her description of the experience of ethical becoming she finds fiction to offer, so too is the ethical value ascribed by James to his relation to Maisie upset by the very terms in which he understands the art of the novel as an achieved formal design. And it is precisely the degree to which he has through his narrative techniques successfully projected Maisie as a living other that makes his use of her as an element of form seem a violation of her subjectivity that points to the exploitative power relations within which acts of othering are situated, even when the experience of voluntary risk or care for the other seems most sincere, most authentic.

We can vividly see the pattern I'm describing at work in Morrison's 2017 book of essays titled *The Origin of Others*. In these essays, Morrison presents the engagement with otherness as the key to her own literary career. She looks back over her major novels and describes both the versions of otherness that she sought to depict and the narrative techniques she systematically devised to do justice to characters valued as others. Her belief in the function of the novel as an ethical task is upheld by statements that indicate her faith in the potential good of the personal encounter with otherness that the novel makes possible. For example, about *A Mercy* (2008) she writes: "Amid all of this struggle, chaos, and unbreakable conflict caused by power distribution within classifications of race and gender, I hoped to draw attention to specific individuals trying to escape harm and mitigate their failures—one narrative at a time. One to one" (73).

And, of course, the way that the narrative technique of this historical novel operates is through a multiperspectivalism that, similar to Faulkner's strategy in *The Sound and the Fury* and *As I Lay Dying*, marks the difference in chapters as a difference in characterological identity.[36] Set in colonial America at the end of the seventeenth century, *A Mercy* represents social states of otherness that are structured by not only race, class, and gender differences but also the emotional condition of outsiderness that defines each character's relation to hegemonic power. These social others include Jacob, the white, Anglo-Dutch immigrant trader; Rebekka, his white English wife, who is a victim of sexual harassment and patriarchal control (resulting in her arranged marriage to Jacob); Florens and her mother, enslaved African Americans; and Lina, Jacob's Native American servant, who lost her tribe to smallpox devastation.[37] Within this diverse group of social others, Morrison makes narrative distinctions. Morrison employs limited third-person omniscience (what James in his prefaces terms reflector narration) for all the characters except Florens, who derives her protagonicity not just from the number of monologues she is granted but also from the first-person narrative stance implied by her second-person mode of address.[38] Florens's mother, also granted a first-person stance, addresses her monologue to Florens. Thus degrees of intimacy are narratively performed both between characters (a strong example of this is the way Morrison represents two white male servants in a single, shared monologue to establish their identity as a loving couple) and in relation to the reader. Certainly a powerful effect of Florens's "I/you" narrative is that it recruits the reader as another addressee. But notably, even though Morrison's narrative protocols make distinctions between the level of intimacy the reader has with different social others, the overall effect of the third-person monologues is to refamiliarize these "strangers." Morrison has accomplished almost too well the task of seeing the stranger from the stranger's point of view.[39] Narratively, there is little register of "what prompts and makes possible this process of entering what one is estranged from—and what disables the foray, for purposes of fiction, into corners of consciousness held off and away from the reach of the writer's imagination" (*Playing in the Dark*, 4).[40] The narrator seems equally at home in each consciousness, and with the use of the first-person, simply more at home in Florens's and her mother's.[41] What is more, historical difference seems just as easily overcome: the imagination of the novelist conquers the otherness of time as well as social positionality.[42]

Especially since *The Origin of Others* dwells on the social conditions and power differentials that make othering a collective cultural act of dehumanization, Morrison's description of *A Mercy* as offering the reader a "one to one" encounter with a range of social others seems to restage the conflict in her thinking between a liberal humanist ethics and an ideological unconscious. The phrase "one to one" emphasizes the ethical task of the reader as a particular individual, presented with the opportunity through literature to know and understand social others. What happens to the political forces (so much on display in the storyworld of *A Mercy*) that create identity as social positionality? A description that Morrison includes in *The Origin of Others* of her participation in a work of performance art at the Vienna Biennale helps to get at the dynamic that connects Morrison's narrative ethics with James's. Morrison tells how she entered a dark room and faced what she thought was a mirror. Gazing into the mirror, she sees a figure in the distance who walks toward her until they are face-to-face. In Morrison's words:

> She placed her palm on the glass and I was instructed to do the same. We stood there face to face, unspeaking, looking into the eyes of the other. Slowly the figure faded and shrank before disappearing altogether. Another woman appeared. We repeated the gesture of touching our palms together and looking into the eyes of the other. This went on for some time. Each woman differed in age, body shape, color, dress. I must say it was extraordinary—this intimacy with a stranger. Silent, knowing. Accepting each other—one to one. (74)

Here is Morrison's ethical optimism: we all regard the world through the mirror of our own point of view, but our ethical capacity to open ourselves intersubjectively (through will, through right affect) transforms self-reflection not just into the apprehension of otherness, but in the conversion of strangeness, into ethical "acceptance." In the ethical moment, solipsism transmogrifies into interpersonal intimacy. Morrison's description is beautifully worded, but it returns me to the kinds of philosophical questions with which I opened this chapter: What kind of otherness? What kind of stranger? What kind of intimacy? What kind of knowledge? What makes the intimacy reciprocal? How do you know you were accepted? What were the material conditions that allowed this kind of social encounter to be curated? Has the Levinasian "face to face" been appropriated for a liberal humanist aesthetic of the "one to one"?

I have been using Morrison's connection to James to argue that it is precisely the conflicted view of ethics that they both share that positions otherness as a rich problematic in relation to the ethics that both attribute to novelistic narrative. To believe in the novel as offering a one-to-one ethical encounter with a characterological other is to forget the material and ideological conditions that throw the ethical value of that encounter into uncertainty. To focus instead on novelistic narrative as the ethical revelation of the inequities of social power—to read *Maisie*, as Morrison does, for the political good of the ideological othering revealed through the narrative depiction of the countess—is to deny the efficacy of individual agency and the significance of interpersonal exchange that is represented in the storyworld of James's novel and is also salient in Morrison's praise of James's ethical rendering of Maisie's otherness. Again, my point is that both positions take the ethical value of otherness as the key value for judging the success or failure of novelistic narrative, and that this problematic (contradictory in itself) works to produce novels as unified works of art.

A quick look at the continuity in the reception history of *What Maisie Knew* can further elucidate this claim. In his preface, James bemoans the reviewers who greeted *Maisie*'s publication by seeing in it only what the terms of their own identity prepared them to see. Blind to the transformative power of the fiction writer's imagination, these early reviewers are, from James's point of view, distinguished by their own lack of responsiveness, their own inability to see otherwise, what Derek Attridge, in other contexts, has described as the failing to be open to the new that leads to the reproduction of what he calls idioculture.[43] James has in mind reviews such as one that appeared in 1897 in a Boston periodical called *Literary World*. The anonymous reviewer ranks *What Maisie Knew* "with the worst schools of French fiction" (454), objecting both to the "immorality" of the behavior of the novel's characters and also to James's immorality in subjecting Maisie to this behavior. And we can see in this 1897 review that the problem of James's own moral behavior is linked directly to his handling of narrative form. For this reviewer, James fails to transform the ugly facts he depicts because his aesthetic purpose corrupts his relationship to Maisie. According to the Boston reviewer,

> [James] exhibits not one ray of pity or dismay at this spectacle of a child with the pure current of its life thus poisoned at its source. To him she is merely the *raison d'être* of a curiously complicated situation, which he can twist and untwist for purposes of fiction. One feels in the reading that every manly feeling, every

possibility of generous sympathy, every comprehension of the higher standards, has become atrophied in Mr. James's nature from long disuse, and that all relation between him and his kind has perished except to serve him coldly by way of "material." (454)

At the heart of this reviewer's criticism is the assumption that a fictional character is somehow not part of the author's material, that characters deserve special representational treatment based on their status as persons, and that the representation of persons demands a provision for their security and ease expressed in the explicit form of the author's stated judgment against those seeking to exploit Maisie and in the more indirectly conveyed sentiment of "manly feeling," construed here as the sympathetic identification of the masculine author with his character's plight. For the reviewer, James's failure to be present in either way in the social world of his novel is an indication of how James's lifelong career as an artist has alienated him from social life *tout court*. On this view, the lifelong pursuit of art is what strangles the ethics of alterity; to it is attributed a corrupting power: it not only removes James from the social world he seeks to depict by closeting him in his study, but causes him to regard that world instrumentally for the aesthetic project it can be made to serve. James's achievement of aesthetic design is thus equated for the reviewer with his designingness. Rather than cultivating the social relation between "him and his kind," James instead develops the firm hand that grasps and plays with the fictional characters it creates, thus failing to treat them as the people they might be.[44]

It is tempting to dismiss this contemporary critic as an unsophisticated reader of novels whose complaint against James is grounded in a too credulous response to novelistic mimesis. But we find James critics a century later, fully informed by poststructuralist literary theory, offering even more vociferous indictments of James's moral character based on an assumed ethical standard for the treatment of fictional characters by their authors. In Chapter 5, I argue that new ethical theory takes on board the characterological basis of the Jamesian novelistic ethics of alterity. But a preview of that argument can begin with Sheila Teahan's 1993 interpretation of James's crimes against his character: "Maisie's ambiguous knowledge and her ultimate scapegoating . . . are themselves produced by the Jamesian representational strategy of the central intelligence, which both brings Maisie into being and sacrifices her in the name of its own antithetical logic."[45] Teahan, as much as the Boston reviewer, understands the aesthetic project of

What Maisie Knew as fundamentally opposed to the ethical representation of Maisie's subjectivity. For Teahan, the manifestation of exploitative aestheticism is located in the misplaced devotion to logical design that leads James to construct his protagonist as a point of view, in the belief that in this way the representation of Maisie's singular consciousness can also conveniently serve as an element of achieved form. For Teahan, as for the Boston reviewer, the palpability of Maisie's formal function in the novel refers us back to the ethical limitation of her maker: it exposes James's "questionable moral sense."[46] And for Teahan this is even more extreme than for the Boston reviewer: Maisie does not just "serve him coldly" but is made to "perish"; James's narrative technique is "fatal" to Maisie (137).[47]

But we can see how in the preface to *Maisie*, James's description of the aesthetic challenge that he set himself, a challenge new to Anglo-American tradition, the challenge of developing an art of the novel, is problematically related in his own mind to the accomplishment of alterity that defines the social value of art. James himself, in other words, both in his writing about the novel as form and in the forms that his novels take, helps to establish the ethical basis for the ad hominem attacks leveled at him by old and new readers, and he supplies in his storyworlds competing models of ethicality through which the reader's own ethical judgment of James might be cast. In developing narrative techniques that he believes deepen the novel's generic capacity for representing characters as other to their author, James also ultimately helps establish the art of the novel as an inimical force to the social world it projects. To the degree that the novelist succeeds in masking his artistic design, he risks being accused of ideological complicity, of pretending to represent the real in an act of veiling the ideological operation of narrative form.[48] To the degree that James makes his design palpable, he may be praised as Derek Attridge praises J. M. Coetzee, for offering "a satisfactory alternative, a different literary practice, willing to reveal its own dependence on convention and its own part in the exercise of power" (*J. M. Coetzee*, 17).[49] I don't wish to argue that either the pessimistic ideological interpretation or the hopeful postideological view of Jamesian narrative is right. My aim is to recapture the role that James has played in promoting the understanding of novel form as a contest between the realization of fictional personhood defined as a type of alterity and the social forces that compromise, inhibit, or extinguish that realization. By recapturing the literary history that has so powerfully freighted novelistic form with the ethical value of alterity, and by appreciating the formative role James played in installing the nineteenth-century realist value of "living others" as an attribute of narrative, we can see how the ethical definition of novelistic aesthetics persists, even as novelists have in the twentieth century changed our notion of where and how this alterity effect might best be produced. To fill in the line of development between James and the contemporary novelist, I want next to show how the strong attempts at the beginning of the twentieth century to develop purely formal aesthetic criteria for the novel as a genre never fully divest themselves of the Jamesian aesthetics of alterity. What is more, even as the formal account of the novel develops over the course of the century into a sophisticated narratological description of the novel's narrative elements, there remains a strong sense among twentieth-century novelists that, no matter how nuanced the understanding of novel form has become, the novel as a genre lives and breathes only by way of its successful engagement with otherness. This thread of the literary history I am tracing runs continuously through the twentieth century, establishing the persistence of James's influence on the critic-novelist's view of the novel as defined by the ethics of alterity it performs through its narrative modes.[50]

"Fascinating and strangely unfamiliar," Virginia Woolf declares Percy Lubbock's new book to be in a 1922 *TLS* review essay.[51] Woolf was referring neither to the literary biographies for which Lubbock was known nor to the novel that he had yet to write but to *The Craft of Fiction*, his recently published study of the novel as a literary art. "To say that it is the best book on the subject is probably true," Woolf judges, "but it is more to the point to say that it is the only one. He has attempted a task which has never been properly attempted, and has tentatively explored a field of inquiry which it is astonishing to find almost untilled."[52] Modernism famously invents itself by imagining the new century as a rupture with the past, and in the first three decades of the twentieth century part of what it meant to fulfill the Poundian imperative to "make it new" was to keep track of the cultural "firsts" as they abounded. The compliment of origination and exceptionalism that Woolf pays to Lubbock is one that in *The Craft of Fiction* and elsewhere Lubbock himself pays to Henry James, the "novelist who carried his research into the theory of the art further than any other—the only real *scholar* in the art."[53] Lubbock particularly has in mind the analysis conducted in the eighteen prefaces that James wrote for the New York Edition of his best work, selected by (as Lubbock, with an even more extravagant display of indebtedness, proclaimed him) "the master" himself.⁵⁴ The prefaces are presented by James as a loving retrospective, an intimate reencounter, with his favorite literary creations. But because, as we have seen for James, the creative enterprise was inseparable from his strong sense of the novel as an aesthetic form, Lubbock found in the prefaces a powerful articulation not of one man's "original quiddity" but of the literary properties common to all novels (*Craft*, 187).

The authentic newness of *The Craft of Fiction* lies in its belief that the art of the novel may be objectively located in its formal properties and objectively analyzed through empirical critical methods. This distinctively modern method, what Lubbock calls a "theory" of the novel, is influenced as much by contemporary science as classical poetics (9, 272). By 1921 Lubbock is wearied by the banality of the critical conversation about novels, the predictability of which reveals more about the limitations of the English reader's critical vision than the novel's actual aesthetic accomplishment: "That Jane Austen was an acute observer, that Dickens was a great humourist, that George Eliot had a deep knowledge of provincial character, that our living romancers are so full of life that they are neither to hold nor to bind—we know, we have repeated, we have told each other a thousand times" (272–273). The "strangely unfamiliar" news announced in *The Craft of Fiction* is that novels have techniques of their own—and good novels can be distinguished from bad novels on aesthetic rather than biographical, historical, sociological, moral, or any other terms outside of autonomous art. *The Craft of Fiction* argues that even novels as different from one another as *Pamela* and *War and Peace* draw from a common store of narrative techniques; rightly employed, these techniques generate aesthetic value, imbuing the novel with its own particular formal beauty. Lubbock thus indirectly answers George Eliot's lament about the novel: it is not that the novel's "absolute technique" does not exist (as Eliot believed) but that it had not yet been discovered. *The Craft of Fiction* will advance the evolution of the genre by allowing future novelists to practice their art self-consciously.⁵⁵ With the formal basis revealed, "the novel may now be starting upon a fresh life." Newly aware of the "immense variety" of technical possibilities "yet untried," the novelist goes forward into the twentieth century, so Lubbock imagines, prepared to perfect the genre not through barbaric cannibalism but through scientific invention, "unheard-of experiments to be made" (173). The publication of *Ulysses* (1922), *Mrs. Dalloway* (1925), and *To the Lighthouse* (1927) must have seemed to Lubbock confirmation of his prediction.

Thus, for all his deference to the master, Lubbock did believe he had an original contribution to make through the methodizing of the Jamesian prefaces into his idea of what a "theory" of fiction (*Craft*, 9) should look like. With "no connected argument, no definition of terms, no formulation of claims," the usual way of discussing novels could never, Lubbock believed, be anything but subjective and ephemeral (272). In the Anglo-American tradition, Lubbock's critical method would produce an enduring description of the novel's narrative properties and the ways that these properties have been effectively (most notably by the master himself) or ineffectively handled. At least through the 1950s *The Craft of Fiction* was a touchstone for academic analysis of the novel, allowing the genre to earn its place on college literature syllabuses. The compositional lessons taught by *The Craft of Fiction* have been so well learned that the critical approach that had seemed "strangely unfamiliar" to Woolf had become by century's end so completely naturalized that it is surprising to remember that aesthetic dicta such as "show, don't tell" (*Craft*, 62) are not universal truths about the art of the novel but were first codified by Lubbock.

But while Lubbock's own techniques of systematic argumentation helped the novel gain recognition as a high art, and while his close-reading method was welcomed by the academy, most practicing novelists—from the beginning to the end of the twentieth century—remained resistant to a purely formal account of the novel art. As late as 1966, David Lodge found the need to repeat Lubbock's plea that the novel be estimated in terms other than the quality of the author's sensibility: "In the last analysis, literary critics can claim special authority not as witnesses to the moral value of works of literature, but as explicators and judges of effective communication, of 'realization.'"[56] The theoretical paradigm has shifted since Lubbock (Lubbock pays almost no attention to the linguistic properties and rhetorical capabilities that for Lodge define the novel as a "realized" form), but forty years after Lubbock, Lodge still found himself arguing that the evaluation of a novel depends upon more than the quality of the author's sensibility, that the "criteria of moral health must be controlled and modified by the aesthetic experience."[57] And at the turn of the new millennium, a writer such as Christine Brooke-Rose, whose work carried on the Lubbockian ideal of "unheard-of experiments," can look back over a thirty-year career and ask, "Have you ever tried to do something very difficult as well as you can, over a long period, and found that nobody notices?"[58] By and large, novelists do not develop the Jamesian aesthetics of alterity through full-scale books with connected arguments, definition of terms, and formulation of claims. There are these, of course, and not surprisingly the most important are written by novelists who happen to be scholars not just by temperament but by profession: Iris Murdoch, Raymond Williams, and Malcolm Bradbury. But as A. S. Byatt recognizes, the English novelist more typically feels that theory has little or nothing to do with the production of great works of art. The resistance to disciplined criticism is, on Byatt's view, not a national failing but the triumph of the novel as an art form. The flourishing of theory in the academy, the writing of "critical texts [that] are full of quotations . . . not from poems or novels" but from "Freud, Marx, Derrida, Foucault," has brought into being, Byatt suggests, a scholarly mastery different from that which Lubbock admired in James. From her perspective at the turn of the millennium, Byatt sees the professional critic subordinating literature to "fit into the boxes and nets of theoretical quotations." Byatt herself learns more about actual novels from ordinary readers whose love of literature irresistibly overflows into critical conversation: readers are "spending more and more time discussing books—all sort of books—in the vulgar tongues and frank language of every day, in book clubs. Or writing messages to the Internet and reviews on Internet bookshop pages."[59] Far from being superseded by new media, the novel is freed from the nets of academic masters by the enlargement of public conversation made possible by the web's extension of Woolf's "common reader."[60]

Byatt's view of the novel as first and foremost a living art points us to a counter-Lubbockian understanding of the genre that looks back to the nineteenth century and develops alongside academic literary theory in the twentieth century. For the novelist-critic the novel's aesthetic power lies not in its formal perfection but in the life it represents, creates—and in itself possesses. A strong proponent of this view is Woolf herself, whose admiration for Lubbock's new method did not extend to the compliment of imitation. Her own pronouncements on the novel are couched in a far more personal style, explicitly addressed to the common reader. Byatt's description of the irrepressible life of the novel, its refusal to be boxed or netted by theory, reverberates with Woolf's explicit and repeated contention that the novel's only aesthetic imperative is to represent life. This is Woolf's own idea, but it is an idea she has also heard from James. As early as "The Art of Fiction" (1884) James declares, "The only reason for the existence of a novel is that it does attempt to represent life" (5). While for Lubbock, James's work points to a rationalized, formal future for the novel, for Woolf the right form of the novel is that which does the best justice to the life it is and the lives it depicts. In "Mr. Bennett and Mrs. Brown" and "Modern Fiction," Woolf lambastes what she terms the "materialist" representation of life pursued by H. G. Wells, Arnold Bennett, and John Galsworthy.[61] But in calling for a view of life that is more "spiritual" ("Modern," 161), Woolf does not mean to return critical conversation to judgments about authorial character that "we have told each other a thousand times" (Lubbock, *Craft*, 273). The vision of life conveyed by a novel is, Woolf insists, a "vague, mysterious thing."[62] Every effort of analysis, every attempt to assign positive attributes to "life" or to locate in the novel its objective correlative, ends in failure. For Woolf the aesthetic achievement of the novel is to project "life" as a life force, as energy, animation, what she calls the "unknown and uncircumscribed spirit."[63] Woolf's mystical pronouncement could not be further from Lubbock's scholarly systems. Yet it is Woolf's formulation that is the one most favored by twentieth-century novelists who have set themselves the public task of talking about the art of the novel.

From the sustained investigations into the novel as an art offered by Vernon Lee, E. M. Forster, Ford Madox Ford, and D. H. Lawrence through Iris Murdoch, Robert Liddell, Brigid Brophy, Laura (Riding) Jackson, Wilson Harris, V. S. Naipaul, Salman Rushdie, and A. S. Byatt, the aesthetics of alterity that begins with James becomes more explicitly equated with what is assumed to be the genre's inherent capacity for otherness, a capacity that comes to life when author and reader participate in a circuit of interanimation, retaining their own subjective particularity even while they are united in their contact with a commonly shared and uncircumscribed spirit (divine or human) that is the basis for their relation. Whether pursuing classic realism or exploring allegory, romance, or other symbolic modalities, a strong line of British novelists committed to the aesthetics of alterity aims to present a "vision of life" (to use James's term) that is a particular kind of self-reflection: that gives a view of what is outside and beyond the self (other to the self) in and through the lens of subjective perspective. Ford Madox Ford offers the term "impressionism" to describe how a successful literary work paradoxically expresses authorial identity by never directly representing it: On the one hand, the "Impressionist author is sedulous to avoid letting his personality appear in the course of his book. On the other hand, his whole book . . . is merely an expression of his personality."[64] The novelist animates the objective world he projects by successfully imbuing it with his own subjectivity, a subjectivity that, godlike, is invisibly visible, everywhere apparent but nowhere directly manifested as his own image.[65] Here Ford develops the Jamesian notion of the novel as the expression of an author's impression of life—and Ford willingly acknowledges James's influence, as in this 1915 paen:

> Let me say at once that I regard the works of Mr. Henry James as those most worthy of attention by the critics—most worthy of attention of all the work that is to-day pouring from the groaning presses of continents. In saying this I conceal for the moment my private opinion . . . that Mr. James is the greatest of living writers and in consequence, for me, the greatest of living men.[66]

But as it becomes consolidated as an aesthetics, accomplished alterity can also be detached from James. For Woolf the master of the novelistic art of alterity is Jane Austen, whom, so Woolf argues, we know only through the refracted light of her supreme acts of achieved alterity, who "pervades every word that she wrote," going "in and out of her people's minds like the blood in their veins."[67]

The continuity of the aesthetics of alterity across the twentieth century, and across untrustworthy divides between modernism and postmodernism, can be illustrated if we juxtapose Salman Rushdie's and D. H. Lawrence's thoughts about fiction. Rushdie, like Woolf, attributes to the novel an interanimating spirit. The novel's generic capacity for depictions of relationality, its refusal to place "one set of values above all others," makes the novel for Rushdie the most socially important genre and the most transformative: "Can art be the third principle that mediates between the material and spiritual worlds; might it, by 'swallowing' both worlds, offer us something new—something that might even be called a secular definition of transcendence?" And his answer is yes.[68] D. H. Lawrence would agree. He regards the novel's performance of irreducible relationality as its only generic "law" and believes as well that the fulfillment of this aesthetic law establishes an animating connection between the material and spiritual worlds.[69] "The novel is the highest example of subtle interrelatedness that man has discovered," Lawrence declares in 1925. "Everything is true in its own time, place, circumstance. . . . If you try to nail anything down, in the novel, either it kills the novel, or the novel gets up and walks away with the nail."[70] The specificity of the novel's depiction of the details of everyday life are not important for their referential value but for the irreducibility of their relatedness, to each other and to the subjects for whom they have meaning. In turn, the irreducible relatedness within the material world is, for Lawrence, upheld and animated by that world's irreducible connection with divinity: "In the great novel, the felt but unknown flame stands behind all the characters, and in their words and gestures there is a flicker of the presence.... The quick is God-flame, in everything. And the dead is dead."[71] The unknown flame is invisibly visible, apprehensible as the flickering flame of life animating not just the storyworld but the novel itself: the novel comes into being as an autonomous art form when it is felt to have irrepressible autonomy, when the form itself seems capable of walking away from any critical attempt to pin it down.

Rushdie's secular transcendence and Lawrence's God-flame are deliberately mysterious energies, like Woolf's notion of "life." What is specified in the novelistic aesthetics of alterity is the ethical challenge and opportunity that irreducible relativism holds for modern society. In the British tradition of novelist-critics that I am focusing on here, the novel's world-swallowing life, as Rushdie postulates it, is a means to society's ethical evolution. "The novel," Rushdie writes, "has always been *about* the way which different languages, values and narratives quarrel, and about the shifting relations between them, which are relations of power."[72] By making cultural difference visible, the novel educates the reader in the irreducible ethical relativity of all value. The novel reader learns that any seemingly objective value is the projection of an interested point of view, a knowledge that in turn leads to self-consciousness about her own standards of evaluation, irreducibly connected with her own subject position.

But the aesthetics of alterity also opens the possibility of seeing through one's point of view to understand the other as other. A novelist's ability to maximize the novel's generic capacity begins not with the right set of tools but with the right emotion. The right emotion, Rushdie argues, is "love," understood as an emotion of self-restraint. Love enables the self to see the other and honor her difference: to accept "that your tastes, your loves, are your business and not mine."[73] Out of such self-discipline comes novel writing's aesthetic discipline. The aesthetic form of alterity fulfills the novel's relativized perspectivalism. To evaluate this success, a critic must be intuitive and responsive, able to circulate himself "like blood" in and out of the author's projected world. As Lawrence puts it, "Design, in art, is recognition of the relation between various things, various elements in the creative flux. You can't *invent* a design. You recognize it, in the fourth dimension. That is, with your blood and your bones, as well as with your eyes."[74]

As I have discussed in Chapter 1, for many twentieth-century novelists, especially liberal humanists, the novel's generic capacity for relativized relationality centers on the aesthetics of character. "The form of the novel so clumsy, verbose, and undramatic, so rich, elastic, and alive, has been evolved," Woolf declares, "to express character."[75] Woolf has in mind the novel's ability to provide a prolonged and detailed rendering of an individual, putting into relation inside and outside views, mental and social activity, an aesthetic goal that requires the writer to give herself wholly up to another, "to steep oneself" in another person's "atmosphere."[76] A related understanding of novelistic alterity stresses the genre's capacity for social abundance and variety, its ability to set into relation characters from every walk of life. Joseph Conrad, Iris Murdoch, and A. S. Byatt, respectively, describe themselves as carrying out the Eliotic project of "enlarging" the spirit of the English citizen by expanding the capacity to respect and honor diversity, to "extend the number and kind of people you are made to take account of."[77] Anticipating Rushdie, Murdoch believes that the multiplicity of social perspectives within the novel is put into a living relation through the quickening power of authorial "love." The novelist is godlike insofar as she feels love not as a will to power but as a will to self-abnegation: the successful novelist is for Murdoch, as it is for Rushdie and Lawrence, the one who successfully practices the "discipline involved in realizing that something real exists other than oneself."[78] As Priscilla Martin notes, "Murdoch said in various interviews that Henry James was a major, or *the* major, influence on her fiction," and we can hear that influence in the way Murdoch stresses that the achievement of discipline is not a God-given capacity but a difficult ethical labor.[79] Explicitly comparing the novelist's achievement of love to the poet's experience of "negative capability," she also suggests a basis of contrast.[80] Whereas for John Keats negative capability describes the feeling of his own effortless absorption in the subjectivity of others, novelistic negative capability—the achievement of an interanimated world of social diversity and multiperspectivalism—is, Murdoch implies, a moral triumph over the ever-present seduction of individual ego. The novelist who successfully practices the self-discipline of love is rewarded as much by the independence of her created characters as she is by her sense of connectedness to them: "the individuals portrayed in the novels are free, independent of their author, and not merely puppets in the exteriorization of some closely locked psychological conflict of his own."[81]

Responding to Lubbock's *The Craft of Fiction* with her own *The Handling of Words* (1923), Vernon Lee anticipates Murdoch in her assertion that characters rendered through "love" are those who will seem to the reader independent of their author. Like James and Woolf, Lee also describes the art of the novel as beginning with the authorial imagination captured by another person, "a person who is not ourselves."[82] In keeping with the aesthetics of characterological alterity I describe, for Lee the art of the novel resides first and foremost in the author's successful projection of autonomous individuals who seem wholly objective. Such characters are not only free from their author but free to be ethically unadmirable. "The Reader may thoroughly detest them," Lee says of aesthetically powerful characters—and she names James's Olive Chancellor as a prime example. But through the quickening spirit of authorial alterity, these characters will live for the reader through their power to "awaken only real feeling."[83] What Woolf calls Lee's poetics of "altruism" thus charts the mutually constitutive circuit of novelistic negative capability, the reciprocating capacity for alterity between author and reader that enables them together to animate and be animated by novelistic characters as autonomous subjects.[84] Lee's discussion of the ethics of novelistic representation leads to an explanation of one of the most enduring and powerful aesthetic effects attributed to fiction: a reader's experience of having an intensely real emotional relationship with imaginary characters whose power lies in their perceived independence from us: "How the person who is not ourselves comes to live, somehow, for our consciousness, with the same reality, the same intimate warmth, that we do."[85]

So accomplished is the novel in creating characters who seem alive, real, and autonomous that over the century many readers and authors have come to believe that the aesthetics of alterity entails a necessary politics. Robert Liddell in 1947 draws the connection this way:

> It would be perverse or whimsical to maintain that fictional characters had duties or rights; yet it is hard to find other words for the conviction that a novelist has certain obligations towards them. Perhaps as they are *simulacra* of human beings, we are shocked if they are not treated as we ought to treat other human beings, as ends in themselves, and not as means to ends of our own.[86]

But as Liddell develops this idea, authorial obligation is less a matter of social contract and more a divine "debt" owed by "a God" to "his creatures."[87] The novelist capable of making his characters so real as to seem as if they deserved human rights is the one who possesses not just the godlike power to create, but the godlike power to love social others as others—and to describe this capacity for alterity, Liddell also reaches for the term "negative capability."[88] Doris Lessing keeps to a secular account of the novel's politics, but her view is equally based upon the profound social value of authorial self-abnegation. Through the others she creates, the novelist expresses her ethical "recognition of man, the responsible individual." The author brings these responsible individuals to life by projecting them as autonomous agents, independent of their author. Such subordination of authorial privilege performs what Lessing believes is the political basis for a democratic community of mutually interconnected individuals, who enact their own human rights through self-conscious restraint: each individual "voluntarily submitting his will to the collective, but never finally; and insisting on making his own personal and private judgments before every act of submission."[89]

For more visionary political novelists such as Laura (Riding) Jackson in the 1930s and Wilson Harris in the 1960s, the novel's aesthetics of alterity directs us away from a politics of human rights and the realist idiom of the simulacrum to symbolist and allegorical modes of fiction harnessed for social transformation and revolution. Jackson and Harris both, respectively, see in "the trembling instability of the [novel's] balance" between materiality and spirituality the opportunity to concretize the difference between what is and what might be (Lawrence, "Morality and the Novel," 150). Especially in her feminist essays, Jackson praises novels that accentuate rather than veil the seam between reality and fiction, between the modalities of verisimilitude and fabrication.[90] The novel best fulfills its generic identity, Jackson argues in 1935, in the open display of the irreducible relationality between truth and fiction, between reality as we know it and reality as it might be imagined. In making legible moments "where story-telling changes naturally into truth telling," the novel includes its reader in the act of reenvisioning the terms of the social contract.[91] To invoke the title of an earlier Jackson polemic, "anarchism is not enough." Unlike her contemporary Wyndham Lewis, whose *Men without Art* champions the overthrow of existing conventions (and pretensions) through the outsider perspective of satire, Jackson advocates the cultivation of alterity as a way to know the other, even the oppressive other, from its own point of view. Her belief that imagination can establish a basis of positive relation even between incommensurable subject positions leads her to find such a negotiation at the heart of the novel's narrative structure. Through its very form the novel puts into relation the ethical claims of irreducible variety and the epistemological need for unified understanding: "The key to Story is bountiful sympathy with the immensely varied actualness of life, as the Key to Truth is bountiful knowledge of actualness, in the immense unity of its significances."[92] For Jackson, the novel can cast its uncircumscribable spirit over both types of bounty, doing equal justice to "varied actualness" and "immense . . . significances," and placing both realms (life and truth) into trembling relation.

From a postcolonial perspective as a Caribbean writer, Wilson Harris provides the most explicit articulation of the novel's contribution to a revolutionary politics of alterity—even as he connects the aesthetics of alterity to his own deeply held religious beliefs. The lack of living spirit that Woolf detected in the "materialists" of her generation is, for Harris, "the supreme casualty" of his own moment in time. The wholly secular world of the realist novel is inseparable, maintains Harris, from the rise of English liberalism and "the death of cosmic love."[93] Any art form that encourages the individual to believe in his constitutive freedom simply masks the "ambitions for power" that underlie liberal humanism.[94] To reinvent the novel as an agent of social transformation, Harris's novelist, like Lawrence's, must put material and spirit into trembling relation. And although Harris feels his belief in spiritual indwelling makes him an outlier to the English literary tradition, he too uses the term "negative capability" to name the power for alterity that is the defining quality of this cosmic love.[95] Whereas creative vision begins for James and Woolf with what Woolf calls the "imposition" of character upon the novelist's imagination, Harris is seized by the alterity that to his mind is divinity itself: "One becomes susceptible to a species of unpredictable arousal, one virtually becomes a species of nature which subsists on both mystery and phenomenon, participating an otherness akin to the terrifying and protean reality of the gods. It is within this instant of arousal that abolishes the 'given' world that one's confession of weakness has really begun."[96] The confession of weakness, the recognition that one is not master but mastered, is the precondition for revolutionary politics. The higher power of the gods may be terrifying, but vulnerability brings humility, a shattering of ego that makes possible a transformative imagination of the world.[97]

The novelist's struggle to find the right modality of novelistic expression, to remodel "a form that has already been broken in the past," establishes a living relation with the uncircumscribable spirit that becomes for Harris the basis of the novel's aesthetic achievement:[98] "This interaction between sovereign ego and intuitive self is the tormenting reality of changing form, the ecstasy as well of the visionary capacity to cleave the prison house of natural bias within a heterogeneous asymmetric context in which the unknowable God—though ceaselessly beyond human patterns—infuses art with unfathomable eternity and grace" ("Frontier," 86–87). Because for Harris this spirit is ancient and intuitive, he looks for the future of fiction in his native traditions ("Tradition," 30; "Closing Statement," 245). This does not mean that the writer is a slave to his own tradition but that he is, if inspirited, able to see his culture as both self and other. On the one hand, the native people are "capable *now*," writes Harris in 1967, "of discovering themselves and continuing to discover themselves so that in one sense one relieves and reverses the 'given' conditions of the past, freeing oneself from catastrophic idolatry and blindness to one's own historical and philosophical conceptions and misconceptions" ("Tradition," 36; emphasis in the original). On the other hand, such discovery accompanies a revelation of the contingency of colonial and postcolonial existence—and of that contingency's resistance to any univocal or unidimensional ways of telling history and of reusing it. Accordingly, the novelist's contingent relation to his own culture, along with the novel's generic capacity for "bewildering variety and surprising complexity of concrete example," will produce the novel as an irreducible multiplicity of cultural perspectives, an achievement that will help combat the social "resistance to alterities."[99]

And the political stakes could not be higher. In 2004 Harris links the social atrocities of the century—the "Holocaust, ethnic cleansing, institutional racism, the gross and terrible exploitation of native and aboriginal peoples"—to the resistance to alterity that drives English liberal culture ("Resistances," 3). Writers from colonized countries like Harris's own Guyana can lead the way for transformational social change. The culture that has suffered through colonial domination has an opportunity not to reproduce it. Political promise lies in the realization that "the prison house of natural bias" can never be eliminated—but can itself be relativized: "Difference rests on diverse cultures, a capacity within diverse cultures to create and re-create windows into the enigma of truth. Each window's susceptibility to rigidity, rigid commandment, breaks, turns . . . into a transitive architecture, a transitive medium into other dimensions within the unfinished genesis of the Imagination."[100]

If Harris's description of the multicultural house of fiction seems a politicized critique of the famous Jamesian figure, it is a revision invited by the figure itself. "The house of fiction," James tells us, "has . . . not one window, but a million—a number of possible windows not be reckoned, rather; every one of which has been pierced, or is still pierceable, in its vast front, by the need of the individual vision and by the pressure of the individual will."[101] Although James's depiction of a house filled with a multiplicity of individual watchers all focused on the social scene privileges the liberal subject deplored by Harris, for James as much as for Harris the novel's architecture is a "transitive medium," the form of realized alterity. The Jamesian conceptualization of the novelist standing at the window is, to borrow Brigid Brophy's formulation, "genuinely not at home."[102] The view from the house of fiction positions the novelist at "the window" of his character's consciousness, which in turn is realized through its operation as a point of view, the establishment of living relation with something outside and beyond the self. That this point of view then becomes available to the reader is part of the novel's power to establish relativized relations. "One of the symptoms of being in love," Brophy tells us, "is that you want to hear everything the other person can or will tell you, not primarily for the information it may give you about life or even about the person concerned, but the preciousness of seeing the world through his eyes."[103] The escape from the prison house of bias is, for the tradition I have been tracing, through the many-mansioned house of fiction, the dwelling described by E. M. Forster (in his treatise on the novel) as "sogged with humanity."[104] The English writer's ethico-religious understanding of the novel as the genre of realized alterity means that there can be no real danger of the death of the genre—and no amount of labor can perfect it as an aesthetic form. As living art, as what Lawrence calls the "bright book of life," the novel is for its twentieth-century creators the genre that keeps its fresh youth because its genesis in irreducible relationality cannot be brought to a halt: it lives its generic life by giving life to the other, a fullness of life that can have no end, since that uncircumscribable spirit is, as Lubbock lamented, "neither to hold nor to bind."[105]

3. Zadie Smith's *On Beauty*
An Ethical Aesthetic as the Problem of Perspectivalism

IN AN INTERVIEW PUBLISHED in *The Atlantic*, Zadie Smith lets it be known, "I don't fuck around with titles."[1] Why then choose for her third novel a title that had already been taken? As she points out in the acknowledgments to *On Beauty* (2005), the title is a direct reference to Elaine Scarry's philosophical meditation, *On Beauty and Being Just* (1999).[2] Smith thanks Scarry "for her wonderful essay 'On Beauty and Being Just,' from which I borrowed a title, a chapter heading and a good deal of inspiration."[3] Smith thus places before her readers an invitation for generic comparison: What is the relation between the novel's treatment of beauty and the philosopher's? Is Smith's novel a novel of ideas, a fictional dramatization of Scarry's philosophy of beauty? Or has she in a more general way been prompted by Scarry to develop her own account of beauty—moving away, perhaps, from Scarry's emphasis on the connection between beauty and justice and emphasizing instead the connection between beauty and human fallibility (the "being wrong" chapter heading she takes from Scarry)? But importantly, in either case, Smith's title asks us to consider as well a question that has not been asked much in the last half century: Is the genre of the novel an artistic enterprise whose aim should include the achievement of aesthetic beauty?[4] And if aesthetic beauty is a generic possibility, why have we heard so little about the beautiful as an attribute of novelistic art?

When asked by the *Atlantic* interviewer to summarize what position her novel takes in regard to beauty, Smith is deliberately vague: "It *is* a book about beauty, but in a very loose sense, and it's about all these other things, as well."[5] Smith does not enumerate what "all these other things" might be, and it seems she uses the phrase deliberately to indicate that there are so many other things the novel is about that one cannot begin to name them all. Yet if Smith's novel is only engaged with beauty "in a very loose sense," then why insist so much on the rightness of its allusive title?

I want to suggest that Smith as a novelist values her title for the difference it seeks to draw between the philosopher's treatment of beauty and the novelist's, between Scarry's phenomenological project and the novelistic aesthetics of alterity that Smith pursues. Whereas Scarry seeks primarily to describe the "felt experience of cognition" (3) that she believes unites all human beings of every culture in their experience of beauty, Smith portrays the particularity and contingency of each individual's apprehension of beauty.[6] And while Scarry aims to enumerate the fundamental qualities of beauty, Smith stresses its relativity and social constructedness. If Smith's repetition of Scarry's title prepares us for a novel of ideas, the novel quickly teaches us that the novel's idea of an idea is different from the philosopher's. In *On Beauty* the lives of Smith's socially diverse characters are filled with aesthetic experience, and their individual attempts to understand that experience—through private contemplation as well as through acts of social exchange—highlight the power relations and social alliances that give meaning to even the most embodied sensory perceptions. In Smith's novel, not only is the "felt experience of cognition" shown to be contingent upon social life, but any abstract idea a character might hold about the operation or value of cognition is shown to be inseparable from an individual's social position within a particular cultural formation.[7]

The citationality of Smith's title thus signals the difference between the philosopher's notion of beauty and the novelist's by calling attention to the social discursivity through which the meaning of beauty is produced. In this way Smith's novelistic aesthetics of alterity is in keeping with Virginia Woolf's description of the novel as the "cannibal art."[8] Smith's allusive title suggests that the novel is most novelistic when the social origins of its languages are highlighted. When Smith chooses *On Beauty* as her title, she knows she is in fact "third in line":[9] Smith's husband, Nick Laird, has written a poem by the same name. Rather than attempting to purify the citation, Smith makes it her own by developing and deepening the way her language use connects her to social others. She not only quotes the entirety of Laird's poem in her novel but adds another layer of social complexity by crediting the poem to the novel's fictional poet, Claire Malcolm (who may or may not be inspired by Jorie Graham). When we also consider that Smith spent a year as a Radcliffe Institute Fellow and that Scarry is Walter M.

Cabot Professor of Aesthetics at Harvard, the title's sociality gains a biographical layer, alluding not just to Smith's personal experience of Scarry's book but to the person who wrote the book. Is it any surprise, then, that *On Beauty and Being Just* turns out to be only the first of the intertexts for Smith's novel? In addition to the framing quotations it deploys—the thank-you to Simon Schama for his work on Rembrandt and the chapter epigraphs that quote philosophers and poets—*On Beauty* enacts, as it were, a global citation, building its very plot through an "hommage" to *Howards End*.[10]

As I have developed in my first two chapters, the aesthetics of alterity that comes to define the art of the Anglo-American novel in the twentieth century includes the ethical belief that the novel realizes its generic potential best when it has maximized the representation of social identities other to the author's own. Whether the aesthetics of alterity is defined as the representation of characters each with a unique point of view or as the ideological subject position that defines a character as a social subject, the novelist's success in the twentieth century is increasingly judged by her capacity to represent the variety and autonomy of lives different from her own. While *The Book of Other People* (2007) is a title that highlights Smith's investment in fiction's capacity to represent characters as persons whose identity is defined by its difference from an authorial self, *On Beauty* draws our attention to beauty's problematic relation to the novel as a literary form. As I have been arguing, the constitutive sociality of the novel's representational project has always put it in tension with the formal control and effects that would most often call forth praise of its beauty. To admire the novel as form is to risk trivializing or objectifying the social alterity that the novel claims as a primary ethical, social, and political good. If beauty were to be had, it resides in these achieved ethical virtues, worked out in the service of bringing to life characters who possess independent points of view; but to strive for beauty as an aesthetic end in itself would be to make the mistake of James's most dastardly villain, Gilbert Osmond, whose evil lies precisely in his attempt to exploit people for his own aesthetic gratification.

While the novel's twentieth-century literary history helps to explain why the beautiful novel develops primarily as an elite tradition and why some of its preeminent achievements, such as *À la recherche du temps perdu*, are distinguished by their failure to represent in any sustained or meaningful way life viewed from a point of view other than the author's own, it also enables us to consider the ways

On Beauty further brings to light the complexities and constitutive contradictions that are at the heart of the novelistic aesthetics of alterity. At issue in the aesthetics of alterity is not just the politicization of formal values like beauty but also the idealization of the novel's representational capacity for the depiction of alterity. As I have discussed in Chapter 2, the novel, on the one hand, is regarded as having a mystical capacity to transcend material conditions: the genre's capacity for otherness comes to life when author and reader participate in a circuit of interanimation, retaining their own subjective particularities even as they are united in their contact with a commonly shared and uncircumscribed spirit (divine or human) that is the basis of that relation. On the other hand, novelistic narrative takes on weight and force as a register of the material and social conditions that impede or limit access to that spiritual animation. The narrative protocols of *What Maisie Knew* and *A Mercy*, freighted with ethical value by the ethical dilemmas and terms set by their respective storyworlds, perform the limits as well as the possibility of ethical alterity. Reading James and Morrison, we ask what kind of ethics and what kind of politics are at play in the narrative representation of others and otherness from a particular author's point of view.

In two of her early essays, "Love, Actually" (2003) and "Read Better" (2007), Smith locates herself in the Jamesian tradition indirectly by accessing James's ideas about the novel through two of his inheritors: the American philosopher Martha Nussbaum (once affiliated with Harvard) and the English philosopher-novelist Iris Murdoch.[11] Smith comes to Jamesian ethics through Martha Nussbaum's *Love Knowledge*.[12] Offering her own account of the ethics of otherness that fiction provides, Smith explicitly builds on Nussbaum's explicitly Jamesian position: "My flag is rather weak in comparison [to Nussbaum's]. It says, 'When we read with *fine attention* [James's term via Nussbaum; emphasis added], we find ourselves caring about people who are various, muddled, uncertain and not quite like us (and this is good).'"[13] James's mediated influence surfaces again when in "Read Better" Smith credits Murdoch with the idea of characterological alterity that she believes is the defining ethical task of the novel as a genre: "It is, Murdoch once said, incredibly hard to make oneself believe that other people really exist in the same way that we do ourselves. It is the great challenge of art to convince ourselves of this fundamental truth—but it's also the challenge of our lives."[14] And we can also see the Jamesian pull in Smith's further description of how otherness is manifested on the molecular level of narrative expression.

Continuing her statement about Murdoch, Smith adds, "I believe further that this relationship can be traced at every level—a sentence can be self-deluded, can show an ulterior motive, can try too hard to please, can lie, can be blind to anything outside itself, can believe itself to be of the utmost importance."[15] Smith's belief that the author's degree of care about people "not quite like us" is made manifest on "every level" of narrative, that this relationship is at stake on both the macro and micro levels of novelistic representation, locates her view of novelistic ethics within the Jamesian aesthetics of alterity.

When Smith does reference James directly, she, like Morrison, quarrels with what she takes as James's idea of form, even while her criticism of James is couched in a Jamesian notion of perspectivalism. Smith's bone of contention is James's 1873 aesthetic evaluation of George Eliot's *Middlemarch*.[16] James judges Eliot's novel to be "a treasurehouse of detail" but "an indifferent whole."[17] Smith dismisses James's opinion, attributing his lack of appreciation for Eliot's accomplishment to constitutive differences between their points of view: "You might say of Henry and George what the novel says of Lydgate and Rosamond: *between him and her indeed there was that total missing of each other's mental track*" ("*Middlemarch* and Everybody," 30; emphasis in the original). James fails as a reader of *Middlemarch*, according to Smith, precisely because he does not open himself up to Eliot's otherness. Locked in his own vision of life, James cannot appreciate the way Eliot's art of the novel brings her characters to life. Using the example of Fred Vincy, Smith argues: "But you can see why Henry hadn't much time for Fred. He's not Henry's type of thing at all—just a simple boy, with a streak of selfishness" (35). Importantly, Smith connects James's failure to appreciate characters not like himself—a simple soul like Fred—to James's equally rigid sense of what novel form should be. Seeking to find in *Middlemarch* his own aesthetic standard—"organized, moulded, balanced composition"—James, according to Smith, will miss Eliot's own version of the novelistic aesthetics of alterity. Smith thus agrees with James—"we must give Henry his due: *Middlemarch* is messy, decentered, unnerving" (39)—in order to suggest that a messy, decentered, unnerving form is in fact the best way to bring to life "people who are various, muddled, uncertain and not quite like us."[18] That James cannot appreciate the success of Eliot's aesthetics of alterity, so Smith implies, is a register of his ethical failure, not Eliot's artistic inability.

Thus we see that Smith joins Morrison in mounting a critique of James that is staged from within the house of fiction that he has built. And so in the *Atlantic* interview, when Smith seems to break even more emphatically with the rules of the novel art (developed out of James by Percy Lubbock) by railing against the creative writing workshop imperative that a novelist should show and not tell, we can see how Smith's rebellion is in fact conducive to advancing the Jamesian aesthetics of alterity. Smith rejects workshop truisms in the service of fashioning better narrative protocols for representing the ethical encounter with otherness: "You're constantly told in college and elsewhere that good taste and good fiction are about not pushing, about not expressing your opinion too forcefully. . . . It's nonsense, and it's time to stop."[19] Smith sees herself leading fiction writing down a new aesthetic path, and indeed she is overturning both modernist pieties about the value of authorial impersonality and postmodernist pieties about the impersonal sources of all subjective agency. But through her conviction that good fiction is not at odds with the expression of strong authorial opinion, that the novelistic world emerges in and through the values and investments of its creator, Smith affirms the perspectivalism upon which the aesthetics of alterity rests. By choosing not to pretend that the social world of the novel is not mediated by the author's specific value system, by rejecting, that is to say, narrative techniques that cultivate the illusion of a storyworld shown and not told, the ethical and representational challenge becomes for Smith how to reconceptualize the novelistic achievement of alterity as derivable from the author's socially embedded viewpoint. How does the novelist bring to life social identities other to her own?[20] Is a failure to achieve alterity an ethical weakness? A deficiency of imagination? A political limit? An artistic incapacity?

To better appreciate how *On Beauty* performs its aesthetics of alterity, it's useful to situate Smith's novel in relation to William Faulkner's *The Sound and the Fury*, a work that positions its beautiful language in relation to a politics of social otherness. The reader's "felt experience of cognition," the apprehension that the language Faulkner uses makes this novel a thing of beauty, is thrown into question by the role beautiful language plays in Faulkner's representation of social others. We can recall the famous moment in *The Sound and the Fury* when Faulkner shifts from the stream of consciousness and interior monologue modes that he deploys to represent the Compson sons to the limited omniscience he uses to depict Dilsey, the Compsons' African American servant. The deviation in the novel's narrative practice at this moment, the switch from the intimacy of stream of consciousness to the performed mediation of the storyworld through narratorial omniscience, is now generally understood by contemporary literary critics as expressive of the politics of positionality.[21] According to the current critical understanding, Faulkner can make vivid in positive terms the private interiorities of three white men, he can honor the alterity of his white heroine (Caddy) by (to use a Faulkner word) refraining to represent her (i.e., by granting her a subjectivity that stands outside of the contamination of the fallen social world depicted in the novel), while his relationship to the black servant is enacted narratively as an encounter with radical social difference. As Wayne Booth rightly noted, the modern novelist's use of stream of consciousness is "omniscience with teeth in it": the novelistic plunge into the mind of a character allows access to interiority that is impossible to achieve outside of literature.[22] The narrator's view of Dilsey is an outside view, a view that begins with the description not of a deep mind but a semiotically saturated body. The limit that Dilsey presents to the novel's norm for characterological personhood not only racializes Faulkner's use of stream of consciousness but politicizes it by referring Faulkner's narrative technique back to the author's subject position. The turn to omniscience thus contributes to this novel's aesthetics of alterity by personalizing Faulkner's ethical relation to the social difference his characters represent. The problem of mind represented by Benjy, the problem of virtue represented by Jason—all these differences are subordinate in this novel to the narrative limits posed by race and gender.

What is less noticed is how the aesthetics of alterity at work in *The Sound and the Fury* functions as a political critique of the lyrical language that accompanies Faulkner's shift to limited omniscience. Dilsey is introduced through Faulkner's high style:

> She had been a big woman once but now her skeleton rose, draped loosely in unpadded skin that tightened again upon a paunch almost dropsical, as though muscle and tissue had been courage or fortitude which the days or the years had consumed until only the indomitable skeleton was left rising like a ruin or a landmark above the somnolent and impervious guts.[23]

The simile, the complication within the simile, the excess of adjectives, the elevated vocabulary—all these features can be understood as Faulkner's bid for lyric power, for literary language that would enhance the aesthetic value of the novel as an artistic achievement. But since *The Sound and the Fury* has by this point established a characterological environment in which fluctuations of vocabulary and tone express both the complexities of individual consciousness as well as the difference between individuals as consciousnesses, the novel teaches the reader to pose the question of situatedness. We ask, Why lyricism here? And whose lyricism? The abandonment of interior monologue, the novelist's inability to imagine Dilsey's alterity as an autonomous consciousness, seems causally related to this lyrical effusion. Faulkner reaches for the high style here as a compensatory act of descriptive ennoblement. Deprived of her inside view, the novelist adorns her outside with a portentous linguistic performance.

Faulkner's turn to the beautiful style thus makes legible both the modern novel's expectation that characters should be rendered as autonomous persons with deep interiorities and the social fact that some social positions resist representation by the white, male novelist. And if the beautiful style marks the social limit of the novelist's capacity to represent social subjects different from himself, it also marks the social positionality of the author.[24] The neologisms, the pile-up of vocabulary, the run-on sentences—the very excessiveness of this lyrical language displays its deviation from the well-wrought poem. Within the perspectival economy of this novel, such stylistic excess repersonalizes literary language as someone's social idea of what literary language should be. What Virginia Woolf termed "the stain of personality" will not be scrubbed away ("Phases," 116). The bid for beauty breaks the illusion of impersonal narration and calls attention to the person who might find such language to be beautiful: the high school dropout, the autodidact, William Faulkner.[25] The novel thus constitutes the author as a perspective indirectly through its acts of style, even in (or especially in) the moments when he strives for literary effects. The outsider's view is homologically rendered through the meaning it drapes over Dilsey's "outside"—even as the literary language deployed for her description strives to establish Faulkner's artistic achievement apart from his social identity, to establish, that is to say, his cultural position as an author through a literary accomplishment, judged by literary standards.[26]

In a novel so devoted to the depiction of the cultural variety of artistic production and consumption, it is significant that *On Beauty* represents no characters who write or read novels. Smith's omission suggests that it is in keeping with the novel's nature as an art form that its aesthetic identity emerges through its discursive acts: its citationality, its representation of social alterity, its authorial style—and the interaction among these categories. By locating her novel explicitly in relation to two other texts bearing the same name, Smith enables us to apprehend the aesthetic qualities particular to the novel inductively, especially through comparison with two other literary genres: the philosophical essay and the lyrical poem. The novel's citationality establishes a perspectival loop: if Scarry's philosophical text gives us ideas about beauty to bring to Smith's novel, Smith's novel gives us ideas about the politics of style to bring to Scarry's philosophical expression. Reading *On Beauty and Being Just* novelistically, we see that the philosophical work makes its own bid for beauty through style—and that this style draws attention to the philosopher's subject position. The philosophical language of logic and abstraction is punctuated by lyrical moments such as the one in which Scarry describes a personal moment of aesthetic revelation:

> My palm tree is an example. Suddenly I am on a balcony and its huge swaying leaves are before me at eye level, arcing, arching, waving, cresting and breaking in the soft air, throwing the yellow sunlight up over itself and catching it on the other side, running its fingers down its own piano keys, then running them back up again, shuffling and dealing glittering decks of aqua, green, yellow, and white. It is everything I have always loved, fernlike, featherlike, fanlike, open—lustrously in love with air and light.[27]

The eruption of lyrical style is accompanied by an attenuated autobiographical reference that places this effusion somewhere between poetry, personal essay, and journal entry. As with the Faulkner passage, the very palpability of the lyricism establishes an opposition with the shadowiness of narrative implied by autobiographical reference. Where is this balcony? Why is the location suppressed? Why does Scarry feel that she is "suddenly" there? Is this experience of effortless travel what it is like for affluent academics to jet to a vacation spot, to touch down amidst exotic scenery? Is the love of beauty a product of a class position that allows the opportunity for leisured contemplation that is experienced by the privileged as "free"? Is her epistemological certainty ("it is everything I have always loved"), the totalizability of emotion and sensuous experience, the interpretive confidence accorded to those who occupy elite professorships?[28] Is it the socially inconsequential nature of those judgments that allows her to be equally sure that aesthetic errors are nothing more than the happy precondition for personal enlightenment?

In drawing attention to the ideological investments and blind spots that connect philosophical works with the people who write them, Smith's citationality does not invalidate Scarry's philosophical project but novelizes it. To make philosophical discourse visible as a social discourse is not to discredit the truth claims made in *On Beauty and Being Just*. The novelistic credo, which could be framed as "no ideas but in people," does not mean that the ideas adopted from others might not be true.[29] Scarry's philosophical text remains key not just to Smith's staging of the characterological apprehension of aesthetic experience within the storyworld of *On Beauty* but also to her own performance of the novel as a novel of ideas, with some of those ideas coming from Elaine Scarry, writer and Harvard professor. The novelist, like the philosopher, writes because she has meaning to convey, beliefs to express, truth to put forward. The poem "On Beauty" that Smith includes in her novel seems in this respect to be a negative example, a way to highlight the categorical difference between poetry on the one hand and philosophy and novels on the other. Identified in the novel as a pantoum, the poem "On Beauty" is constructed as a puzzle, a semantic game played through regulated line repetition. Its own aesthetic beauty lies in the clever managing of the expressive rules that define it, the different meanings that accrue to lines and phrases as they inhabit different syntactical positions. In contrast to Scarry's philosophical project, which is dedicated to elucidating the meaning of beauty, "On Beauty" the poem flirts with such definitional projects even while defying them: "No, we could not itemize the list / of sins they can't forgive us. / The beautiful don't lack the wound. / It is always beginning to snow" (*On Beauty*, 153). The hope that we might discover the poet's definition of the beautiful frames our engagement with its semantic opacity. We read and reread waiting for comprehension to click. But we also know that poems don't have to mean—and we can think them beautiful for the strategies they use to resist paraphrasability, to attenuate narrativization, to stymie perspectivalism.

By situating her novel between the universality of the philosopher's truth claim and the gamesmanship of contemporary poetry, Smith seems to be issuing a Foucauldian warning about the way discourses belonging to the ideologically elite cultivate social forgetfulness. Her novel shows, however, that the social practices of beauty making, truth telling, and literary creation persist, despite the rational understanding of their ideological instrumentality. *On Beauty* depicts the pursuit of beauty in the same way it depicts truth-telling: as a socially constructed act of cognition whose socially constructed nature is unavailable to the spontaneity that defines it as cognitive experience. The flash of certainty, the call of beauty—these judgments seem to come to us as unmediated insights, no matter how much we also know through our reflective knowledge that their very irresistibility is the sign of our ideological investment and social position.

If we find ourselves posing Zora Belsey's theory-head question to the novel that she is in—"But after Foucault . . . where is there to go with that stuff?"—the reply might be that *On Beauty* simply refuses to be scandalized by the knowledge that aesthetics and philosophy serve as ideological instruments through their discursive erasure of the social agents who produce them (*On Beauty*, 219). On Smith's view, the conflict between the cognitive need to trust spontaneous apprehension (this is what I know, this is beautiful to me) and the epistemological doubt derived from the knowledge that the "this" one knows and feels is socially produced and politically consequential is the defining structure of knowledge within contemporary secular society. Smith does not strive to eliminate the conflict between perspectivalism and authorial belief. Unlike Foucauldians and Marxists, Smith does not chastise the novel for its contribution to the social production of bad political formations like the liberal subject.[30] For Smith the issue is not how the novel might be reformed to avoid bad politics but how the risk of bad politics attends any and all ways of knowing.[31] To feel that one knows a truth about the world is to think that this truth is by definition valid beyond the contingencies of personal experience. To express this personal belief by way of an art form is at once to abstract and to aestheticize socially contingent values. The power of Smith's novel is to show the novel's power as a genre to dramatize the oppositional but mutually defining nature of these modes of knowing: in the moment of the lived apprehension of truth and beauty, we forget that we see only from a point of view.

Smith's own philosophical expression about novelistic aesthetics that inform *On Beauty* can be found in three nonfiction essays that she published in *The Guardian*, two of which I have already referenced: "Love, Actually" (2003), "Fail Better" (2007), and "Read Better" (2007). At one point Smith intended to collect these essays under the title *Fail Better: The Morality of the Novel*.[32] Although she "changed her mind" about the collection, taken together the essays do indeed represent a serious attempt to articulate a theory of the positive value of literature as an ethical discourse, which is to say, an aesthetic discourse that raises the question of its own status as a social discourse.[33] As Smith boldly asserts in "Fail Better," the defining feature of literary art is "style": style should not be understood, she cautions, as "fanciful syntax, or as the flamboyant icing atop a plain literary cake, nor as the uncontrollable result of some mysterious velocity coiled within language itself" ("Fail Better," par. 8). Style is for Smith nothing less than the authentic revelation of personal identity through the artistic choices a writer makes. Like a fingerprint, style can neither be chosen nor denied: it is, she declares, "the only possible expression of a particular human consciousness" (par. 8). Style is not just a matter of vocabulary and tonality but extends to the very form a writer chooses. According to Smith, poem or novel, romance or play—each represents a belief about the world, and all the representational choices that follow are attempts to "truthfully describe the world as it is experienced by [the author's] particular self" (par. 13). Artistic achievement is thus for Smith inseparable from what she calls "ethical" qualities. There is no such thing, on her view, as pure poetics, a "Platonic ideal" of literary form. "Bad aesthetic choices" are always an index of the author's "pesky self—vain, deluded, myopic, cowardly, great" (par. 7). The artwork's attachment to the person who produces it is not only inexpungible but the relation that makes authorial identity legible. Who you are, in other words, determines how good your literary creation will be: "literary success or failure, by this measure, depends not only on the refinement of words on a page, but in the refinement of a consciousness, what Aristotle called the education of the emotions" (par. 8).

Given how important ethical virtue is to Smith's theory of literature's social value, we might wonder why Smith believes that something as indirect as style would be the optimal manifestation of the moral quality of authorial consciousness. One might imagine that an author's ethics could be better ascertained outside of fiction, through direct statements in journals, letters, nonfiction essays, or interviews, or through a biographical account of how the author chose to live life. For Smith it is precisely the uncontrollable revelation of value through the representational choices made by an author that makes literature a privileged discourse for knowing identity. "Fictional truth," Smith declares in "Fail Better," is "a question of perspective, not autobiography" (par. 19). One can falsify a description of oneself or lie in a statement of belief, but one can't counterfeit the way one sees, the point of view from which one makes sense of the world. It is this "way of being in the world"—of one's perspectival position—from which an author "can't help tell if [she] write[s] well" (par. 19). We can extrapolate that if the author writes poorly, she will also convey her core beliefs and values—but they will be ones that are hardly worth the reader's time. Poor writing includes works whose style is imitative or insincere, revealing an author who either does not have the courage of her convictions or enough insight to have a point of view of her own. Great writers, on the other hand, understand that the art of writing demands self-revelation; they have, in Smith's formulation, a "duty to express accurately their way of being in the world" (par. 18). Yet precisely because "a way of being in the world" is something that is lived by the author, it can never be fully known by her: the artist may try to take the exact measure of her pesky self but her way of seeing can never be wholly visible to her. The ethical artist is always doomed to fail; but, Smith asserts, "the art is in the attempt"—thus her advice to writers to make it their ethical work to "fail better" (par. 22).

Although Smith casts her theoretical claims in general terms, arguing for the nature of "art," "writing," and "literature," it is not surprising to find that in "Fail Better" all of her examples are from novels. The novel is not only the genre best accounted for by Smith's theory, but as the dominant literary genre of the twentieth and twenty-first centuries, it is the genre that defines literature for her cultural moment.[34] Even if we don't go so far as Percy Lubbock to declare that "the whole intricate question of method, in the craft of fiction . . . [is] governed by the question of the point of view," the novel as a cultural agent has contributed to the modern belief in personal identity as grounded in perspectival relativity.[35] What better way to fulfill one's authorial "duty," to "express accurately" one's "way of being in the world," than to express that way of being through an art form that takes perspectivalism for granted—whose primary aesthetic dictum has been that a novelist's worldview is best told when it is shown?

In Chapter 1 I made the case for tracking Smith's view of novelistic ethics back to Henry James through the act of embodiment that both use as a figure for the authorial accomplishment of characterological alterity. I discussed there how in "Fail Better" Smith updates James's notion of the ethics of alterity by bringing to self-consciousness its implied politics through her example of a fictional novelist named Clive who fails to bring to life "the character of the corrupt Hispanic government economist, Maria Gomez. . . . He found it hard to get into her silk blouse, her pencil skirt—even harder to get under her skin" ("Fail Better," par. 2). In keeping with the logic of the novelistic aesthetics of alterity, Clive's failure lies in (as Smith imagines it in free indirect style) "not simply flaws of language or design, but rather flaws of . . . what? Him" (par. 2). For Smith, the ethical imperative to represent one's authentic self through the act of style is, in the novel, always only achieved through the narrative act that will also serve to bring into being the identity of a social other.[36] In the novelistic ethics of alterity, one can imagine the author as possessing a unitary and coherent self only in relation to the social other he attempts to depict.[37] We come to know Clive by the social identity that limits his view of Maria to the outside—a view that cannot seem to overcome the differences in gender, ethnicity, and professional occupation that define them and, Smith implies, that even sexualize Clive's relation to his fictional character.

To choose the novel as one's aesthetic form of self-expression is thus for Smith to display a self-conscious awareness about the paradox of perspectivalism. To believe that the world is apprehended from the position of an individual point of view is to forget that the contingent and particular experiences afforded by social life produced the point of view that the individual experiences as her own. As worked out from the logic of Smith's views, the form of the novel suits the expression of this paradox because it can represent homologically the doubleness of perspectivalism. On the one hand, the vision of life the author projects through the novel can be said to instantiate the author's constitutive way of seeing: her vision of life is told by the novel, taken as an expressive whole. On the other hand, within the novel itself point of view is formally structured as an ongoing negotiation between interpreting subject and interpreted world. To understand the novel as a whole as the expression of the author's individual point of view is to forget the way the novel itself insists on the social contexts that produce and mediate authorial vision. And to understand authorial identity as point of view (from the point of view of the novel's form) is, in turn, to forget that the novelist has created the storyworld that she pretends to recount and to find the objective measure of her perspective in the difference between her valuation of this world and its own autonomous existence.

We can see, then, that the Jamesian theory of identity that has strong Romantic roots (the notion that individuals are inherently unique, that consciousness is the source of their difference and substance, and that successful self-expression is an ethical act of bravery) is developed by Smith in ways that bring the novelistic aesthetics of alterity into self-consciousness as an ethical aesthetic. When in "Fail Better" Smith praises literature generally for giving readers access to individualized points of view that are unavailable to us in real life, she sounds the Romantic note: "You can never know, no matter how long you live, no matter how many people you love . . . the experience of the world through a consciousness other than your own" (par. 20). And in keeping with the Romantic sensibility, her belief in the power of the novel as a literary form to do just that—to enable authors to represent consciousnesses other than their own—is, for Smith, the "intimation of a metaphysical event" (par. 20). But it is precisely the notion of a metaphysical understanding of persons that is interrogated by novel form, as Smith understands it. The novel not only gives the reader access to a consciousness other than her own, but also best teaches the reader to appreciate that consciousness as a social other. The novelistic experience of alterity as the "intimation of a metaphysical event" is grounded in the felt difference between one's own consciousness and a consciousnesses other than one's own. In Smith's description of literary effects, the encounter with alterity that the novel provides is not accomplished through a willing suspension of disbelief. In the novel, the experience of alterity comes through a struggle with belief. To understand the experience of the world through a consciousness other than their own is, Smith asserts, for novel readers to "allow into their own mind a picture of human consciousness so radically different from their own as to be almost offensive to reason" (par. 25). Smith describes this readerly experience—the reader's experience of the author's way of experiencing—as highly emotional and so powerful as to be felt as self-obliteration: "Great writing forces you to submit to its vision" (par. 21). Release is not guaranteed upon closing the book. In Smith's description, the great fiction writers enable you not just to experience their experience of the world while you are reading but to continue to see your own world through their vision even after you stop: "You spend the morning reading Chekhov and in the afternoon, walking through your neighbourhood, the world has turned Chekhovian" (par. 21).

The novel reader's encounter with alterity is so profound that it may seem as if the reader's own identity has been evacuated, that she has become simply a vessel for the author's more powerful vision of life. But this is not the case. Crucially, in Smith's version of the aesthetics of alterity, what remains of readerly identity is the structural noncoincidence of perspective preserved by the reader's own ethical act of will. A reader may feel forced to submit to the author's vision, but this is a submission that she has invited in her choice to be a novel reader. Her own volition is retained through the reading experience by an equally powerful feeling, the feeling of estrangement that enables the reader to register the "radical difference" between the way of being that she knows to be hers and the way of being that she identifies as the author's. The novel's performance of perspectivalism, in other words, does not end with the mimetic depiction of the author as a point of view on the storyworld. By making authorial identity available to the reader *as* perspective—through style, form, and characterological point of view—the novel also encourages the reader not to mistake the author's perspective for the reader's own. Whereas a lyric poem may encourage identification—I have loved daffodils, too, or now I know how to love nature as Wordsworth does—novelistic perspectivalism discourages the reader from collapsing the difference between self and other, from treating someone else's point of view as one's own—even as one sees one's own world through the eyes of Chekhov.

"Great styles," Smith declares, "represent the interface of 'world' and 'I,' and the very notion of such an interface being different in kind and quality from your own is where the power of fiction resides" ("Fail Better," par. 21). The "great joy of fiction" is thus the ethical good of alterity understood not just as the "variety" of authorial perspectives we encounter through reading different novels, but also as the way novels represent the apprehension of alterity as itself a perspectival event. The novel stages the encounter between points of view not as a meeting between two discrete and autonomous entities—the collision, say, of two marbles—but as an event that can itself be known only from a particular point of view. In the largest sense, the encounter with alterity provided by the novel is grounded in the ethical belief that, although it is impossible to have an unmediated knowledge of the other, one can approximate the other's alterity in better or worse ways. "This matter of understanding-that-which-is-outside-of-ourselves using only what we have inside ourselves" is, on Smith's view, "the hardest intellectual and emotional work you'll ever do"—and the basis of the novel's positive social value (par. 23).

The name Smith gives to this intellectual and emotional work is "love"—and she thus locates herself in a liberal humanist line of ethical criticism of the novel that, as I elaborate in other chapters, includes Vernon Lee, develops through

Lionel Trilling and Iris Murdoch, and finds a recent exponent in Martha Nussbaum.[38] *On Beauty* in fact invokes Murdoch by naming the Belseys' beloved family dog after her. As we have seen, Iris Murdoch makes grand ethical claims for what she regards as the novel's generic fitness for representing the good of social diversity, of achieved characterological personhood defined as the achieved ethical value of the encounter with difference; for Murdoch, the novel's characterological project is the best evidence there is that modern society is "likely to flourish" ("The Sublime and the Beautiful," 263). She adds that "the feature that most interests me in the un-Hegelian nature of . . . great novels is simply this: that they contain a number of different people" (257). The love that the novelist holds for people different from herself is for Murdoch the root of social justice: "A great novelist is essentially tolerant, that is, displays a real apprehension of persons other than the author as having a right to exist and to have a separate mode of being which is important and interesting to themselves" (257). Like Smith, Murdoch believes that the novelist who maximizes the novel's capacity for alterity has accomplished a significant ethical achievement, which, as I have discussed in Chapter 2, Murdoch expresses by offering a Kantian gloss on Keats: "In a special sense [the artist] *is* the good man: the lover who, nothing himself, lets other things be through him. And that also, I am sure, is what is meant by 'negative capability'" (270; emphasis in the original).[39] But for Smith love is neither so disciplined nor so altruistic. In this regard Smith comes close to Martha Nussbaum's argument in *Love's Knowledge*:[40] on Nussbaum's view, dispassionate goodness is itself an ethical limitation. And Smith makes her own departure from Murdoch clear when she asserts, "Tolerance falls short of love." ("Love, Actually," par. 16).

It is precisely the unruly nature of love that makes it for Smith the key to alterity, its power to create social bonds between people that are based on investments other than simple "appreciation." The power of human emotion makes ethics (both in life and in the novel) "a messy human concoction" ("Love, Actually," par. 24). The author's perspectival investment, her uneven treatment of different characters within a novel or even the same character over the course of a novel, helps make authorial identity, the fingerprint conveyed as style, legible. In other words, the degree to which the author fails to be the kind of lover who "nothing himself, lets other things be through him" is the degree to which characters in a novel seem to come alive as human beings: their subjectivity is made to seem ontologically equal to the author's. Love in general is for Smith "stickier, more shameful" than tolerance—and the novelists that Smith deems great are ones, such as E. M. Forster, whose characters inspire unruly feelings in their author (par. 24). Although Smith follows Murdoch in using the Keatsian term "negative capability" to describe the workings of novelistic alterity, it is, fittingly, Keats's other definition of the term that Smith has in mind: "when man is capable of being in uncertainties, mysteries, doubts, without any irritable reaching after fact and reason" ("Love, Actually," par. 20; qtd. from Keats).[41]

If Murdoch's notion of tolerant alterity evokes a Christian economy of sacrifice (the good novelist eliminates her own identity in order that her characters may live), Smith's notion of sticky love insists on both the impossibility and undesirability of authorial impersonality. On Smith's view, it is not self-sacrifice but our sense of self-restriction, of limited positionality, that allows us to believe that life outside the self is more than the self—uncertain, uncontrollable, and mysterious. Smith argues that Forster's preoccupation with the tendentiousness of his own point of view becomes the basis for the love that he bestows upon his characters. In other words, Forster's sense of self-limit is directly linked to the social factors that define point of view as a subject position. His privileged class position makes "him feel that he could not understand the experience of the great majority of his fellow men," Smith argues, while his socially taboo sexuality limits the full public expression of his identity in life and in art ("Love, Actually," par. 15). It is Forster's acute awareness of the social factors that bind his own identity that leads him to embrace novelistic negative capability as an encounter with unknowability rather than an act of self-purification. Forster's love for characters in his own novels who "are so muddled they barely know their own name" suggests, Smith declares, that "there might be some ethical advantage in not always pursuing a perfect and unyielding rationality" (par. 16).

Smith's notion that the ethics of alterity is produced through the experience of self-limit helps to explain the way *On Beauty* accords ethical value to its own perspectivalism.[42] Why does a novel that begins with the narrative promise of telling the story of Kiki Belsey, an African American woman married to Howard Belsey, a white Englishman, end up dominated by Howard's point of view? The story of Kiki Belsey, Florida native, Massachusetts resident, mother, nurse, empathetic individual, "strong black woman" (as her son calls her), feminist, is one that we have not heard much.[43] While Faulkner's imagination cannot get past the outside view of a "big woman" now "draped loosely in unpadded skin that tightened again upon a paunch almost dropsical," Smith readily installs us inside the large body and interesting mind of an African American woman who weighs 250 pounds. But Smith does not stay there. *On Beauty* goes in and out of minds at a dizzying pace. The family members all take a turn as center of consciousness; the minds of family friends suddenly open up; and Smith seems even to display the sheer unpredictability of her multiperspectivalism by almost gratuitously taking us for a few isolated pages into the mind of Katie Armstrong, one of Howard's students (249–253). That even such a minor character can suddenly and momentarily blossom into subjective presence establishes an ethical standard for the representation of characters as persons: because the social world of *On Beauty* belongs equally to any and all of its characters—because, in other words, the novel emphasizes that all of its characters have the capacity for protagonicity—the uneven distribution of points of view, the narrative rhythm and pacing of the novel's multiperspectivalism, becomes weighted with ethical value. On the macro level, this ethics of alterity comes to a climax in the final pages of the novel. Why does the characterological potentiality of Smith's omniscience narrow down to the white, male academic's perspective? Why by the end of the novel is the capacious presence of Kiki's mind closed off to the reader? Why does Smith rewrite Forster's novel as Howard's end? What does it mean that a novel that displays its capacity to write a new cultural narrative, Kiki's narrative, falls into the same old story, the Updikean-Bellowian-Rothian male, midlife-crisis sexual romp?

The ethics of alterity that drives the novel's storyworld action sets the terms for answering these questions about Kiki's characterological representation. After Kiki moves out of the Belsey home, she disappears from the novel, only to reappear as an unexpected member of the audience assembled to hear Howard's academic lecture on Rembrandt. Howard's joy in seeing her (the profound compensation for his disastrous professional performance) gives Kiki's reappearance in the storyworld the feel of a happy ending: "He looked out across the crowd to find the man responsible for this special [lighting] effect and found instead Kiki, sixth row, far right, looking up with interest at the image behind him. . . . She wore a scarlet ribbon threaded through her plait, and her shoulders were bare and gleaming" (442). The final narrative portrayal of Kiki is all from Howard's point of view—and it is infused with the love and hope her presence inspires in him. The novel closes with Howard's rapturous upwelling of feeling for Kiki: "Howard looked at Kiki. In her face, his life." The private communication that he establishes with her amidst his public humiliation suggests the renewal of their intimacy and marital union. "He smiled at her. She smiled. She looked away, but she smiled" (442–443). The Rembrandt paintings that were to be the subject of his political critique now in this context ironically suggest their humanist value: the enduring expression of the love a man holds for a particular woman.

This final scene is thus poised between the ethical value of Kiki's implied forgiveness of Howard—her capacity for sticky love, her acceptance of her love for Howard as against all reason and therefore a measure of his ethical singularity—and the narrative erasure of her point of view. The novel's ethics of alterity thus develops the aesthetic intensity of this final scene by weighting the narrative with incommensurable interpretive options. To the degree that Kiki's protagonicity is fulfilled through an ethical ideal of obtained otherness (the love that leads her back to Howard), Howard's portrayal (in the force of its emotion and its personal need) suggests the limits of his own capacity for otherness. Although from Howard's point of view the reunion with Kiki seems certain, the novel ends with no verification of his interpretation of Kiki's intentions or feelings. In fact, according to the ethics of alterity developed through *On Beauty*, Howard's rapture, and the beautiful style of its expression, may either be the redemptive representation of his personhood (the expression of his love for Kiki as a move beyond narcissism to vulnerability and need) or be another instance of the novel's portrayal of his co-optation of her identity, the ways "we refuse to be each other."

This citation, from the political philosopher H. J. Blackham, serves as the epigraph to the novel's first chapter and thus establishes the ethics of otherness as the novel's presiding concern, even as it (like the use of Scarry's title) also invites consideration of the difference between the philosopher's definitive knowledge claim ("we refuse to be each other") and the novel's ethical investigation of the possibilities for knowing others (as points of view) and the limits to this encounter.[44] The ethical stakes of the final scene between Howard and Kiki have been developed through Smith's portrayal of a social world where personal identity is inextricable from social positionality. At the center of this social web is the Belsey family, mixed race and middle class. The drama of Kiki and Howard's marital conflict, framed as a problem of identity difference (the difference between English and American, black and white, male and female), sets the terms for the failed attempts of their three children to forge friendships or love relations with people different from themselves. For example, in attempting to justify his repeated infidelity, Howard blames not his lack of self-control but his gender identity: "It's true that men—they respond to beauty" (207). The novel exposes the fallacy of Howard's appeal to a gendered world of natural otherness (women are the beautiful objects, men the erotic responders) by dramatizing his daughter Zora's response to the beautiful body of Carl Thomas. Serendipitously, both Carl and Zora are swimming at the same pool:

> For the time it takes to swim one length she stood by the side of the lifeguard's chair and watched the smiling sun make its way through the water, watched the initial seal-pup flip-flop of the boy's torso, the ploughing and lifting of two dark arms in turbine motion, the grinding muscles of the shoulders, the streamlined legs. (133)

But although in this case Howard's identitarian logic (male desire is naturally different from female desire) is undermined by the novel, the irony points to the material conditions that create the feeling of a natural condition of otherness. Zora's failed attempt to attract Carl culminates in an accusation from Carl that sums up a view of the instrumentalization of alterity important to the novel's ethical investigation: "People like me are just toys to people like you. . . . I'm just some experiment for you to play with" (418). Howard may be wrong about the natural state of male desire, but in the storyworld of the novel, Carl seems right about the othering power of class difference. Both in the storyworld and in the distribution of point of view, class difference defines an otherness that cannot be refused. The storyworld thus frames the terms of value for the novel's ethics of point of view. In this regard, Chantelle's lack of point of view is as significant as Kiki's preponderance of point of view. Exploited for her beauty by her mentor, Monty Kipps, Chantelle is also an object of aesthetic interest for the poet Claire Malcolm. The narrator reports that Claire longs to hear "that saturnine young lady's startling accounts of ghetto life in a bad Boston neighborhood," and that Claire "was spellbound by this news of lives so different from her own as to seem interplanetary" (215). For Smith the task of the novelist is not just to listen to the stories of others but to depict that otherness as the defining feature of the novel as a social world, in its form as well as its content. And the narrative ethics of alterity refers the degree and kind of characterological otherness portrayed in the novel back to the author's ethical capacity to represent consciousnesses other to her own. Does Smith's management of point of view ultimately bespeak her own failure—like Faulkner—to imagine fully the alterity of this black woman, so different from Smith's own identity? Or is the ascendance of Howard's point of view an even deeper accomplishment of alterity? Is it the harder ethical task for a woman like Smith to sympathetically occupy the consciousness of the white male in midlife crisis? To make this cultural cliché viable as an individual with whom a reader can empathize?

The very fact that *On Beauty* asks us to understand the meaning of its management of point of view as an ethics of alterity also indicates how as readers the lines of our sympathy and judgment are shown to be related to values that attend our own social positionality. If you find Howard's sexcapades amusing and I find them wearying, or if you regard Kiki as the novel's feminist center and another reader sees her as hopelessly male-dominated, then we may come to believe that our difference in judgment is based as much on differences in subject position as on the novel's artistry in portraying these characters as formal points of view. The ethics of alterity that governs novel reading recalls Smith's description of Henry James's inability to appreciate *Middlemarch*: "You might say of Henry and George what the novel says of Lydgate and Rosamond: *between him and her indeed there was that total missing of each other's mental track*" ("*Middlemarch* and Everybody," 30; emphasis in the original). And as we have seen, the aesthetics of alterity illuminates not only the social values that drive judgment but also the idea of novel form that readers bring to the novel. Two early reviews of *On Beauty*, one positive and one critical, illustrate the perspectivalism of readerly aesthetic evaluation. Frank Rich locates the aesthetic achievement of *On Beauty* in what he regards as the match between style and content performed in the service of representing the "beauty of culture itself."[45] For Rich, this hymn to culture is delivered especially in what he regards as the novel's joyous descriptions of the pleasure to be had through the experience of monumental cultural achievements that include Hampstead Heath, Mozart's music, and Rembrandt's paintings. Rich thus misses all the ways the novel problematizes a unified idea of beauty, as well as a unified idea of culture, by its politicization of at least two of the three achievements he lists. Debates about how to estimate the value of Rembrandt's paintings fuel the conflict between Howard and Kipps, while Smith's interest in depicting the Requiem lies in the disagreement within the Belsey family about the music's aesthetic power and social agency. Smith's depiction of the Belsey family listening to the Requiem is, of course, a politicized reworking of Forster's famous description of a performance of Beethoven's Fifth Symphony in *Howards End*. The novelistic aesthetics of alterity suggests that when a person like Rich approaches the novel with a belief that gardens, music, and painting are absolute cultural goods, he overlooks—indeed he cannot see—the perspectival mediation and citationality that make these moments of "joyous apprehension" depicted in Smith's novel as always socially situated, an index of subject position and personal value.

In fact, Smith powerfully stages the description of the Requiem as a demystification of a universal and absolute view of cultural values. Beginning a new chapter, the description first invokes a decontextualized "you" that seems to belong to anyone who listens: "Mozart's Requiem begins with you walking toward a huge pit. The pit is on the other side of a precipice, which you cannot see over until you are right at its edge. . . . Your will is a clarinet and your footsteps are attended by all the violins" (69). But having been recruited into this universalized aesthetic response, the reader discovers that the "you" is in fact a particular "you," a view that belongs not just to a specific character but a character whose point of view is defined by a specific social positionality—even when she is thinking of herself, to herself: "You peer over the precipice: a burst of ethereal noise crashes over you. In the pit is a great choir, like the one you joined for two months in Wellington in which you were the only black woman" (69). What does the cultural monument of Mozart's Requiem mean for this black woman living in a white world? Jerome's tearful response to the music is proof for Kiki that her son understands what she cannot, the masterworks of white culture. Her thoughts about his cultivation are her thoughts about the music. The meaning of Mozart is that her son is "a young black man of intelligence and sensibility, and *I* have raised him" (70). Between Howard Belsey's stated dislike of music that "tries to fake [him] into some metaphysical idea by the back door," his son Jerome's strong emotional response to the music through silent tears, and his mother's racial pride in Jerome's emotional response, the social politics of beauty could not be more emphatically depicted (72).

Rich, blind to the operation of perspectivalism in the description of the Requiem, counts Smith's achievement to be beautiful; Frank Kermode, who only partially sees the novel's perspectivalism, counts the same passage an aesthetic mistake. With a (Lubbockian) creative-writing-workshop sense that point of view should always only operate systematically, Kermode judges Smith's move from a generalized you to Kiki's point of view as a lapse in her formal control. Zeroing in on lines describing Kiki's response that he finds particularly egregious, Kermode insists that "a pedestrian editor would have eliminated the blunder and a good editor the entire passage. It hardly helps that the Forster original is just as bad."[46] As with the debates about James's handling of Maisie's point of view, the critical disagreements about *On Beauty*'s aesthetic accomplishment are drawn into the ethics of alterity: coming to the novel with points of view that are their own, can readers open themselves up to the otherness conveyed by this particular novel? Can novel reading upset rather than confirm the reader's expectation of what cultural value might be and how novelistic aesthetics might successfully operate?

While the management of point of view in *On Beauty* leaves readers to ponder their own subject positions and ethical values—and the limits both place on any individual's capacity for alterity—the novel's management of narrative poses another set of questions about the values implied by other features of Smith's novelistic style. Why is a novel so dedicated to perspectivalism undergirded with a well-wrought plot? This aspect of the style of *On Beauty* is especially interesting, since Smith, in her discussion of E. M. Forster, equates his empathetic superiority with his formal incompetence.[47] Sticky emotions like empathetic love, Smith argues, yield a "muddled style" ("Love, Actually," par. 19). It is Forster's capacity for alterity that, to use a phrase from his own *Aspects of the Novel*, "sogs" his novels "with humanity."[48] As Forster's novels follow out the points of view of their various characters, the form of the novel gets, in Smith's words, "all bent out of shape" ("Love, Actually," par. 12). But if Smith believes this about Forster, what does it mean for her view of alterity that her own novel is so beautifully plotted? That the characters' lives are muddled and messy but not the novel itself?

I want to suggest that in the same way that the economy of power between Howard's and Kiki's points of view becomes the flashpoint for the political understanding of characterological alterity offered by the novel, Smith's tour-de-force plot is a flashpoint for thinking beyond poetic adornment in the consideration of novelistic aesthetics.[49] As I have discussed, ever since the novel was first theorized as a literary form, the conflict between alterity and artistic design has organized the debate about its generic identity. The personalization and contextualization of style insisted upon by novelistic narration means that plot, like lyrical style, has the force of an authorial instrument of power, an attempt by the novelist to impose art upon life, an authorial act of domination that encroaches on the life of the storyworld. The modern novel's commitment to the creation of autonomous characters positions any act of narration as a potential encroachment on the existential freedom of that character. The constant threat of aesthetic exploitation bolsters the novelistic aesthetics of characterological freedom, the reader's intense apprehension that fictional characters are autonomous, living beings—even to the point of seeming entitled to the rights of real people. The understanding of the novel as caught between its social and aesthetic nature is, in ways I hope I have now made clear through my discussion of Smith, constitutive of novelistic aesthetics, conceived of as an aesthetics of alterity. A fictional character like Chantelle can be felt to be no different from a real human being to the degree that her functional positionality seems like a restriction of her potentiality, a limit to the full freedom that she has the right to enjoy beyond the artistic uses that the novel puts her to. The characters in *On Beauty* are "living" to the degree that we feel the artificial plot does an injustice to their potentiality. Kiki is more alive, more discussable as "real," to the degree that the novel has failed to make her equal to its aesthetic enterprise.

With this understanding of the politics of positionality as it relates to Smith's representation of character, we can now appreciate a related element of Smith's novelistic aesthetic: the act of style by which she communicates the beauty of truth claims. In a mode of omniscient narration particular to this novel, *On Beauty* offers us highly specific acts of interpretation and judgment that seem to come from the author herself. In her frequent use of aphorisms, Smith is clearly invoking a feature of the nineteenth-century English novel, especially the novels of George Eliot. But once again, the incipient ethics of narration in Eliot's aphoristic style becomes for the twenty-first-century novelist a marker of the quality of the author's interface with the social world she represents. More often than not, these acts of interpretation take their own specific form in the novel: they are aphorisms presented through or near free indirect discourse and usually offer generalizations about human nature suggestive of lived experience. Here are some examples, gathered from across the novel:

> When you are guilty, all you can ask for is a deferral of the judgment. (13)
>
> The ill-pitched greetings that compassionate age sings to mysterious youth rang out. (56)

> Time is not what it is but how it is felt. (129)
>
> She did what girls generally do when they don't feel the part. (129)
>
> Here were people. Here were tastes and buying habits and physical attributes. (210)
>
> He stretched his arms around her solid nakedness. In a whisper he began begging for—and, as the sun set, received—the concession people always beg for: a little more time. (398)

As Smith deploys it, the aphorism potentially emanates from three different enunciatory scenarios. The authoritative homeliness of its insights (usually framed as a social generalization: girls do this, people are like that) suggests strongly that the statement is issued by an omniscient narrator who expresses the opinions that the author has gained through perspicacious living. But the embeddedness of the aphorism within the context of free indirect discourse also invites us to consider that the expressed judgment is the opinion of one of the characters, voiced by a helpful narrator. Finally, the shift in tonality that characterizes the aphorism invites us to consider a third enunciatory source. The compression of their formulation, the deployment of rhetorical flourishes, and the resonance of their authoritative voice give these statements a poetic quality that stands out from the rest of the prose. Through these elements of its form, the truth claim seems to exceed the limited view of any ordinary individual (character or author) and to invoke the transcendental insight of the literary author as genius, as seer.[50]

In contrast to Faulkner's leap to beautiful language (which cast a veil over what he did not know he did not know), Smith's aphorisms stage for the reader the vexed relation between the seemingly spontaneous call of beauty and truth, on the one hand, and the social embeddedness of our response, on the other hand. By situating the aphorism at the intersection of these vectors of speakerly positionality, *On Beauty* involves the reader in the act of comparing the sociality of all knowledge claims. As with any knowledge claim made in a novel, the reader asks of the aphorism, Whose insight is it? The multiplication of its potential enunciatory sources—Smith, narrator-for-character, seer—asks the reader to consider what difference it makes to the wisdom claim if it is ascribed to one speaker and not another. Or, if it can in some way belong to all speakers, then what difference does this consensus make for our assent or dissent from the claim's proposition? The multiplication of enunciatory positions staged through the narration of *On Beauty*'s aphorisms demands that readers inductively locate their own positionality in relation to the possibilities before them. Readers thus know that they know through positionality—but the wisdom claim itself simultaneously suggests that knowing entails the limitation of perspectivalism, even if this limitation is itself situational and temporally contingent.

But what distinguishes the narration of aphorism in *On Beauty* from other novelistic representations of positionality is the form of their content. Why do Smith's aphorisms routinely formulate positive knowledge claims that are based in normativizing generalizations about social types? If this is the voice of the seer, then what the seer sees in the world of the novel is the shared behavior and attitudes that define social groups. The multiplied choice of enunciatory sources for the aphorism is interestingly counterbalanced by the unifying singularity of its social proposition. In the particular politics of *On Beauty*'s narration, the act of knowing people other to oneself is made possible through the sense that otherness is apprehensible only through the identification of qualities that are repeated and shared. The aphorisms in *On Beauty* show knowledge of the other to be rooted in empirical experience that uses inductive reasoning to posit classifying generalizations (she is like this, people are like that). The aphorism thus stages in all three of its aspects—point of view, social positionality, and inductive wisdom claim—the cognitive, ethical, and political pressure to know the identities of other people through the simplification and unification of their subjectivities. To the degree that readers assent to the content claims of the aphorism, they can feel that these simplifications have been successful, that perspicacious induction can be sensitive and accurate, that the narrator utters not just wisdom claims but wisdom itself, the way the poet, the seer, and the prophet have been felt to do—however homely this wisdom may be in its acts of social typification. But Smith's narrativization of the aphorism also performs the ethical and political risk of the wisdom claim: that such generalizations can be shallow and reifying, engaging in the injustice of social stereotyping or the bathetic simplification of individuality.[51]

On Beauty's narration of aphorism suggests that within both life and literature there is the need to know the world by the truth claims people offer as well as by the social identities implied by their acts of style. To know Zadie Smith by the "watermark" (one of her favorite critical terms) of her style is thus to know her through her capacity for alterity and the limits of that capacity; it is also to know her from the truths she posits, borrows, and tests.[52] The lyrical beauty of Smith's aphorisms—their figuration, cadence, and elevated tone—thus becomes an important element in the novel's depiction of the complex social nature of aesthetic experience and judgment. By dramatizing the negotiation between positionality and proposition that takes place in and through a social world, *On Beauty* encourages us to question the source of aesthetic judgments as well as showing how difficult it is to justify or share the personal experience of beauty. If it seems a mistake to ask "Is *On Beauty* beautiful?," that potential error is, as I hope I have shown, exactly what Smith seeks to point out through her understanding of the art of the novel as a perspectival endeavor and an ethical task. But as *On Beauty* also shows, it is equally an error to ignore the question of beauty—beauty as a question—posed by novelistic acts of style. By inviting the question of beauty, Smith's novel calls attention to the stylistic resources and effects as well as the theoretical assumptions about character and form that in the twentieth and twenty-first centuries have become the basis for understanding the craft of fiction as a novelistic aesthetics of alterity.

Since Zadie Smith's early essays have usefully helped in the articulation of her contribution to the novelistic aesthetics of alterity, I want to close this chapter by investigating what it might mean for her to have jettisoned her plans to include them in a collection that had the projected title "Fail Better: The Morality of the Novel," publishing instead a volume entitled *Changing My Mind* (2009). Although "Fail Better," "Read Better," and "Love, Actually" are missing from *Changing My Mind*, there is nothing in the volume to suggest that Smith has moved away from the idea that novelistic aesthetics is inherently bound up with the ethics of alterity—and in fact her view of the novel as the book of other people is restated ten years later in "Fascinated to Presume: In Defense of Fiction" (2019). I want to suggest, though, that one of the reasons why *Changing My Mind* seems a lightweight offering is that the notion of perspectivalism that so much enriches the ethico-artistic task of her novels collapses when she takes on the role of public intellectual into a weaker ethical notion of the self's frictionless capacity for endless change. This is an ethical good that she comes to, tellingly, not through and as the encounter with other people but introspective self-reflection. As she states in the foreword to *Changing My Mind*, "I'm forced to recognize that ideological inconsistency is, for me, practically an article of faith."[53] The grounding in an ungrounded identity (whose key value is not the ethical effort to transcend ideological limits but the confident ability simply to refuse them) marks the paradoxicality of Smith's knowledge project as a public intellectual. Her essays exist to articulate her opinions and insights—the truth of her beliefs. But by also claiming an identity that is defined not just by inconsistent beliefs but incommensurable beliefs (willed changes in ideological positioning), Smith implies that the stated beliefs in any given essay are not to be believed. Rather than following out the ethical dilemma raised by such a stance, Smith instead nominates the capacity for change as an inherently ethical condition. Do I contradict myself between that essay and this? Then, yes, I have only proven my virtuous ideological inconsistency.[54] But as I want to show, the positive value that Smith in her foreword to *Changing My Mind* attributes to her own cultivation of relativity marks the difference between the aesthetics of alterity that she pursues in her fiction and the watered-down multiculturalism that as a public intellectual she holds out as a political good.

A useful way to register what it means for Smith to write as a public intellectual rather than a novelist is to compare the essay on E. M. Forster that she includes in *Changing My Mind* with "Love, Actually," the 2003 discussion of Forster that appeared in *The Guardian*. There is a striking difference between the complex account Smith gives of Forster's novelistic achievement in "Love, Actually" and the praise she offers for Forster as a public commentator in "E. M. Forster, Middle Manager."[55] As I have been discussing, in "Love, Actually" Smith holds up Forster as a consummate example of a novelist whose willingness to fail according to traditional stylistic expectations is both a sign of the superiority of his ethical endeavor and the key to his aesthetic success. The criticisms that have been made of Forster's lack of artistic control—his uneven style, his erratically developed (or wholly underdeveloped) characters, his direct expression of personal views (views that are, moreover, sometimes bathetic), his reliance on chance as a plot device—are for Smith the basis of what is most novelistic about good novelistic aesthetics. On her view, the novel as an ethical discourse defines itself against moral authorities from any quarter (including the academy) whose literary judgments are so consistent, certain, and prefabricated that they are most comfortably expressed through rationalized, distinctively nonliterary genres such as the "mission statement," a "piece of public policy," "social history," or one might add, moral philosophy ("Love, Actually," par. 3).[56] Smith argues that Forster self-consciously positions himself against the kind of moralist whose mind is made up, who is closed to new experience, by portraying such people as flat characters in his novels. For Smith, Forster as novelist spectacularly fails to be self-consistent for two related reasons: because his moral judgments are inseparable from his emotional investments in his characters, making his judgments of these characters "unfair" because not impartial; and because the primary emotion that drives him as a novelist is that of empathetic identification with his characters, which makes him incapable of judging them by any formalized set of rules or codes.

When Smith turns away from Forster the novelist, though, to take a look at Forster the public intellectual, a popularizing literary critic for the BBC, she finds Forster's project now to be wholly unmysterious, fully nameable, easily explained and judged. The excesses of style, the lack of system, the airing of sometimes embarrassing beliefs that worked for Smith as a novelistic aesthetic strategy—that projected the novel as "a life" through its resistance to perfected and rationalized formalizations of its value—this same unevenness Smith sees in the BBC lectures. But now, without the generic resources of the novel to give them ethical stake and social consequence—without, in other words, the novelistic aesthetics of alterity—Forster the public lecturer is for Smith not a higher force for a better ethicality but only comfortably middlebrow. Smith still says she "loves" Forster, but to love this Forster, to love the public lecturer rather than the novelist, is to experience love as an altogether different emotion. Instead of sticky love, instead of the experience of being ruled by an outside power, instead of "being in mystery," the stylistic unevenness of Forster's lectures leads Smith to a fully composed knowledge of Forster's fully graspable identity; to understand this Forster, one need only "*reconcile* oneself to the *admixture* of banality and brilliance that was his, as he had done himself" (16; emphasis added). In contrast to the novelist's productive ethical muddle that sustains itself through its openness to alterity, his emotional engagement with the other people he represents, the lecturer's highs and lows, his brilliance and banality, neatly combine for Smith into the "admixture" of middlebrowness.[57]

These two different essays on Forster thus do not represent a change of mind but a consistent view of why the difference between the novelist's capacity for muddlement and the lecturer's "admixture" of brilliance and banality is the difference between the encounter with alterity offered by the novel as a genre (as performed through its acts of narrative) and the encounter with the directly stated opinions of a single individual offered through the lecture. As lecturer, Forster finds himself shoring up his public role by asserting the logic of the selfsame. Smith quotes Forster's public reply to the demands of his heterogeneous listeners: "I've had nice letters from people regretting that my talks are above them, and other equally nice regretting that they are below; so hadn't I better pursue the even tenor of my way?" (18). Smith calls this Forster's decision to "plow the middle course," a decision whose sensibility she defends. But it is important to see what is lost when the value of the aesthetic muddle is exchanged for the value of the public middle.[58] In "pursuing the even tenor" of his way, in pursuing the self as an even tenor, Forster effectively stops striving for ethical alterity. The public (in general, taken en masse rather than through individual relation) are all nice people, distinguished by classifiable differences (high and low), a gradation that can measure and validate Forster's own position as itself classifiable (a midway between extremes). We hear a weak echo of the novelistic project of achieving aesthetic beauty through the ethical pursuit of "being in mystery and uncertainty" when Smith sums up Forster's achievement as a public lecturer in this way: "There's magic and beauty in Forster, and weakness, and a little laziness, and some stupidity. He's like us. Many people love him for it" (18).

We can vividly see Smith plowing her own middle course in "Speaking in Tongues," an essay on Obama's successful campaign for the US presidency.[59] What especially interests me about this essay is that it shows how in the attempt to "do" politics, to pursue the topics of ethicality and social alterity by weighing in on current events, Smith forgets what as a novelist she cannot not know: the social and material forces that create social difference. I interpret this forgetting as itself in keeping with the public discourse of the Obama campaign, which contributed to the larger cultural desire for individual efficacy and transformative social action through the valorization of positive thinking per se—"Yes, we can"—which was linked to the official campaign slogan, "Change we can believe in." Central to the campaign strategy was the projection of a positive conception of racial and ethnic difference as a social pluralism that could lead to the election of an African American president through the notion of democratic cultural reconciliation and admixture: "Yes, *we* can." Smith's brief in "Speaking in Tongues" is to argue for Obama as a public figure who also possesses the representative capacity for social alterity that distinguishes the literary artist. She explicitly reinvokes the value of Keatsian negative capability to define Obama's political achievement as an ethical achievement, the ability of "'being in uncertainties, Mysteries, doubts, without any irritable reaching after fact and reason'" (144). But unlike the sticky love that leads the novel reader (through his emotional engagement and investments with author and characters) to the conceptualization of ethical uncertainty as a perspectival event, informed by the power relations inherent in the different subject positions occupied by novelist, characters, and readers, Smith's composed appreciation of Obama leads her tellingly to invoke an entirely different lineage for literary alterity: not the novel but the drama.

Now, as she elucidates the ethicality of negative capability, Smith invokes Shaw and Shakespeare rather than Forster. This move from novel to drama brings with it the excising of social mediation, of the accomplishment of alterity in and through power relations, so that in "Speaking in Tongues" the ethical achievement of alterity is conceptualized by Smith not as a complicated negotiation between self and other through emotional engagement and differential subjective investments, but through the effortless gift of literary "genius." Smith lauds Shaw and Shakespeare for their ability to populate the stage with people who they socially are not, but who they nonetheless imaginatively can somehow be. For Smith (following Keats), Shakespeare is the paragon of this version of negative capability. The mediating power of history, language, genre, actors, and performance context is wholly absent in Smith's conceptualization of the drama. Without the obvious mediating instrument of narration, the drama can seem to her the expression of the authorial capacity for nonconflictual multiperspectivalism. For her, Shakespeare's literary and ethical supremacy both are products of his capacious identificatory capacity: "In his plays he *is* woman, man, black, white, believer, heretic, Catholic, Protestant, Jew, Muslim" (143; emphasis added). The novelistic alterity that informs Smith's understanding of sticky love now is posed as a wholly one-sided authorial act: the social others—woman, black, Jew—are social heterogeneities all equally available to the responding imagination of the literary artist, and this capacity for alterity is precisely what, on this model, defines the literary artist as ethically superior to the social types he depicts. In fact, the logic of this version of negative capability creates a necessary ethical distinction between the negative capability of the playwright and the monolithic point of view that defines his characters, since it is only by representing characters as self-consistent, through the logic of the same, that social diversity is made legible so that the playwright's capacity for alterity can be manifested.

The playwright standing outside and above social determination, with no single voice of his own, is thus distinguished from his characters, who, without the "gift" of literary imagination that might enable them to also be defined through their capacity for identificatory alterity, instead are themselves made identifiable as social subjects through their unchanging social positions: woman, man, black, white, believer, heretic, Catholic, Protestant, Jew, Muslim. The absolute difference between the playwright and his characters is underscored through Smith's discussion of *Pygmalion*. The plight of Eliza Doolittle, as Smith sees it, is precisely that of a woman whose attempt to change her station, to speak the language of the upper classes, leads not to the achievement of a change in social positioning but rather to social alienation. Because she is a woman, because she was a flower girl, Eliza will never be at home in high society, even if she can master the language.

But why can Shaw succeed where Eliza cannot? In her mystification of the literary imagination as the ethical agent of alterity, Smith does not consider the social factors that legitimize Shaw's representational authority, that give him the cultural privilege to project as social types Eliza, her father, and Professor Higgins. Nor does she consider the difference between representing these lives as characters in a play and encountering them as social subjects. This difference is residually suggested, though, and precisely, in the moment when she appeals to the magical, alterity-giving properties of the literary imagination to explain the difference between Shaw's multivocality and Eliza's self-division. Shaw can bring to life social types as various as Professor Henry Higgins, Eliza Doolittle, and Alfred Doolittle without losing his own life, without becoming caught in between, because, Smith claims, he is in "possession of a gift he wouldn't, or couldn't, give Eliza: he spoke in tongues" ("Speaking," 134). It is the couldn't or wouldn't in this statement that points to the difference between Smith's novelistic aesthetics of alterity, predicated not only on such subjective investments and uncertainties but also on the necessary power relations between author and character, and the nonconflictual version of social diversity that she finds in great plays.

But since Smith's project in "Speaking in Tongues" is to make the case for Barrack Obama as the equal to Shakespeare or Shaw in his possession of the gift of social alterity, she does need to consider how someone who is not a literary genius can accomplish the ethical act of representing social others as social others through the mimetic reproduction of their identities. She believes that

Obama's ethical achievement is what makes him a better political representative: he represents the people because he incorporates social heterogeneity into his being. What is more, he can represent this social heterogeneity by reproducing social others in their own terms, without mediation: "This new president doesn't just speak for his people. He can speak them" (136). On Smith's view, "the tale [Obama] tells is all about addition. His is the story of a genuinely many-voiced man. If it has a moral, it is that each man must be true to his selves, plural." The implication is that the plural self is an ethical accomplishment, that for Obama as for the literary artist the condition of personal plurality comes from the openness to beliefs and views that are not your own, that belong to other social subjects.

But without the literary "gift," what accounts for Obama's ethical achievement? In the 1980s, in work by Henry Louis Gates, Houston Baker, and Barbara Johnson, Obama's exceptionalism would have been explained by the double vision afforded him through the subaltern position he occupies as a biracial man in a hegemonically white society.[60] For a moment in "Speaking in Tongues" the issue of race seems to lead Smith away from the mystifying power of her account of literary imagination to consider the social and material factors that have caused Obama to construct himself as a socially plural self and to value social plurality as a supreme ethical and political good. Smith nods to the influential Du Boisian account of the African American identity as always already a double identity because it is caught between two separate social worlds, white and black—but she refuses to accept the Du Boisian estimation of that condition as tragically split owing to the asymmetries of social power. On Smith's view, Obama's biracial identity does not provide him with social experience that results in insight into the operation of social power but instead puts him in touch with a universal truth: that "everything is doubled, everything is various. You have no choice but to cross borders and speak in tongues" (138). While Du Bois yearns for and works toward a social future where African Americans can be un-self-divided because empowered as social equals, a condition that will allow them an authentic relation to the transcendental self available to white philosophers such as Ralph Waldo Emerson, Smith's happy construction of the experience of doubled personhood is grounded in a purely secular philosophy of identity, one that makes a virtue of the relativity of all value in a world without God, without transcendence. To be biracial, at least from the perspective of Zadie Smith, is to get an early introduction to the frictionless accomplishment of ideological inconsistency. Of her own biracial identity she says, "I felt a sort of wonder at the flexibility of the thing. Like being alive twice" (133).

Smith's references to Obama's biography and to her own experiences of relativized "variousness" thus function not as a material explanation for why she believes Obama grasps the ethics of alterity when other politicians do not, but as convenient examples of what Smith ultimately formulates as the universal condition of personhood in the era of globalization: the disinstantiation of identity that comes from the shared cultural condition of living between social worlds, of border crossing, of speaking not through one's own voice as an instrument of self-expression but through other social languages—the "tongues" that make voice a figure for selfsame identity now a figure for self-contingency and social pluralism. As Smith would have it, Obama's biracial identity is simply one version of the experience of Americans who in their "daily lives, conjure contrasting voices and seek a synthesis between disparate things" (138). Obama, it turns out, does not just "speak the people" in all their social diversity, but in being the kind of person who can speak the people becomes a person with whom the people can identify—not because he only speaks their tongue but because they too feel themselves, as Eliza Doolittle did, constituted by a social multiplicity. Americans voted for Obama, on this view, not to effect a certain program of political action but as an act of self-recognition. When Smith declares that "only a many-voiced man could have spoken to that many people" (140), she means not only that the heterogeneous American public identified with Obama because he spoke in all their social voices, but also that they identified with the universal condition of multiperspectivalism, of necessary social pluralism, that Obama projected through his capacity for vocal mimicry.

In describing Obama's ability to inspire this kind of mass identification, Smith calls Obama, after Pauline Kael's term for Cary Grant, the man from Dream City. But Kael's point about Archibald Leach is that through the social institution of the entertainment industry he projects himself as a social ideal, a man from nowhere, who exists only on-screen, a cultural imaginary, the Cary Grant that even Archie Leach would like to be. And it is my argument that it is exactly in this sense that Obama occupies a social ideal for Smith: that of social relativity without social conflict, ethical incommensurability without disagreement, social diversity without the differential of political power relations. The desire to imagine the "way forward," to theorize a positive account of individual agency based in an understanding of social diversity as a benign plurality rather than an effect of social power, leads Smith to ignore the violent history of American civil rights that gives both cultural specificity and a sense of embattlement to the African American pursuit of a "dream." The occasion of Smith's essay is her review of Obama's memoir, *Dreams from My Father*. And significantly, Smith's understanding of this title deemphasizes Obama's own reference to lineage and inheritance. Obama does not inherit a patriarchal dream, Smith argues, but is placed by both his parents in the experiential state of "occupy[ing] a dream, to exist in a dreamed space" (137). This is the ideological space, I would submit, of the "Yes, we can" campaign rhetoric, taken by Smith not as a political strategy but as a social reality.

It is Smith who is dreaming the possibility of a better future here, and this social dream is not of postracial politics but of postpolitical ethics. The dream space for Smith is not the political world of campaign speeches, bank bailouts, and health care reform bills but the ethical space of individual identity, which for her is the mind of the universally pluralized social subject. We can see this not only in her account of social alterity as always only an experiential phenomenon but also in the "theory" of ethics that she offers at the conclusion of her analysis of Obama.

> My little theory sketches four developmental stages. The first stage in the evolution is contingent and cannot be contrived. In this first stage, the voice, by no fault of its own, finds itself trapped between two poles, two competing belief systems. And so this first stage necessitates the second: the voice learns to be flexible between these two fixed points, even to the point of equivocation. Then the third stage: this native flexibility leads to a sense of being able to "see a thing from both sides." And then the final stage, which I think of as the mark of a certain kind of genius: the voice relinquishes ownership of itself, develops a creative sense of disassociation in which the claims that are particular to it seem no stronger than anyone else's. There it is my little theory—I'd rather call it a story. It is a story about a wonderful voice, occasionally used by citizens, rarely by men of power. (146)

This is an account of ethical value in which the ethical agent has been rendered almost wholly passive. And it is not surprising, given the subordination of agency here, that "genius" is invoked to explain the transition between a model of social determination (the first stage, the encounter with incommensurable social positions) and the last stage: the "creative disassociation" from localisms, from ideology, from belief.

Smith implies that there is in fact a fifth stage to her developmental model: to have achieved disassociation from any personal claim is to embrace social alterity as both the form of truth and a preeminent ethical good. Shakespeare could inhabit a variety of social positions because, Smith argues, through his creative disassociation from his own beliefs he could make "himself a diffuse, uncertain thing, a mass of contradictory, irresolvable voices that speak truth plurally" (144). This is also what she believes Obama is able to do, and she believes this is the experiential source of his ethical rejection of dogmatism, his pursuit of "flexibility" as an ethical good, his commitment to having an open mind—and to changing his mind—as paths toward accomplishing positive social transformation. But unlike the poet, the politician must act as well as be. Can the capacity for being in mystery and uncertainty translate into ethical political action? When Smith views Obama's public policies, she celebrates them along similar lines as she does Forster's BBC lectures. But for Obama she implies a causal relation: the man who has achieved the disassociation from belief that comes through multiperspectivalism is the politician who can plow the middle way. Smith makes this explicit in her defense of the "'great statesman of the Privy Council, set up to mediate between Parliament and Crown as London burned,'" George Savile, Marquis of Halifax (1633–1695), whose reputation as a "trimmer," a politician who steers the course between extremes in order to forge a middle ground, represents for Smith the positive capacity for compromise, admixture, and the possibility for reconciliation (145). In Smith's essay, our final view of the man from Dream City is Obama, middle manager. The "flexibility" that Smith says Obama has won through his superior capacity for negative capability—his accomplishment, in other words, of social alterity and social multiperspectivalism—allows him to accept the middle way, to settle for the doable rather than the ideal. The representative who meets the dreams of the public through the self-identification his multivocality affords turns out to be the politician whose campaign slogans of promise and faith in futurity—change, hope, yes we can—lead to political solutions that are adequations, middle courses, acceptances of what can *possibly* be rather than the pursuit of what belief would deem *should* be.

I've spent so long detailing the logical tensions in "E. M. Forster: Middle Manager" and "Speaking in Tongues" because these essays show how Smith holds fast to the nonrelativized belief in social alterity as an ultimate ethical good, no matter what else she may change her mind about. Indeed, as I have suggested, it is her belief in this value that leads her to believe that changing one's mind is itself an ethical good—as long as one does not change one's mind, one supposes, about the ethical value of the social contingency of all value judgments. And in tracing the reconfiguration of Smith's notion of how ethical alterity can be achieved, I have tried to suggest that in occupying the role of the public intellectual, Smith forgets what she knows as a novelist: that the disinstantiation from social identity that allows for the benign acceptance of truth as always only socially relative is forestalled by the material forces that create social differences to begin with. In her own novels and in her discussion of the novel as a form, Smith is aware of the way power relations mediate and mitigate social diversity and of the way rational forms of knowledge are necessarily pursued in the face of the ethical ideal of ever-expanding alterity. But as a public intellectual Smith performs instead an ethical act of hope, which might help remedy the power politics that make the novel so apposite for our own cultural moment. Her hope for Obama is that he will prove to be the leader whose acceptance of social relativity and whose respect for otherness will turn social difference into "a proper and decent human harmony" (148).

The impulse that leads Smith to first propose a "theory" of ethical development that she then redescribes as "a story" is emblematic of the way as an essayist she appeals to an inherent fictionality that she ascribes to narrative, in contrast to the ethics of alterity that as a novelist she credits to characterological perspectivalism. As narrative, truth claims are posed as contingent, partial, and contextual. As story, narrative further implies that all knowledge is an act of fictionality, a projection of a possible truth, even a counterfactual truth. In her stance as a public intellectual, Smith performs an act of pious discourse that she hopes will enable social transformation. Whatever logical contradictions there may be within her argument, part of the hope is that the act of articulation holds transformative power: that material and social conditions will change through the act of saying so. And if the projection proves to be wrong, then the stakes are low, since after all, it is only a story. Bruce Robbins notes that this "defiant floating of all final knowledge" is an enduring description of literature's particular power, a power that is also understood as "literature's freedom to reimagine and recreate the social world."[61] But as we have seen, neither virtuous irresolution nor boundless imaginative freedom are qualities of the novel as developed through the Jamesian tradition. Instead the novelistic aesthetics of alterity shows how "the social significance of literature is proportional to the resistance that the (unfree) imagination overcomes or at least recognizes and confronts"[62]—both in the attempt to represent social others and in the attempt to "push the novel's form to its limits" (Smith, "*Middlemarch* and Everybody," 41) by first constituting it through an ethics of alterity as an aesthetic form that has generic limits.[63]

J. M. Coetzee's *Elizabeth Costello*
The Tradition as the Sum of Its Parts

J. M. COETZEE'S NOVELS have provoked and attracted readers by the peculiar, sometimes perverse, and frequently violent social relations they depict. The ethical evaluation of this social world is explicitly invited by the self-questioning undertaken by the protagonists as each confronts the problem of how best to live in personal and social circumstances that are suddenly and radically altered. Significantly, the disruption of quotidian life in many of Coetzee's novels is inextricably linked to the intense emotional connection that the protagonist develops with an enigmatic social other. In *Waiting for the Barbarians* (1980), for example, a magistrate at a colonial outpost develops an erotic attachment to a native woman whose political victimage has left her mostly blind. Eventually the magistrate comes to see that his obsession with her body is a displacement for a more abstract kind of desire, the knowledge of her closed-off personhood: "I hunt back and forth seeking entry. Is this how her torturers felt hunting their secret, whatever they thought it was? For the first time I feel a dry pity for them: how natural a mistake to believe that you can burn or tear or hack your way into the secret body of the other!"[1] This formulation poses otherness as an ethical provocation: Is the magistrate's failure to know the other a failure of his ethical responsibility? Or is it the result of an ideological barrier, the power relations that render her identity a "secret" from his subject position? Should the magistrate attempt to overcome otherness, to try to know her identity from "within"? Or is the right ethical choice to honor the difference in social identity and respect that it will remain forever unknowable from the magistrate's gendered and racialized point of view? The magistrate's dilemma sets the terms for Coetzee's representation of the native woman. Has he as author succeeded where the magistrate failed?

In *Age of Iron* (1990), Mrs. Curren, a retired, white South African classics professor, dying from cancer while race riots rage in the streets of Cape Town, chooses to make a homeless man, Mr. Verceuil, her most intimate social relation.

Curren devotes her final days to attempting to understand the ethical call of Mr. Verceuil's otherness. The novel is a record of the wins and losses in a volatile ethical journey that for her is never finalized, is done and undone by new circumstances, unanticipated feelings, surprising revelations from the past. When Mrs. Curren first meets Mr. Verceuil, she posits that they share a common ground of identity, within their different states of being: "He is and is not I" (19). Humiliated by her own bodily mortification, she identifies with Mr. Verceuil as "a rubbish person" (47) who emblematizes the "state of shame" (119) that is the ultimate human condition. Through that felt sense of shared human frailty, she seeks to establish with him a friendship based not on charity but "heart to heart" mutuality (22). But does Mr. Verceuil share this sense of himself and of their relation? Is a felt sense of personal shame the basis upon which he would reciprocate friendship? Is friendship even what he wants from Mrs. Curren? Or is Mrs. Curren's belief in the possibility of friendship as an ethical good simply a marker of the class difference that constitutes their unbreachable otherness? Again the ethical questions extend to Coetzee's narrative portrayal. To use a phrase from David Lurie in *Disgrace*, does Coetzee "have it in him to be the woman?," Mrs. Curren? Can he write from her first-person point of view? If he is successful, does this mean that his representation of her is grounded in his sense of their shared humanity? "She is I." Or does the artistic achievement lie in representing her as "not I"? If Coetzee is successful in his representation of the otherness of Mrs. Curren, does that mean his characterological representation of Verceuil reproduces her sense of Verceuil as other?[2] Or does Coetzee treat both characters equally as ethical subjects who "are and are not" versions of a shared humanity?[3]

In *Disgrace* (1999), Coetzee's most controversial depiction of the violence of social difference, Lucy, a white woman who lives alone on a farm, reports that she is raped by two black men and a boy. Lucy's father, David Lurie, is visiting her; the men set him on fire. Lucy and her father struggle to understand the reasons for the attack. Have the men perpetrated an immoral act that deserves social punishment? Should the rape be understood as violating Lucy's honor and virtue? If so, will punishing the men rehabilitate Lucy's moral condition? Or should the attack on both of them be understood impersonally, as either South Africa's "history speaking through them [the men]" (156) or the ideological expression of gender oppression: "what women undergo at the hands of men" (111)? Lucy herself rejects all these socially oriented interpretations, insisting instead that the attack is "a purely private matter" (112) and claiming her right to decide for herself the meaning of the attack for her own life.⁴

What relation can there be between the urgent ethical imperatives raised by these novels, an oeuvre that has won Coetzee international crucial acclaim and a Nobel Prize, and *Elizabeth Costello* (2003), a work that depicts the life of a celebrity novelist mainly through the lectures, addresses, and conversations about literature that she engages in as a well-paid guest speaker in the sequestered public venues of the college lecture hall, the academic conference room, and various dining rooms? *Elizabeth Costello* is not only devoid of the searing social drama of *Waiting for the Barbarians*, *Age of Iron*, and *Disgrace* but possesses so few of the attributes that are commonly associated with the novel as a literary form that it might justly be asked if it counts as a novel at all. With no continuous storyworld action or time frame, with little attention to setting and physical description, with a minimum of backstory for its characters (even for the protagonist) and some anomalies of fact (such as John Bernard's marital status), *Elizabeth Costello* may seem to be less a novel than the deconstruction of a novel—yet another postmodern "gasp and squeal" (to use David Foster Wallace's phrase).⁵

But I want to suggest that *Elizabeth Costello*, so different in storyworld drama and narrative construction from Coetzee's major novels, links itself to those powerful portraits of contemporary sociopolitical life through its reflection on the way literary representation participates in the ethical project of attempting to know social others.⁶ If the magistrate in *Waiting for the Barbarians*, the retired classics professor of *Age of Iron*, and the female farm dweller of *Disgrace* all allow Coetzee to depict ethical value as the attempt of socially embedded individuals to understand people other to themselves, *Elizabeth Costello* dramatizes the encounter with alterity that writers and readers credit to their engagement with literary texts.⁷ As I have been arguing, the ethical value attributed to literature turns out to be the quality par excellence of one genre: the novel. The novel's participation in the ethics of alterity is the explicit subject of Elizabeth Costello's lectures and addresses, a main topic of conversation among other people in the social world of the novel, and also the framework of value guiding *Elizabeth Costello*'s own narrative management. What Coetzee asks us to consider through the form and content of *Elizabeth Costello* is that, by the close of the twentieth century, a cultural assumption about the ethics of otherness that inheres in novelistic narrative has elevated the novel to the most socially significant of literary genres. *Elizabeth Costello* develops the philosophical complexity of this ethical view of the novel as a genre by dramatizing Costello's deep commitment as a writer to the idea that novelistic creation is inextricably linked to the achievement of alterity, that for the novel writer "'it is the otherness that is the challenge. Making up someone other than yourself. Making up a world for him to move in. Making up an Australia.'"[8] And it is precisely the difficulty of bringing this otherness to life—"'if it were easy it wouldn't be worth doing'"—that makes the achievement of alterity a twinned accomplishment: the author's ethical capacity for goodness, to imagine on behalf of another, must be matched by her mastery of the narrative resources of fiction if the personhood of characters and the social world of fiction are to be successfully rendered as autonomies.[9] The novel's storyworld events show that Elizabeth Costello's ethical view of the novel is culturally widespread: other novel writers and readers also express the idea that the novel as a genre is socially valuable because of the ethics of alterity that they assume is an attribute of its narrative structure.[10] In a work that otherwise seems so discontinuous, whose storyworld events seem so minimally narrativized, the unifying concern, from beginning to end, is the topic of the novel's narrative ethics. In the same way that the protagonists in *Waiting for the Barbarians*, *Age of Iron*, and *Disgrace* are reduced to the bare minimum of a social state (a state defined by the ethical relation between self and other), so too is *Elizabeth Costello* as a novel stripped to its bare minimum as a genre: the unifying concern, from beginning to end, is the discussion and performance of the novel's ethics of alterity, real or aesthetic.[11]

Even more specifically, *Elizabeth Costello*'s depiction of the characters' investment in narrative ethics draws attention to the formalism that underwrites their collective understanding of novelistic alterity. Coetzee shows that almost all the characters in the novel take two things for granted: first, that the value of the novel lies in its formal resources for the depiction of otherness; and second, that through its narrative structure the novel stages an ethical encounter between author and reader, author and character, and reader and character. Coetzee interrogates this formalist view of novelistic ethics precisely by exposing it as a cultural orthodoxy. As I will discuss, the characters self-consciously debate about the kind of otherness the novel brings to life and which formal resources are most important for that generic task—while Coetzee's staging of disagreement works to draw attention to the unexamined basis of agreement: that novels are socially valuable because of the ethical encounter with otherness that they provide. In my close reading of this novel I want to show how the myriad disagreements that characters have about the nature and location of the novel's generic performance of ethical alterity catalogue a plethora of novelistic narrative techniques, each made visible and aesthetically interesting by the ethical qualities ascribed to it. Thus, through the characters' analysis of narrative technique and through his own acts of style in *Elizabeth Costello*, Coetzee makes a positive case for the aesthetic intensity that is accorded to the novel as a genre when narrative is assumed to be an ethical activity—even as he also cultivates a skeptical attitude toward the cultural assumptions that attribute an absolute ethics to novel form. As *Elizabeth Costello* so powerfully vivifies, novelistic prose could by century's end, through the ethics of alterity ascribed to it, be regarded as possessing a narrative form as dense and intricate as any sonnet stanza. *Elizabeth Costello* suggests that the problem that the novel presented for Henry James and the modernists who followed him—the notion that the novel as a genre might be anything at all and thus defy artistic method and control—is putatively solved by the ethical value the Anglo-American literary tradition comes to ascribe to the novel's capacity for heterogeneity. The "cannibal art" (to use Virginia Woolf's term) comes to be understood not as a self-consuming artifact but as a welcoming host for otherness. As I will show, by the end of the twentieth century, the cultural assumption that the novel's devotion to difference is the source of its ethical value allows even a novel as citational, narratively discontinuous, and unpsychological as *Elizabeth Costello* to achieve aesthetic success as a well-wrought, artistic unity.

Elizabeth Costello belongs in the self-conscious tradition that Robert Alter identifies in *Partial Magic*. Alter tracks this novelistic tradition back to Cervantes and through the major accomplishments of Sterne, Diderot, and Nabokov. On Alter's analysis, through the narrative strategies of these novels the author "pointedly asks us to watch how he makes his novel, what is involved technically and theoretically in the making, as the novel unfolds."[12] To open *Elizabeth Costello* and find that the chapters are listed in the table of contents as "lessons" is from the start to be pointed in the direction of pedagogy. The watching reader discovers that this novel conveys its lessons both through the content of Elizabeth Costello's lectures and addresses and through the narrativization of these lectures; thus the lack of vigorous linearity in the storyworld plotline helps call attention to Coetzee's self-conscious demonstration of the novel's metanarrative, the story of what is involved technically and theoretically not just in the making of this novel but for the cultural construction of literary value in our own contemporary moment.

Part of what it means to watch this novel unfold technically and theoretically is to track the tensions and contradictions in Elizabeth Costello's statements about the value of literature in general and the novel in particular. Do her ideas finally hang together as an ethical defense of literary value? The novel invites this question of judgment even as it dramatizes Elizabeth Costello's own personal stake in being right. Her belief in the ethical value of fiction is the commitment that has guided her life. Forsaking other professional endeavors and other types of social engagement (her children huddle outside the study door, begging for her attention, making "tiny whining sounds"), she stays at her desk, "confronting, day after day, year after year, while her hair slowly goes from black to grey, the blank page" (4). To Jonathan Franzen's query—"You ask yourself, why am I bothering to write these books?"—Costello believes she has an answer. As she states of another novelist, he must be "'as good a man can be who is also a novelist, that is to say, perhaps not good at all, but tending nevertheless to the good, in some ultimate sense, otherwise why write?'" (180). *Elizabeth Costello* the novel asks us to consider whether this complicated statement is true, who else in her social world might agree with her, whether or not there is a philosophical or evidentiary basis for her belief, and what narrative form or forms best express the putative ultimate goodness of the writer.

The connection between *Elizabeth Costello* and Coetzee's other works comes even more firmly into view once we see that each of its eight lessons is devoted to a different philosophical aspect of the ethical task of knowing and representing alterity, and that over the course of the eight lessons the problem of alterity is connected to different modes of novelistic representation: Defoe's formal realism (the technique of *Disgrace*), the Richardsonian epistle (the technique of *The Age of Iron*), Borgesian metafiction (the technique of *Slow Man*), Kafkaesque allegory (the technique of *The Childhood of Jesus*), and postmodern citationality (the technique of *Foe*).[13] To read *Elizabeth Costello* as a novel is to see how it reflects on the variety of modes through which the novel as a genre can engage with the ethical value of representing otherness, modes that Coetzee himself cannot not use.

In this regard, it might seem as if *Elizabeth Costello*'s overarching narrative structure stages a pilgrim's progress for its reader through the novel's literary history, beginning as it does with a first lesson on "Realism," the eighteenth-century novel's defining feature as well as *Elizabeth Costello*'s own dominant mode, and ending with a fragment of postmodern citationality: Coetzee's fictional rewriting of Hugo von Hofmannsthal's fictional "Letter of Lord Chandos to Lord Bacon" (1902, set in 1603). The final pages of *Elizabeth Costello* leave behind any trace of the social world in which each lesson has been set—and even leave behind the bildungsroman convention of a titular protagonist whose lived life is coextensive with and homologous to the novel's narrative. Left in the novel's final lesson waiting at a gate that seems to allegorize the threshold to the afterlife, Elizabeth Costello makes no appearance in the postscript. As a narrative component of this self-conscious novel, the postscript thus suggests that the novel as a form can continue beyond realism, beyond character-based modes of narration that carry with them (so postmodernists such as Roland Barthes, Alain Robbe-Grillet, John Barth, Thomas Pynchon, and others have said) anachronistic notions of personhood.[14] But the eight lessons that this novel gives us in how to read for novelistic alterity also provide the clue for understanding that the literary history it performs through its narration is not supersessive, not the story of realism's rise and fall, but the story of the continued availability of all novelistic modes to the contemporary writer.[15] The realism that is both deployed and an object of characterological analysis is not disabled so much as supplemented: Coetzee's capacious understanding of the modes of representation available to the contemporary novelist, modes that have been developed through the Anglo-American and European tradition he draws upon, function as stylistic choices fully available to the twenty-first-century fiction writer.[16] The novel still can be, as James and Woolf declared, anything at all—but this variety coalesces into an art form when it can be comprehended through or as an ethics of alterity. So thoroughgoing is the ethics of alterity at work in *Elizabeth Costello* that even the postscript's imitation of Hofmannsthal becomes a final opportunity for a novelistic act of otherness: can Coetzee re-create the fictional world projected by Hofmannsthal by reversing its gender orientation? As an epistle penned by another Elizabeth, Lady Chandos? The postscript thus repurposes postmodernist play by drawing citationality into a novelistic ethics of otherness. And in doing so the novel ends where it begins: by Coetzee as author calling attention to the relation between his own gendered identity and that of his protagonists, whose textual status and fictional condition do not prevent them from being brought to life as characterological others, whose personhood is defined as a social relation to himself. In its opening sentences, *Elizabeth Costello* announces its alterity project as "a simple bridging problem." But while it might indeed seem a simple thing for readers to position themselves in relation to the imagined world that fiction creates, *Elizabeth Costello* shows, through its form and content, how complex the ethics ascribed to that act has become.

In the same way that the narrative sequencing of *Elizabeth Costello* reflects on the different modalities of novelistic form, so too does it unfold the degrees and types of alterity at stake in different modalities of otherness. Like the number and variety of words that Eskimos are said to have for snow, the novelist's task, as understood at century's end, is so completely equated with the task of representing otherness that the notion of alterity has expanded to include the problem not just of knowing other people but of knowing alterity in a whole range of different states. *Elizabeth Costello* defines the ethics of alterity in terms of a philosophical problematic, a family of ideas that raises questions about the ideological conditions that produce social otherness (the relative weight of race, class, and gender differences); the power of ethical attitudes to alienate humans from their own humanity, turning them into moral monsters; the possibility of a nonanthropomorphic understanding of animals as different species; and the achievability of knowing about / dwelling in other ontological states of being: divinity, life after death, and also fiction as its own ontology.[17] In this chapter I want first to explore the family of ideas that constitute the novel's formulation of the ethics of alterity and then examine the narrative techniques that make the novel as a genre, from this novel's point of view, not just the book of other people (to use Zadie Smith's phrase) but the book of other states of being.[18]

As I will show, the ethics of alterity reproduces as a task for the novel form the difficulty of knowing states of being from a particular embodied subject position. This is the same problem that Coetzee's protagonists confront in his other novels. How can the fictional character be known as other from the point of view of the authorial self? Can the social self of the author be fully transcended through the successful operation of the sympathetic imagination? Should the writer strive, as Mrs. Curren does, to see the other "as you really are" (*Age of Iron*, 179)? Or should the novelist accept the fact that "when I write about him I write about myself" (131)? Is the novelist's task to establish the right emotional state of intimacy with her character, to "love him because I do not love him" (131)? Is the author responsible for the lives of fictional others who come "without being invited" to her imagination (179)? Or does the author occupy a hostile relation to the states of being that she attempts to render, believing that she can "burn or tear or hack your way into the secret body of the other" (*Waiting*, 49)?

Questions like these are at the heart of the novelistic ethics of alterity as it is developed over *Elizabeth Costello* as a whole, from the first lesson through the postscript. What emerges is a notion of novel form that views narrative as a location of ethical engagement among author, character, and reader. The lessons in novelistic alterity encourage readers to attend to the author's narrative choices, judging whether he succeeds in representing the character as other to himself and what the terms of achieved otherness should be. Do the novelist's narrative choices achieve characterological otherness by representing characterological personhood in and for itself? Or is the narrative figuration of character mediated by the author's sense of his reader's expectations? Has he represented characterological identity, in other words, on behalf of the reader? And does the author project through his narrative management a view of his reader as the same as or different from himself? A similar set of possibilities describes the choices that structure the individual novel reader's task as a narrative ethics. Has the reader been able to open himself up to the experience of knowing others offered through narrative figuration? Does the reader experience his location in narrative as enabling intimacy with the characterological other? Is the reader's relation to the storyworld obstructed by the narrative register of authorial identity? Or does the structure of novelistic narrative allow the reader to encounter both the fictional character and the novel's author as autonomous others? How can readers who disagree about the ethical experience given to them through narrative structure adjudicate their differences? Does readerly difference necessitate different experiences of ethical reading?

Sympathetic Imagination as Ethical Emplacement

Elizabeth Costello's philosophical investigation into the novel's capacity for alterity is, importantly, turned over to its characters. The metafictional aspects of the project highlight Coetzee's successful creation of characters who seem to think for themselves, who have their own beliefs. Most of the characters in *Elizabeth*

Costello are literary professionals: their social lives are devoted to either the writing or reading of literature, and almost everyone is engaged with some aspect of the social distribution of literature. Commercial media such as radio and television extend the audience for literature through the interviews they conduct with authors. Academic scholars and teachers from their institutional positions create a literary public through the journals they edit and the required reading assigned to their students. Large sums of prize money are bestowed upon novelists deemed to be socially significant. *Elizabeth Costello* shows that each of these professionals comes to literature with an urgent, sometimes passionate sense of its ethical value. The belief that literature is an ethical good fuels debates about how to describe and where to locate literature's ethical value. The meaning that draws them to the writing and reading of literature seems to answer questions about how best to live that are of great urgency for each person. But as Coetzee shows, for most of the characters in the novel, the question of how best to live is inseparable from the question of how to know and honor states of being different from one's own. And the writers who obtain celebrity status are those whose work connects the ethical value of alterity with the political good of a just society.

Elizabeth Costello most powerfully stages the link between knowing alterity and bettering society in the two lessons devoted to the lives of animals. This is the position explicitly advanced in a lecture given by Elizabeth Costello at Appleton College. Costello believes that raising animals in order to eat them is "a crime of stupefying proportion" (114). She feels that to go to dinner and be offered at the dining table "Corpses. Fragments of corpses that they bought for money" is "as if I were to visit friends, and to make some polite remark about the lamp in their living room, and they were to say, 'Yes, it's nice, isn't it? Polish-Jewish skin it's made of, we find that's best, the skins of young Polish-Jewish virgins'" (114, 115). Costello uses her descriptive powers as a fiction writer to defamiliarize the social practice of meat-eating, but the identity she posits between the lives of Jews and the lives of animals is passionately critiqued from a different ethical understanding of the sacred difference between human and animal life as well as the singularity of the Holocaust as an ethical event. As Abraham Stern reasons in a letter he addresses to Costello:

> You took over for your own purposes the familiar comparison between the murdered Jews of Europe and slaughtered cattle. The Jews died like cattle, therefore cattle die like Jews, you say. That is a trick with words which I will

not accept. You misunderstand the nature of likenesses; I would even say you misunderstand willfully, to the point of blasphemy. (94)

Who is right? The lesson that the novel teaches is that the ethics of alterity can be debated from different grounding principles. One person's belief that an other is like the self becomes another person's occasion to reaffirm absolute difference, to view the terms in which identity is established between self and other as merely a "trick with words."

But descriptive defamiliarization and logical syllogisms are not Costello's only methods for comparing the inhumanity of Nazi Germany with the moral crime of raising animals for slaughter. She develops in her lecture a philosophical notion of the sympathetic imagination that is also a defense of establishing "likenesses," not through words or logic but as an ethical task undertaken by each individual. Likeness, as Costello describes it, is the embodied effort to imagine sympathetically a similarity between self and other that cannot be logically sustained or defended. What should the Nazis have done? What is the right ethical act that would have prevented the Holocaust, that would also put an end to treating animals like "prisoners of war" (104)? The Nazis, she says, "'closed their hearts. The heart is the seat of a faculty, *sympathy*, that allows us to share at times the being of another'" (79; emphasis in the original). Undertaken by each individual alone, sympathy is what brings the humanity of the other home to the self. Costello's notion of sympathy thus favors an ethics of embodied individual feeling as a means of bridging difference, one to one (to use Toni Morrison's phrase), as contrasted to moral commandments, formulated through political hegemony, that uphold the power hierarchies between self and other.[19] As she puts it, Nazi Germany's "'crime against humanity,' is not that despite a humanity shared with their victims, the killers treated them like lice. That is too abstract. The horror is that the killers refused to think themselves into the place of their victims, as did everyone else'" (79).[20]

To share in the being of another is thus, as Costello develops the notion, to feel one's difference even as one likens one's own state of being to another's.[21] This is a tricky distinction. On the one hand, likeness is an effortful act of imagination that does not pretend to know another's experience *as* that other. One can't know the experience of a particular person in a Nazi death camp, and one can't know the experience of a steer rounded up for slaughter. On the other hand, Costello suggests that by thinking oneself into the *place* of the victims a bridge of understanding can be established. It's not exactly clear how place is defined in this context. But it seems that as Costello describes it, "sharing in the being of another" is an embodied act of imagination that puts one's own knowable experience in the service of understanding an other by asking what it would be like for oneself to be in this same situation, this place. What would I feel if I were in the death camp?

> "They [the killers] said, 'It is *they* in those cattle cars rattling past.' They did not say, 'It is I who am in the cattle car.' They said, 'It must be the dead who are being burned today, making the air stink and falling in ash on my cabbages.' They did not say, 'How would it be if I were burning?' They did not say, 'I am burning, I am falling in ash.'" (79)

I for the other, my life in the place of theirs. The ethical act of imagination comes from feeling what I do know, my own embodied feelings and states of being, on behalf of the other whom I can never know but whose equality with me I can establish through this act of emplacement. Through the experience of putting myself in the place of the other, I also become aware of the unjust social conditions that create the material conditions of identity and my own position within the social hierarchy of power.[22]

Importantly, this imagined emplacement is never not hierarchical: the other is the other because of its/his/her/their disempowerment, victimage, abjection. The self who strives to know this other does so from a position of security that can *only* imagine subaltern experience through personal approximations that are real for the imagining self but that also don't pretend to be equivalents to the condition of otherness that the self cannot know, which is to say, the other's embodied experience. The act of sympathetic imagination on Costello's view produces feeling for the other but, crucially, does not eliminate or pretend to eliminate the social difference that produces otherness. In the words of Mrs. Curren, "he is and is not I." And as Costello emphasizes, "sympathy has everything to do with the subject and little to do with the object, the 'another'" (79). In the case of hierarchies of social power, the sympathetic act is not reciprocal: it is the task of the socially empowered, those who occupy the social position of selves, to cultivate an ethical imagination that will repersonalize the other through an experience of feeling attributable to his condition. But Costello believes that such ethical acts of imagination are a step toward redressing the material and structural conditions that produce inhuman crimes of violence and undoing the power relations that allow masters to regard others as inhuman. Thus the "trick with words" of which Costello is accused—the trick that putatively equalizes unequal conditions of ethical being (the abbatoirs and the Nazi death camps)—contrasts with the theory of ethical imagination that Costello puts forward, a theory that on her view emphasizes the material and social inequalities that produce the alienation constitutive to the self/other relation while allowing for the ethical value of imagining from a position of security denied to the other what it might be like to be the other.

Elizabeth Costello's explicit disagreement with the philosopher Thomas Nagel lies precisely in her belief about the imaginative availability of likeness as an ethical experience.[23] On her view, Nagel's position rests on a mistake about identification as the sole mode of accessing states of being other to one's own. Nagel's position, she believes, is based on the assumption that for humans to understand the life of an animal they need to be embodied as that animal: in her paraphrase of Nagel's example, "'to experience bat life through the sense modalities of a bat'" (77). Applying her own view of the ethical work of the sympathetic imagination to the problem of animal alterity, Costello argues instead that the human self can understand what it is like to be a bat by putting her own experience in the place of the bat. What is tricky, of course, is figuring out what that place might be. Is it behind bars at the zoo? Is it in the abbatoir? It turns out that for Costello the place of animal identity is its own body. She takes it as axiomatic that the being of animal nature is based in bodily sensation. To know the animal, to sympathize with the bat, is to make one's own experience of embodiment—a body "full of being"—the basis of feeling what it is like to be a bat. There is no need to experience the world *as* a bat, with the bat's particular sense modalities, because for Costello the task is not to *be* the bat but to put one's own sense of embodiment in the place of bat being. By this means an ethical likeness is established between self and other that does not presume equivalence or identification, or eliminate the conditions of power that privilege human life over bat life, the conditions that produce humans as selves and animals as others. But from within these structures of power, the act of imaginative feeling on behalf of the other provides the self with the ethical experience of why it is wrong to treat the animal as "'a slave: a being whose life and death are in the hands of another'" (156). On Costello's model of the sympathetic imagination, to know "'embodiedness, the sensation of being ... of being a body with limbs that have extension in space, of being alive to the world'" (78) is to know the bat not just as a life but as a life that takes "joy" in its life, valuing its experience of life as much as we do ours, even if animal life is defined only as the pleasure in and right to freedom of movement.[24] Costello again attributes so much efficacy to the imaginative act of putting oneself in the place of the other that she believes ethical action makes social change possible; to imagine oneself in the place of the subaltern, to find the basis of likeness between you who have power and they who do not, is, she believes, to understand why it is "a crime of stupefying proportion" to be the human who places animal corpses on a dining room table.

"The Lives of Animals" thus establishes Costello's belief in the ethical capacities of imagination, and also theorizes acts of imaginative emplacement undertaken by embodied individuals, as having the most consequential stakes for the ethical betterment of society: individual acts of ethical imagination can lead directly to large-scale social reform. But has she persuaded anyone in the social world of the novel that her theory has merit? Her lecture inspires strong criticism from the academic audience, along with some uncomfortable attempts to isolate an idea or two for the performance of polite agreement in the dinner-table conversation that follows. We learn in Lesson Six that the lecture was so controversial that the international media have covered it. She has been "attacked in the pages of *Commentary* (belittling the Holocaust, that was the charge) and defended by people whose support for the most part embarrassed her: covert anti-Semites, animal-rights sentimentalists" (156). But interestingly, at no point in "The Lives of Animals" is her theory tested experientially. Not one of her many interlocuters testifies to either succeeding or failing in the act of imagination that Costello has proposed as the heart of the ethics of alterity. The closest remark is one that dismisses her theory in its own terms, as it were, as being the product of a person who has too much imagination. The philosophy professor, Thomas O'Hearne, argues that "'it is only among certain very imaginative human beings that one encounters a horror of dying so acute that they then project it on to [*sic*] other beings, including animals'" (109). This criticism adds another layer to the debate about the ethics of alterity: the source of otherness is not just the difference between the human being and animal being, and it is not just the difference between humans and animals created by the inequities of social power; now O'Hearne nominates Elizabeth Costello herself as an aberrant other, made different from other humans first by what she lacks—the fortitude to deal with the fear of death—and then by what she has too much of—imagination. O'Hearne's implication is that rather than successfully using her imagination on behalf of the other, rather than beginning to bridge the difference between self and other by acts of emplacement, Elizabeth is so horrified by the thought of her mortality that she is especially incapable of understanding others different from herself, be they animals or other people who fail to share her obsession with death. O'Hearne thus brings the debate about ethical otherness around to the question of what a specific, embodied individual can know about human experience generally. In Costello's case, he clearly believes that her excesses and deficiencies make her unlike the majority of humans and thus unqualified to offer philosophical generalizations based in her own, minority experience.

As a philosopher, O'Hearne should know better than to invoke the genetic fallacy: the theory of ethical imagination proposed by Costello might be true even if she is also a very imaginative human being. But O'Hearne's comment usefully directs us to the question of whether Costello's theory of ethical imagination might be a way of understanding literature, as a creative act undertaken precisely by people who, like Costello, have an abundance of imagination. Do the imaginative acts of creating and reading literature have an ethics? And if so, can the ethical experience offered by reading literature lead to social and political betterment? Or, from the negative point of view introduced by O'Hearne, is the "man of imagination" (to use James's descriptor for the novelist) the person who believes he has the ability to know and represent otherness but whose excessive imagination only reproduces self-identity under the guise of otherness?[25] Although most of the novel's eight lessons develop Costello's own views about how the writer's sympathetic imagination manifests itself as a novelistic ethics of alterity, the views of other writers and readers are also dramatized, many of whom share her belief in the novel's capacity for otherness but have different accounts of how alterity should be philosophically defined and where its novelistic effects should be formally located. While writers and readers disagree (and, as we shall see, while Costello is herself inconsistent in her philosophical defense of the novel's ethical alterity), the range of ideas about how to define the ethics of alterity that is credited to the novel works to unify the novel's generic identity and this novel as an artwork, even as it complexifies and intensifies the notion of what novel form might be.[26] It is to the art of the novel understood as an ethics of alterity to which I now turn.

The Poet and the Novelist

From Costello's point of view, O'Hearne's criticism is no criticism at all. Not only does she agree with the description of herself as having more imagination than most, but she sees this quality as the distinguishing feature in the portrait of the artist that she develops through her lectures, interviews, and dialogues about the nature of literature and literary value. Costello herself makes no distinction between the poet and the novelist in this regard: both are privileged ethical agents who not only appreciate the value of alterity but know how to deploy the faculty of sympathetic imagination to bridge difference. In her lecture the evening before, discussing Wolfgang Kohler's research into the mental abilities of apes, she had proclaimed that "the poet" (here understood generally as the literary writer) more than the scientist could understand what it was like to think like an ape because the writer's imagination could give her "a feel for the ape's experience" (74). In the same way that ethical imagination can allow humans to know bats through the human experience of embodied being, so too does the writer, more than the unimaginative scientist or even the average zoo-goer, access her capacity for embodied feeling on behalf of the other—now to use the act of imaginative emplacement as a source of creativity that can bring that other into literary being as what is and is not I. But significantly, as I want to show, when Costello invokes the example of poetry's ethical alterity, it is worked out in terms that are on a continuum with what is ultimately her more comprehensive account of the novel as the ethical genre par excellence. In other words, the evaluation of genre is perspectival: from Elizabeth Costello's point of view, poets possess the capacity for ethical imagination, but the engagement with alterity that poetry offers (represented in the novel by the short lyrics Costello teaches and reads) is less multifaceted and variegated than that provided by novelistic form.

We can see how Costello makes the case for the poet in the seminar, titled "The Poets and the Animals," that she offers at Appleton College the day after her controversial lecture. Only very briefly represented in the storyworld of the novel, the seminar is used by Costello to argue for Ted Hughes as superior to Rainer Maria Rilke in the ethical representation of the lives of animals. Costello praises Hughes's jaguar poems for what amounts to an act of sympathetic emplacement, for "'feeling his way towards a different kind of being-in-the-world, which is not entirely foreign to us'" (95). As this statement indicates, the sympathetic act of emplacement as performed by the literary artist is rendered through literary representation to include the reader: through literary techniques, readers are placed to have their own experience of the "not entirely foreign" state of being that is the life of a bat, the life of a jaguar. Hughes's poems achieve this degree of sameness and difference, Costello argues, because Hughes does not strive to "'find an idea in the animal, that is not about the animal, but is instead the record of an engagement with him'" (96). Consistent with the ideas about animal lives articulated in her lecture, she praises Hughes for representing the being of the jaguar not as he "seems" but as "'the body moves, or as the currents of life move within it'" (95–96). And what Hughes's poem offers the reader, according to Costello, is the opportunity "'to imagine our way into that way of moving, to inhabit that body'" by bringing our own experience of embodied movement to our feeling for the jaguar (96).

But in keeping with this novel's investigation into the ethics of alterity, does Hughes really deserve Costello's praise? Or is she interpreting his poetry in light of her own novelistic values and concerns? As we have already seen, at the outset of this novel she states her commitment to achieved alterity and couches her view of achieved alterity in novelistic terms: "'It is the otherness that is the challenge. Making up someone other than yourself. Making up a world for him to move in. Making up an Australia'" (12). Coetzee seems to suggest that Costello reads poetry in light of her novelistic values, since the only poems that engage her interest are those that can be interpreted as striving to depict states of otherness. In a later lesson Costello sits reading a different poem, one that gets her thinking about how humans might be able to apprehend godly states of being. The poem that prompts this meditation is "Erotikon: (a commentary on *Amor and Psyche*)" by Susan Mitchell. Costello's first thought is to wonder why so many American poets are drawn to the story of Psyche: "Do they find something American in her, the girl who, not content with the ecstasies provided night after night by the visitor to her bed, must light a lamp, peel back the darkness, gaze on him naked? In her restlessness, her inability to leave well alone, do they see something of themselves?" (184). But as Costello develops her idea, to see something of themselves in the story of Psyche is not the end of the relationship between self and other (not a knowledge that comes from identification, in other words) but a toehold, a favorable cultural predisposition to work out a likeness between different states of being that opens up the means of understanding not just the human life of Psyche but the life of Eros as god, godliness as a state of being different from the human condition.

The question that Costello poses to herself—whether we can "*be one* with a god profoundly enough to apprehend, to *get a sense of*, a god's being" (188; emphasis in the original)—is answered affirmatively and in the same ethical terms that she brings to bear on Hughes's depiction of the jaguar. She in effect extends the ethical logic of the human relation to animal lives: in the same way that the human sense of joy in movement becomes the basis of likeness with animal lives, so too does the human sense of embodiment's restrictions make it possible for humans to have the feeling, to get a sense of, divine states of being. Literature that brings home an animal's being does not "try to find an idea in the animal, that is not about the animal, but is instead the record of an engagement with him" (96); literature that brings home a sense of a god's being is also the record of an embodied engagement with the other, but in this case the human experience of confinement gives the feeling of divine lives. And the way that literature can render that engagement is neither through the idea of a god nor through being the god but through the act of trying to imagine what it must be like for a god to take on the restrictions of human embodiment. To have a feeling for a god's being is to draw on our experience of embodied limitation and put that in the place of, in the ethical service of, understanding divinity. Through their experience of embodiment, humans know from their reifying position of mastery what it is like to be a bat, and they know from their position of subaltern restriction what it is like to be a god (the sense of a soul encaged by a body).[27]

The logic that guides Costello's interest in and admiration for the poems of Hughes and Mitchell raises the question of how the mental activity of reading can produce the feel for experience that is specifically defined as the feeling of and for embodiment. We are given insight into how Costello might answer this question when, in a digression she makes in her Appleton College lecture, she extends her discussion of the literary writer's feel for animal states of being (through the joy of embodied motion) to include her feel for a state of alterity defined by the body's lifelessness. She tells her Appleton audience: "'I know what it is like to be a corpse'" (77). As Costello elaborates this position, we see that in her description the ethical imagination works not just to establish bases of likeness (how would I feel, being who I am, if I were in this other body) but to disable reason. The cognitive act of imagination, in other words, cultivates mental states of logical paradox, thereby, according to Costello, giving the mind the feeling of alterity felt as embodied experience: "'For a moment we *are* that knowledge. We live the impossible: we live beyond our death, look back on it, yet look back as only a dead self can'" (77; emphasis in the original).

> "Do I know what it is like for me to be a corpse or do I know what it is like for a corpse to be a corpse? The distinction seems to me trivial. What I know is what a corpse cannot know: that it is extinct, that it knows nothing and will never know anything more. For an instant, before my whole structure of knowledge collapses in panic, I am alive inside that contradiction, dead and alive at the same time." (77)

"I am alive inside that contradiction": by disabling reason, the imagination (of paradox) creates an embodied experience of alterity, the feeling of being "dead and alive at the same time," of placing one's own experience of life in service of the otherness of extinction. This experience is necessarily fleeting, an act of mind that works through the hierarchal mental dominance of reason to momentarily disable reason through the imagination of paradoxical states.[28] As her account of Hughes's animal poetry suggests, these are the moments of dislocation that literature can provide to the reader: the solicitation of reason in order to disable it and to promote the embodied experience of literary reading as a lived state of paradoxicality, the sense of being alive within a contradiction, of simultaneously being I and not I, of being one's self and an other—a jaguar, a god, Elizabeth Costello.

To put Costello's view of imagination this way is to begin to see the novelistic quality of her praise of the poets.[29] Even when she is conceptualizing the human imagination of nonhuman states, her idea of the sympathetic imagination is profoundly characterological.[30] The general condition of embodied paradoxicality that she ascribes to literature generally finds its fullest realization in the novelist's focus on the individual, embodied experience of a particular human who attempts to know states of being other than her own. And with a closer look at Costello's engagement with Mitchell's poem we can see how the novelist picks up what she takes to be the poet's task of conveying the feel for divinity, imaginatively developing the poem's scenario as she reads and thinks—a process that organically leads to her beginning to write. Costello's imagination of the experience of encounter between a mortal, Anchises, who slept with a goddess,

Aphrodite, focuses on the particular moment of sexual congress—and more particularly, it imagines the encounter with alterity as experienced by an individual as an embodied encounter. And in keeping with the logic of novelistic alterity, Costello imagines the embodied nature of Anchises' point of view as inseparable from his own consideration of Aphrodite's point of view:

> So there was nothing left for a prudent fellow to do but lose himself, last thing at night, in drowsy memories: how it had felt, man's flesh lapped in god flesh; or else, when he was in a more sober, more philosophically inclined mood, to wonder: since the physical mingling of two orders of being, and in specific the interplay of human organs with whatever stands in for organs in the biology of gods, is strictly speaking not possible, not while the laws of nature continue to hold, what kind of being, what hybrid of slave body and god soul, must it have been that laughter-loving Aphrodite transformed herself into, for the space of a night, in order to consort with him? Where was the mighty soul when he took in his arms the incomparable body? Tucked away in some out-of-the-way compartment, in a tiny gland in the skull, for instance; or spread harmlessly through the physical whole as a glow, an aura? Yet even if, for his sake, the soul of the goddess was hidden, how could he not, when her limbs gripped him, have felt the fire of godly appetite—felt it and been scorched by it? (185–186).

Like the state of being a corpse, these questions defy reason. But for the novelist to undertake the project of representing what it might be like for a human to have a sense of divine identity, the "mingling of two order of beings" must be depicted as someone's experience, as the paradoxical state of otherness experienced by a particular self in a particular body. Where was the mighty soul of the god while she occupied the human body? What was it like for Anchises to feel godly appetite? Of course these terms are human terms: no human can be the god. But there is also no way of being Anchises. It is precisely Anchises' difference from Costello that prompts the novelist's need to imagine his experience. The novelist's ethical imagination thus begins with the project of knowing others different from herself and accomplishes this by discovering bases of likeness (this is what I would feel like if I were in Anchises' place) that are structured within a paradoxicality that both relies on reason but also (temporarily, but also again and again) disables reason. We can't be Anchises, but through the imagination of his embodied experience and point of view, the novelist places herself in his position, and as readers we thus place ourselves in relation to Costello's narrative othering, a process that paradoxically brings the fictional character to life as a person who is and is not like Elizabeth Costello, and who is and is not like the reader of her work.

In this lesson, Coetzee further portrays the workings of the novelistic imagination as the act not just of "making up someone other than yourself" but, as Costello has told the interviewer at the outset of the novel, of "'making up a world for him to move in. Making up an Australia'" (12). In her imagination of what it is like to have an encounter with the divine, Costello makes up the world of Mary of Nazareth. As Costello sets to the task of imagining the embodied experience of encounter between human and divine states of being, she attributes the question that is the basis of her own act of ethical imagination to the people in Mary's social world: "What was it like, how did it feel, how did you bear it?" Thus we see the novelist's alterity project expanding and compounding: Costello not only wants to get the feel for divine alterity through the imagination of Mary's embodied experience and point of view, but she also makes up a world for Mary to move in by imagining that the exceptionalism of Mary's encounter with divinity becomes a basis of communal identity and inquiry for her social world. What the novelist wants to know, in other words, takes characterological form as what other people want to know about Mary:

> How did she bear it? They must have whispered among themselves. *It must have been like being fucked by a whale. It must have been like being fucked by the Leviathan*; blushing as they spoke the word, those barefoot children of the tribe of Judah, as she, Elizabeth Costello, almost catches herself blushing too, setting it down on paper. Rude enough among Mary's countryfolk; positively indecent in someone two millennia older and wiser. (187; emphasis in the original)

Costello's feeling of indecency is the sign that difference has been preserved, that the self has not overtaken the other (in this case the historical other, two millennia older) but forged a likeness, the experience of a self that is and is not the same. In achieving this bridge to the divine through the imagination of Mary's embodied state, embedded in the point of view of the country folk within her social world, and by intensifying the dramatization of their feelings about Mary and her situation by skipping from the word "whale" to the more biblically resonant word "Leviathan," Coetzee shows how Costello's act of novel writing springs from the authorial engagement with the ethical good of encountered alterity. For Costello to novelize Mitchell's poem is for the narrative resources of the novel to be drawn into the ethical task of achieved otherness: characterological interiority, the mobility of point of view, descriptive individuation through detail, and most especially, the capacity of novelistic structure to refer simultaneously back to the social life of its author and away to the autonomy of the fictional world are enlisted in the project of bringing to life states of being different from the author's own. The author's ethical capacity for goodness, to imagine on behalf of another, must be matched by her mastery of the narrative resources of fiction if the personhood of characters and the social world of fiction are to be successfully rendered as autonomous.

The Novel's Ethical Aesthetic

The many fans of Elizabeth Costello's novels praise her for achieving the match between the ethical good of realized alterity and the formal good of narrative control. And the first lesson *Elizabeth Costello* teaches, the lesson of Lesson One, is that although her admirers all agree that Costello's novels are superior works of art because of the match between their ethical and formal achievements, they disagree about the conception of alterity that is foundational to these works as well as which modalities of narrative best realize alterity.

Lesson One is mainly narrated from the point of view of one of Elizabeth Costello's most invested readers: John Bernard, her adult son. For John, the reading experience of his mother's novels confirms the success of her ethical endeavor. Exchanging opinions about his mother's work with a feminist literary critic named Susan, John echoes his mother's views about the value of her writing, defining his mother's literary accomplishment specifically as the achievement of knowing and bringing to life other states of being: "'But my mother has been a man,'" John declares. "'She has also been a dog. She can think her way into other people, into other existences. I have read her; I know. It is within her powers. Isn't that what is most important about fiction: that it take us out of ourselves, into other lives?'" (22–23). John clearly associates his mother's ethical ability to "think her way into other existences" with her narrative ability to make the lives of others available to the reader. Through the novel, both author and reader are taken out of the self, "into other lives." That this capacity did not lead Elizabeth Costello to open the door of her study to respond to the whimpering of John and his sister further suggests that novel writing and reading are exceptional ethical states. In a way that is not possible in everyday social life, novels take us out of ourselves and into other lives. Thus, even though he also finds his mother to be "[by] no means a comforting writer," whose "insight" has the power to "shake" her readers in a way that seems "cruel" and even "positively indecent" (5), such affective effects are in fact ethical elements of the novel's narrative structure that are as important as the writer's imagination in the full achievement of the novel's ethical value. The novelist's achievement lies not just in imagining a dog's state of being but in narrating this condition in a way that allows readers to experience the effort toward likeness as disrupting their identitarian position of security, whether defined in terms of social or species positionality.

John finds his mother's imagination of otherness to be so successful that he believes her to be a "genius," the very opposite of the flawed human that O'Hearne takes her to be. Although this judgment might easily be dismissed as the hyperbole of a proud son, the term effectively works to develop further the logic of ethical alterity as the sole standard within the social world of the novel for conceptualizing the novel's possibility and value. John does not imagine that his mother has had sexual congress with the gods but that the power of divine creation, the power to bring other states of being to life, resides within her. How else to explain her capacity to exceed the bounds of what is humanly possible, to transcend social, material, and species limits to know and occupy the lives of others—a dog, a man?

But not all her admiring readers understand Costello's achievement of alterity in these terms. Susan, the radio interviewer and feminist literary critic (to whom John is speaking when he describes his mother's novelistic accomplishment), challenges his view. Susan argues against John that Costello's representation of other states of being is irreducibly ideological, reflective of political values that are constitutive of Elizabeth Costello's social identity, an identity that does not vanish when the novelist engages in the creative act of representing states of being other than her own. Against John's view of his mother's divine power of creation, Susan asserts that "'whatever she does, she does as a woman. She inhabits her characters as a woman does, not as a man'" (23). When John disagrees, saying "'I find her men perfectly believable,'" Susan replies by invoking the ideological logic of his own subject position: "'You don't see because you wouldn't see. Only a woman would see. It is something between women. If her men are believable, good, I'm glad to hear so, but finally it is just mimicry. Women are good at mimicry, better at it than men'" (23). For Susan, the cultural construction of gender identity is so strong that it not only dictates the limits of an author's imaginative conception but also produces novel readers, men and women (in her binary logic), who occupy two completely different subject positions and thus two different states of being.[31]

Susan's political critique may seem to refute both John's view of his mother's achieved alterity and the ethical value of alterity itself. On Susan's view, Costello makes her feminist contribution by *not* being other. It is precisely Elizabeth Costello's *failure* to be the man that for Susan is both an ethical and a political accomplishment. But in fact Susan's interpretation of Costello's success as a novelist is equally based on the ethical value of alterity—only now instead of being defined by the artist's willed capacity to inhabit other states of being, achieved alterity is understood as Costello's self-conscious representation of the subaltern status conferred upon women by patriarchal hegemony. In Susan's logic of ethical alterity, Costello's artistic achievement lies in her deployment of narrative to represent the impossibility of female identity understood as a positive state of being. Susan most admires Costello's use of narrative indirection: the narrative gendering of character relation that marks Costello's work as a "woman's" novel— she "'inhabit[s] her characters'" not *as* a woman but "'as a woman *does*'" (23; emphasis added). Not surprisingly, then, Susan singles out for praise Costello's use of narrative mimicry. Narrative mimicry performs woman's otherness not just to male characters but also to the metaphysical notion of self that men take for granted. On Susan's view, then, the ethical and artistic triumph of Costello's novels is not to pretend to overcome alterity but to expose its political structure.

By staging this disagreement between two of Costello's admiring readers, Coetzee underscores the basis of agreement that both take for granted: for both Susan and John, the value of Elizabeth Costello's literary achievement is inseparable from the ethics of alterity. While John (and the humanist readers he stands for) believes that his mother, in the person of an old and frail woman, performing in her novelist's outfit, becomes when she writes "a mouthpiece for the divine" (31) through her capacity to be another, and whereas Susan (and feminists like her) believe that Elizabeth Costello's novels, despite what the author believes or states about them, are great because they narratively embody a woman's point of view—both types of readers link the formal triumph of Elizabeth Costello's novels to the ethics of otherness: John to the ethical good of bringing characters to life as individual autonomies through techniques such as point of view, and Susan to the ethical good of unveiling through narrative the patriarchal power that others a woman's experience of the self. John and Susan further agree, indirectly, that the novel reader is included through the structure of narrative in the novel's ethical project: whether that reader reads as an everyman, the way John does (and is shaken by the novel), or reads as a feminist, the way Susan does (and is affirmed by the novel), both agree that the exceptional kind of ethical experience offered through reading novels leads to social betterment.

Thus, even as Coetzee dramatizes the inextricability of narrative ethics from the cultural understanding of the novel's form and value in our contemporary moment, he also begins to denaturalize this long-standing view of the novel by portraying how in the storyworld ethical alterity is everywhere invoked as a literary good and yet rarely worked out as a defensible understanding of novel form. The professional writers and readers in the storyworld have notions about alterity that have been derived from within conflicting theoretical schools of academic thought. John's humanism, for example, resonates with Martha Nussbaum's account of Henry James; Susan's feminism resonates with Gayatri Spivak's account of Mary Shelley and Charlotte Brontë.[32] But notably, the novel readers and writers in *Elizabeth Costello* draw on these academic notions of alterity quite loosely; they are more interested in referring novelistic effects of alterity to their own reader response. Coetzee further underscores the indefensibility of each character's claims about the formal intrinsicality of narrative ethics by dramatizing the monologic nature of their literary debates: although characters in the novel constantly discuss how the ethics of literature should best be defined, conversation changes no one's mind. Indeed, as the novel's chapter structure dramatizes, what is taken to be the single, defining feature of the novel as a genre, its capacity for alterity, is understood by fiction writers and readers in a multitude of different ways. While narrating Costello's life as a series of compartmentalized scenes, the chapter structure also sketches an anatomy of the novelistic ethics of alterity in our contemporary moment that, by isolating different aspects of the philosophical problematic, reinforces the sense that these views are partitioned, nondialogical, and certainly nondialectical. Moving from Lesson One through Lesson Eight, the reader explores novelistic ethics via a humanist appreciation of "living" characters ("Realism"); an ideological analysis of social otherness (the relative weight of race, class, and gender differences dramatized in "The Novel in Africa"); a posthumanist meditation on the knowable alterity of animals ("The Lives of Animals"); a defense of novels as ethical guides in an age of secular perplexity ("The Humanities in Africa"); a moral analysis of states of inhumanity ("The Problem of Evil"); an ontological inquiry into the achievability of knowing about / dwelling in states of divinity ("Eros"); the imagination of what state of being might follow death ("At the Gate"); and finally, the exploration of fiction as its own ontological state of being (postscript to "Letter of Elizabeth, Lady Chandos").

And Coetzee doesn't simply multiply chapter by chapter the ways that interpreters of novels assume narrative to be linked to ethical alterity. Over the course of the novel, he depicts his protagonist as an *unsystematic* interpreter of the narrative ethics of alterity. For example, in a visit to Altona College to receive the Stowe Award, Costello, first in a public lecture and then in a private conversation, offers two different interpretations of the meaning of narrative in Franz Kafka's well-known short story "A Report to an Academy" (1917). Written as a monologue delivered by an ape named Red Peter, the story tells the tale of the ape's mastery of human behavior. Both of Costello's interpretations make the case for the literary greatness of Kafka's short story through the ethics of alterity that Costello believes is at stake in the story's narrative construction. But both interpretations also locate that narrative ethics in completely different descriptions of the story's narrative form. It's worth dwelling on the details of Costello's two interpretations, because what is at issue is the crucial duality of contemporary narrative ethics. On the one hand, Costello makes absolute but contradictory claims for the ethics she attributes to novelistic narrative; on the other hand, the idea of novel form is enriched and variegated by the ethical value she attributes to it.[33]

On her first interpretation, Costello correlates Kafka's ethics of alterity with his deployment of first-person narration. She argues that because Kafka writes the story as an address, as a monologue delivered by a character in the first person, he achieves an ethics of characterological autonomy. Because the monologue is limited to the speaker's own words, with no narrative frame—or as she puts it, with no formal "'means for either speaker or audience to be inspected with an outsider's eye'" (18)—the use of first-person narration honors the speaker's autonomy. Costello argues further that the lack of narrative frame installs the reader in an ethical relation with Kafka's character. Guided by no narrative authority, deprived of an impersonal or even a subjective view of the speaker and the storyworld, the reader must make conclusions about the speaker's identity through an unmediated encounter with that identity. The ethics that Costello assigns to this narrative technique are intensified by the particular question of species difference that she believes Kafka's story raises. With no outside authority to enforce social conventions for identity difference, can the reader be sure that Kafka's speaker really is an ape? Might it be a human performing as an ape?, Costello asks. And if the reader decides that the character is an ape, then what in the speaker's rhetorical performance confirms this? Conversely, if the reader can find no evidence of ape identity in the monologue, then Kafka has still achieved the proper ethical stance toward his character because he has brought home to the reader that the animal other is in fact closer to the human condition than humans assume. In this lecture, Costello's final point about the ethics of Kafka's narrative lies in the identitarian ambiguity that it sustains: her conclusion that one will "'never know, with certainty, what is really going on in this story'" (19). The reader's ultimate perplexity casts ethics as an affective response to the singularity of another's identity, ungraspable through predetermined assumptions about what distinguishes states of being.

But although Costello's lecture at Altona College has thus developed a complex and extensive account of the way that Kafka's narrative manages the ethics of alterity, Costello offers a completely different interpretation of the ethics of alterity at work in "A Report to an Academy" when her son John discusses her lecture with her on their trip together back to Australia. Whereas in Costello's first interpretation Kafka's management of the first-person monologue derived its ethical value from its refusal to provide a perspective on the speaker other than the speaker's own, now, on this account, the narrative structure of "A Report to an Academy" instantiates a very personal relation between Kafka as author and his fictional character.

> "Kafka had time to wonder where and how his poor educated ape was going to find a mate. And what it was going to be like when he was left in the dark with the bewildered, half-tamed female that his keepers eventually produced for his use. Kafka's ape is embedded in life. It is the embeddedness that is important,

not the life itself. His ape is embedded as we are embedded, you in me, I in you. That ape is followed through to the end, to the bitter, unsayable end, whether or not there are traces left on the page. Kafka stays awake, during the gaps when we are sleeping." (32)[34]

Importantly, the sole attribute that Costello assigns to Kafka's perspective is again an ethical one: what is conveyed through novelistic narrative is Kafka's capacity to care for the other, the other as ape but also as his fictional progeny. Now the narrative qualities that are most important are the achieved autonomy of the ape's experience as a register of Kafka's capacity to turn his own life over to the life of another. On the one hand, there is the ethical good of a life narrativized, "followed through to the end," tracked and culminating in its own terms. But there is also the ethical good of realist detail that brings the ape and a world "to life" through social embedding.[35] The quality of narrative that now matters is the particularity mobilized by Kafka to depict a struggling subjectivity with psychological and emotional depth. On Costello's new interpretation, "whether or not there are traces left on the page" of a personal authorial or narratorial voice, Kafka's successful use of narrative detail to convey the autonomy of characterological self and storyworld registers his ethical copresence as an attendant to that life. Fiction's narrative structure unfolds as a continuous ethical task for the author: Will the author see her character through to the end? Identity is still a performance, but now it is the performance of an author's ethical care for his character. Costello now defines ethics as a life dedicated to witnessing the life of another: Kafka "'stays awake during the gaps when we are sleeping'" (32). And the implication is that witnessing is not a clinical activity but a bond of ethical intimacy, an overcoming of otherness in the embedding of "you in me, and I in you." On this second interpretation, Kafka's care for his fictional character is no different from the feeling that binds mother to son.

Neither Elizabeth Costello nor her son remarks upon the disjunction between Costello's two different interpretations of Kafka's narrative ethics. Coetzee's reader is left to decide between them, to treat each skeptically, to try to reconcile them—and also, of course, to consider whether a connection should be made with Coetzee's own narrative practice in this and other novels. Does Coetzee embed his characters in a social world? Does he stay awake during the gaps when we are sleeping? But of course the shifting modalities of Coetzee's own narrative practice are not limited to just those identified and discussed by the characters in the novel. The fact that two conflicting interpretations are given of Kafka's narrative ethics does not mean that these are the only possible interpretations of his narrative practice—or of any novelistic narrative. This is precisely the point of Coetzee's organization of *Elizabeth Costello* according to different modalities of novelistic representation (realism, Kafkaesque modernism, postmodernist citationality). To see Costello hold two different views about Kafka's narrative is to have the ethics of alterity pointed out as a defining framework for understanding novelistic aesthetics and an invitation to Coetzee's reader to see in his narrative modulations the varying formulation of the ethics of alterity.

For example, Costello's stress on the author's omnipresence as an ethical feature of fictional narrative might disrupt the realist frame of Lesson One by inviting a metafictional reading of what authorial care might look like from the character's point of view. If we read Coetzee's text figuratively, if we read, that is to say, John's relationship to his mother as a likeness for the relationship of a character to his maker, as giving us through that likeness a feel for the state of being a fictional character might possibly inhabit, then we might conclude that Coetzee occasionally deploys narrative to follow his characters to their "bitter, unsayable end" by imagining from their point of view what that end might be. The closing sentences of the first lesson describe John's vision of Costello not as a genius infused by creative divinity but as completely corporeal. Sitting next to his sleeping mother on the plane, "he can see up her nostrils, into her mouth, down the back of her throat. And what he cannot see he can imagine: the gullet, pink and ugly, contracting as it swallows, like a python, drawing things down to the pear-shaped belly-sac" (34). With this vision of his maker as only and wholly a body, John recoils from his embedded relation to her: "No, he tells himself, that is not where I come from, that is not it" (34). Thus the son who would cast off the blood tie with his mother and the filial duties that attend that relation is also the fictional character who is depicted by Coetzee as breaking the realist frame to look back upon his divine maker and appalled to find that maker to be so grossly embodied. It is the fictional character who is granted the imagination to complete the vision of his maker as embodied human: "What John cannot see he can imagine." His vision figures the embedded nature of character and author from the perspective of the character's lived state of vulnerable ontological dependence.[36] The autonomy that fictional characters seem to possess can at any time be swallowed back up into the human bodies to which they are connected.

John Bernard and Elizabeth Costello can both, in other words, cease to exist in and for themselves and always only be understood as expressions of their human origin, of their author and master, J. M. Coetzee.

Henry James in Africa

Lesson Two, "The Novel in Africa," stages the debate about novelistic ethics as a disagreement between Elizabeth Costello and the (fictional) African novelist Emmanuel Egudu. As with the conversation between Susan and John, neither writer disputes the fact that narrative form carries an ethics and that this ethics is tied to the relation that novelistic narrative establishes between self and other. In keeping with the cultural view that the novel is the genre most distinguished by the ethics of alterity, however, the two novelists do not recognize this fundamental basis of agreement, focused as they are on their divergent senses of how novels perform an ethics of alterity. I want to look at the terms of this debate not only because Coetzee uses it to develop his sense of how readers and writers with very different politics equally praise the ethics of alterity that they credit to the novel but also because the literary history of the novel offered by Egudu shows how this tradition comes back to Henry James—even when, or perhaps especially when, James's role in establishing the ethical value of the novel becomes a weapon used against him.

As is the self-conscious novelistic practice of this novel, Egudu's views on the novel are socially embedded. He and Elizabeth Costello are featured speakers in a program aboard a cruise ship that caters to retired people interested in continuing education. In his lecture, titled "The Novel in Africa," Egudu defines novelistic narration not as a condition of divine inspiration, as John Bernard views it, that makes the author exceptional, godlike in her capacity for knowing states of being, but instead as the authentic register of the African novelist's lived identity, which on his view is defined by a communal self, other to the Western individualistic conception of self. The most important feature of the African novel, according to Egudu, is the orality that he believes to be definitional of African culture. On his view, the African narrator speaks his story, using storytelling methods practiced in his community. The story he tells portrays the oral cultural of which he is part. Oral culture is, Egudu stresses, an embodied culture. The African novel brings African voices to life, but, he insists, can do this accurately only by depicting in the storyworld "the way that people live in their bodies. The way they move their hands. The way they walk. The way they smile or frown. The lilt of their speech" (44).

Egudu's belief that the novel gains its ethical power from the narrative resources that allow it to depict embodied lives thus clearly puts his view on a continuum with Costello's theory of the sympathetic imagination as an embodied act of ethical emplacement. But, although both writers find the novel's value in the embodied otherness that it makes available for ethical encounter, the task of the African author, as Egudu sees it, is not to put oneself in the place of another but through novelistic representation to make the personhood of the African self a body, a narrative place, that the Western reader's sympathetic imagination can access.

As Egudu works out his own version of the logic of sympathetic embodiment, he theorizes that novelistic representation creates a bridge between the African self and the Western other by inviting the Western reader to participate in the experience of oral culture. According to Egudu, the voice that is embodied in the narrative structure of the African novel is "'inert, only half alive [on the page]; it wakes up when the voice, from deep in the body, breathes life into the words, speaks them aloud'" (45). On this view, the novel performs its ethics of alterity by allowing the novel reader to know what it might be like to live the life of a cultural other, defined by its embodied orality. Western readers who speak the African novel aloud discover in the use they make of their own body the shared "place" of the body that bridges the difference between African and Western states of being. Western readers do not project their voices onto to the African novel but, through the physical act of intoning, perform an act of self-restriction and acceptance of the identity of the other that "breathes life into the words," bestowing upon the African novel its own life and unity as an art form.

Elizabeth Costello, who has listened to Egudu deliver "The Novel in Africa," is intensely critical of his theory of the African novel. In conversation with Egudu after his lecture, Elizabeth scornfully suggests that he wants the novel to be a "pocket-sized block of paper that is at the same time a living being" (50). But doesn't she praise Ted Hughes for accomplishing something similar through his poetry? Doesn't she credit him with using words to mingle "breath and sense" in such a way as "to bring the living [animal] body into being within ourselves" (98)? It would seem that Costello objects more to Egudu's notion of how the novel achieves its ethics of alterity than to his understanding of the novel as a "pocket-sized block of paper that is at the same time a living being." We remember that for Costello the ethical value of novelistic otherness cannot be separated from the difficulty of the task: as she says to the interviewer in Lesson One, "'If it were easy it wouldn't be worth doing'" (12). Her real objection to Egudu's position, I would argue, is that his idea of the African oral novel too effortlessly resolves the contradiction between Western and African identities—between the colonializing power of the novel as an instrument of Western hegemony and what she regards as Egudu's optimistic sense that geopolitical material realities can be significantly undone by the act of a Westerner reading aloud. In other words, for Costello, Egudu's solution to the problem of otherness counts too much on the shared human condition of embodiment to bridge cultural differences through bodily action (reading aloud) and does not properly acknowledge, on her view, the effortful role of the creative and responding imagination in performing the ethical task of novelistic alterity.[37]

In the question-and-answer period that follows his lecture, Egudu acknowledges that other African novelists have formulated the problem of alterity along different philosophical lines, and his description of the work of Ben Okri comes closer to the narrative ethics endorsed by Elizabeth Costello. Egudu cites Okri's work as an excellent example of narrative that "'negotiates the contradictions of being himself for other people'" (48). Here is the kind of intellectual paradox of which Costello approves. How to be Elizabeth Costello and Mary of Nazareth? In Egudu's formulation, the task for Okri is symmetrical but flipped: how to be African in a way that can be recognized as culturally significant for Westerners; how to retain one's own indigenous standards of selfhood and yet communicate those qualities through a Western lens of value. These are the difficulties, according to Costello's view of the novel, that if managed properly will jam reason and yield the imagination of embodied alterity: "'For an instant, before my whole structure of knowledge collapses in panic, I am alive inside that contradiction, dead and alive at the same time'" (77). The debate between Egudu and Costello thus performs the difference in their cultural values, and that difference supports Egudu's sense that the Westerner values the power of the mind over the body. (Costello must use one power of the mind, imagination, to disable the ruling power, reason, in order to gain a living experience of embodied otherness, whereas the African begins with a sense of embodied cultural identity and looks for a way through the body to give Westerners a feel for African identity.)

Coetzee's interest in the metafictional project of recovering the literary history that promotes the view of the novel as defined by an ethics of alterity is furthered by the lesson that this section gives on how the European birth and development of the novel as a literary form is regarded from the perspective of the colonized. According to Egudu, the novel signals its colonial origins first and foremost by being written. From the perspective of a culture defined by embodied orality, writing of any kind is an inimical cultural practice, the legacy of Western domination. Indirectly echoing Claude Lévi-Strauss's position in *Tristes Tropiques*, Egudu argues further that the West's belief that writing is the product of advanced civilization reflects cultural bias: the development of writing as a social practice is from Egudu's point of view an expression of the West's overvaluing of acts of the mind over embodied experience. On this view, writing is not an absolute good but the expression of identity, an identity different from the African's. Egudu argues further that the quality of abstraction that from his point of view defines writing also allows it to function effectively as a technology of power: endlessly reproducible, infinitely relocatable, writing spreads the European mode of being "across the world like a cancer," stifling indigenous modes of localized face-to-face social organization through the cultivation of "silence and solitude" as the proper material conditions for the production and consumption of literature. Thus even Egudu's project of writing the oral novel can be incorporated into Costello's view of ethical alterity; the task of his narrative technique is to find a place created through the logic of contradiction: how to make it seem as if writing can be a mode of orality, how to bridge the difference, to find a basis of likeness.

Egudu, of course, would resist this view of his alterity project. Although he does not try to deny or retheorize the novel's connection to Western identity through and as writing, the literary history he constructs counters Western hegemony by positioning the African oral novel as a return to the genre's origins, the reinstatement of the novel's proper generic identity before it was distorted by its Western upbringing. In other words, Egudu distinguishes between the novel's essential identity and what happened to that identity when, like Africa itself, it was taken over and colonized by the West. What is the novel's original nature according to Egudu? It is precisely the quality that Henry James and the modernists who followed him formulate as a problem for the Western artist to solve: the novel's protean nature, its capacity to be anything at all. From the perspective that Egudu offers, to call the novel for this reason "the cannibal art," as Woolf does, reveals exactly the kind of cultural bias that distorts a true view of the genre's identity while also exposing the kind of racism that derives from mistaking a cultural preference—in this case, for unity and aesthetic order—for truth.[38] Egudu reminds his shipboard audience that the term "novel," "'when it entered the languages of Europe, had the vaguest of meanings: it meant the form of writing that was formless, that had no rules, that made up its own rules as it went along'" (44–45). It is only as it was developed and disciplined within the Western tradition that the novel became, according to Egudu, an increasingly "disembodied" mode of written expression (45). Egudu believes that the African writer returns the novel to its original formlessness by putting writing in the service of storytelling: to the degree that novel writing could be infused with orality, it could counter the quality of abstraction that allows novels to be regarded as if they possessed material properties distinct and different from storytelling as an embedded social discourse.

Where does Egudu locate the apex of the Western novel's development into disembodiment? That would be the dawn of twentieth-century modernism, the era, as we have seen, when novelistic formlessness was equated with cannibalism, the era represented for Egudu by two names: Henry James and Marcel Proust (45). While Egudu regards both of these writers, and by implication the modernist art project more generally, as the moment in its literary history when the novel's natural link to embodied storytelling is most fully betrayed, the cluster of ideas that he uses to characterize Western abstraction suggests that James more than Proust is the salient culprit. The train of association is clear and goes something like this: the Jamesian style—known for its cerebral demands (its abstract language, vague pronoun references, and extended figurative associations)—so successfully disassociates language from the bodies of those who use it that the novel after James is approached not just as writing but, even more abstractly, as writing that has a quality that can figuratively be thought of as so plastic as to be form itself. What is more, once perceivable as form, the novel in the West can through this process of abstraction be further restricted: its nature can be judged narrowly as an achievement of form only, a form that can be right or wrong, better or worse. As I have discussed, even though James explicitly criticized Walter Besant's rule-bound approach to the art of the novel, the rules that James's followers developed out of the prefaces have routinely been credited to James. I believe it is this line of the Jamesian novel tradition that Egudu has in mind when he describes the African tradition by contrast as turning its back on this late Western view of the novel to reclaim the novel as the "form of writing that was formless, that had no rules, that made up its own rules as it went along" (26).

But through another line of the Jamesian legacy, the line I have been developing, we can see that Egudu's own theory of the novel is more Jamesian than he knows.[39] To say that Egudu misrepresents James's view of the novel by omitting the role of perspectivalism in James's theory and practice is simply to say that Coetzee, in representing Egudu, dramatizes the relativization of value that James's novel theory grapples with. As we have seen in Toni Morrison's interpretation of James's depiction of the countess in *What Maisie Knew*, to read James's form as the expression of hegemonic identity is to turn the lesson of the master back onto the master. Morrison and Egudu may have different senses about which aspects of Jamesian narrative embody ideological identity (just as they have different ideas about how to define the content of that ideological identity), but as *Elizabeth Costello* has been devoted to displaying, the disagreement among readers and writers about which properties of the novel realize the ethics of alterity is less important than the agreement that the ethics of alterity defines the value of the novelistic enterprise. If we work out the metafictional dimensions of Egudu's characterological representation, his discussion of James can be likened to John's view of his mother. In both cases, the novel figuratively gives a character's perspective on its maker: John, through the fictional character's alienated view of the fleshly authorial body from which he has sprung; and Egudu, who refers us back to Coetzee's own attempt to occupy the position of otherness that a black African novelist poses for him—and for whom he imagines that the marker of difference would be his negative attitude toward Henry James.

Ethics or Aesthetics

To have the author held to account for the lives of his characters is to be pointed back to the question of how to evaluate the ethics that informs Coetzee's narrative practice in this novel and all of his work. But to conduct the task of ethical evaluation, the reader needs to settle on a particular philosophical framework for understanding narrative ethics—which, as I have been arguing, is exactly what the novel throws into question. For example, when J. M. Coetzee takes up the project of bringing to life his female protagonist, Elizabeth Costello, which model of ethical alterity applies?[40] Is it the effortful and successful imagination of female identity accomplished by a gendered other—as in John's view? Or should we apply Susan's standard and read the novel's narrative details for traces of Coetzee's untranscendable subject position, the masculinist views that might betray the ideological limits to his grasp of female identity (perhaps revealed in his frequent privileging of John's point of view or when he attributes to Elizabeth Costello a view about the female body: that "nothing is more humanly beautiful than a woman's breasts" [150]). Or is Coetzee's ethical accomplishment evidenced by the monologues he bestows upon Elizabeth Costello, allowing her like Kafka's speaker to represent herself in her own words? Or does the novel's narrative ethics lie in the ethical care that Coetzee bestows on his protagonist by seeing her through to the end? Indeed, the last chapter of the novel, "At the Gate," places Costello in a deliberately Kafkaesque landscape to see her through to what she believes is her mortal end.

By refusing to provide a clear philosophical grounding for narrative ethics, has Coetzee recast ethics as aesthetics? Is this novel asking us to consider whether the unprovable, multiple, and undecidable claims for the ethics of narrative form can persist as a novelistic aesthetics—even if the bases for these claims are untrue? Detached from belief, can the ethics of alterity still provide the novel with an artistic unity?

In the novel's final lesson (the chapter written in the Kafkaesque idiom), Coetzee has Elizabeth Costello confront the state of otherness represented by her own death. The threshold between one state of being and another is figured by a gate that she must get permission to enter. The tribunal of judges who decide whether to grant her passage requires that Costello provide them with a statement of her beliefs. Costello declares that as a novelist her duty is to hold no beliefs: "'It is not my profession to believe, just to write'" (194). Not surprisingly, this statement of Costello's presents yet another configuration of novel writing as an ethical task. As she explains to the judges, beliefs of her own would "stand in the way" of knowing what is beyond the self. As a novelist, she seeks not to judge others but to "make sure I have heard right." In *this* formulation of the ethical task of alterity, her artistic practice demands that she hold a relativized view of her own beliefs, treating them as a screen of attitudes and biases that work as "resistances" to knowing and encountering alterity. "'To put it another way,'" she states to the tribunal, "'I have beliefs, but I do not believe them'" (200).[41]

This relativization of belief that Costello describes—to have beliefs but not believe them—might be a way of understanding how the ethics of alterity collapses into an aesthetic. Aesthetics distinguishes itself from ethics because it requires no true belief. Form can be read *as if* it held ethical value. The searing ethical encounters that are missing from *Elizabeth Costello*'s storyworld are arguably restaged in the novel as the lively aesthetic intensity of narrative form generated by the possible and conflicting ways of conceptualizing otherness as and through narrative. But what Costello's address to the tribunal also suggests is that for the contemporary novelist all beliefs are relativizable except the belief that the value of the novel lies in the achievement of ethical otherness. The negative capability that Costello strives for is explicitly in service of "knowing" and doing justice to "what is beyond the self." As *Elizabeth Costello* so stunningly proves, even when beliefs about the novel's ethical capacities are explicitly thrown into question, this questioning is conducted in service of formulating a better literary ethics.

When the tribunal asks Elizabeth Costello to provide rational grounds for the faith she places in the authenticity of her capacity for alterity—"'How do you know where your voices come from?'"—she is suddenly overwhelmed by what she calls "the literariness of it all" (204). "Have they not the wit to come up with something new?" she wonders (204).[42] What strikes her as literary, apparently, are the two kinds of questioning that this final scene brings together: Costello's resistance to her own beliefs and the tribunal's resistance to Costello's ethics of alterity as a justification of her artistic practice. The literary is thus defined in this novel not as the suspension of belief but as an ethical mode of questioning belief, especially beliefs about ethics. In the hands of a contemporary writer such as Coetzee, there is no plot for the novel other than the plot of ethical inquiry. And there is no other value to narrative form than the value of ethics. *Elizabeth Costello*'s achievement as a literary work is self-consciously defined by the tradition it throws into question yet cannot move beyond. And it cannot move beyond that tradition precisely because it formulates its questioning of the tradition as itself an ethical act. Coetzee's complex and relentless investigation of the problem of novelistic alterity makes me want to revise the claim Victor Shklovsky makes for *Tristram Shandy* and dub *Elizabeth Costello* as "the most typical novel in world literature"—at least for our time, place, and culture. Now that Coetzee has helped bring to light the literary history that has so long linked the novel's literary identity to its ethics of alterity, future novelists may indeed have "the wit to come up with something new"—a new basis for establishing the social value of literature—but given the endurance and richness of the tradition Coetzee sketches for us, they just as likely will, as Coetzee has done, use their wit to deepen and extend the novel's ethical tradition.

5 The New Ethics in the Academy
The Lesson of the Master, the Master as the Lesson

THE DIALOGUE WITH REAL-LIFE PHILOSOPHERS and literary critics conducted by both *On Beauty* and *Elizabeth Costello* invites us to explore the connection between the literary tradition I have been tracing and the defenses of literature's ethical value pursued by contemporary theorists within the Anglo-American academy.[1] With the unfolding of the new century, a body of scholarship has burgeoned forth, fueling a debate not over whether ethical questions should be pursued but how this new ethical inquiry might best be conducted.[2] For many poststructuralist critics and theorists, the return to ethics is not just the attempt to recuperate the agency of individuals for positive political action but also an attempt to theorize for our contemporary moment the positive social value of literature and literary study.[3] In this chapter, I want to investigate why these recent defenses of the ethical value of literature are made through the particular example of the novel genre—and why this defense so often refers the question of ethics to the novels of Henry James.[4]

In contrast to determinist social theories that locate the negative political value of selves and literary works in the interpellated "outside" of "forces, powers, surveillances" (Miller, *Ethics*, 8), the theorists upon whom I focus all argue for the ethical value of the readerly self that is produced from "within" literature, through the experience of literary reading.[5] These theorists all agree that to open a literary work is to open oneself up to a type of decision-making that is itself inherently ethical. Will I submit to the alterity that literature allows? In contrast to the unconscious operation of ideology, the will to read ethically is theorized as a self-conscious choice. In the phenomenological models of reader response proposed by new ethical theory, an affirmative answer launches the reader into a transactional relation with another agent, an agent defined by its difference from the reader. This agent is made available as an ethical other by two related readerly acts: the act of self-subordination that enables the apprehension of alterity, and a prior act that makes self-subordination itself possible—the will to believe in the possibility of alterity. The social good of diversity and cultural difference can be accomplished, these new ethical theories argue, as much through the felt efficacy of reading—reading as a personal and affective activity—as through legal judgments or state policy. The reader's experience of free submission, the personal response to the "hailing" performed by a specific literary work, becomes, for the new ethics, a necessary condition for the social achievement of diversity, a training in the honoring of difference, which is theorized as the defining ethical property of literature generally.

The particularity of the novel's generic suitability for this ethical experience is everywhere assumed but rarely taken as a topic of theoretical reflection.[6] In choosing the novel as the prime example of literary ethics, theorists implicitly tie the encounter with otherness that literature affords to the particular imaginative and affective experience offered by novels. In this chapter, I explore how the new ethical defense of literary value develops the Jamesian novel tradition's view of ethics not in a monolithic way but, as we saw in *Elizabeth Costello*, by taking for granted different aspects of the literary tradition's understanding of why the novel—as narrative, as fictional, as representing heterogeneous social worlds, as devoted to the storyworld exploration of difficult ethical decision-making, etc.—is particularly qualified to offer the reader an ethical encounter with alterity. I begin my analysis of the new ethics with a comparison between Martha Nussbaum and Judith Butler to argue that, although the new ethics is most associated with literary critics working within a poststructuralist philosophical framework (whose master thinkers in this context include Foucault, Levinas, and Derrida), a shared understanding of ethics as an ethics of alterity and a shared understanding of the novel as the genre of ethical alterity link self-described liberal humanist critics such as Nussbaum with poststructuralist critics such as Butler.[7] In my comparison of Nussbaum and Butler, I show that their respective phenomenological descriptions of reader response carry forward long-standing assumptions about the novel's capacity to foster not just readerly emotion but ethical emotions, ones that begin with the reader's feelings toward characters. The poststructuralist notion of the subject that informs Levinasian/Derridean new ethical theory does not result in an approach to literature that eliminates the understanding of characters as individuals whose narrative representation should be honored and respected (as

Alain Robbe-Grillet and Roland Barthes at midcentury had advised and believed to be inevitable). What is more, the aesthetics of alterity that develops through the Jamesian tradition allows new ethical theorists to privilege literary works as ethical agents without seeming to partition either ethics or aesthetics from politics. By appealing to the notion that novelistic narrative mediates the reader's access to otherness, new ethical theorists thus can seem to define the act of literary reading as both ethical and political, that is to say, as offering an ethical experience that is defined by the self-awareness novelistic narrative offers about the conditions of possibility—material, political, ideological, and/or psychological—that restrict or allow access to the other. The art of the novel, as developed in twentieth-century literary practice as an aesthetics of alterity, helps to naturalize this ethico-political view of narrative to the point where contemporary academic theorists can treat it as an objective truth, the grounding plank of their new ethical phenomenology of literary reading.

In the introduction to a 2002 special issue of *diacritics* on ethics and interdisciplinarity, Mark Sanders asks us to consider, "What points of contact, if any, are there between the current investment in ethics in literary theory, and the elaboration of ethics in contemporary philosophy?"[8] Yet the question behind this question—the one that motivates his selection of essays for the issue—is why literary critics and theorists have drawn their ideas about ethics from Emmanuel Levinas, Jacques Derrida, Michel Foucault, Giorgio Agamben, and Alain Badiou with little or no felt need to consult past or present moral philosophers. As Sanders goes on to note, while "in North America and the Anglophone world generally, the tendency in ethics has been to bring moral reflection to bear on questions in political theory," there "has been relatively little attention among literary theorists to developments in disciplinary philosophy."[9]

Sanders's observation of this disconnect is particularly intriguing when we consider that the return to moral reflection in contemporary literary theory is in fact a double return: the pursuit of ethics has been accompanied by a new celebration of literature, and it is in the imbrication of these endeavors—the new pursuit of ethics leading to a new defense of literature—that literary theory and moral philosophy find common ground in the twenty-first-century academy.[10] No moral philosopher has been more enthusiastic or more vocal about the positive social value of literature than Martha Nussbaum. But the mere mention of the author of *Love's Knowledge* and *Poetic Justice* may seem to take the mystery out of Sanders's question. Isn't Martha Nussbaum—self-described humanist, avowed liberal, public excoriator of Judith Butler's "defeatist" feminism—the prima facie evidence of moral philosophy's failure to get what is "new" about the new ethics?[11] While literary theorists pride themselves on pursuing ethics and assessing literary value in light of and response to complex and difficult poststructuralist truths, Nussbaum in particular and moral philosophy in general seem to remain, as Andrew Gibson has said, "pre-Barthesian."[12] While Gibson identifies the "pre-Barthesian" as a throwback to mid-twentieth-century naïve humanism (epitomized for him by Trilling, with whom he groups Nussbaum), others have found Nussbaum so retro as to be antiquity itself: "Nussbaum is defiantly Aristotelian and therefore pre-Enlightenment; her slogan might be 'Antiquity—An Incomplete Project.'"[13]

Those hostile to Nussbaum find it fitting that the pre-Barthesian who unembarrassedly confesses her love of literature, who argues not just for the positive social value of literature but for the superiority of literature to other types of social discourse, and who even goes so far as to claim that "literary people" (authors and readers of literature) are "best equipped" to perform ethical inquiry, would be in love with Henry James.[14] It is one thing for Lionel Trilling in 1948 to hold up the Jamesian novel as an ethical ideal, to see literature generally and novels in particular as a moral corrective to the "cold potatoes" of social reform through government policies.[15] After all, Trilling's defense of the social value of literature is rooted in a prestructuralist sense of the liberal individual, usefully defined from the post-Foucauldian perspective of D. A. Miller as "the subject whose private life, mental or domestic, is felt to provide constant inarguable evidence of his constitutive 'freedom.'"[16] This is the kind of freedom that Trilling invokes when he argues that the imperialism of US public policy can be checked only by the cultivation of the "free play of the moral imagination" and that "for our time the most effective agent of the moral imagination" has been a product of the literary imagination: "the novel of the last two hundred years."[17] For Trilling the ethical enterprise that is fiction—defined by its lack of utility, its anti-instrumentality, its nonequivalence to state law—culminates in the work of an aesthete, Henry James.

But by 1990 shouldn't Martha Nussbaum have learned from literary critics the political lessons of Jamesian aestheticism? In *The Political Unconscious* Fredric Jameson declares James's creation of an aesthetics of the novel to have such profound social consequences as to be "a genuinely historical act," a crucial cultural formation in the development of late capitalism.[18] For Jameson, James's refinement and glorification of point of view—both as a narrative technique and as a philosophy of perspectival individualism—serve as a "strategic loc[us] for the fully constituted or centered bourgeois subject or monadic ego," enabling capitalism to "produce and institutionalize the new subjectivity of the bourgeois individual."[19] In the years since Jameson made this claim, literary critics have fleshed out the list of Henry James's political offenses. Many of these critics follow Jameson in their belief that James's formal practices—and the aesthetic value that James attributed to novelistic form—are the key to his bad politics. James's dedication to developing the novel into a high art form is understood as part of a more general effort on the part of nineteenth-century white male writers to make up in cultural capital what they were losing in sales figures. The ideological production of the aesthetic as a "discrete entity," Michael Gilmore and others have proposed, was the "creation of white male fiction writers reacting against the commercial triumphs of the feminine novel."[20]

In the post-Marxist and post-Foucauldian understanding of the development of the novel, James is indeed a culmination of the last two hundred years, and that culmination does produce, as Trilling believed, the liberal imagination. But for these critics the belief in the liberal imagination is precisely the problem that needs political reform. It has been the work of literary studies at least from the 1980s forward to show that the "free play" of the moral imagination is anything but free: it is an agent of regulation, discipline, instrumentality, and ideological delusion. Through its affective power and strategic representation of society, the novel creates a reader who (to quote D. A. Miller again) "seems to recognize himself most fully only when he forgets or disavows his functional implication in a system of carceral restraints or disciplinary injunctions."[21] In a similar line of argumentation, Nancy Armstrong finds the novel's conservative political power to lie in its genre strategies of "disavowal," which transmogrify the "material body" as a social and political reality into a "metaphysical object" of "language and emotion"[22]—an aesthetic act of partitioning that leads individual subjects to think of themselves as universal subjects.[23]

Is Nussbaum's defense of literature in general and Henry James in particular anything more than the disavowal of her own social positionality? The literary values she admires, notes John Horton, "openness, subtlety of discrimination, a delicately nuanced understanding and a precisely graded emotional responsiveness [are] . . . perhaps not surprisingly, the virtues of a liberal literary intellectual."[24] And indeed Nussbaum's conception of literature generally and the novel in particular is predicated on the ethical value they confer upon private emotion: literature, she says, gives "ethical relevance" to "particularity and to the epistemological value of feeling" (*Love's Knowledge*, 175). The novel distinguishes itself as a genre by its "profound" commitment "to the emotions" (40). This means, for Nussbaum, that the novel both communicates its meaning through emotion and communicates the ethical value of certain types of emotion. One such ethical emotion is the feeling of possibility: novels, she tells us, engage "readers in relevant activities of searching and feeling, especially feeling concerning their own possibilities as well as those of the characters" (46). Our feeling of possibility is, for Nussbaum, an outgrowth of a more foundational ethical feeling: love. To feel that we love is at once involuntary proof of our deepest values—what we authentically care about, what we can't not care about—and a means of developing better social practices, since our love for others allows us to make their cares, their values, our own, extending our experience by widening our "range of concerns" (47). Nussbaum proposes that the art of the novel is first and foremost a performance of—and education in—the care we should have (and for those of us who "love" literature, that we do have) for the ethical goods of alterity, particularity, complexity, emotion, variety, and indeterminacy.

The value that Nussbaum places on love thus clearly signals her affinity with the development of the Jamesian aesthetics of alterity developed within the British novelistic tradition discussed in Chapter 2. It also provides a further basis of comparison with Trilling's argument for the novel's generic preeminence as an ethical agent. Anticipating Nussbaum, Trilling also takes as axiomatic Nussbaum's belief that the novel "widens our range of concerns." Trilling's claim in 1948 that the novel has "taught us, as no other genre ever did, the extent of human variety and the value of variety" echoes George Eliot's even earlier view of the novel as fostering in its readers not just the recognition of social difference but the emotional experience that enables them to extend their concern to "those who differ from themselves in everything but the broad fact of being struggling erring human creatures."[25] But whereas Eliot appeals broadly to sympathy as the novel's ethical emotion, Trilling argues for the novel's ethical training in "love," making his case by appealing to what he takes to be the distinguishing feature of the genre, developed over the centuries through novelistic practice: the depiction in the storyworld of "a reciprocating subject in a relationship of affection."[26] The implication of Trilling's position seems to be that novel readers, schooled by such experts as Forster and James (to take his examples), will learn that the appreciation of social "variety and modulation" through the cultivation of loving friendship is the key to human flourishing.[27] The novel's power lies in its ability to foster a love of humanity in the reader, through the affection that is created for and displayed by novelistic characters who bridge social difference. Novels that present blueprints for social policy dampen the novel's generic capacity for ethical alterity, since they fail to hail the reader into Trilling's liberal humanist version of emotional binding, fail to install the reader into an individually chosen, loving relation with the characters as social others.[28] Trilling goes so far as to imply that the reader who submits to the novel's emotional training may come to reject programmatic political action altogether: the true recognition of the difference that constitutes the other as a "reciprocating subject" leads Trilling to an ethical critique of the "moral" defense of policies that make social others "the object of pity, then of our wisdom, ultimately of our coercion."[29] Cultivated by the novel, the voluntary self-restriction promoted by ethical love—the ability to appreciate others for themselves and for their difference from oneself—is thus for Trilling the antidote to the self-seeking "nature of moral passion" that devises plans for social liberation by imposing social restrictions abroad that are driven by the failure to imagine other ways of being.

For the Foucauldian cultural critic, "love's knowledge" stands as strong testimony to the particular way the novel performs its ideological work, the way that novelistic aesthetics contributes to the hegemonic political formation of the bourgeois subject. The novel as a producer and agent of care certainly fits into D. A. Miller's account of the way the novel administers the "regime of the norm."[30] For the Foucauldian, readerly love becomes the basis for (in Miller's words) "the subject's own contribution to the intensive and continuous 'pastoral' care that liberal society proposes to take of each and every one of its charges."[31] Nussbaum's (and Trilling's and Eliot's) notion that the problem of human flourishing is first and foremost a private and "practical" affair, a problem pursued through and solved in relation to our emotional experience of "life" and, most intensely, through our emotional experience of life as represented in novels (*Love's*

Knowledge, 21), is for the political critic confirmation of the liberal subject's valorization of psychological interiority through its mystification.

A key moment in *Love's Knowledge* provides a powerful example of how novels might be said to lead Nussbaum herself into liberal disavowal. She quotes at length a passage from *David Copperfield* that describes the "comfort" David derives from the characters he meets through novel reading. The passage that Nussbaum cites ends with David's memory of "sitting on my bed, reading as if for life" (*Love's Knowledge*, 230). For a chapter title, and elsewhere in *Love's Knowledge*, Nussbaum restyles Dickens's phrase "reading as if for life" as "reading for life." Her substitution seems to perform the erasure of the materiality of social reality by the "free play" of the liberal imagination. To forget the "as if" is to equate reading with life, is to disavow the ideological nature of reading, the particular social conditions that encourage Nussbaum herself to believe that there could be no significant difference between life and its fictional representation, between reading as a private and individual experience and reading as cultural work. To forget this difference is to project both life and the reader as mystified essences, metaphysical objects.

It thus may seem the logical conclusion of Nussbaum's liberalism that the political program she develops in *Love's Knowledge* locates the path to social reform in the consciousness of a fictional character, and a Jamesian consciousness at that. The first thing that contemporary literary critics should teach the world in order to improve it, Nussbaum declares, is how "to confront reigning models of political and economic rationality with the consciousness of Strether" (192). The man of imagination, as James calls Lambert Strether in his preface to *The Ambassadors*, is for Nussbaum the epitome of right ethical value, brought into being by James's own ethical act: the creation of a novel that models through its narrative structure the "finely aware and richly responsible" acts of perception (the phrase is James's) that are for Nussbaum the key to human flourishing (148). What do politicians and law-keepers have to learn from James's representation of Strether's consciousness? That "the well-lived life is a work of literary art" (148). That this sentiment echoes the villainous aesthete Gilbert Osmond, who advises Isabel Archer in *The Portrait of a Lady* that "one ought to make one's life a work of art," seems to suggest the limits and dangers of living "for" life by living life "as if" it were no different from art.[32] To want to confront power with Strether seems a confession of one's addiction to imaginary solutions for real political problems. In a postmodern world of pop culture, globalism, and multiculturalism, we might instead take it as a sign of our own cultural distance from the "genuinely historical act" of high capitalist subject formation that most readers at this moment in the twenty-first century, academic and nonacademic, feel the spectacular irrelevance of the Edwardian aesthete, either Strether or his maker. We might take it as the end of disavowal that we can say with Cynthia Ozick, "The truth of our little age is this: nowadays no one gives a damn about what Henry James knew."[33]

But as it has been the work of this book to argue, even if no one thinks they give a damn about what Henry James knew, the modern novel that James helped to invent and the tradition of novel theory that he inaugurated provide a foundational aesthetics of alterity for the novel that underlies both Nussbaum's ethical philosophy and the poststructuralist new ethical theory that has developed in the attempt to articulate the positive social value of literature for our postmodern age. To mention J. Hillis Miller, Gayatri Spivak, Judith Butler, Derek Attridge, Geoffrey Galt Harpham, Michael André Bernstein, and Adam Zachary Newton is to invoke some of the most influential contributors to the new ethical defense of literary value. And while these theorists do indeed, as Sanders observes, derive their ethics from diverse political theorists (Foucault, Agamben, Adorno, Benjamin, Levinas, and Derrida), what Sanders and others have yet to note is that the heterogeneity of these political influences has coalesced in a surprisingly unified account of literary value.[34] By showing how this ethical good is at stake both for the "pre-Barthesian" Nussbaum and the poststructuralist Judith Butler, I want to establish as well how Nussbaum's explicit privileging of the Jamesian view of the novel alerts us to the implicit privileging of the novel as the literary form par excellence for poststructural ethical theorists.[35]

Ultimately, Nussbaum and Butler contribute to the development in the twentieth century of a novelistic aesthetics of alterity that can be distinguished from aesthetics understood invidiously as the pleasure derived from "mere" form, or in J. Hillis Miller's words, the "pure, irresponsible pleasures of aesthetic form."[36] As it emerges through new ethical thought, the value of novel form cannot be adequately explained (away) by the ideological notion of disavowal since the avowal of disavowal is part of what novelistic narrative demands—and this formal operation is what defines it as an aesthetics. By recapturing James's role in this tradition, we can appreciate how the new ethical view of the novel's social value redeems the novel's aesthetic value by defining its aesthetics as promoting the reader's ideological self-consciousness. As I will show, new ethical theory accords to novelistic narrative an absolute ethical agency that it then takes as the basis of its phenomenological description of ethical reading without acknowledging the aesthetic privilege that it confers on the novel or the possibility, clear from the point of view of literary history, that the ethical value ascribed to novelistic narrative may be no more than an effect of its art, as constructed through the Jamesian tradition.

My interest in the new ethics was whetted when I read an article by Judith Butler titled "Values of Difficulty" (2003), an address to leftist activists that makes recommendations about ways of "crossing cultural barriers in a nonimperialist fashion," specifically by "learning to speak across various languages in ways that do not assimilate [the] variety of languages" to an ideal of a "common language" (205). Why, I wondered, does an argument that begins with an analysis of AIDS activism in the 1980s culminate in an analysis of *Washington Square*? The political problem of cultural and social difference as Butler defines it ("learning to speak across various languages in ways that do not assimilate [the] variety of languages" to the ideal of a "common language") has a strong resonance with the Bakhtinian notions of heteroglossia and dialogism, but to note this is simply to make Butler's turn to James even less obvious: if there was ever an example in Bakhtinian terms of the monological writer—the writer who muffles the heterogeneity of discourse, whose novels strive to obtain the status of high art by suppressing their status as social discourse and whose characters all speak in the voice of their author—that would be Henry James.[37]

The ethical value Butler finds in James lies not in any claim for *Washington Square*'s referential reproduction of "the extent of human variety and the value of variety" (Trilling) but in the ethical affect that James's management of narrative offers to the engaged reader. Butler turns to James, she says, "not because he is a political hero or because he represents brilliant class politics, but because the kind of difficulty he represents for us is one with a clear ethical implication" (206). Butler's example of ethical affect comes from the last page of *Washington Square*. If this ending is not as spectacularly indeterminate as the ending of *Portrait*, the quietness of its narrative shift resonates with the end of *What Maisie Knew*, and the fact that Butler finds so much meaning in such a small move makes clear how her view of the novel takes for granted that narrative protocols are steeped in ethical value. The novel closes with Catherine Sloper declining a proposal of marriage. In Butler's reading of the passage, Catherine not only refuses Morris but also refuses to explain her refusal. "These refusals," according to Butler, "make her virtually incomprehensible to everyone" (207). On Butler's view, Catherine's refusal to speak—along with the narrator's refusal to speak for her—produces the interpretive difficulty that advances the reader's ethical education. Catherine's sudden silence, Butler declares, is a linguistic performance deployed by James to mark the limit of translation. While Catherine's silence leads in the storyworld to Morris's negative judgment of her, on Butler's view James's narrative positioning of the reader in relation to that silence secures an affective response that marks the limit for the reader not just of judgment but of sympathy as well. The depiction of Catherine's reserve, her refusal to make her "own terms" available to the reader, closes her off as a point of view. Catherine, according to Butler, thus defines her autonomy (for the other characters and for the reader) not through the attempt at positive self-characterization but by "marking the limits of all speaking that seeks to bind her, that offers itself to her as a way of binding herself" (208). Catherine's withdrawal marks the limit to readerly sympathy with Catherine as well, thus effectively stymieing what Gayatri Spivak has in another context called "the imperialism" of identification with the other.[38] Catherine's refusal to speak is, Butler argues, a positive provocation to the reader to regard Catherine as possessing qualities of personhood that are beyond social expectation, that exceed the norms of knowability—to understand alterity itself as the ethical limit to translatability. We might further note that Butler's reading of Catherine can also be developed to explain why the cutting off of Catherine's point of view marks the end of the novel: when James as well ceases to speak for Catherine, the linguistic act that is the novel, the linguistic act of projecting characters as real social others and attempting to speak as each, must also come to an end.

But what Butler does not acknowledge is how much her reading of *Washington Square* is a response to the ethics of alterity that James works out on a thematic and formal level. Butler may elucidate the notion of personhood from within a Levinasian framework, but James's artistic project is what invites her to describe the experience of incomprehensibility in ethical terms as honoring the ethical otherness of another person's life, even if that person is a fictional character. What has the plot of *Washington Square* been but the ethical calculation of the degree and kind of narcissism and cold-bloodedness that motivate Dr. Sloper and Morris? What has James's ironic use of point of view encouraged if not an appreciation of Catherine's particularity and powerlessness? Butler can take for granted the ethical positioning she finds in the novel's handling of point of view because James—in a way that makes a Levinasian reading possible—has freighted his artwork with the problem of doing justice to people different from oneself.

Butler thus is following out James's thematics when she reads Catherine's disappearance as a point of view as an ethical opportunity for the reader: the opportunity to be released from the position of judgment in which the narrative installs the reader:

> If we cannot join with Morris and the other chatterers to judge [Catherine], then perhaps we are asked to understand the limits of judgment and to cease judging, paradoxically, in the name of ethics, to cease judging in a way that assumes we already know in advance what there is to be known. And this suspension of judgment brings us closer to a different conception of ethics, one that honors what cannot be fully known or captured about the Other. (208)

When Jamesian narrative stymies our comprehension, Butler tells us "the reader is . . . left, in a sense, exasperated, cursing, staring"—and this emotion, which for Butler marks the limits of translation, thus recognizes and honors the other's ethical personhood as more than her social identity. To cease judging is, in other words, to cease trying to understand Catherine and instead value her for the ethical other she is. To the degree that the reader's judgment can be converted into recognition of/for Catherine is the degree to which we read "for *a* life" (214; emphasis added). Importantly, readers can encounter this ethical life only by first binding themselves to the experience of limited positionality offered by narrative. Ethics begins when readers willingly restrict their own point of view: when they assent to occupying the relation to the social world that the novel's narrative holds out to them. Being narratively bound (to the judgments that constitute the social norm, to the narrative conventions for depicting characters as persons, to the withdrawal of Catherine's point of view that ends the novel), readers "have" (as James himself might say) their ethical experience: "We *undergo* what is previously unknown . . . we learn something about the limits of our ways of knowing; and in this way we experience as well the anxiety and the promise of what is different, what is possible, what is waiting for us if we do not foreclose it in advance" (209; emphasis added).

The comparison between Butler's notion of limited translation and Bakhtin's concept of heteroglossia is worth pursuing for a minute as we think through the novel's role as an agent of alterity in new ethical theory. For Bakhtin, the novel is the preeminent linguistic manifestation not just of heteroglossia but of "the internally dialogized double-voiced discourse" that enables translation, that enables the self to say "'I am me' in someone else's language, and in my own language, 'I am other.'"[39] For Bakhtin the novelist's dialogic imagination can overcome the otherness produced by social positionality, but the novel itself remains first and foremost for Bakhtin a social document, an imaging of the heteroglossia that belongs to a specific cultural moment with a particular social history. For new ethical theorists the novel is not this kind of social document; its social value cannot be separated from its status as *fiction*. The reader's experience through the novel of the social limits to self-translation is, for the new ethicist, offset by the possibility that fiction itself generates for knowing and being other. The novel's transformation of storyworld actualities into narrative contingencies and its throwing ethical judgment into uncertainty make possibility possible. The "as if" of fiction allows repetition with a difference.

The poststructuralist emphasis on the ethics of fiction, of fiction as a property of ethics, guides us to a more specific understanding of how novelistic narrative is conceptualized both as an epistemological limit for encountering characters as ethical others and as a structure that brings readerly self-consciousness about the sociopolitical nature of those limits. We can begin to limn this ethics of fictionality by comparing Nussbaum's revision of Dickens's "reading as if for life" with the ethical value Judith Butler finds in the phrase "for life, as it were." The phrase that interests Butler is, importantly, Henry James's—and it ends the last sentence of *Washington Square*, the novel that Butler has used to make her own case for James's ethical insights. Here's the full last line of James's novel: "Catherine, meanwhile, in the parlour, picking up her morsel of fancy-work, had seated herself with it again—for life, as it were."[40] The phrase "as it were" opens up semantic ambiguities that result in irresolvable ethical questions. Is the narrator suggesting that Catherine's renunciation leads her to live the rest of her life as only a pale shadow of the rich "reality" that she might have otherwise lived? Does "as it were" mark a deliberate refraining from real life? Or does "as it were" suggest that Catherine has chosen to make life as she would have it be: that her morsel of fancy-work is a more satisfying way for her to live because it is a chosen way, a life she picks up and commits herself to (for life). Butler doesn't spell all of this out, and we could go even further and add that the word "fancy-work" contributes to the ambiguating power of "as it were," since it might connote either the idling away of a life or an escape from life (into fancy) or a delusion about life (a fancy) or a positive engagement with life (through fancy) that is a source of imaginative and emotional connection to life on her own terms.[41]

According to Butler, the semantic tensions created through the phrase "as it were" epitomize the ethical power of fictional representation, of representation as fiction. Butler understands the conditional phrase ("for life, as it were") as James's insight into the necessary condition of meaning-making not just in literature but in life. In Butler's version of unverifiability as an essential quality of ethical experience, the quality of fictionality found in the novel is coextensive with the fictionality that attends any act of representation. It is not just the fact that James demands ethical judgments that remain unverifiable; any act of representation both implies a referent and stages its difference from that referent.[42] "As it were" works as a phrase of semantic ambiguation, as a narratorial comment that implies judgment but disallows judgment owing to the insufficiency of information provided by the narrator, both about his own view of Catherine's decision and what the decision itself might be. But "as it were" is also a testament to the figuration that is an element of any linguistic act. Unverifiability is the ethical condition of any attempt to formulate truth claims. Fiction, and more particularly the Jamesian novel, thus emblematizes the ethical condition for Butler in that it not only performs the difference between representation and reality but performs it as a hypothetical: that there might be a reality that one can know as other and that there might also be a better reality that one can imagine and project as a real future. What is more, the "as it were" of fiction marks the difference between determinative social and material forces and the emotion that ratifies the reader's ethical encounter with alterity. On a metalevel, realist fiction asks to be understood both as the world is and how it might be. The attempt to translate representation as referent together with the jamming of that translation through semantic ambiguity contributes to the new ethical view that characters can be ethically experienced when the reader is "disarmed and . . . become[s], suddenly, unknowing" (214).[43] It is through the ethical emotion generated by fiction's handling of its own fictionality that the reader learns that not just judgment but any "posture of dogmatism" that "may well sidetrack us from the evanescence, if not the ineffability, of *a* life" (214; emphasis added).

Because Butler sees all meaning-making as an act of figuration, of the "as if" imposition of order and coherence onto experience, not just reading but any act of knowing is, on Butler's view, created through the act of restyling "reading as if for life" as "reading for life." For Butler, human understanding comes into being through the oscillation between reading for life and reading as if for life. Reading for life, we ignore or forget the conditionality of our understanding. Reading as if for life, we are self-consciously aware that our certainty is all hypothetical: we understand that we create the meaning we think we find; we know that when we feel most certain, we are taking for fact exactly what we pretend to be.[44] Our experience of how literature binds us (to characters, to its emotional effects) is thus the happy psychological condition that frees us from our usual epistemological limits. The felt condition of our own binding makes possible, in other words, our knowledge of life "as it were." Through the affective experience delivered to the reader by the novel, incomprehension of the other yields knowledge of the self: we are made to recognize our operative interpretive categories as our own "regime of the norm." Butler implies that Catherine's refusal to explain herself—and James's refusal to explain to us *for* her—is experienced by the reader as an emotional upset that both reveals the reader's own participation in the everyday binding we all perform on people we pretend to know and opens the reader to the possibility that persons and personhood can be different and should be more than social identity. And this felt recognition of the limits of our ways of knowing opens up, for Butler, the possibility that we might change for the better, that we might actively try to judge less and undergo more.

The sociopsychological model that underpins Butler's account of readerly affect means this ethical lesson cannot be learned once and for all. Our capacity for undergoing is dependent upon our continuing to judge: alterity can only be registered positively by our experience of its power to disrupt us, to leave us, in a sense, exasperated, cursing, staring. Our avowal of our epistemological limits is something that must be freshly performed, undergone again and again. Indeed, the hope of Butler's model lies in her belief that the ethical autonomy and significance of *a* life, of any one life, always exceeds the social "system of carceral restraints or disciplinary injunctions" by which we know it.⁴⁵ For Butler, alterity is defined by the endless potential to resist comprehension, to trouble certainty. And it is precisely the endless possibility for psychological upset that creates the positive conditions for personal and social change. The end of the liberal subject's feeling of "constitutive 'freedom'" defined by private life begins with the individual's emotional experience of the private life as confounded, invaded. Vulnerability allows change.⁴⁶ Anxiety, ethical promise.

How does Butler's "as it were" help us to understand Nussbaum's erasure of Dickens's "as if"? I believe it opens up for our appreciation a strong basis of connection for their shared understanding of literature's ethical value as the novelistic experience of otherness. For Nussbaum the conversion of "reading as if for life" to "reading for life" is, as it is for Butler, grounded in two types of alterity: the reader's honoring of the characterological lives depicted in the novel and the work of literature as itself a "life." For Nussbaum, as for Butler, it is the encounter with alterity—what Nussbaum calls the new—that produces "pains and sudden joys"—emotions that are themselves ethical in this context (*Love's Knowledge*, 53). The narrative strategies of the novel—"complex," "allusive," and "attentive to particulars" (3)—position the reader to care "about what happens" (3-4), to be "lucidly bewildered, surprised by the intelligence of love" (53) into an openness to the new and different. Nussbaum says she learns from Strether the "willingness to surrender invulnerability, to take up a posture of agency that is porous and susceptible of influence" (180). "The life of perception feels perplexed, difficult, unsafe.... But this life also seems to Strether—and to us—to be richer, fuller of enjoyment, fuller too of whatever is worth calling knowledge of the world" (181). Literary texts thus display to Nussbaum what Butler's essay title terms "Values of Difficulty." For Nussbaum, novels engage the reader in "the complexity, the indeterminacy, the sheer *difficulty* of moral choice ... the refusal of life involved in fixing everything in advance according to some system of inviolable rules" (141–142; emphasis in the original). For Nussbaum as for Butler, we negotiate between the "conceptions" (29), the "rules and principles" (44), the categories for judgment that we bring to the text, and our willingness to be "in some sense passive and malleable, open to new and sometimes mysterious influences" (238). This vulnerability, she believes, "is a part of the transaction [with literary texts] and part of its value" (238). To be truly vulnerable, to have authentically risked, is to honor the power of the life of the other through the feeling of "surrender," "succumbing" (*Love's Knowledge* 237; qtd. from Booth).

Nussbaum's liberal humanist account of the novel thus ultimately distinguishes itself from Trilling's—and does so, moreover, in a way that complements the poststructuralist political critique of Trilling.[47] For Nussbaum, the reader's experience of the free play of her moral imagination ends in her experience of social restraint, of binding and being bound to the life of the other.[48] In *Poetic Justice* Nussbaum comes even closer to Butler in her meditation on the way literary representation produces "otherness" through figuration. Nussbaum's term for figuration is "fancy"—and her definition of fancy neatly glosses why, in the James passage that so interests Butler, Catherine Sloper's act of refusal is accompanied by the picking up of her fancy-work. Nussbaum tells us: "Fancy is the novel's name for the ability to see one thing as another, to see one thing in another. We might therefore call it the metaphorical imagination" (36). For Nussbaum, as for Butler, figuration enables us not only to apprehend alterity (to see one thing as another, to see one thing in another)—but to inhabit the conditions of possibility that allow us to imagine a future different from our "now": that "other things [can be] seen in immediate things" (36).

One reason the connection between Nussbaum and the poststructuralist new ethicists might be hard to see is that the name given by poststructuralists to their valorization of readerly experience is anything but love. But to find this much common ground between Nussbaum and Butler puts us in a position to understand how the names poststructuralist theorists give to literary experience—names such as estrangement, defamiliarization, and difficulty—are, like Nussbaum's "love," an attempt to answer Foucauldian and Marxist subjective functionalism by offering an alternative theory of private interiority. Rather than being the "constant inarguable evidence of . . . constitutive 'freedom,'" our interiority is, for Nussbaum and poststructuralist ethicists alike, the constant inarguable evidence of our constitutive sociality, a sociality felt as self-restraint. The disavowal of social positionality entailed by reading "for life" is countered by the avowal of social positionality necessitated by reading for life "as it were." The psychological necessity of oscillating between disavowal and avowal is, for both Nussbaum and Butler as well as in new ethical theory generally, what makes possibility possible.

Butler's new ethics helps us recognize novelistic aesthetics as an inherently politicized aesthetics by showing how novel form positions readers to experience themselves as "free" through their experience of being socially bound. Readers experience the free play of imagination as produced through a power struggle with a social other. The struggle to bind turns back upon the reader, enabling him to experience himself as unfree, as in a constitutive relation with the other, who in turn binds him. And because the reader experiences his own binding as both a private and an emotional condition, as a relationship with the characterological lives represented by a novel as well as the literary text as itself a life, for the new ethicist literature is theorized as conferring a felt encounter with alterity that is not simply compensatory for social positionality but outside of systematic discipline. In the new ethical defense of literary value as the values of novelized form, reading produces not false ideology but a true experience of how possibility is produced in and through the operation of social constraint.

In new ethical theory, literature provides not just (or for some, not even) the fictional imagination of social reform projected through the realist idiom of a storyworld. Novel reading does not yield a portable list of rules or tips to guide conduct. For the new ethicist, literature does not technically teach us anything at all—unless we understand learning as the overthrow of epistemology by experience, the troubling of certainty by an apprehension that comes through surprised feeling. Ethical knowledge is the experience of irresistible encounter with what one does not try to know, what one cannot help but know. It is knowledge that is beyond reason, of the emotions, and so intuitive as to seem a bodily knowing. To formulate this knowledge as epistemology, as we must do, is to register the moment that we move from being bound to binding, and back again. But the felt conversion of knowing into knowledge is what enables the process to continue—and to be felt as an ethical progress. Readers feel they come to know more about the sociopolitical construction of otherness each time their current knowledge is confounded. Ethical encounter is made possible by every felt failure to know and made new through every repetition.

That the reader's ethical experience of alterity begins with the encounter with literary character is an aspect of poststructuralist ethics that provides the literary-historical link to James. James's creation of deep psychological characters leads readers, and himself as rereader of his own work, to regard these characters as possessing an autonomy of their own, an autonomy that encourages the cultural belief—for writers and readers alike—that fictional creations have a right to human rights. Yet James's subjectification of narrative through point of view simultaneously calls attention to the way novels construct the personhood of characters from particular subject positions. The new ethics helps us to see that the belief that characterological freedom should be honored and respected is made possible not just by the agency the storyworld accords characters as representations of persons, but through the aesthetic functionalism that the novel as an art form assigns them. Judith Butler can talk about Catherine as if she were an actual person not because James's use of point of view bestows upon her a full subjectivity indistinguishable from our own, but because as point of view, and in other ways, Catherine as character is also an instrument of the novel's form—and thus seems ethically violated.

Notably, in defining the reader's ethical response to character as the experience of spontaneous emotion, the new ethical model of alterity reaches beyond love, vulnerability, or anxiety to theorize a meta-ethical emotion: unverifiability. The unverifiability of the otherness constructed and encountered by the novel reader retains the poststructuralist's skeptical regard for reason as a tool of hegemony while bestowing upon epistemological uncertainty a positive (and absolute) ethical content. From the post-Foucauldian perspective, self-conscious unverifiability protects the new ethical defense of literature from the charge of participating in the treatment of artworks as metaphysical objects. It was, of course, precisely to correct such a mystified view of aesthetics that Foucauldians such as D. A. Miller and Nancy Armstrong, as well as Marxists such as Fredric Jameson and Raymond Williams, launched their political accounts of the novel's cultural work.[49] The otherness prized by new ethical theory returns poststructuralists to a description of the artwork as autonomous and the reading experience as unified, but the unverifiability of these totalities—readers understanding that the otherness they experience may in fact be a fiction—prevents the new ethical model from reproducing the mystified view of aesthetics (i.e., the artwork as existing outside the social world, in a transcendental realm). Not only are readers made self-conscious about the epistemological uncertainty that attends the knowing of characters as others, but this uncertainty extends to the autonomy of the novel's social world, which they feel they apprehend but in fact must imaginatively project. The coherence of a character's life and of the social whole extends to the unity of an artwork—these are all totalities that are delivered by the novel to the ethical reader with the right way of reading, which is understood as the ability to be open to the otherness that they cannot be sure of but feel they experience owing to their will to believe in the possibility of alterity.⁵⁰ Further proof of James's centrality to the new ethical defense of literary value lies in the number of works published since 1987 (the date of J. Hillis Miller's *The Ethics of Reading*) that feature James as a grounding example of the ethics that literature provides.⁵¹ I want now to focus on this body of James criticism to show how thoroughly James's novelistic aesthetics of alterity pervades the poststructuralist understanding of narrative ethics. As I continue to chart the phenomenology of novel reading developed through the new ethics, I want to focus on how the creative position of the novelist, as it has been described from within the literary tradition I have been tracing, is extended to the new ethical reader. In the same way that the novelist in the Jamesian tradition feels responsible for the life of the fictional people that he has projected out of the words on the page, as well as feeling ruled by their will, so is the task of the reader, as developed by new ethical theory, to project the literary text as a state of being other to one's own, an autonomy with the power to enhance self-consciousness about the limits that define one's own state of being.

Reminiscent of Coetzee's depiction of Elizabeth Costello offering two completely different interpretations of the narrative ethics at work in Kafka's "A Report to an Academy," the theorists who are most explicitly invested in James's novelistic practice—Adam Zachary Newton, Andrew Gibson, and J. Hillis Miller—disagree about which narrative modes best offer the reader an ethical encounter with alterity, but all are certain that what is most at stake in James's novels is the possibility of the reader having such an encounter. In keeping with the argument I have been making about the difference between the philosophical and novelistic approaches to ethics, these theorists each make the case for the ethical value of literature through the authority of a particular philosophical framework they bring to bear on literary texts generally and James's work in particular: Newton couples Cavell and Levinas; Gibson argues for the proper philosophical understanding of Levinas as antiphenomenological; and J. Hillis Miller develops his notion of ethical conduct by linking J. L. Austin's speech act theory to Derridean deconstruction. So invested are these thinkers in reading James through the authority of a particular philosophical approach that they fail to see how much James's novel theory and practice guide the claims they each make for how literature delivers its ethical experience to readers. The power structure that James takes to be inherent in the act of fictional representation—the power of the author over his character, the power of the author to do ethical justice to people different from himself—is still in play for these theorists. But whereas for James the ethical value of narrative structure depends upon its relation to the ethical problems and actions represented in the storyworld, the new ethicists assign absolute ethical value to particular narrative modes (first- or third-person, for example). The new ethicists judge James by the ethical capacity they find unambiguously expressed through his handling of the alterity that now is assumed to be a defining feature of narrative itself. Thus the contingency that for James is a feature of novelistic aesthetics—the Jamesian view that narrative stances don't hold absolute ethical value but gain ethical value in relation to storyworld action—is traded for an absolute phenomenological claim about the ethical value inherent in the reader's narrative experience of epistemological aporia.

Although for new ethicists narrative modes reflect the unambiguous ethics of the author, the literary text, not the author, provides readers with their direct encounter with alterity. For Newton, Gibson, and Miller the function of characterological otherness is to direct the reader to the literary text as an othermaker (to use Sanders's phrase). Theorized as the embodiment of or material container for alterity, the literary text is granted autonomous agency and even, to some degree, a subjectivity of its own that tasks the reader with a specific ethical response. As agents, vehicles, and embodiments of otherness, literary texts are championed by new ethicists as not just ethically and politically valuable but, for at least one theorist, as sacred.

I want to turn first to Adam Zachary Newton's treatment of James in *Narrative Ethics* (1995) because we can see most vividly through Newton's argumentation how James's idea of characterological alterity modulates into more abstract claims about otherness as a feature of literary texts. Newton's idea of how to apply Levinasian ethics to literature is explicitly grounded in the personhood Newton accords to fictional characters. Newton doesn't mention that James also credits his fictional characters with personhood. But it seems that Newton might have in mind James's description of Isabel Archer, who, James relates, pops into his imagination "altogether in the sense of a single character," even though she possesses none of the usual specifications of social identity, which James describes as so much artistic detailing to be "super-added."[52] Newton in fact begins his investigation into James by inquiring into the ethics of such authorial superadditions: "What limits exist," he asks, "for the authoring, that is the imaginative filling in, of persons?" (127). The form of the question registers Newton's refusal to take for granted the altruism of authorial imagination. In his equation, authoring as an act of imagination risks violating the ethical limit between self and other. On Newton's view, the free play of the authorial imagination (which in his interpretation of James is expressed both as the gratuitous elaboration of characterological detail and the simplification of personhood into social types) registers the author's ethical failure to practice self-restraint. The difference between the personhood of characters and the personhood of their author marks for Newton the narrative boundary between ethics and aesthetics: imaginative acts practiced on behalf of ethical alterity (the bringing into being of the personhood of characters) and those undertaken for the pleasure of self-gratification: imagination for imagination's sake, or pure aestheticism.

Newton's overall project is to distinguish between novelists who self-indulgently fail to rein in their imagination (treating characters as elements of art) and novelists who admirably engage in ethical self-restriction, who assume a posture of receptivity to the singularity of characterological personhood (pursuing "the founding condition of intersubjective relation: the ethical separateness of persons") (172). Importantly for my argument, Newton deduces an author's ethical sense not from biographical information or from extraliterary sources but from the operation of narrative form. Newton postulates that "narrators, listeners, and witnesses assume the responsibilities of ethical relation in discharging their 'roles and functions'" (128). What are these roles and functions? The ethical absolute of narrative fiction begins for Newton with the belief that "narrational roles and responsibilities [are] emblematic of the moral separateness of persons" (128). For Newton, the shared body of narrative form bestows upon narrators and readers, as well as authors and characters, an equality of personhood. To succeed in the ethical task that fiction writing offers is for the author to restrain his will to imagination by honoring and maximizing the a priori personhood not just of characters but also of narratorial agents. Narrative ethics begins with Newton's sense that narrative itself is a cure for the novelistic imagination: narrative provides "boundaries" between narrative subjects, boundaries authors can choose either to maximize or else transgress.

To argue as I am that Newton's formalism, his belief that fictional narrative establishes a necessary ethical relation among narrative agents who are regarded as equal subjects, owes more to James than it does to Levinas might seem counterintuitive, since Newton nominates James's fiction as a failure of ethics, as an example of narrative management that violates the personhood of characters precisely through the failure of self-binding that manifests itself as a will to fiction/authorship. But as we have seen with Morrison, Smith, and Coetzee's fictional novelist, Emmanuel Egudu, Newton develops his ethical critique of James by extending James's own investigation into the limits and possibilities of fiction's capacity for achieved alterity. In the narrative ethics that Newton develops, characterological alterity cannot be done justice to through the love that Nussbaum credits to Jamesian narrative or to the Jamesian "as it were" that for Butler creates ethical anxiety. For Newton, to be ethical, narrative must perform not just the author's openness to persons different from himself but the influence that the fictional other has had on the authorial self. The question Newton states that he would like to "put to James himself" is "How much of the *I* who shapes the character is in fact an *I* who has been shaped by characters?" (144; emphasis in the original). By adding this ethical imperative to the family of ideas about how otherness should be defined and located in the literary text, ideas that have grown out of the Jamesian tradition, Newton can deem James an ethical monster. He characterizes his chapter on James as an ethical retort, an indictment of James's narrative practice on behalf of those he has wronged: "a rebuke of the exercise of authorial 'lordship' which sentences characters to textual 'bondage'" (129). Whereas on Butler's view, James's failure to find positive terms for the representation of Catherine's otherness could be understood as a narrative aporia that honored her difference, on Newton's view, James's failure to render the otherness of character can only be explained as a violation of the personhood of characters (132). Not to bind the self is to put the other in bondage. James's handling of narrative is for Newton expressive of a "proprietary attitude, a *lèse majesté*, to acts of representation" (127), and he goes so far as to equate this "ruthless 'sovereignty'" with "a certain, shall we say, totalitarianism" (129).

Newton's interpretation of the artist figure who narrates "The Real Thing" establishes the foundation for Newton's more specific argument that authorship itself is an act of oppression. The proprietary attitude toward acts of representation turns out to be a love of representation per se as against the personhood of the represented. The selfish pleasure the author takes in exercising his imagination means that the bondage the character endures at the hands of its author passes beyond servitude to final extinction: the "de-realization" of person into text (129). This formulation suggests that Newton understands textuality as mere representation, representation that has lost touch with the persons embedded in narrative, that has overcome the ethical boundaries supplied by narrative structure through the preponderance of "filling in" that has turned persons into nothing but fictional characters. According to Newton, "The Real Thing" narratively dramatizes "the descent of person into type, in a double sense of the word: general class and merely *graphic* character" (131; emphasis in the original). The novella thus performs in his reading "the fate that looms over every literary character—a shrinkage of person within representational space." The "*aesthetic* forms which give them textual life . . . efface their personhood" (132; emphasis in the original). The author who prefers to fill in characters rather than be influenced by them chooses the practice and self-gratification of representation over establishing narratively a "face to face" relation with character (143). On Newton's view, James's lack of regard for the value of the intersubjective encounter, let alone the ethical act of "placing oneself in hostage-for-another" (142), makes him an aesthete. The implication is that James's deficient ethical sensibility, his narcissism, not only drives him to extinguish the personhood of his characters but makes him prefer the solitary satisfactions of aesthetic design to human relation.

Newton makes his case against James by focusing on three novellas, two told in the first person ("The Real Thing" and "The Aspern Papers") and one in the limited third person ("In The Cage"). Although his theory of narrative structure might suggest that the types of boundaries enforced through narrative would be differently constituted according to narrative stance, Newton's interpretation of the roles and responsibilities of the Jamesian narrator in all three stories tell the same ethical story: the exploitation of characters for the obtainment of artistic capital. It's easy to see how the ethically compromised, first-person narrators of "The Real Thing" and "The Aspern Papers" pose the question of the possibility of authorial exploitation, but Newton's analysis of "In the Cage" reveals how determined he is to read all narrative stances through the lens of James's ethical culpability. Newton interprets the narrator as embroiled in a rivalrous relation with the telegraph operator whose point of view focalizes the narrative discourse. At issue for Newton is the social difference between the telegraph operator who "simply could not tell her own story, as is not the case for more polished and linguistically sophisticated narrators like those of 'The Real Thing' or *The Aspern*

Papers" (171) and the author himself, who ostentatiously steps in to loan his sophistication and aesthetic sensibility to the operator. Although we have seen in my discussion of *What Maisie Knew* the multivalence with which James treats the narrative ethics of such a relation, Newton's monolithic interpretation of James's narrative ethics rests on two assumptions. First of all, he seems to accept the class divide that he sees performed by the narrative, taking for granted that the operator is in an absolute sense not capable of telling her own story. Second, the privilege he extends to characters as persons leads him to regard authorial language used on behalf of a character as always only suspect, as an act of domination rather than of generous assistance or even neutral translation. On Newton's view, for James as author to bestow on the protagonist "special literary powers of vision" as well as sophisticated language use is indicative of an ethical failure in self-binding. Rather than holding back, rather than attempting to know the operator as other to him, James makes his protagonist into a version of himself.

These assumptions about the ethical quality of the relation between author and character lead Newton to develop a complicated account of how James's representational practices invest other narrative agents in the ethical circuit of alterity. According to Newton, the narrator, incensed by the author's crediting to the protagonist powers of narration that rightly belong to his narrative position, seeks revenge on the character for "daring to poach on his premises" (172). As Newton describes it, the narrator "gets back" at the operator by getting to her: so at one is the narrator with the protagonist that he performs a "seamless telepathy into her thoughts" (172).[53] He gets back at her, in other words, precisely by violating the "ethical separateness of persons" (172). For Newton, the narration of characterological consciousness through the stance of the Jamesian "reflector" can have only one ethical value: the violation of personhood, the turning of a person into a literary character. Thus, on Newton's interpretation, the author exploits the operator by bestowing upon her his class identity and aesthetic talent, which goads the narrator in turn into exploiting the operator by invading her consciousness and textualizing its contents.

While he thus contrasts with Nussbaum and Butler in his negative estimation of James's ethical treatment of his characters—understood as a respect for the personhood that Newton believes belongs to literary characters before they become literary characters—Newton does credit James with a self-consciousness about his complicity in exercising narrative power. But unlike Nussbaum and

Butler, who see the avowal of disavowal as an ethical recognition of the normative judgments or ideological barriers that necessarily attend every attempt to raise the ethical impulse to alterity to the level of knowledge, Newton regards James's self-conscious depiction of the risks and responsibilities of authorial power as so much bad faith. Newton implies that, because such avowals do nothing to alter the operation of power, even as they pretend they might, James's depiction in his storyworlds of "authorial privilege and authorial culpability" projects a "*kynicism*," a resistance to dominating authority, that "should not itself escape critique" (131). Thus Newton sets the stage for theorizing the ethics that literature offers the reader: the critique that the reader levels at James's authorial intentions becomes the means for redirecting the reader's attention away from the operation of narrative power in the novelistic ethics of alterity to a more purely Levinasian notion of affective encounter, achieved by the reader in relation with that better other, the literary text.

Endorsing an idea that he credits to Stanley Cavell, Newton argues that fiction does not present its readers with an "observational, distanced look at life" but instead "offers up for encounter . . . hard facts of distance, separation, and alterity which seem familiar as 'facts of life,' but which gain extra pathos and piquancy when framed by the special boundaries of art" (129). Love, anxiety—pathos and piquancy. For Newton, as for Nussbaum and Butler, the power relation that attends novelistic narrative can be temporarily offset by the spontaneous welling up of readerly emotion that new ethical theorists regard as a nonappropriative recognition of the value of otherness. On Newton's view, the reader's ethical emotion is not prompted by the refined and detailed perception of characterological subjectivity (Nussbaum) or shifts in point of view (Butler) but through a more abstract experience of representational instability that is a quality of literary texts, which as he defines it are texts "framed by the special boundaries of art." It turns out that in Newton's full understanding of fiction's aesthetic project, a literary text functions as a complicated totality, an achieved autonomy governed by what he calls an "ethical structure," of which the rivalrous subjective economy of narrative ethics that I have been discussing is only one part. In contrast to the debased aesthetic project that Newton equates with the play of the author's unrestrained addiction to imaginative acts (rather than the ethical real of personhood), the artwork, defined as a unified and autonomous structure, functions as a three-dimensional repository for, as well as an active agent of, alterity. The narrative body that links author, narrator, and character turns out to be only the "textual surface." Inherent to the text is an ethical force that breaks this surface "from behind and below," creating "gaps and traces" that serve as the reader's entry point into "the 'upsurge' of alterity" that somehow resides within the artwork, described as a three-dimensional form (172–173). Thus the ethical experience offered by literary texts is ultimately, for Newton, defined as the reader's perception of the text's broken surface. But although readerly apprehension is cast in these material terms—so as to seem a direct contact with the energy of alterity exuded by the text—the apprehension of these gaps and traces also seems to require a high level of interpretive abstraction, since it launches the reader, according to Newton, into a philosophical inquiry, which he describes as the "putting-into-question of a self's 'boundless freedom,' and the investing of it as critique" (172). For Newton the putting into question is, importantly, not the reader's own complicity in characterological othering, but James's. The upsurge of alterity is the reader's experience of the text's preservation of the ethical imperative as a norm that binds the reader through an individually experienced emotional response to an ethical absolute that serves as a standard against which to judge James's narrative failure.

In his *Postmodernity, Ethics and the Novel* (1999), Andrew Gibson launches his own defense of literary value by quarreling with Newton on a philosophical basis. Gibson believes that Newton's new ethical theory rests on a misunderstanding of Levinas and offers his own theory as correction. Specifically, Gibson objects to Newton's deriving a "phenomenology of reading" (*Postmodernity*, 13) from Levinas when on Gibson's view Levinas's ethical project takes "phenomenology to task" (188). But I want to show that in fact the account I have been giving of the new ethical phenomenological model—an account that includes Nussbaum and Butler as well as Newton—takes on board what Gibson describes as Levinas's specific objection to the Husserlian version of phenomenology defined as the "'self-awareness' of cognitive life" (188). As I have been arguing, Newton as well as other new ethical theorists build into their phenomenological model a self-conscious understanding of the limits to rational understanding, an apprehension that is conveyed through the embodied experience of emotional knowledge. Thus Gibson seems inaccurate when he argues that the "ethical limits of reception theory" lie in "its failure to think affect" (188). He also seems not to have read Newton fully when he declares that "reception theory has never really been about *receptivity*. It has been concerned with production (the production of meaning) not reception or openness to alterity" (188). It is precisely the experience of conflict between the production of meaning—bringing the value of alterity to self-conscious understanding, interpreting narrative protocols as operations of power—and the experience of affect—love, anxiety, pathos, and piquancy—that is at stake in the investment of the new ethics in novelistic representation. That Gibson does not recognize this suggests that perhaps his focus on the philosophical frameworks that separate them rather than the literary tradition that unites them has led him to miss the import of the close readings that Nussbaum, Butler, and Newton perform, as well as the way their new ethical phenomenology functions (whatever its philosophical origin) when applied to literary texts, especially novels.

Looking at how Gibson conducts his own readings, we find that his points of departure are strikingly similar to Newton's. Like Newton, he ascribes to different narrative modes an absolute ethical value. Omniscience, third-person limited, first person, "each of these distinctions—distinctions between what is apparently known and what is presented as beyond the frame of narratorial knowledge—has an ethical dimension. Indeed, the relevant distinction ultimately expressed the ethics of the text in question" (26). We saw where Newton's assumptions about the roles and responsibilities inherent to narrative positioning led: to a description of Jamesian narrative as a circuit of rivalry among novelistic agents. Gibson, by contrast, credits to Jamesian narrative the positive accomplishment of ethical alterity. But homologous to Newton, this positive evaluation of James's narrative ethics is equated with a particular mode of narration—in this case the Jamesian "reflector-narration"—to which Gibson assigns absolute ethical value. What is more, when Gibson describes the ethical structure of reflector-narration, it hardly sounds different from Newton's description of the same narrative mode. What is of concern for both theorists is the relation between description and experience performed by a reflector-narrator. But, rather than stipulating the autonomy and equality of narrative agents—author, narrator, character—Gibson attributes a special ontological status to the narrator, the ability to be simultaneously inside and outside of the storyworld: "The narrator is also an experiencer. He or she is engaged, involved in the world narrated. Thus narration as reflection appears to supervene upon pre-reflective experience" (27). Yet despite this more fluid understanding of the narrator's positionality, Gibson arrives at the same conclusion as Newton in terms of the ethical value of the narrator's function: it (the narrator's positionality) "problematizes the relationship between narrating subject and narrated object [i.e. character]" (36). And like Newton he believes that to problematize the relationship between subject and narrated object is to draw attention to the potential for domination that inheres in the narrator's role as the mediator of characterological experience. But more than Newton, Gibson links narratorial domination to narratorial report: the knowledge claims that are made about the represented world. While for Newton, the reflector-narrator attempts to get back at the telegraph operator by violating her privacy (publishing her thoughts), for Gibson the reflector-narrator works in a positive way to "destabilize the identity principle."

In Gibson's example, when the narrator in *The Golden Bowl* represents Maggie's thoughts, he does not revenge himself upon the character but instead creates "an aporia," an unresolvable ambiguity as to whether the passage of thought belongs to "Maggie, the author, or the narrator" (33). "The ambiguous voice of the reflector . . . crosses and blurs the boundaries between categories on which . . . power depends" (34). According to Gibson, at such moments the reflector-narrator enacts a simultaneity of possibilities rather than an exclusionary rivalry: "It hovers, hesitates, is either, neither, both" (33). Through this productive encounter with the otherness of—and created by—the reflector-narrator, Gibson's reader is forced to abandon literary reading as an epistemological project. The readerly encounter with alterity described by Gibson resonates strongly with Butler's account of how literary ethics entails the reader's self-conscious experience of the limits that define personal identity. As Gibson puts it, the failure of epistemology creates within the reader a "spontaneous and *immediate* desire to escape the limits of self, a desire generated as those limits are experienced in their narrowness, even their sheer absurdity. It is . . . the principle of unease within and inseparable from the self that is of a different order to being and more profound than it" (37; emphasis in the original). Love, anxiety, pathos, piquancy—unease. And in a way that strengthens the case for the connection I have made between Nussbaum and Butler, Gibson sounds a good deal like Nussbaum when he describes the ethical lesson that narrative teaches the reader: the lesson of "openness and attentiveness. . . . A capacity for being mastered, a receptiveness which even precedes cognition and makes cognition possible" (Gibson, *Postmodernity*, 162). This chimes with Nussbaum's description of the ethical reader's willingness to be "in some sense passive and malleable, open to new and sometimes mysterious influences,"[54] to "take up a position of agency that is porous and susceptible to influence" in order to become "lucidly bewildered."[55] What is more, Gibson's account of narrative structure as participating in the ethics of social transformation resonates both with Butler's "as it were" and Nussbaum's "fancy" ("the novel's name for the ability to see one thing as another, to see one thing in another"[56]). Narrative, Gibson declares, represents the "unreality of what is represented and the possibility of . . . 'a world that could be so different'" (173; qtd. from Rhys, *Good Morning, Midnight*).

Gibson believes that his new ethical understanding of narrative poses an alternative to classical narratology, which to his mind makes the mistake of conceptualizing narrative as a "'frame of knowledge' whose conditions are separation, distanciation, structures of opposition." According to Gibson, in classical narratology, "an entity deemed to be identical with itself . . . holds the other at bay, at a 'knowing' or '*scrutinizing* distance.'" He proposes instead that narrative be reconceptualized as transactional, enacting "constitutive ambivalences, exchanges and substitutions." In this way, he argues, the other is no longer held off but "enters into composition with, is invaded by or questioned in relation to this other" (36; emphasis in the original). But in seeking to define narrative representation as inherently ethical, has Gibson really abandoned the "frame of knowledge" model that he criticizes? It is not just that his own project is framed through Levinas, whose idea of ethics holds other ideas about ethics at bay, at a scrutinizing distance (to the point where Gibson feels the need to correct Newton's understanding of Levinas), but that Gibson's idea of narrative is grounded in the idea that otherness makes itself felt as an "invasion," a "questioning" of the self that it enters into. What has the Jamesian aesthetics of alterity allowed but the conception of narrative as operating through "ambivalences, exchanges, and substitutions"? Gibson discounts the positionality that still obtains in his alternative model of narrative, the feature of narrative that has from the beginning of the Jamesian tradition been the register of the degree and kind of ethical contact between self and other.

For all his work in narrative theory, J. Hillis Miller is the new ethical theorist least interested in making explicit claims for narrative as a privileged ethical mode. At the same time, he is the poststructuralist theorist most invested in James: *Literature as Conduct* (2005) works out its ethical theory through the sole example of James's fiction, with the aim of proving that "literature can conduct its readers to believe or to behave in new ways" (2). If we thought that deconstruction is what took us away from ethics (either because from its linguistic perspective ethics could be viewed as metaphysical and therefore hegemonic or because it seemed in retrospect to authorize the wartime acts of Paul de Man, one of its leading theorists), it turns out we were wrong, since, as Miller tells us, "deconstruction is nothing more or less than good reading as such" (*Ethics of Reading*, 10), which he regards as a precondition for the ethical encounter with alterity offered by literature. Deconstruction now means for Miller a conception of the act of reading as a particular and "concrete" encounter between particular and concrete readers and texts: "It begins with and returns to the man or woman *face to face* with words on the page"—and then asks, "'What kind of responsibility to whom or to what' is involved in this action?" (4; emphasis added). Miller's emphasis on the particular and concrete is especially striking given that the whole point of deconstructive play is, as Roland Barthes famously argues, to unbind the text from the literary work, to disseminate the text by "dispersing it within the field of infinite difference."[57] I want to show how Miller's commitment to defining ethical value in terms of otherness (and to defining otherness in terms that would distinguish his new ethical theory from old, liberal humanist theories of character) leads him to rebind the text, to overvalue its material properties (words on the page) as a basis for a physical integrity and autonomy through which the ethical reader can construct the semantic integrity and autonomy to which she will respond. It is on this material basis that the text can provide the reader with an ethical experience, an encounter between self and other.

If the surprise of Miller's position in *The Ethics of Reading* (1987) is that deconstruction turns out to be about "concrete" and direct realities (students and teachers, readers and texts, face-to-face experience), the surprise of *Literature as Conduct* is that Althusserian "hailing" can be understood as the positive condition of authentic ethical action. By the time he wrote *Literature as Conduct*, Miller had developed his notion of readerly responsibility to include the text's interpellation of the reader as an individual: "The call is addressed to me, personally. I alone must act, must respond. I cannot let anyone else read for me" (14). Whereas for Althusser the individual's identification with the social position created for her marks the insidious operation of social control, the ideological delusion of the liberal subject who believes that she has freely chosen what is in fact assigned to her—an interpellation that on Althusser's view casts resisting subjects as "bad subjects"—for Miller the literary phenomenon of textual "calling" constructs the reader as a good reader, an ethical individual. And it does so for Miller by generating readerly freedom out of a textual necessity. The call to the reader is a call to submit to something outside the self. Through this submission, the reader is produced as an indispensable and irreplaceable co-creator of alterity. Responding to the call commits the reader to action that is defined as ethical by its nontransferability, its performance by each "I alone." Althusserian hailing is thus revised by Miller as the basis of literary ethics—responding to the call of the text puts the reader in the position of responsibility to the text.

That Miller prefers the term "text" as a descriptor for the hailing agent, the other that commands responsibility from the reader, reveals both the highly abstracted nature of his account of literature's distinguishing formal properties as well as the covert operation of the novelistic view of alterity at work in his new ethical theory. Miller imbues the Jamesian subjectification of narrative with another level of materiality through his implicit description of the reader's face-to-face relation with the words on the page. The text as other, as brought to life as an other, dons the human face of Levinasian singularity. As in a Jamesian novel, out of words come persons. Text takes on the subjectivity imputed to it. It is to this personified textual face that the reader (like the Jamesian novelist to his characters) bears responsibility.

Although Miller does not explicitly acknowledge how his figurative description of textuality is itself an act of conduct that makes literary texts available to readers as if texts were concrete, delimited, autonomous wholes (so that the reader can respond to them as though they were ethical agents of otherness), his large-scale theoretical position allows not just for the fact of such conduct but for its necessity. In Miller's formulation, the literary text takes on its human face in part because readers, in their quest for meaning, treat the text as though it possessed an inside and an outside: the reader approaches the literary work with a "hermeneutic model of penetration within or behind or below the data to reach a hidden meaning" (26). Responding to the call of the text to "'Read me!'" the reader attempts to develop an account of the text that is "cognitively" (Miller's word as well as Gibson's)[58] formulated as a "completely verifiable assertion" (83). But the ethical power of literature, according to Miller, lies in the demands it makes on readers to interpret a meaning that seems to lie within or beneath its surface, yet through its ambiguities and "blanks" (his word as well as Newton's) prevents readers from accessing that interior (22). The reader's failure to reach a hidden meaning—the fact that literary reading confounds rather than reveals meaning—offers the ethical experience of personal interpretive failure that leads to the "discrediting" of this "mistaken paradigm." This recognition includes the realization that the hermeneutic model inhibits the "achievement of real knowledge" as well as the understanding that such acts of rational investigation enact an ethical transgression of an other's being (26).

In keeping with other new ethicists, Miller thus poses bodily knowledge as the alternative to the transgressive nature of reason. But by bringing Austin's speech act theory to bear on Derridean ethics, Miller adds a new element to the new ethical paradigm: he theorizes bodily knowing not just as affect—although it is that, in that unease, anxiety, perplexity are all at play in his theory—but as a type of "doing." For Miller, the alternative to epistemological knowledge is "the blind, bodily material kind [of knowledge] that cannot be narrated. We only witness to it, in another speech act" (22). I find this conception of bodily knowledge difficult to understand—but perhaps that is exactly Miller's point: it cannot be narrated or even made directly available to reason. By calling this knowledge "material," Miller seems to mean that knowledge of the other and knowledge as a condition of otherness is so beyond reason as to be intuitive, corporeal, performed through and as action. Understood this way, bodily knowledge would refuse the hermeneutical mistake of thinking that meaning resides within the body, that the body is the container for meaning. As Miller puts it, "What the reader learns [through the experience of reading] is not definite knowledge. It is at most a bodily understanding of what he or she cannot in principle objectively and impersonally know, but can only do, perform, act" (26).

To be uncertain—to have no definite knowledge—and yet still to have to act is for Miller precisely the human condition that defines ethics. Miller takes a deontological view of ethical conduct; indeed, he defines ethical conduct explicitly as that which is "never fully justifiable by rational explanations" (83). The confounded reader thus, on Miller's new ethical model, does not simply oscillate between ethical feeling and epistemological certainty but comes to understand ethics as taking responsibility for actions and decisions that are unjustifiable in that they can never be defended on grounds other than the responsibility that the individual must take for what she does. Miller stresses that in this sense any interpretation of a literary work qualifies as an ethical action: "Reading a literary work confers a responsibility on the reader to make an accounting of his or her act of reading" (3). Guided by Paul de Man's understanding of allegory as a figure for reading, Miller further explains that "any writing down of a reading necessarily involves synecdoche, part for whole, the insolence of choice in the selection of details to cite and single out for comment. For that choice the commentator must take responsibility" (49).[59]

While for Butler, James's novel teaches the ethical lesson that one should try to stop judging, for Miller, James's work teaches the opposite lesson: that the reader must continue to judge in the face of indefensible choices. According to Miller, James demonstrates this understanding of ethics first by putting at the center of many of his works the cognitive labor of narrators and characters who seek to understand the hidden nature of other people, and then by linking these acts of cognitive labor to ethical evaluation. Pointing to the narrator of "The Aspern Papers," for example, Miller argues that the first-person narrator emerges as a voice that "seemingly speaks in response to a demand for an accounting" (13). On this view, the narrator of the "The Aspern Papers" wants not just to know (about the papers, about the past) but wants his narrative "above all to justify itself" (13). From whom does he seek justification? Miller argues that the reader is both the agent who places a demand upon the narrator to justify himself and the agent who, in turn, takes on "the responsibility of evaluating [his narrative] for plausibility and credibility, then judging it." James thus puts the reader in a position that demands the pronouncement of a verdict: "'Guilty' or 'Innocent'"—even though this verdict cannot itself be justified (14).

Although the example of "The Aspern Papers" highlights the role of first-person narration in the ethical address the literary work makes to the reader, in *Literature as Conduct* Miller argues more generally that the reader's invitation to judgment begins with the reader's relation to narrators and characters as ethical agents. *The Portrait of a Lady*, for example, holds out a standard of ethical conduct through its narrative of Isabel Archer's ethical education. At the outset of the novel, Isabel is defined by the pride she takes in ethical self-scrutiny and justifiable self-conduct. She marries Gilbert Osmond in the sincere belief that she grasps the secret of Osmond's being better than anyone else in her social world, a performance of what Miller would term cognitive apprehension that justifies her decision to marry him even though everyone else in the novel thinks she has made a mistake. In fact Isabel has indeed made a mistake—and, reading the plot through Miller's new ethical model, James thus represents her ethical education as beginning with her own felt experience of the inadequacy of reasoned justification for one's actions. Isabel's ethical journey thus allegorizes the nature of ethical conduct in general, a lesson that is brought home to James's readers through the experience of reading James's narrative: "To read James is to be put in the pickle of being made responsible for judgment when the grounds for judgment are not entirely certain" (Miller, *Literature as Conduct*, 15).

To explain how the reader's own epistemological quest to develop a justifiable interpretation of Isabel is narratively confounded, Miller directs us to the kiss between Isabel and Caspar Goodwood and the famously indeterminate conclusion of *Portrait*: "The novel does not tell the reader enough to confirm a reading. It leaves the reader unable to understand Isabel's decision, therefore unable, if the reader does not import something from *outside the text*, to pass judgment on her decision as good or bad" (79; emphasis added). Importantly, the language of inside and outside recurs in Miller's description of the reader's relation to the text, but in keeping with his definition of bodily knowing as a material knowing, the inside of the text ultimately functions not as a depth to be penetrated but a materialized other to be honored, honored through the reader's realization that "he or she cannot in principle objectively and impersonally know, but can only do, perform, act" (26). The reader, knowing that she doesn't know, still must meet James's demand to judge. The insufficiency of information provided by the text

> does not prevent decisions from being made, nor does it even prevent us from saying that they ought to be made, that they must be made. Nor does it prevent the reader from taking upon himself or herself the responsibility for filling in the gap between the kiss and the knowledge that follows it with one or another of the explanations I have proposed. This is your decision, but you are on your own in making it, just as you are on your own in making any decision. (80–81)

Whereas for Butler the "as it were" of fiction prompted and brought to self-consciousness both the possibilities for identity that might belong to the characterological other and the limits to epistemological knowledge as the politically conditioned performance of certitude, for Miller the "unverifiable hypotheses" that the reader generates in response to James's narrative aporia ultimately become the ground of the reader's own "bodily" action, his willed interpretation of the text, an interpretation that cannot defer to the authority of the text or to the author or to literary critics as experts or even to other readers but honors the otherness of the literary text by taking responsibility for what he takes it to be. In Miller's formulation: "For that repetition the one who repeats must take responsibility. The doer must take responsibility, that is, for what he or she does not know, but can only perhaps succeed in reinscribing. He or she reinscribes it in a new, singular, unheard-of way, with incalculable effects on the future" (29).

In striking contrast to the experience of unverifiability that for Miller is the ethical value offered by literary texts generally and James's fiction in particular, Miller finds no ambiguity in the ethics he attributes to James's narrative modes. For example, similar to Newton and in contrast to Gibson, Miller describes James's reflector-narrator as the repository of subjectivities who are in a rivalrous relation for power. Miller sounds most like Newton when he draws an analogy between Gilbert Osmond's relation to Isabel Archer and the narrator's relation to Isabel: "Such mind-reading is, one might argue, even more sinister than Osmond's surveillance of Isabel, since Isabel is at least aware that the latter is taking place, whereas it is a rule of third person telepathic narrations that the characters are never aware of the narrator" (71). While Newton explicitly argues that James's ethical failure is the failure to ask of himself, "How much of the *I* who shapes the character is in fact an *I* who has been shaped by characters"? (144; emphasis in the original), Miller's criticism implicitly mobilizes the same value: that the personhood of a fictional character has equal status to that of the narrator. The reflector-narrator, or what Miller calls "telepathic narration," fails to honor characters as ethical others. And just as Newton holds James responsible for the dominating and instrumentalizing narrators to be found in his fiction, Miller suggests that a flaw in James's own character inspires his fiction writing: "There may be something sinister in the secret surveillance of social life that generates works of fiction—James's, for example" (71).

Miller isn't completely clear as to whether he is attributing secret surveillance specifically to James and the kind of fiction he writes or if he is implying as well that fiction per se sinisterly surveilles the social world, instrumentalizing its autonomy for its own aesthetic agenda. If the latter, this negative judgment of fiction seems at odds with the positive ethical value that he theorizes through his idea of literature as conduct. The only way I can understand Miller's antifiction stance in this passage is by way of the literary tradition that has installed a belief in the rivalry of narrative subjects even when it is unwarranted by Miller's new ethical theory. Miller is, I believe, too eager to dismiss literary history, which he derides as springing from the university's "search for a narratable historical truth" and which he holds up as a signal example of the repressive "commitment to truth-seeking in our culture" (21). But to say that Miller critiques literary history is simply to say that he critiques any and all beliefs in historical knowledge as a variety of the bad ethics of epistemology.

But as we have seen, as much as Miller insists on the groundlessness of ethical judgment, his ethical theory is grounded in the absolute value of achieved alterity. The text as an ethical other hails the reader into a face-to-face encounter. The reader, like the narrator of J. M. Coetzee's *Waiting for the Barbarians* who seeks to know the secret identity of the native woman, can "hunt back and forth seeking entry" to the text, but, as in Coetzee's novel, that quest for determinate knowledge will prove futile.[60] The failed act of understanding the text is the precondition that allows the reader's fuller submission to the text's identity as ontological other. The reader serves as host for the text's otherness, as it is incorporated into the reader's body as a material, unnarratable knowledge. Through the "doing," the speech acts, the conduct, that "reinscribe" the material knowledge derived from the reader's encounter with the literary text, the life of the text, the text as a life, extends into the future. The ethics of alterity that structures Miller's account of literary value thus tethers the radical constructivism that Miller attributes to subjectivity in passages like this:

> Subjectivity has no solid basis in a perdurable, pre-existing and indestructible selfhood. Selfhood is created and created anew from moment to moment by speech acts. You do not have a self first and then decide on the basis of that. You decide, for reasons that remain ineffably mysterious and unaccountable. The decision gives you a self. This means a new decision will give you a new self. (78)

What is the ineffable, mysterious, and unaccountable reason but the life of the text making its presence felt as a nonnarratable force? And how new can the self be if that incorporated material knowledge lives on, even as it is passed on (repeated, reinscribed)? If a new decision produces a new self, that self remains tethered to the otherness that it cannot know but embodies. Thus, although Miller's new ethics does not contribute to the understanding of the ethics of alterity as a politics—although, in other words, it does not link the limits of ethical alterity to ideological, material, political, and psychological determinates—it does follow out the formalism of the Jamesian novelistic aesthetics of alterity by crediting the literary text with the power to bind the reader in ethical relation, and through the narrative journey of that relation, enhance personal self-consciousness about the limits that define the reader's own state of being.

Self-Restriction as the Re-grounding of a Discipline

While new ethical theory thus emphasizes that the reader who reads for "I alone" does so in order to make personally experienced, embodied contact with the others represented by literary texts and the other that the literary text is, another branch of the Jamesian project ends up providing literary critics with a new basis for establishing the value not just of literature but of professional training in literary study. Following the Lubbockian line of inheritance, this new ethical stance endorses the need for academic training in literary critical interpretation in order that readers may respond fully to the encounter with alterity offered by literary texts. Indeed, the new ethical attempt to move past the Foucauldian critique of literature as the expression of class privilege generally and the novel more particularly as an instrument of nineteenth-century social discipline inspires a new defense of literary criticism as an academic discipline: as the training of readers in the ethical act of self-discipline through the honoring of the alterity to be found in literary texts. It turns out that the literary critic who is professionally trained to decode and articulate the ethical value of novelistic techniques is necessary to the regulation of ordinary readers—initiating these readers into the discipline of literary studies, the discipline of self-disciplined interpretation. Thus we find a poststructuralist theorist such as Gayatri Spivak echoing Wayne Booth's midcentury insistence that readers need training in narrative theory in order to properly decode the ethics at stake in the particular strategies at play in particular novels.[61] Significantly, Spivak makes the case for disciplined interpretation in an essay that takes as its prime example Coetzee's novel *Disgrace*—and thus vivifies the continuum between James and Coetzee that I have been establishing.[62] Spivak's essay offers its own "lesson" in the ethics of narrative, referring us indirectly back to Coetzee's term for the chapters of *Elizabeth Costello* and the lesson of the master—the lesson about narrative form as an ethical problem of mastery—inaugurated by Henry James.

Spivak argues in "Ethics and Politics in Tagore, Coetzee, and Certain Scenes of Teaching" (2002) that literary reading has to be "learned" (22). She believes that the literary critic's "training" in literary technique is the basis of what literary studies has to offer as its own specialized discipline (26). Although she is more explicitly committed to interdisciplinary alliances than J. Hillis Miller, she too holds up the reader's active engagement with the alterity represented in and as a concrete literary text as being the antidote to monolithic political interpretation: "If the social sciences describe the rules of the game, literary reading teaches how to play" (22). We see Spivak invoking here a disciplined notion of deconstructive play that emerges, as it did for Miller, from her ethical project, the project of mobilizing a poststructuralist understanding of subjectivity and meaning-making on behalf of an achieved ethics of alterity. And in her willingness to pronounce on the positive social consequences of good reading as end-oriented, ethical play marks a distinct shift from the hermeneutics of suspicion operative in Foucauldian critique: "If Paul Wolfowitz [a housemate of Spivak's when she was in graduate school who later served as deputy secretary of defense under George W. Bush] had had serious training in literary reading and/or the imagining of the enemy as human, his position on Iraq would not be so inflexible" (23). The clear—and high-stakes—implication is that if Wolfowitz had majored in English and not political science, he would have made ethically superior political decisions.

Spivak defines the literary critic as an expert in "textural change": "Each discipline has its own species of 'setting-to-work'—and the texture of the imagination belongs to the teacher of literary reading" (26). In her reading of *Disgrace*, textural change is charted by apprehending microshifts in narrative positioning that, taken as an integrated whole, embody the quality of the literary work's ethical imagination. But training in right literary reading also means that the "readerly imagination" is trained to respond rightly to the "rhetorical signals" that Spivak believes are inherent in literary texts. The competent literary reader is for Spivak the reader who can occupy the position prepared for him by the text by accurately decoding (affectively and ethically) the values implied in specific and concrete narrative choices. The step-by-step interpretive adventure of this "canny reader" ends in the apprehension of the dominant moral value "authorized" by the novel as a whole (22). On Spivak's reading of *Disgrace*, the stakes of right reading are again incredibly high: the reader who fails to apprehend the full ethical position embedded in the novel's handing of narrative modes will conclude that the novel "can be made to say every racist thing" (24). In other words, the untrained reader, the reader who has not been schooled in the complexities of narrative modes, complexities of both form and ethical meaning, will misinterpret Coetzee's novel by thinking that its reflector-narrator, its third-person focalization of narration through David Lurie's point of view, validates Lurie's interpretation of events. On Spivak's interpretation, for the reader to believe that the novel endorses Lurie's point of view is to accept "the limited perfect validity of the liberal white ex-colonizer's understanding." For Spivak, this would mean reprehensibly accepting an ethical view that would define social progress as blaming the subaltern that the colonist has othered for the violence that colonialism has enacted, a political program that in terms of the novel's storyline would begin with the "education of Pollux, the young rapist" (24). But if the reader has read accurately, according to Spivak, he will have attended to the limits that the novel sets to Lurie's point of view—limits set by what Spivak understands as the novel's performance of an ethics of alterity. Spivak argues that Lurie's dominating point of view is politicized—politicized because it is ironized—through the narrative representation of Lurie's daughter, Lucy, the victim of the rape. In an interpretive move that recalls the case Butler makes for Catherine's representation in *Washington Square*, Spivak argues that *Disgrace*'s refusal to explain Lucy—its insistence on retaining "the enigma of Lucy" (24)—exposes the ideological assumptions in Lurie's account of his daughter as "patient and agent" (22). Spivak argues more specifically that what is at stake in terms of literary training is the need for the reader to recognize not just that some general "dramatic irony" is at work in the representation of Lurie's dominating narrative, but an ethics and politics that are operative through "the rhetorical signal" that the text makes available to the "active reader" (22). Properly trained, this reader understands that the narrative representation of Lucy is a call to what Spivak terms "counterfocalization."

To my knowledge, the concept of counterfocalization is Spivak's original contribution to narrative studies, and in keeping with my larger argument, it takes for granted the necessary ethico-political nature of novelistic representation. Spivak specifically defines the ethical content of counterfocalization in terms of readerly affect. In contrast to the easy sympathy rhetorically signaled by the reflector-narrator of Lurie's point of view, counterfocalization is defined by its "effortfulness":

This shuttle between focalization and the making of an alternative narrative as the reader's running commentary, as it were, used to be designated by the prim phrase "dramatic irony" when I was an undergraduate. You will see immediately how much more effortful and active this counterfocalization is than what that term can indicate. The provocation into counterfocalization is the "political" in political fiction—the transformation of a tendency into a crisis. (324)

I take the notion of tendency at stake here to be Spivak's way of characterizing the reader's imaginative processing of the dominance of Lurie's perspective as not just emblematic of hegemony but arising from Lurie's own personal affiliation with that hegemony. What seems allowable as a contingency or for a limited amount of time—the dominating view of a reflector-narrator—functions politically to veil the consolidation of power. For the reader to effortfully imagine that a tendency can become a norm is for novelistic narrative to have installed the reader in an ethical journey through which he experiences the effects of hegemony as leading to a political crisis, which fosters in him the need to deploy critical redescription as an act of ethical disruption, a refusal to accept the tendencies of hegemony.

But should we accept Spivak's assertion that counterfocalization bears political value whereas dramatic irony does not? And should we even accept the assumption that somehow it is more effortful to counterfocalize than to detect irony? Once again I see phenomenological claims being made in place of literary historical contingencies. Spivak can make these elevated claims for the political stakes of counterfocalization because her understanding of narrative is completely conditioned by the Jamesian ethics of characterological subjectivity. Counterfocalization is more political because it is related to imagining the personhood of characters, characters as other to their author and characters as other to their narrator. Lucy is subaltern as much because of her narrative position as because of what happens to her in the storyworld. We can see how Spivak extends this novelistic aesthetics of alterity to literature generally. Invoking Martin Luther King Jr.'s endorsement in "Beyond Vietnam" of the "difficult but no less necessary task . . . to speak for those who have been designated as our enemies," Spivak defines the ethical work of fiction as trying "to imagine the other again and again" (23). This she calls "the literary impulse: to imagine the other who does not resemble the self" (23; King qtd. by Spivak).

By refusing to focalize Lucy, by representing her narratively as an enigma, Coetzee distinguishes himself from Lurie (so Spivak implies) by keeping open the possibilities of her personhood—keeping open her personhood as possibility—by avowing both the novel's complicity (any novel's complicity) in the operation of social power: "In the arrangement of counterfocalization within the validating institution of the novel in English, the second half of *Disgrace* makes the subaltern speak, but does not presume to give 'voice,' either to Petrus or Lucy. This is not the novel's failure, but rather a politically fastidious awareness of the limits of its power" (24). The avowal of complicity performs the author's ethical self-binding. Lucy as enigma disrupts "the affective value-system [the patriarchal system of knowing-loving] attached to reproductive heteronormativity as it is accepted as the currency to measure human dignity" (21). She thus stands as "an originary 'nothing,' a scary beginning" (21). The ethical values of this new beginning are so other to Enlightenment liberal values that they defy positive articulation. Lucy's narrative representation as an enigma thus for Spivak highlights the way fiction ethically promotes acts of imagination that are self-consciously speculative, hypothetical, the imagination of possibility. To counterfocalize is to know that Lucy as other cannot be known cognitively, that her otherness defies epistemological certainty, that every act of imagination on her behalf is (as Butler described the working of language itself) a figuration of meaning that demands an equal effort of "dis-figuration" (21).

Mobile self-positioning is thus profoundly for Spivak, as it is for the other theorists I have been discussing, the ethical activity that literature most enables through the self-binding of the reader that it requires. Fiction is an "event," she says, "an indeterminate 'sharing' between writer and reader, where the effort of reading is to taste the impossible status of being figured as object in the web of the other" (18).[63] "The web of the other," the call of the text, the anxiety from estrangement: in all these new ethical paradigms, "sharing" is made possible only by the reader's willingness to submit. If this theory has erotic overtones, they are ones that are, as in a John Donne poem, themselves bound by a religious sensibility. As Spivak herself declares, the readerly experience of voluntary self-binding is nothing less than the manifestation of the "sacred" for a secular world (18)[64]—sacred not just because of the act of gaining righteousness through the abdication of self, but also because of the condition of this ethical revelation: the willingness to hold the belief that literary meaning can be divined, that it broods, visibly invisible, not on Milton's vast abyss but in the concrete particularity of texts. "Literary reading," Spivak asserts, "teaches us to learn from the singular and the unverifiable" (23). And it is the responsible objectification that reading promotes which allows texts themselves to serve as common ground: "The only way a reading establishes itself—without guarantees—is by sharing the steps of the reading. . . . Unless you take a step with me, there will be no interdisciplinarity, only the tedium of turf battles" (23).[65] The "as if" of the novel puts us in touch with the "particular," the singular—and although we then abstract from our experience to generalize about ethical values, to make moral judgments, we learn from fiction that these judgments themselves are as unverifiable as the social world we project through novel reading. "Taking a step with" is to take a leap into the dark: both are predicated on the will to believe in alterity, in the possibility of a law outside and different from the self, the possibility of translation and the limits to translation.[66]

Developed through the Jamesian tradition, the ethics of alterity distinguishes the novel as the secular mode for the sacred social good of honoring otherness. In a mixture of the spiritualism of Virginia Woolf and Wilson Harris with the religious philosophy of Emmanuel Levinas, novelistic aesthetics develops out of modernism and into the contemporary moment as an ethico-political formalism. The novelistic aesthetics of alterity conceptualizes the relation between the novelistic self and the other through a range of possible interpretive positions. The triple nature of novelistic narrative—its allegiance to the characterological life embedded in it, its reflection of the author's ethical capacity, and its function as an element of aesthetic form—has inspired the debates and assumptions about how the novel's ethical nature should best be realized through narrative practice. In arguing for, or in some cases, simply assuming the merit of one of these positions, novel readers tend to make absolute claims about the nature of narrative ethics. A common starting point for understanding the novel's narrative ethics is the notion that the representation of character in the novel is never free from the threat of instrumentality, either from the subjective source of narration or the threat of objectification posed by literary design. As it has been the work of this book to show, out of this notion of narrative power come a variety of different claims about how novelistic narrative accomplishes the ethical achievement of alterity. As we have seen, for some critics fictional characters are produced as "human" precisely by the perceived limitation from both sources that novelistic form places on their autonomy. Fictional characters can be felt to be no different from real human beings to the degree that their functional positionality seems like a restriction of their subjective potentiality, a limit to the full freedom that they have a right to enjoy beyond their representation by and within the novel. This leads some critics to view novelistic narrative is inherently hegemonic, a force that must be countered through ethical response. The all too visible incarceration of subjectivity by artistic design is decried as an abuse of representational power. The author who must more or less use his character for his own expressive ends is felt to be exploitative. The doubleness of novelistic subjectivity (as person, as artistic instrument) is perhaps best emblematized by the novel's third-person narrator, whose subjectivity is constantly imputed as the more than or the excess beyond the functional role as storyteller to which he is bound.

For others, training in the subtlety of novelistic narrative protocols will reveal the novel's ethical response to the circulation of power, through its capacity, in Virginia Woolf's words, to convey the "unknown and uncircumscribed spirit" that defines a human life; in Wilson Harris's words, to "overcome the prison house of natural bias"; or in the Levinasian mode of Spivak's formulation, to "taste the impossible status of being figured as object in the web of the other."[67] In the positive view of ethics as a position of insight, creativity, or self-empowerment that stands outside of the operation of social power, there is also praise for the author who, so some readers feel, uses narrative structure to replicate social structures of reifying otherness in order to make them visible, diagnose them, and make them available for social transformation. There is praise as well for the novelist who is said to use narrative to install the reader in a position of psychological or emotional identification, allowing a privileged intersubjective relation with a social other. For other critics, the achievement of alterity is a more effortful task for the reader to perform. Will the reader respond to the call of the text? Will she open herself up to the imagination of a fictional character that might bring a feeling of endangerment? And what should she regard as the right ethical affect to hold in relation to fictional others? Can "identification" be achieved in some pure state? Or does the trace of the self, either in terms of individual power or social positionality, inflect the quality of identification? Should the reader who identifies with a character worry about emotional colonization? Or, from the opposite emotional perspective, should the reader and author who feel only the aesthetic thrill of a character's fate carry the guilt of the voyeur?

The politics of ethical challenge and possibility that the new ethicists in the academy find in literature generally are at the heart of Henry James's anxious consideration in his prefaces and elsewhere of the lives bound up in his fictions. The aesthetics of alterity allows us to understand the untheorized privileging of novel form that undergirds both the cultural critic's and the ethical theorist's investment in the genre. The new ethical defense of literary value thus importantly casts new light on the development of novelistic aesthetics in the twentieth century. New ethical theory allows us to see that the craft of fiction carries with it a complex and powerful set of cultural values that have been developed through a rich literary history. These values are at play even in timeworn creative writing workshop dicta such as "Show, don't tell," "write about what you know," and "be consistent in the handling of point of view." The new ethical theory also helps us see that what I have elsewhere called the social formalism at the heart of the Jamesian tradition of novel theory—the belief that the novel instantiates social identity through its form—is not a theoretical mistake about the nature of novelistic form but an abiding response to the Jamesian notion of the art of the novel as an ethics of otherness that is carried through the twentieth century and into our own cultural moment by the novelists and novel readers whom James helped to inspire.

CODA
Henry James in the Clinician's Office

THE CONVERGENCE OF the Jamesian novel tradition with poststructuralist new ethical theory has been such a powerful force within the academy that it serves not just as a ground for redisciplinizing the study of literature but also as an inspiration for a whole new interdisciplinary field: narrative medicine. The work of Rita Charon, a leader in Columbia University's graduate program in narrative medicine, has done much to shape this new field. Among the skills she seeks to impart are lessons in ethical alterity that clinicians can learn from Henry James's novels. Charon reports in an interview that the "first time I read Henry James, I'd picked up *The Wings of the Dove* off a pile that someone had thrown away on the Upper West Side. It was in good shape, and it was a hardcover book, and I was on my way to a week at the beach." Opening the book, she found that James wasn't quite the light vacation reading she had sought. His high art project and demanding style required "a serious disciplinary knowledge of, How does writing work? The craft of it."[1] What better allegory could there be for the making and remaking of the value of Jamesian aesthetics? For anyone who thought James's idea of the art of the novel belonged to a past era, that for the contemporary reader the leisured social world he depicts and the difficulty of his terms of representation were so much rubbish, Charon's anecdote suggests instead not just the attraction his work holds for new readers but also the power of his style to make new readers feel that a "disciplinary knowledge" of the art of writing is a requirement for a full understanding of his work. Judged by her contribution to the field of narrative medicine, what Charon has learned from literary experts engaged in the disciplined study of writing is that Jamesian style performs an ethics of alterity.

Beginning with her 1999 dissertation, Charon's career-long engagement with James has been fueled by her belief that the practice of medicine can be crucially improved if clinicians can master the narrative ethics she finds in James's work. Laudably, she wants physicians to treat patients not as objects of medical knowledge but as subjects who demand ethical recognition, who should be treated by the physician with "singularity, humility, accountability, and empathy."[2] Like so many other new ethical theorists, she comes to narrative ethics with the purpose of theorizing a basis for individual efficacy in the face of institutional power.[3] Motivating her work in narrative medicine is her desire to redress the institutionalized hierarchies of power and knowledge—and knowledge as power—in medical practice. Charon believes this reform begins with the medical practitioner understanding the relation to a patient as one of ethical responsibility. Invoking Levinas, Charon describes this relation as a "face to face" encounter: the physician, meeting the patient, is installed in an absolute ethical relation. Heeding the ethical call of that stranger means not just attempting to cure the ailing body but honoring the singularity of that person as an ethical other. Why is narrative the key to this ethical project? As I want to show, Charon believes that James's narrative practice provides a model of virtuous self/other relation that can and should guide interpersonal relations generally, because narrative is in play in any act of telling, oral or written. But she also believes that medical practitioners are also narrative authors through the work they do and therefore that their own narrative practices can benefit from emulating James's narrative methods—which she deems virtuous—and from understanding the virtuous ethical power that she accords to narrative per se, which when effectively mobilized (as James has shown how to do) can profoundly aid the medical practitioner's goal of doing justice to the patient's personhood. In bringing James to the clinician's office, Charon thus follows the new ethical model of deriving absolute ethical value from James's contingent novelistic practice. If noting the tensions in Charon's thinking about narrative ethics stands as a critique of the programmatic use she tries to make of James's ethical aesthetic, it also shows how the extension of Jamesian ethics into the social practice of medicine participates in and keeps alive the family of ideas that make up the Jamesian tradition of novelistic alterity.

What can the medical practitioner learn about ethical alterity from reading Henry James? First of all, the clinician who reads James learns to emulate what Charon understands as James's capacity to know and represent his characters from their own point of view: "The teller or writer is absorbed in the task of understanding, from the inside, the situation of the other. When a writer does it, the other is an imaginary being, a creation, who springs from any number of origins.... When a doctor does it, the other is a relative stranger, generally sick or fearing sickness" ("Perilous Fate," 433). The doctor must strive to achieve "an inside view" by converting the meeting with a new patient into an encounter with the otherness that defines the stranger as an ethical being. As with the other new ethical theorists I have discussed, Charon sees this lesson in alterity performed through James's choice to express his vision of life through and as narrative. Narrative, she believes, holds the absolute virtue of an ethical willingness to "share" personal experience with strangers. James's virtue lies in his artistic ability to make his own experience available for that unknown reader as readerly experience. More specifically, this means for Charon that James is to be credited with the capacity for self-restriction that enables him to express himself best by giving life to characterological others. Charon thus implicitly allies herself with Zadie Smith's Romantic understanding of style as the watermark of authorial identity. But notably, in Charon's formulation, style is generally narrowed down to narrative technique in particular: "The author's style, perhaps more than plot, creates and demonstrates the conditions for . . . representation. The narrative method seems even more revelatory of the aims of the artist than the actual story events or even the metaphors adopted in its telling" ("Perilous Fate," 422).

James's successful authorial performance of ethical alterity sets the standard for Charon's understanding of the conditions for representation performed by James's narrative method. For example, on Charon's interpretation of "The Bench of Desolation," James's narrative enacts a story of virtuous self-restriction through the use it makes of narratorial mediation. Charon notes that in this short story the narrative moves from being highly mediated by the narrator's presence to seeming wholly unmediated. According to Charon, the narrator thus repeats James's standard of authorial alterity: the narrator performs his capacity to be for the other by restricting the desire for self-indulgent self-expression and instead generously serving both the reader and the character by putting their respective personhoods in direct relation. As Charon puts it, "In effect, the teller of 'The Bench of Desolation' *transfigures* himself, rendering himself transparent, so that the reader slowly finds himself or herself in the unmediated presence of the characters, watching them in their dilemmas and also, maybe, accruing valuable experience by *watching*" (425; emphasis in the original). Of course, as I have discussed above, a long line of ethical criticism has faulted James and his characters exactly for their penchant for watching rather than doing, understood by some as voyeurism rather than ethical commitment, by others as occupying the Foucauldian position of surveillance in relation to the characterological subjects James only pretends to make free. But one reason why Charon can credit a positive ethics to this narrative effect is that she implicitly understands it as a materialized achievement of the Levinasian face-to-face ethical encounter. Freed of narratorial mediation, autonomous characters and readers are positioned face-to-face. That the characters do not see the reader's face fits the logic of the Levinasian ethical scene: it is the (readerly) self who is tasked with bringing the other into ethical being, which is to say, with converting physical proximity into ethical recognition. This is also how Charon describes the ethical scene as it unfolds in the clinician's office: one to one with the patient as stranger, the doctor must strive to move from the outside perspective to the inner view. And it is the doctor's own narrative practice that according to Charon can make this transfiguration possible.[4]

How does the doctor as teller or writer—as, in other words, the empowered representor of the patient's point of view—use narrative to bring the otherness of the patient into recognition? Charon's answer might at first seem surprising: the best way to honor the singularity of the patient, the best way to understand the patient from the inside, is by amassing precise medical notation of her bodily functions. Although this idea of seeing with the patient is so different from the usual way of thinking about Jamesian characters as deep, private consciousness, it weirdly extends the notions of embodied alterity shared by other new ethicists, and has especially interesting affinities with J. Hillis Miller's idea of material knowledge as the trace of the encounter with otherness incorporated into the body. In Charon's version, bodily knowledge of the other is available to the doctor through the minute description of a particular person that is made possible through the language of medical measurement and testing:

> Corporeal singularity is nowhere more pronounced and heard than in the clinic: the particularizing measurement of physical components of a patient's body (the concentration of potassium in your serum is 4.1 millimoles per liter); the temporal characterization of repetitive events (the time it takes for depolarization of your cardiac muscle cells is 0.04 seconds); the meticulous accounting for tissues and individual cells in pathological biopsies (your ovarian cancer is

a malignant endometriod epithelial tumor); and the precision of complexly derived visualization of the body (your supraspinatus and infraspinatus tendons are frayed without evidence of full-thickness tear). ("Perilous Fate," 428–429)

Charon asks us to understand these physical measurements as constituting the patient as an ethical being: they establish that "there is only one such person in the universe" (429). The visibility that medical discourse confers on the body accomplishes the ethical act of seeing persons in their full particularity.[5] Charon doesn't spell out the ethical logic here, but if we remember how J. Hillis Miller invoked bodily knowing as an alternative to the dualist conception of personhood, then we might understand Charon as saying that to achieve an inside view of a person is to understand that bodies are not containers for souls but are life forces, signatures of a radically individual way of being and the key to the continuance of this particular life. In Charon's new ethical model, medical data is the language of the other's embodied ethicality. The medical practitioner, trained in this specialized language of embodied otherness, can recognize and honor the patient as ethical other through the narratives he composes that address this language of embodied otherness to others, making this life available "for" other professionals and also "for" the patient as a reader/listener of the story of her embodied singularity.

Significantly for the tradition I am tracing, Charon's approach to James and to ethics more generally intertwines a number of different philosophical sources. In this case, she gets the term "corporeal singularity" from Judith Butler's *Giving an Account of Oneself* (2005).[6] But because Charon fails to grasp the political dimension of Butler's ethical theory, on display as I have shown in Butler's own reading of *Washington Square*, Charon overrates the virtuous alterity of medical description. Is personhood as blood pressure rate really what Butler, following Levinas, has in mind when she defines the other "as fundamentally exposed, visible, seen, existing in a bodily way and of necessity in the domain of appearance" ("Perilous Fate," 427; qtd. from Butler)? As is clear from Butler's interpretation of *Washington Square*, on Butler's Foucauldian view the domain of appearance is constituted by the operation of political power that unevenly distributes social visibility. But Charon seems to understand Butler as saying that any and all domains of appearance possess equal ethicality. Could there be a more vivid example of how the new ethics—interpreted from within the Jamesian novelistic tradition—risks sidestepping rather than solving the problem of Foucauldian determinism? Charon seems to think that the Foucauldian description of medical discourse as a technology for the surveillance and normativization of social identity can be reversed through her redescription of the doctor's chart as the performance of narrative ethics.

Charon is not unaware that the institutionalized protocols of medical care have been the focus of extensive critique: "Now, these gestures may be and usually are taken as reductive assaults on the patient's selfhood." But it is symptomatic of her sense of ethics as existing in a realm apart from politics that she thinks this conflict can be dispensed with simply with a change in point of view: "*They can also be appreciated as singularizing descriptions of this and only this human being*" (429; emphasis in the original). And here we see an unacknowledged Jamesian influence, the influence of Jamesian perspectivalism. Like Zadie Smith in the role of public intellectual that she adopts in *Changing My Mind*, Charon encourages us to think that the political critique of medical knowledge as a discourse of normativization can be dispensed with simply by changing one's mind. Indeed, the call to change is highlighted by Charon's italics. And the call itself is cast in the language of ethical work: medical notation as an ethical art can be appreciated by those—like the Jamesian reader—who have learned the master's lesson, who know and practice the absolute virtue of ethical otherness.

We see in Charon's thinking more generally how the virtue she ascribes to embodied knowing risks displacing and editing out an understanding of narrative as linked to power relations. Although when she interprets James's fictional narratives, as we have seen in her reading of "The Bench of Desolation," Charon is alert to the degree and kind of narratorial mediation that James establishes as a necessary element of narrative ethics, when she reads the narratives that she herself writes in her professional capacity, she accords to narrative per se the virtuous power to make her own experience available "for" her as a reader—in other words, to offer her through narrative the recognition of her own ethicality. Detached from fictional characters, James's notion of narrative alterity now serves as a privileged mode for self-apprehension, specifically for insight into the way one's body performs ethical alterity outside and beyond one's rational understanding. Here's Charon's description of rereading a medical report she had written:

> When I described the office visit with the elderly woman, I *placed* myself bodily with her. I found myself describing our spatial relations, specifying, for example,

that I was on my knees in front of her. Only on rereading it did I realize that I put myself on my knees twice in the short description . . . emphasizing the meanings of being on one's knees in front of another—worship, service, awe. I recognized myself as embodied in her presence—on my knees, using my hands on her feet" ("Novelization," 40; emphasis in the original).

The medical report surprises Charon with a vision of her own ethical action: rereading her narrative, she now sees that her appointment with the patient as stranger became a face-to-face encounter with ethical otherness that she unknowingly performed through and as bodily knowing. Implied in this analysis is that the medical report, as narrative, carries with it an intrinsic ethical power: it makes visible—in this case offers to self-apprehension, to Charon as the reader of her own work—her virtuous act of embodied recognition, bestowed upon the patient as ethical other. As Charon has described it, narrative is the virtuous embodiment of alterity: it offers her as reader a place to view her past action, and through its methods of depiction, it also makes available for self-apprehension a view of one's own body, which cannot be witnessed in the moment of performance. Charon's understanding of her bodily performance as a virtuous emplacement thus literalizes, by physicalizing, Elizabeth Costello's notion of the ethics of alterity as an imaginative emplacement. Narrative seems so fully to do justice to the ethics of alterity, conceived as bodily knowing, that Charon's "recognition" of herself as an ethical agent need not consider the political and cultural construction of the body that dictates who can touch whom in the clinician's office, who might be clothed and who unclothed. Charon might be on her knees, in a posture that evokes in her the ethical emotions of worship, service, and awe, but to feel the virtue of this self-restriction, this subordination of the self to the good of the other, is also not to be the medical authority dictating the terms of the patient/doctor relation, a relation governed by institutional policies and legal codes. But on Charon's view of narrative ethics, the impersonal forces that mediate social relations more generally disappear with the closing of the door of the consulting room.

Charon's theory of narrative medicine thus imbibes James's formalism along with his ethics of alterity. Indeed, Charon's notion of the ethical otherness that narrative makes available (and the strangers to whom its ethics of alterity are addressed) is grounded in her understanding of social relations and material forces as radically restricted in nature and effect, even while at the same time

Charon endorses the idea of ethical power as limitless. We can see this balance in play in her interpretation of a key scene from *The Golden Bowl*, the scene when Maggie negotiates her ethical relation to Charlotte:

> In the same way that insulin's effect on one liver cell is amplified to influence the whole body and, in rippling effects, the family and the workplace and the society, the effects that occur between characters ripple outward in discernible, albeit diffusing, arcs of change. Mightn't the events on the terrace influence not only Maggie and Charlotte but also their extended family, the city of London, or even the stratified class structure of late capitalism? *Hors texte*, James's novel and, indeed, his whole oeuvre influences Western civilization's concept of gender roles, the institution of marriage, the status of the novel. ("Novelization," 45).

Charon is making here a general case for ethics as a social and political force even as she includes as part of her case the particular power *The Golden Bowl* has to "influence Western civilization's concept of gender roles, the institution of marriage, [and] the status of the novel." These are high stakes indeed, but even if we were to accept them (along with the monolithic conceptualization of Western civilization that is operative here), it seems harder to grant the assumption that this rippling effect flows only in one direction: outward from the face-to-face encounter and outward from one novel to the whole world. Acknowledgment of the stratified class structure and the operation of gender roles impedes neither Charon's sense of Jamesian narrative as a triumph of achieved alterity nor her faith in the "mutual transformations undergone by our patient and doctor in the course of their clinical encounter" ("Novelization," 45).

In the same way that Charon is aware that she needs at least to acknowledge that class structure, gender roles, and medical notation have been regarded as political and cultural restrictions to the voluntary self-restriction of ethical otherness (even if only to sidestep this counter-position), so too as a James scholar she feels the need to address the enduring ethical criticism of James, especially the view that equates his investment in the art of the novel with self-directed gratification rather than other-oriented ethical accomplishment. Charon defends James from this charge by again appealing to her ripple model of ethical effects: "Unlike the hermetic model of art, which holes up the artist in his or her own private aesthetics, James's art forms a bridge from the work to the world, to the universe, and, ultimately, to other human contacts with whom to share what he sees, making him grateful toward and dependent on the readers who agree to accept what is offered" ("Perilous Fate," 428). This formulation vivifies the extravagant discrepancy between narrative as the limited place for a delimited social encounter (the ethical encounter with otherness staged as the relation between author, narrator, character, and reader) and the limitless social effects that Charon accords this narrative experience. James, sitting in his study, can transfigure not just the world but the whole universe, and he can do this through the way he has mobilized the ethical power inherent in narrative to "share what he sees," making that personal vision of life available for all who come into embodied "contact" with the life that his novels both contain and perform.

The bridge from the work to the world is, of course, exactly what the academic discipline of narrative medicine is devoted to constructing. In Charon's hands, the Jamesian novel first bridges English departments (the repository of disciplinized professional training) and medical schools, and then, on a larger scale, the academy and the social locations of medical practice: the hospital, the consulting room. More often than not, Charon describes this bridge in terms of a repetition: the lesson learned in English departments about the art of narrative ethics can be handed over to medical students, who then practice that lesson upon their patients. But within this repetition Charon performs revisions that reflect the distinctive way that her version of new ethical theory occludes the power of social forces. For example, in *Narrative Medicine* (2006), Charon's elaboration of the ethicality that inheres in narrative resonates with Toni Morrison's description of the ethical "danger zones" that Morrison seeks as a reader and writer of fiction:

> The narrative impulse does not evacuate the unknown beyond recognition. It does not sanitize it of danger; it does not consign it to sameness with other such predicaments. . . . It celebrates the uniqueness and respects the unity of the event while representing it. Expansive rather than restrictive, multiplying possibilities instead of reducing them, narrative practices enable the observer or the participant to live in the face of contingency without trying to eradicate it. Writing and reading are, in the end, expeditions into the mysterious, potentially dangerous, uncharted continent of the contingent. (50)

While Charon's championing of "expeditions into the mysterious, potentially dangerous, uncharted continent" echoes Toni Morrison's praise for the "risk" that characters as ethical others pose for her as a writer and reader of fiction,

Charon's notion of risk seems far more reduced than Morrison's. Confronting the hitherto unknown or attempting to approximate what is ultimately unknowable are for Charon ethical tasks that, as we have seen, are solved by narrative—by the ethical "impulse" that she believes resides in narrative and ultimately through the absolute value that she assigns to "writing and reading" any and all modes of narrative, not just novelistic narratives that depict fictional social others in a social world. Whatever expedition is taken into the unknown, narrative's power to stage the "recognition of our common concerns and shared goals" provides the terms of a happy ending. Doctor and patient, patient and doctor, are "storytellers all, bearing witness to one another's ideals, celebrating our common heritage as listeners around the campfire, creating our identities in the stories we tell" (11). The figure of the campfire reflects Charon's belief that ethics inheres in narrative per se rather than in relation to the social conditions in which storytelling occurs (and in this regard vividly contrasts with Walter Benjamin's notion of the storyteller).[7] It is the "magic" (her word) of story that creates "uncanny intimacy" between doctor and patient (48, 55). It is precisely because her model of narrative alterity fails to take into account the social conditions that it celebrates (locality, particularity, situatedness, contingency, etc.) that it enables Charon to locate our "common heritage" in a campfire scene: the campfire is her figure for the primacy of storytelling as not just a human but a humanizing act. But where is this campfire? Who gets to speak first? Who gets to sit at the fire? What counts as a story for those assembled? The absence of these social specifications enables a staggering formulation of nonhistorical, noncultural self-fashioning: we "create our identities in the stories we tell" (11).

Even with such an absolute and capacious sense of narrative's ethical value, Charon still makes a special case for reading what she calls "great literary texts." To bear witness to another's ideals is the common starting place for storytelling, but apparently clinicians need more specialized training in the complex techniques of storytelling if they are to appreciate the full gift of the patient's identity, conveyed as a story to the doctor and then re-represented as the doctor's story.[8] But we can see how a statement about literary interpretation as a discipline—"Close reading takes practice, skill, and long experience with many texts" (x)—modulates into a claim about close reading as itself an ethical act: "We introduce them to great literary texts and give them the tools *to make authentic contact* with works of fiction, poetry, and drama" (x; emphasis in the original).⁹ Close reading (for Charon as for J. Hillis Miller) is not just a mode of interpretation but the way the reader can see the other that is the literary text. The New Critical injunction against paraphrase is thus reproduced as the new ethical valuing of representational particularity and specificity. Once again ethical otherness hovers between a notion of spiritual singularity (authentic contact) and liberal humanist, individualizing detailing.

But when Charon isn't reading James, it isn't clear that close reading is the method she herself employs. In *Narrative Medicine*, great literary texts are primarily quoted for the wisdom they hold. Charon finds that canonical literary authors—John Donne, William Carlos Williams, Leo Tolstoy, James Joyce, and T. S Eliot—express ethical beliefs that coincide with her own. Since many of the quotations she uses are from poetry, we can only conclude that the narrative ethics of "great literature" lies in its ability to express beautifully and poignantly well-worn sentiments—a safe return to the familiar rather than a voyage to the unknown. Thus we learn of Holy Sonnet Ten: "In stripping poor death of its haughtiness, Donne achieves an expansiveness of life despite its measured end. If 'soonest our best men with thee do go,' then we who go, including my patient, are also of the best" (35). And of *The Four Quartets*: "T. S. Eliot's 'still point of the turning world' indeed refers to the timelessness within the shell of time that, perhaps, best explains the sick person's dwelling in temporality" (44).

Charon's approach to literature thus does not provide narrative medicine with a philosophically viable theory of literature's absolute ethical value but models for general readers the value that literature holds as a repository of ethical wisdom. The insights into the human condition that Charon finds in literary texts, if taken to heart, might make the doctor/patient relationship more humane, might set a personalized standard of care and lead to a program of training that could result in long-term institutional reform. But as it has been the work of this book to demonstrate, for authors, readers, and professional literary critics alike the defense of literary value mounted through the Jamesian ethics of alterity is less about the success of robust philosophical arguments and more about the novel becoming generically legible by the cultural construction of its narrative ethics of alterity. To dismiss either Charon's understanding of James or Levinasian ethics more generally as merely "pious discourse"—the term is from Alain Badiou's critique of Levinas—would be to miss the way the ethics of alterity defines a literary tradition that has spanned a century, includes a diversity of writers, and encompasses a variety of narrative modes.[10] When Charon makes the case for the achievement of the ethical good of otherness, in and outside of literary texts, from the English department to the clinician's office, her thought carries forward the salient features of the tradition. The uneasy logic, the switches in perspective from writer to reader, the appeal to the objectifying power of narrative, the larger instability and contradiction in the way that materiality is conceptualized, the confusion as to whether otherness as an ethical good constitutes a spiritual state or social condition: these tensions are precisely what distinguish the Jamesian novel tradition from pious discourse—and from any type of programmatic or systematic position-taking. In this tradition the ethics of alterity is a problem to be addressed, actively confronted by characters in the storyworld, by novelists who attempt to honor their characters' personhood and by readers who, even if they are not ethically improved by the novels they read, have learned to regard the lives novels seem to hold and seem to be as ethical others.

Notes

Preface

1. For example, do David Comer Kidd and Emanuele Castano really present us with important findings when they conclude from their 2013 empathy study that "whereas many of our mundane social experiences may be scripted by convention and informed by stereotypes, those presented in literary fiction often disrupt our expectations"? Kidd and Castano admit that their study does not "fully capture the concept of literariness, which includes among others, aesthetic and stylistic matters not addressed in this research." But while Kidd and Castano seem confident that the qualities of literariness can be distinguished from the ethical operations of literary fiction, they simultaneously assume literariness as a distinguishing feature of their archive. What they don't seem to recognize is how they have in advance of their empirical findings assumed that what defines literary fiction as literary is its ethical power. Their operative assumption is that literary fiction distinguishes itself from popular fiction and nonfiction through the techniques that literary fiction uses to "expand our knowledge of others' lives, helping us recognize our similarity to them" and thus reducing "the strangeness of others" ("Reading Fiction Improves Theory of Mind," 377). We can see the mutually supporting nature of sociological and literary study in a follow-up report on Kidd and Castano for the *New York Times* (Belluck, "For Better Social Skills, Scientists Recommend a Little Chekhov"). When asked their opinion of Kidd and Costano's findings, professors of literature overwhelmingly regarded them as happy confirmation of what they already know about literary fiction, rather than as findings that "disrupt" or alter their own expectations (pars. 21–22). In a follow-up opinion piece for the *Times*, Gregory Currie points to the uncontroversial nature of the assumption that "exposure to challenging works of literary fiction is good for us" and asks, "Why would anyone need evidence for something so obviously right?" ("Does Great Literature Make Us Better People?," pars. 1–2).

2. Tellingly, Kidd and Castano cite M. M. Bakhtin and Roland Barthes as authorities for their view of literary fiction as fostering readerly participation (and thereby Theory of Mind) without taking into account the ways that both of these theorists have also been

interpreted as theorizing the limits of not just empathy but the centered subjectivity upon which the notion of empathy depends.

3. For other recent critical studies of ethics as a narrative practice, see Berman, *Modernist Commitments*; Childs and Green, *Aesthetics and Ethics in Twenty-First Century British Novels*; Glowacka and Boos, *Between Ethics and Aesthetics*; Hughes, *Ethics, Aesthetics, and the Beyond of Language*; Jottkandt, *Acting Beautifully*; Larson, *Ethics and Narrative in the English Novel, 1880–1914*; Levinson, *Aesthetics and Ethics*; Masters, *Novel Style*; Öztürk, *Evolutionary Aesthetics of Human Ethics in Hardy's Tragic Narratives*; and Serpell, *Seven Modes of Uncertainty*.

4. On the lyric as apostrophe, see Jonathan Culler's *Theory of the Lyric* and Barbara Johnson's "Apostrophe, Animation, and Abortion."

5. Terry Eagleton provides an excellent example of a critic whose view of the novel as a genre recapitulates the sense of both the limitlessness and the restriction that I am describing. In his introduction to *The English Novel*, Eagleton asserts that the novel as a genre can be anything at all, that "there seems to be nothing it cannot do," that its anarchic nature "cannibalizes other literary modes and mixes the bits and pieces promiscuously together" (1). But in the English tradition that is the topic of his study, the novel's limitless generic possibility is self-restricted to the protocols of the realist novel and the premium it places on the representation of characters within a social world.

6. See Ross, "Modernist Ethics, Critique, and Utopia" for an alternative view of the nature of modernist ethics. Following Max Horkheimer and Theodor Adorno, Ross argues, "I presume and argue for a fundamental ethics to modernism: modernism was a fundamentally ethical set of projects, even when specific modernists disagreed with one another over the specific content of the ethics they sought. In this regard, my reading is somewhat at odds both with older understandings of high modernism as amoral and with the more recent critical models that have concentrated on restoring the full breadth of modernist cultural production" (49). See also Berman, *Modernist Commitments*, who similarly draws on Adorno but qualifies his understanding of modernism: "Though [Adorno's] theory helps us understand the possibilities of a noninstrumental politics, the way back to the world that emerges out of radically experimental texts, and the potential for critique in the fractured forms and languages of many varieties of modernism, it posits the work's autonomy and its disengagement from reality as a first principle. As I have argued, literary modernism knits together aesthetics and the ethico-political experience of modernity so that the world becomes the problematic to be addressed, transformed, configured, and reconfigured, rather than refused" (25–26).

7. For example, although Henry James uses "ethics" and "morals" as synonyms in his review of J. W. Cross's 1885 biography of Eliot, "moral" and "morality" are by far the preferred terms to describe what James sees as Eliot's didactic tendencies: "the author's

general attitude in regard to the novel, which for her, was not primarily a picture of life, capable of deriving a high value from its form, but a moralized fable, the last word of a philosophy endeavoring to teach by example" (50). By contrast, the transitional sense of "morality" to an ethics of novelistic form is reflected in James's statement that "the essence of moral energy is to survey the whole field, and I should . . . say not that the English novel has a purpose, but that it has a diffidence. To what degree a purpose in a work of art is a source of corruption I shall not attempt to inquire; the one that seems to me least dangerous is the purpose of making a perfect work" ("Art of Fiction," 25).

8. James's deep admiration for Eliot always struggled with his exasperation at what he calls "the absence of free aesthetic life." See James's review of Cross's biography (esp. 49–52) and also James's review of *Middlemarch*, in which he declares that novel "a treasure-house of details but . . . an indifferent whole" (424).

9. Hale, *Social Formalism*, 22.

10. Fowles, *The French Lieutenant's Woman*, 96.

11. Proust, *In Search of Lost Time*, vol. 1: *Swann's Way*, 91.

12. Ibid., 92. See Genette, *Narrative Discourse*, 175–186.

13. In her interview with Smith for *The Telegraph*, Gaby Wood ends her brief summary of Smith's family biography by emphasizing the close temporal connection between Smith's name change and her reading of *Their Eyes Were Watching God*: "[Zadie was] a studious girl and precocious author of sonorous words (at 14, around the time her mother gave her Zora Neale Hurston to read, she changed her name from Sadie to Zadie)" ("The Return of Zadie Smith," par. 23).

Chapter 1: The New Ethics and Contemporary Fiction

1. Marilynne Robinson develops her notion of the ethics of alterity throughout her essays and interviews. For example, in a 2006 conversation with Sarah Flynn, Thomas King, and Adam O'Connor Rodriguez, she describes the origin of *Gilead* (2004): "I have a very strong imagination of John Ames that was generated by the fact that I thought of him as a voice in my head. I was surprised to have a male narrator. I trusted this voice. I felt as if someone were speaking" (88). In a 2008 interview with the *Paris Review*, Robinson advocates for the ethical treatment of characterological personhood: "I don't believe in exploiting or treating with disrespect even an imagined person" ("Art of Fiction, No. 198").

2. Wallace, "*E Unibus Pluram*," 81.

3. For critical studies of the "new sincerity" ushered in by Wallace, see Balliro, *The New Sincerity in American Literature*; Fitzgerald, *Not Your Mother's Morals*; and Kelly, "Dialectic of Sincerity" and "The New Sincerity." For a dramatic treatment, see Alena Smith's play *The New Sincerity*.

4. Woolf, "Narrow Bridge of Art," 13. Robinson's statements about novelistic technique establish the link between contemporary and modernist views of the novel's protean style and also indicate how an ethics of alterity grounds that style. In conversation with Flynn and others, Robinson states, "I always tell my students that you can do anything you can get away with, that implausibility is a problem of style" (79). She adds, "The most successful third-person writers break all the rules" (93). In the *Paris Review*, she elaborates that the best narrative style is that which makes the novel a living form: "I don't try to teach technique, because frankly most technical problems go away when a writer realizes where the *life* of a story lies ("Art of Fiction, No. 198"; emphasis added).

5. This chapter focuses on the contemporary novelist's view of character as a problem of ethical alterity. Chapter 5 links the ethical turn in the academy specifically to the Jamesian investment in the ethics of characterological representation. But it should be noted here, at the outset of my study, that the renewed critical interest in character more generally is noted by Rita Felski in her introduction to the 2011 special issue of *New Literary History* that includes essays by Sarah Ahmed, Amanda Anderson, Catherine Gallagher, Suzanne Keen, Julian Murphet, Andrea Sauchelli and Paisley Livingstone, and Murray Smith. Felski observes that *NLH* last took up the problem of character in 1974. Since then, she states, a "conception of a core selfhood imbued with a moral and social typology had been dissolved in the acid bath of critical theory, or superseded by linguistic and performative theories of identity," which led literary critics to abandon the study of character. She accounts for the revival of character as a topic of critical interest through the slow development of a new "conviction that literary character can disclose rather than disguise; that, via the specifics of its formal shaping, it offers otherwise unattainable insights into the historical inflection of personhood" as well as insight into "our intellectual curiosity about, and emotional attachment to, people who do not exist" (v–vi).

Felski rightly singles out Alex Woloch's *The One vs. the Many* as offering a new formal theory of character that has inspired its own school of criticism. Woloch's project has appealed to so many in part because it brings together ideological theories of novel form with narratological approaches. On the one hand, Woloch brings forward and develops in his own terms Jameson's notion of a politicized narrative character system in *The Political Unconscious* (see esp. 166–179). On the other hand, Woloch explicitly describes his approach as contributing to the formal description of novelistic narrative pursued by narratology. In self-statements such as "My interpretative method rests above all in the combination of two new narratological categories which I will formulate and continually return to: *character-space* (that particular and charged encounter between an individual human personality and a determined space and position within the narrative as a whole) and the *character-system* (the arrangement of multiple and differentiated character-spaces—differentiated configurations and manipulations of the human figure—into a unified narrative structure)" (14), we can see how Woloch implicitly draws on Vladimir Propp's structuralist study of character to establish common ground between Jamesonian Marxism and narratological formalism (see Jameson's discussion of Propp's *Morphology of the Folk Tale* [1928] in *The Political Unconscious* [119–129]). As I discuss in the next chapter, Jameson's ideological theory of novelistic narrative as objectifying the political unconscious and Woloch's theory of character-space as politically structured both stand as an example of a claim I make at the end of this chapter: that contemporary theories of narrative when applied to nineteenth-century novels establish an aesthetics of form grounded in the value of otherness (in Woloch's case, characters as having a right to the full representation of their full human personality; for Jameson, the ability of some novelists more than others to construct socially symbolic narratives expressive of the class dialectic of their historical moment).

See Marta Figlerowicz's *Flat Protagonists* for an example of the innovative thinking that Woloch's work has inspired. Figlerowicz identifies an Anglo-European novel tradition (Aphra Behn, Isabelle de Charrière, Françoise de Graffigny, Thomas Hardy, and Marcel Proust) whose central characters "represented self-expression and ties to others contract and simplify over the course of a novel. . . . Their behaviors are increasingly stereotypical and predictable, and their means of responsiveness and expression progressively diminish, until other characters no longer even contradict, but simply disregard, what they say" (2). See also Kitzinger, "Illusion and Instrument."

To appreciate the way Woloch's approach to narratology differs from the rhetorical approach developed out of Wayne Booth's work and the Chicago School more generally, see James Phelan's *Living to Tell about It* and Katherine Saunders Nash's *Feminist Narrative Ethics*.

Maria DiBattista's *Novel Characters* is on the leading edge of the critical trend that Felski describes. DiBattista emphasizes a key quality in the Jamesian tradition I am tracing: the portrayal of characters as expressions and representations of the uniqueness of human beings, especially of their creativity and capacity to surprise: "Novelistic characters in particular are notorious for defying as much as fulfilling our expectations and hopes for them. We need to acknowledge and accept this fact about them—that they would not be novelistic characters if they did not possess and exercise their capacity to surprise—including the capacity to surprise themselves. This capacity for surprise is a measure of their freedom *as* novelistic characters" (10; emphasis in the original).

6. Robbe-Grillet, "On Several Obsolete Notions," 28.

7. Roland Barthes, *S/Z*, 95. Robbe-Grillet defines the contemporary period as one of "administrative numbers," an economic transformation that, on his view, reflects that "the world's destiny has ceased, for us, to be identified with the rise or fall of certain men,

of certain families," and also that "the exclusive cult of the 'human' has given way to a larger consciousness, one that is less anthropocentric" (29).

8. Dominic Head, thinking skeptically about the academic formation of the new ethical criticism, observes that "the novel has, surely, always been a crucible for the investigation of the self, and for examining the relationship between self and other, and between private and public realms" (*Ian McEwan*, 15). There could not be a truer statement, but it misses the modernist equation of this characterological dimension of the novel with a new ethics of narrative form.

9. Jessica Berman's *Modernist Commitments* provides a paradigmatic understanding of the modern novel's narrative ethics of alterity. She argues, "In narrative we put ethics into play and begin to imagine justice, acting to generate and respond to the social relationships and obligations that shape the future of our common world. The ethical demands of alterity infuse the narrative situation and the process by which we attempt to respond to it even as the narrative itself takes place as an ethical event between writers and readers that responds to, intervenes in, and changes its rhetorical and social situation" (6).

10. Over the course of the twentieth century, the notion that novelistic narrative objectifies the "real" becomes the basis for a more self-conscious understanding of novel form as an ethics of alterity. Different critical schools have, of course, offered various accounts of how novel form instantiates the real. But whether theorized at the outset of novel theory as the recovery of perception (Shklovsky, "Art as Technique," 12) or the social heteroglossia of novelistic language (Bakhtin, "Discourse in the Novel"); or after midcentury, as the writerly play of signification (Barthes, *S/Z*, 4) or the political unconscious (Jameson, *Political Unconscious*, 13); whether attributed to the cultural difference represented through the storyworld (Appiah, *Ethics of Identity*: "By follow[ing] a narrative and conjur[ing] a world, . . . we learn about the extraordinary diversity of human responses to our world and the myriad points of intersection of those various responses" [258]) or the technical capacity of narrative fiction to represent other minds (Palmer, *Fictional Minds*; Young, *Imagining Minds*; Zunshine, *Why We Read Fiction*) or the "unnatural" nature of fictionality, the real that is revealed through the novel has become more and more allied with the novel's privileged capacity to "approximate and conceptualize Otherness" (Alber and Heinze, introduction to *Unnatural Narratives*, 2).

11. See Elias, "Postmodern Metafiction," for a useful overview of the modes and varieties of American metafiction (esp. 18–24 for her situation of John Barth's oeuvre in this tradition). See Widiss, *Obscure Invitations*, for an important account of how twentieth-century American novels resist the death of the author.

12. This first chapter takes up this literary history from the novelist's point of view. To appreciate how developments in criticism respond to the contemporary writer's renewed concern with ethical character, we can note the shift in Catherine Gallagher's theory of

fiction, which is first developed as a historical argument that views fiction as a cultural invention that begins in the need to develop fictional characters as an authorial protection against the libel laws instituted in eighteenth-century England (*Nobody's Story*, 92–137), but later is framed as a philosophical description of the "ontological lack" that Gallagher now claims distinguishes fictional characters from the representation of "known historical figures" in novels ("What Would Napoleon Do?," 317–318). For another important recent critical theory of characterological ontology, see Ruttenburg, "The Human Document" (and my discussion of her argument in note 17 of Chap. 4).

13. James, *Psychology*, 168.

14. Jameson, *Political Unconscious*, 221. For Jameson's more recent formulation of the reification he takes to be inherent in Jamesian point of view and modernism more generally, see *Antinomies of Realism*, 21–26, 181–186.

15. Elizabeth Strout qtd. in Levy, "Elizabeth Strout's Long Homecoming."

16. Kingsolver, "Dave Eggers's New Novel," par. 9.

17. As I will discuss in Chapter 5, alterity has become popularized as a term for otherness owing to the school of new ethical thought derived from Emmanuel Levinas's body of work. But my point here is that through popular usage the term has expanded to include a family of ideas about otherness as manifested in and as novel form that connect with an older twentieth-century novelistic view of ethical otherness. For the Levinasian source of the term, see especially his *Alterity and Transcendence*, *Ethics and Infinity*, *Otherwise than Being*, and *Totality and Infinity*. Jacques Derrida develops the deconstructive potential of Levinasian ethics and in doing so becomes a crucial influence for the return to ethics within the academy. See especially *Adieu: To Emmanuel Levinas*; *The Animal That Therefore I Am* (e.g., "Nothing will have ever given me more food for thinking through this absolute alterity of the neighbor or of the next(-door) than these moments when I see myself seen naked under the gaze of a cat" [11]); *Ethics, Institutions, and the Right to Philosophy*; and *The Gift of Death and Literature in Secret* (esp. 82–116).

For strong examples of the expansion of the Levinasian/Derridean notion of alterity, see Baudrillard and Guillaume, *Radical Alterity*; Cornell, *Philosophy of the Limit*; Critchley, *Ethics of Deconstruction* and *Ethics, Politics, Subjectivity*; Eaglestone, *Ethical Criticism*; and Glowacka and Boos, introduction to *Between Ethics and Aesthetics*. Glowacka and Boos trace the French development of Levinasian ethics through Jean-François Lyotard, Jean-Luc Nancy, Maurice Blanchot, and Jacques Derrida and characterize that French poststructuralist project as a search for "ways to articulate the exteriority that transcends thought itself and therefore remains nonrepresentable" (3).

For strong examples of the application of the Levinasian/Derridean notion of alterity to literary texts, see Avelar, *Letter of Violence*; Black, *Fiction across Borders*; Herbrechter,

Lawrence Durrell; Hollander, *Narrative Hospitality*; Nealon, *Alterity Politics*; Rainsford and Woods, *Critical Ethics*; Reynier and Ganteau, *Ethics of Alterity*; and Rospide and Sorlin, *Ethics and Poetics of Alterity*.

Although the Levinasian/Derridean tradition is most important for new ethical literary criticism, the term "alterity" also has a significant Anglo-Protestant religio-humanist provenance. An *OED* search reveals that as early as 1642 Henry More used the term in his *Psychodia Platonica*: "O life of Time, and all Alterity!'" (second stanza). In volume 3 of his *History of Philosophy*, Thomas Stanley writes: "The Maker of all things took Union and Division, and Identity, and Alterity, and Station and Motion to compleat the soul" (53). "Alterity" also occurs in George Berkeley's *Siris . . . Virtues of Tar-Water*, 161; and Coleridge's *Table-Talk*: "In the Trinity there is, 1. Ipseity. 2. Alterity. 3. Community," 86. A 1934 translation of Plato's *Parmenides* by A. E. Taylor includes the more object-oriented definition: "*Alterity*, the character of being . . . a thing which is diverse from something else" (101).

In the psychoanalytic context, some of the earliest instances can be found in Jacques Lacan's work. See especially "Aggressiveness in Psychoanalysis" and "Introduction and Reply to Jean Hyppolite's Presentation of Freud's *Verneinung*," but the term is used throughout the essays assembled in *Écrits*. See also Julia Kristeva, *Desire in Language*, and Luce Irigaray, *To Be Two*, for the development of "alterity" within psychoanalytic feminist theory.

18. In an early review of *Atonement* ("Who's Afraid of Influence?"), Geoff Dyer makes the case for Woolf being the primary influence in this highly allusive novel. Dyer understands McEwan's self-conscious engagement with the modern novel as "creatively extending and hauling a defining part of the British literary tradition up to and into the twenty-first century." Ann Marie Adams, in "Mr. McEwan and Mrs. Woolf," notes that the relation of contemporary novelists to the modernists has been underrecognized because "extended references to modernist works are assumed to be homages, an assumption that does little to help a critic explain how a novel like McEwan's [her example is *Saturday*] could criticize what it also seeks to recover in Woolf's writing" (550). For a discussion of McEwan in relation to modernist novels beyond Woolf, see Finney, "Briony's Stand" (esp. 71–72). See also Robinson, "The Modernism of Ian McEwan's *Atonement*," for a comparison of *Atonement* with Henry James's *What Maisie Knew* (484–487). Robinson describes the inheritance from James specifically in terms of ethical subjectivism: "*Atonement* particularly benefits from *What Maisie Knew* in exploring the idea that 'point of view' is not a merely visual perspectivism but a moral way of looking at the world—and thus one that can be exploited" (484).

19. See, for example, Belluck, "For Better Social Skills, Scientists Recommend a Little Chekhov"; Currie, "Does Great Literature Make Us Better People?"; Fassler's interview

with Marilynne Robinson, "Marilynne Robinson on Democracy, Reading, and Religion in America"; and Zalewski, "Background Hum."

20. Niedzviecki, "Winning the Appropriation Prize" (qtd. in Schuessler, "Editor Resigns").

21. George Eliot to Charles Bray, July 4, 1859, in *The George Eliot Letters*, 3:111; emphasis in the original.

22. Eliot, *Middlemarch*, 175. In "*Middlemarch* and Everybody," Zadie Smith explicitly draws the connection among Eliot's ethics of characterological perspectivalism, the influence Eliot's narrative method had on Henry James, and Smith's own novelistic project—and she cites this famous passage from *Middlemarch* as representing the crux of the literary tradition she is tracing (30). See Chapter 3 for further discussion of how this essay links Smith and James.

23. As Raymond Williams astutely argues in *The Country and the City*, "George Eliot extends the plots of her novels to include the farmers and the craftsmen, and also the disinherited. But just as she finds it difficult to individuate working people—falling back on a choral mode, a generalising description or an endowment with her own awkwardly translated consciousness—so she finds it difficult to conceive whole actions which spring from the substance of these lives and which can be worked through in relation to their interests" (173).

24. See Michaels, *Shape of the Signifier*. In Michaels's example, people who do not believe in Islam treat those who do believe in Islam not as if "they have false beliefs" but as social others, fundamentally different from themselves. "People who *believe* differently are treated as people who *are* different" (171; emphasis in the original).

25. In 2014, *Every Day* was required reading for all students at the Bentley Upper School, Lafayette, California.

26. Levithan, *Every Day*, 1.

27. Jen, *Tiger Writing*, 96.

28. In *Fiction across Borders*, Shameem Black argues that Jen mobilizes her comic sense as a novelistic technique of alterity: "Although her fiction addresses serious and sometimes even tragic subjects, Jen's distinctive prose style finds something to laugh at within even the most troubled circumstances of modern life. In continually returning to a comic mode, Jen suggests that humor comprises a necessary aspect of her border-crossing fiction. As she invites us to laugh at and with her characters as they develop their distinctive crowded selves, she uses comedy not to satirically undermine their performances of alterity but to satirically endorse them" (119).

29. *A Sensation Novel* was first performed on January 30, 1871, and first published in 1912. Its music was composed not by Arthur Sullivan but by Thomas German Reed, and then new music was later added by "Florian Pascal," pseudonym for Joseph Williams Jr.

30. Gilbert, *A Sensation Novel*, 52.

31. Ibid.

32. In the passage from which the play takes its title, we can see how the director as a socially empowered authority figure is also an ontological equal (i.e., possessing personhood no different from that of the actors) and thus functions as a diminished substitute for the lost narrative author whose representational task locates character identity within a structure of value:

> **Usher** [*timidly*]: There are some people here asking for you.
> [*The* **Director** *and the* **Actors** *are amazed as they look down from the stage into the audience.*]
> **Director** [*again in a rage*]: But this is a rehearsal. And certainly you know that during rehearsals no one is allowed in. [*Addressing himself to the rear.*] Who are you, please? What can I do for you?
> **Father** [*coming forward, followed by the others, as far as one of the two staircases*]: We are here in search of an author.
> **Director** [*confused and angry*]: An author? What author?
> **Father**: Any author, sir.
> **Director**: But there's no author here. We are not rehearsing a new play.
> (Pirandello, *Six Characters*, 11)

33. Lukács, *Theory of the Novel*, 41.

34. For recent treatments of Eliot's narratorial sympathy and its limits, see Argyos, "Without Any Check of Proud Reserve"; Fulmer, *George Eliot's Moral Aesthetic*; Greiner, *Sympathetic Realism*; and Nunning, "'The Extension of Our Sympathies.'"

35. Jen, *Tiger Writing*, 6.

36. Ibid., 62.

37. Ibid., 59.

38. See Chen and Yu, "The Parallax Gap," for a Žižekian approach to Jen's representation of otherness in *The Love Wife*. While Chen and Yu pose the problem of otherness in terms of perspective—"The truth of the very gap between Blondie and Lan is one of parallax: they appear different due simply to a gap in perspectives" (396)—their reading of the novel somewhat surprisingly does not explore the relationship between Jen's narrative methods and her otherness project. Perhaps this is due to the critical tendency to solve the literary problem of representing alterity through the systematics of critical theory, in this case through the application of "Slavoj Žižek's notion of Pauline Love" (396).

39. For example, we can see the strong vocal continuum Jen establishes between Carnegie and Lan in the cross-cutting between the characters' interior monologues that

breaks from the control of Carnegie's first-person interior monologue into dialogue that more resembles the lyricism of Woolf's *The Waves* than the dramatic mode of "Nighttown" in Joyce's *Ulysses*, but refers back equally to both modernist experiments:

> Thinking thus, I almost missed how straightening her back, she continued the motion up through her smooth, long neck—a time-lapse film of a fiddlehead fern, she seemed, every moment less fiddlehead and more fern—until suddenly she seemed, impossibly, to be raising her head, turning and tilting it toward me; and still the motion upward; until her face was lifted too, and her eyebrows, and her gaze.
>
> **Lan** / *He was rich. American. Sexy. He seemed gentle, and perhaps loving. I had never had a man who was loving. Who made you shiver. And look how he had helped me already. He was kind. He was not short.*
> **Carnegie** /—Thank you, she said.
> Her gaze was shiny and honest and slightly cross-eyed, her pupils black and enormous.
> I could not speak.
> —You do so much for me, she said. You should not.
> **Lan** / *I felt so grateful, in my heart, for his help.* (235; italics in the original)

40. Jen orients Lan's identity through a spectrum of conventions employed to represent her self-expression. Idiomatic markers signify her position as a foreign speaker of English, which makes the moments when her expression is characterized by an effortless fluidity suggest that her thoughts are being translated by the narrator. Compare, for example, the idiomatic rendering of "*I thought that* **Harry [Dirty Harry]** *very strange. What kind of hero was that? So rude. But sexy, it was true. I thought that* **Clint Eastwood** *almost as handsome as* **Gregory Peck**" (221), with the fluidity of "*My father was, before Liberation, an English and French and Russian teacher, as well as the principal of a small high school his parents had bought for him to run. My mother was a Communist who left him for an officer in the People's Army. After all, she was beautiful and young. Why should she stay with trouble?*" (95; italics and bold in the original). As I have discussed in the previous note, Jen uses lyricism to establish a "human" language of intense emotional experience available to persons, regardless of positionality.

41. For example, Dewey Dell's monologues represent her social position through quoted dialogue cast in idiomatic dialect (e.g., "'Go on, now. I done put supper on and I'll be there soon as I milk'") while representing the profundity of her thinking with lyrical language (e.g., "The dead air shapes the dead earth in the dead darkness, further away than seeing shapes the dead earth. It lies dead and warm upon me, touching me naked through my clothes") (Faulkner, *As I Lay Dying*, 63–64). For my analysis of how this

method of representation establishes an ethics as well as a politics of authorial relation, see Chapter 3. See also my "*As I Lay Dying*'s Heterogeneous Discourse."

42. See, e.g., Franklin, "Narrative Management"; and Pilkington, *Heart of Yoknapatawpha* (esp. 94).

43. See my interpretation of "Women and Fiction" in *The Novel*, 566–570.

44. Eliot, "Silly Novels," 324.

45. Jen, *Tiger Writing*, 22.

46. Ibid., 136.

47. Robinson echoes James's characterological view of the novel in her 1994 interview with Thomas Schaub: "'Plot' is a word that I think embarrasses writers. I think that's universally true. I can't think of anything that Ruth thinks about without thinking of what happens to her and what she does. At the same time, when I was writing I was aware of movements of mind not mine, that I didn't know the solution to" (241). Her trilogy *Gilead* (2004), *Home* (2008), and *Lila* (2014) carries forward the Jamesian perspectival tradition through the narration of the same story from three different character's perspectives, but unlike James, who in the prefaces decries the "looseness" of the first-person as a narrative mode, Robinson advocates for her first-person approach: "I don't know if I will ever write other than in first-person. But I feel like I'm being faithful to a voice that is not mine and that's where the first-person comes in" ("Conversation with Marilynne Robinson," 92).

48. Daniel Zalewski further notes that "McEwan twice cited Henry James's dictum that the only obligation of a novel 'is that it be interesting'" (par. 9). But as I am arguing, James models for McEwan the way that interest can be located in narrative ethics.

49. See Abrams, *The Mirror and the Lamp*, for the deeper literary historical roots of style regarded as an index of identity. Abrams notes that by 1760 "the opinion was already commonplace that although poetry is imitation, style is the man. This assertion was not self-contradictory, for, it was affirmed, it is the matter which mirrors the world, and the manner which mirrors the man" (231). Abrams argues that the view of poetry as "an indirect and disguised expression of the author's temperament" was "theological in its origin, and Kantian in the philosophical vocabulary by which it was justified" (236).

50. As with Gilbert's operetta *A Sensation Novel*, James's description of the novelist as in a bodily relation with his character had become so standard by the beginning of the twentieth century that Frank Norris, a novelist writing at the same time that James was penning his prefaces and whose subject matter was as different from James's as was his politics, nonetheless uses this same figure to describe the novelistic depiction of what we might call historical alterity. In regard to *Ivanhoe*, Norris states that Scott "got beneath the clothes of an epoch and got the heart of it, and the spirit of it (different essentially and vitally from ours or from every other, the spirit of feudalism); and he put forth a masterpiece" ("True Reward," 17).

51. For a more detailed reading of this key passage from the prefaces, see my *Social Formalism* (esp. 42–45).

52. See esp. "Queer Performativity." Sedgwick writes of James's relation to Christopher Newman: "The wooing in these scenes of pederastic revision is not unidirectional, however; even the age differential can be figured quite differently, as when James finds himself, on rereading *The American*, 'clinging to my hero as to a tall, protective, good-natured elder brother in a rough place'" (10–11).

53. *Atonement* remains the locus classicus for discussions of McEwan's narrative ethics not only because of the narrative twist that reveals Briony to be (within the storyworld) the author of the novel but also because of McEwan's incorporation into the novel of quotations from a memoir published in 1977 by Lucilla Andrews, an indebtedness honored only in a general way in his acknowledgments to the novel. See Cowell, "Eyebrows Are Raised"; and Alden, "Words of War."

Sweet Tooth (2012), *Nutshell* (2016), and *Machines Like Me* (2019) carry forward the alterity project by depicting, respectively, the attempt of a male author to occupy the point of view of the woman he loves, the first-person perspective of an unborn fetus, and an investigation into the moment of "singularity," when a robot assumes human personhood. The sophisticated and witty language use that McEwan grants the fetus in *Nutshell* plays up (through a first-person narrative stance) many of the comic effects that James achieves through bestowing his sophisticated language and insights on young Maisie, which I discuss in Chapter 2. See Dobrogoszcz, *Family and Relationships*, for a reading of *Nutshell* that refers the fetus's language back to McEwan himself. For example, after quoting a passage from the novel, Dobrogoszcz argues, "Such remarks are much more likely to be coming not from a fetus, but from a middle-aged writer, who earlier that year prompted criticism from human rights campaigners for inadvertently expressing a risky opinion in a transgender debate" (222). In "Postmodernism and the Ethics of Fiction in *Atonement*," Alistair Cormack indirectly locates McEwan in relation to James through his discussion of McEwan in relation to F. R. Leavis's *The Great Tradition*, a critical work that firmly established Henry James within the liberal humanist view of the novel's ethical enterprise.

54. McEwan, "Nihilism, the Novel and Political Creativity."

55. McEwan reiterates this view in a 2005 interview conducted by Zadie Smith: "At least since the early '80s, it's began [*sic*] to fill out for me as an idea in fiction, that there's something very entwined about imagination and morals. That one of the great values of fiction was exactly this process of being able to enter other people's minds. Which is why I think cinema is a very inferior, unsophisticated medium" (Smith and McEwan, "Zadie Smith Talks," 212). McEwan's opinion about the novel's superiority to film is shared by Franzen (qtd. at the end of this chapter).

56. James Wood would seem to agree. In *How Fiction Works* he implies that John Updike is at fault for failing to take full advantage of the novel's capacity for alterity. The implication is that Updike lacks either the moral courage or the imagination (or both) that would allow him to occupy fully the point of view of his character Ahmad, an American Muslim. In a statement that supports my sense of James's foundational importance to the novelistic ethics of alterity, Wood's criticism of Updike also serves to praise James: "How willing Henry James was, by contrast, to let us inhabit Maisie's mind. . . . But Updike is unsure about entering Ahmad's mind, and crucially, unsure about *our* entering Ahmad's mind, and so he plants his big authorial flags all over his mental site" (29; emphasis in the original). As is clear from my reading of *Maisie*, I think Wood oversimplifies both James's sense of his project and his narrative execution of that project, but that oversimplification in turn supports my point about how the ethics of alterity has become a baseline assumption about "how fiction works," distinguished from rigorous philosophical conceptions of alterity.

57. Janine Utell's explicitly Levinasian interpretation of McEwan's early novel *On Chesil Beach* makes my point about how the novelistic ethics of alterity provides common ground between liberal humanist and poststructuralist ethics. Utell argues, "As we read ethically, placing texts in conversation with each other and holding spaces open for multiplicity and doubt, we model what McEwan's characters might not be able to do: moving below the surface, moving beyond misperception, and rejecting the impulse to reduce the other to a single meaning" ("*On Chesil Beach*," 91). In "Briony's Being-For," David K. O'Hara makes a similar ethical argument about McEwan's narrative technique in *Atonement*: "Self-conscious narrative, in the case of McEwan, is oftentimes utilized in order to reassert an *ethical* complex that lies between author and reader, text and world" (74; emphasis in the original). O'Hara asserts that McEwan offers "an affirmative narrative ethics" (74) that, following Paul Ricoeur, "allows the self to appreciate just how necessary Others are to our own self-awareness. For it is only by feeling for the Other in this way that we understand what narrative identity is all about" (92).

58. See Serpell, *Seven Modes of Uncertainty*, for a Deleuzian interpretation of the ethical problems and potentials raised by *Atonement* (79–117). Charles Cornelius Pastoor ("Authorial Atonement," 304) asks why McEwan would "so shamelessly recycle the same 'surprise' literary device" in *Sweet Tooth*. He goes on to point out that the narrative feature distinguishing the two novels is a shift away from godlike authorial power over the fictional world toward ethical collaboration with the reader (305–306).

59. Naomi Booth ("Restricted View," 862) reads this passage as replacing "McEwan's idealistic versions of empathy with the grubby pleasures of spying and sexual role-play."

60. The plot of *Every Day* similarly draws upon the particular ethical situation of the lover understanding the beloved through embodiment. In keeping with Levithan's

more utopian view of novelistic alterity, the protagonist is able to transcend social barriers in order to experience the world from within the beloved's skin while simultaneously setting limits on the degree and kind of allowable inhabitation. This act of self-limitation is initiated out of love and is regarded by the protagonist as an ethical stance that conveys respect for the beloved by honoring her autonomy and privacy from a position within her.

61. Laura Savu Walker ("'A Balance of Power,'" 495–496) argues that the condition of "covert authorship" stands as a figure for the nature of freedom within ideology. Walker's interpretation of *Sweet Tooth* reads the novel through the lens of the ethics of alterity: "By portraying a (writing) self that acknowledges the other both outside and inside itself, McEwan shows that writing can also be driven by the will, or rather openness to love, which is irreducible to ideology." She adds: "More specifically, McEwan continues here his project of reimagining the agency of the male writer and thus re-engendering authorship by foregrounding the perspective of a female spy.... Herein... lies the ethical function of an authorial self that is connected to an other—in this case, a significant other—rather than complicit with the power he is trying to deconstruct" (496). In *Family and Relationships in Ian McEwan's Fiction*, Tomasz Dobrogoszcz explicitly agrees with Walker's reading of the novel but casts the notion of otherness from within a more particularized Lacanian framework (see esp. 201). Irena Ksiezopolska reads *Sweet Tooth* as McEwan's attempt after *Atonement* to find a "way of restoring faith in fiction" (McEwan's phrase) and makes that ethical achievement sound suspect: "*Sweet Tooth* flounces to excess the novel's intertextuality and thereby foregrounds the reader's entanglement in the textual web, simultaneously offering that reader the possibility to become the master spider in this pattern of deception" ("Turning Tables," 416). Attuned to the darker note implied by Ksiezopolska, Naomi Booth ("Restricted View," 845) argues that spying in *Sweet Tooth* represents "the pleasures of literature as the pleasures of surveillance, reporting back on the impossibility of a literary point of view that is non-ideological or non-tendentious: writing here is depicted as a decidedly dirty pleasure, where politics are always in play and artistic freedom is an illusion; where 'all writers are spies' serving a secret regime and narrative is the product of a pointedly restricted view."

62. Ermarth, *Realism and Consensus*, xxii.

63. See Sedgwick, "Paranoid Reading." For an analysis of how Sedgwick's notion of reparative reading has fostered a view of the novel in particular as a spatialized ideological form, see my "The Place of the Novel in Reparative Reading," 104–105.

64. In *Tiger Writing*, Gish Jen also appeals to social science for verification of her assumptions about reading, in this case to the sociologist Qi Wang (see esp. 58–71).

65. We can hear a strong echo of Jean-Paul Sartre in Franzen's ethical assumptions. But whereas Sartre emphasizes the philosophical condition of free commitment in the

reader's collaboration with the author, Franzen emphasizes the social product of co-collaboration: the imaginative bringing-into-being of a social world that seems to possess its own autonomy (see esp. Sartre, "Why Write?," 58–65).

66. To explore the resonances between Franzen's notion of "gift-giving" and the Derridean notion of "hospitality" as applied to Gish Jen's work, see Sokolowski, "The Limits of Hospitality."

67. In his *New Yorker* essay on Edith Wharton, Franzen explores the more familiar affective term "sympathy" in his analysis of readerly participation. Significantly, the way he defines sympathy is specifically in terms of the experience of otherness that is so important for George Eliot, and which leads into the Jamesian aesthetics of alterity: "But sympathy in novels need not be simply a matter of the reader's direct identification with a fictional character. It can also be driven by, say, my admiration of a character who is long on virtues I am short on (the moral courage of Atticus Finch, the limpid goodness of Alyosha Karamazov), or, most interestingly, by my wish to be a character who is unlike me in ways I don't admire or even like. One of the great perplexities of fiction—and the quality that makes the novel the quintessentially liberal art form—is that we experience sympathy so readily for characters we wouldn't like in real life." ("A Rooting Interest," par. 13)

68. Zadie Smith concludes her essay on Henry James's critical analysis of *Middlemarch* with a statement that echoes James's view of the novel as both protean and limitable. In crediting this view to Eliot's practice in *Middlemarch*, Smith's comment underscores the difference that Jamesian theory makes for the novel understood as an art form: "What twenty-first-century novelists inherit from Eliot is the radical freedom to push the novel's form to its limits, whatever they may be" ("*Middlemarch* and Everybody," 41).

Chapter 2: Henry James and the Development of the Novelistic Aesthetics of Alterity

1. Morrison, *Playing in the Dark*, 3.

2. Peter Brooks (*Henry James Goes to Paris*) agrees that James's "radical perspectivalism" is the basis of his "theory of fiction" but tracks this not to an aesthetics of alterity but to an "epistemological fervor" (2, 52).

3. See Zwinger, *Telling in Henry James*, for an interpretation of the narrative representation of otherness in *The Europeans* that attends to the novel's use of linguistic alterity: "Just as foreign objects . . . lurk within and yet also constitute the domestic, so the italicized and the non-italicized foreign languages that comprise our 'own' language tell us that we are indeed, as the English title of the French book written by Julia Kristeva (whose first language is neither) would have it, 'strangers to ourselves'" (39).

4. See Chapter 1 for my discussion of Thackeray and Trollope.

5. Irene Tucker also calls attention to the two different models of ethical agency at

work in this scene. Note that Tucker concludes by holding James ethically accountable for this clash of ethical models: "James the fiction-maker ends up looking a lot like Beale the manipulator" ("What Maisie Promised," 348).

6. Walter Benn Michaels ("Jim Crow Henry James?") agrees with Morrison that *What Maisie Knew* is informed by a political unconscious, but he argues that, rather than expressing the Jim Crow attitudes about race emerging in the period that authorized social segregation, James's representation of the countess expresses James's class views on the threat the market economy poses to the quality of social life (see esp. 289). See Johnson, "The Scarlet Feather," for an overview of the critical debate launched specifically in response to Morrison's interpretation of the countess.

7. See Keen, *Empathy and the Novel*, for a comprehensive account of the literary historical tradition of novelistic empathy and its relation to kindred identificatory emotions such as altruism and sympathy.

8. See Woloch, *The One vs. the Many*, for a theory of novelistic character that similarly takes into account the variable and dynamic representation of characterological personhood across narrative space and time.

9. For the range of strong opinion concerning James's ethical vision, cp. the entries in the Bibliography for Millicent Bell, Leo Bersani, Wayne Booth, Richard Chase, Samuel Cross, Jonathan Freedman, Dorothea Krook, Jil Larson, F. R. Leavis, Juliet Mitchell, Iris Murdoch, Robert Pippin, Richard Poirier, Sally Sears, Dorothy Van Ghent, J. A. Ward, James Wood, and Ruth Yeazell. See Chapter 5 for my discussion of Andrew Gibson, J. Hillis Miller, Adam Zachary Newton, Martha Nussbaum, and Lionel Trilling.

10. Cp., e.g., Poirier, *Comic Sense of Henry James*, on the ethicality of James's methods for representing character (esp. 9, 250), with Tanner, *Henry James* (esp. 104), and Butler, "Values of Difficulty" (discussed in Chapter 5).

11. See esp. Murdoch, "The Sublime and the Beautiful Revisited," Nussbaum, *Love's Knowledge*, and Trilling, "Manners, Morals, and the Novel," for an interpretation of James as devoted to an ethics of love (discussed below and in Chapter 5). See Hanson, "Screwing with Children," Silverman, "Too Early / Too Late," Stevens, "Queer Henry *In the Cage*," and Zwinger ("Bodies That Don't Matter," esp. 673–675) for the argument that James's children are erotically constituted.

12. For Alfred Hitchcock's statement about actors as cattle, see McGilligan (*Alfred Hitchcock*, 210–211, 277). For his statement about actors as props, see Truffaut (*Hitchcock*, 111). For scholarship that explicitly works out the comparison between James and Hitchcock, see Griffen and Nadel, *Men Who Knew Too Much*.

13. I will discuss in more detail later the unsigned review of the novel published in *Literary World* (1897).

14. Margaret Walters argues that James takes with Maisie "a connoisseur's pleasure

in the violation of her innocence . . . a pleasure detached, voyeuristic, almost pornographic" ("'Keeping the Place Tidy,'" 197). See Habegger (*Henry James and the "Woman Business,"* esp. 156) for the comparison between James and Humbert Humbert, and see Hurst, *Voice of the Child*, for the comparison between Lolita and Humbert Humbert and Maisie and Sir Claude (esp. 35). See Stevens, "Queer Henry," for a more positive view of James as "the playful erotic punner, the teaser, taking pleasure in weaving a polyvalent erotic web which flickers between revelation and concealment" (132). Ellis Hanson similarly describes James as "being naughty and joining us in this playful erotics of children" ("Screwing with Children," 372).

15. See Pick, "Miracles of Arrangement," for a more general discussion of Jamesian instrumentality situated within a Levinasian ethical framework. See Tanner, *Henry James*, for the liberal humanist ethical formulation of the moral "evil" James attributes to "the callous manipulation and selfish appropriation of other peoples' lives" (110).

16. See Himmelfarb, "Manners into Morals," for the Victorian background to this liberal humanist ethical model (esp. 231). See Tucker, "What Maisie Promised," for an in-depth analysis of the workings of the liberal notion of contract in *Maisie*.

17. Dan McCall reads the novel as the story of Maisie's inevitable "soiling" ("What Maisie Saw," 52).

18. Wayne Booth believes that James's best work "does not just present virtue and vice in conflict; the story itself consists of the conflict of defensible moral or ethical stances" ("Why Ethical Criticism," 26). He goes on to argue that the conflict is ultimately decidable through the right reading of James's fictional technique for the complex formulation of ethical value. In *The Rhetoric of Fiction*, Booth takes care to distinguish between what on his view characterizes James's successful and unsuccessful aesthetic expressions of complex ethical value.

19. As Carren Osna Kaston observes, "In the *Maisie* world, the impulses of caring and the arts of use are both hard to tell apart and difficult to combine for any length of time" ("Houses of Fiction," 31). Tony Tanner describes more generally the effect of James's depiction of the "concealed predatory nature of much of what passes for generosity" (*Henry James*, 13).

20. See Leavis, "What Maisie Knew" (esp. 126, 128); and Banta ("Quality of Experience," 492).

21. Marius Bewley heralds Maisie's "triumphant escape" at the end, crediting her with having "literally saved herself spiritually" (*Complex Fate*, 141).

22. Juliet Mitchell stands as a good example of this position ("*What Maisie Knew*"; see esp. 169).

23. Martha Banta similarly uses the language of gamesmanship to describe what she believes is Maisie's happy development from "mere spectatorship" to mature

"self-determination" ("Quality of Experience," 492). To regard ethical achievement as a game is arguably, for both Pippin and Banta, to some degree to have imbibed the cynicism of the adults in the novel.

24. James Gargano provides a good overview of the critical divide between those who argue for Maisie's development and those who insist on her static intrinsicality ("*What Maisie Knew*," 33–34). Gargano supports the development model (see esp. 39).

25. Marius Bewley maintains that "Maisie's innocence remains uncontaminated throughout" (*Complex Fate*, 97). Tony Tanner takes Maisie as James's moral ideal: through her depiction, James "is also demonstrating what, to him, was the most valuable way of responding to experience—with generous, unselfish wonder" (*Henry James*, 90).

26. Marius Bewley also makes this comparison with *The Turn of the Screw* (*Complex Fate*, 108).

27. I've inverted the phrases of James's sentence.

28. See Jeff Westover for a reading of the novel that credits Sir Claude's "kindness and care" with "nurturing Maisie's autonomy" ("Handing Over Power," 211).

29. Christopher Brown argues that the novel's last lines convey the triumph of "balanced antitheses: sentiment and irony, resolution and dubiety, verbal skill and a sense of its cost" ("Rhetoric of Closure," 65). Michelle Phillips, on the other hand, feels that "what it promises with one hand it denies with the other" ("'Partagé Child,'" 105).

30. See Silverman, "Too Early / Too Late ," where she argues that Maisie grows not into "power and social integration, but to loss and isolation" (162).

31. The alterity project articulated in the preface to *Maisie* is usefully compared to that formulated in the preface to *Portrait*, in which the absolute ethical value that James places on the novel's narrative resources for representing characterological autonomy problematizes any other aesthetic goals that the author might also wish to achieve. Thus, in the preface to *Portrait* James seems to denigrate the integrity of personhood that he seeks to honor in Isabel Archer when he refers her successful "expression" (to use Woolf's term) to his own artistic talent: as he undertook the writing of *Portrait*, he remembers thinking to himself, "To depend upon her and her little concerns to see you through will necessitate ... your really 'doing' her" (52). James so successfully makes the case in both his fiction and his nonfiction writing about fiction for the author's self-subordination, for his handing the novel over to his characters, that any self-crediting for the success of her representation seems to reinstate the hierarchical operation of power from which the novel was to free "the smaller female fry." To "do" Isabel Archer is for James as an artist to take for granted that she is "for so considerable a time all curiously at my disposal" (48). The ethical power of the narrative relation that James forges with Isabel Archer through his management of point of view, the never-before-attempted rendering of "*her* vision, *her* conception, *her* interpretation" (preface to *The American*, 37; my pronoun revision

and emphasis) in chapter 42, stands against James's larger intention to write the novel as an aesthetic whole, as a unified composition. For James thus to dispose of Isabel Archer by making her "the single small corner-stone" of the "square and spacious house" that was to be *Portrait of a Lady* seems a self-serving instrumentalization of the very personhood that he has so convincingly brought to life. For James to pride himself on the "technical rigor" that enables him to erect the "literary monument" that he feels he achieves in *Portrait of a Lady* is for the person, Isabel Archer, to stand in tension with the projection of the novel as an autonomous aesthetic object: for Archer to be reduced to the condition of the "neat and careful and proportioned pile of bricks and arches" that James believes are necessary to the artist's larger purpose of projecting the novel as an aesthetic whole (53).

32. Judith Ryan argues that James's model of consciousness is consonant with that developed by William James ("Vanishing Subject," 860).

33. Richard Poirier is one of the first critics to describe the micro-effects of the aesthetics of alterity: "The question is felt on every page—who is exploiting the life of another human being? . . . 'Am I guilty,' James seems always to be asking, 'of violating the dramatic freedom of this character in order to place him in some system of meaning?'" (*Comic Sense of Henry James*, 9).

34. The aesthetics of alterity that I am describing is integrally related to James's use of free indirect discourse. But readings of *Maisie* that focus on that use only begin to tap the complex and dynamic positioning that James establishes between narrator and character. See, e.g., Wood, *How Fiction Works*, 18.

35. Joseph Conrad thus concludes more generally about James's depiction of such complexity that "a fine conscience is naturally a virtuous one" ("Henry James," 18).

36. See e.g. Wyatt, "Failed Messages," 142; Wyatt, in arguing that Morrison represents Florens as lacking "what cognitive scientists call Theory of Mind," suggests another interesting basis for comparing Morrison's linguistic strategy for Florens's monologue with Faulkner's representation of Benjy in *The Sound and the Fury*.

37. See Strehle, "'I Am a Thing Apart,'" for a useful overview of the different critical interpretations of Florens's language use, including Morrison's own characterization of the combined "innocence" and "sophistication" that she was aiming at in composing Florens's monologues (120; qtd. from Smallwood, "Back Talk"). Important for my argument, Morrison's description echoes the contradictory qualities that James's language bestows on Maisie. Strehle also quotes Caroline Moore, who, in describing Florens's diction as an "improbable amalgam of would-be lyricism, folksy illiteracy, . . . and contemporary slang," invites a connection with Faulkner's narrative practice (120; qtd. from Moore, review of *A Mercy*). The "would-be lyricism" especially connects to the shift in diction in *The Sound and the Fury* that I describe in Chapter 3, while the antimimetic shifts in register carry on the practice of *As I Lay Dying*, which I discuss in Chapter 1. Strehle's own position is

that Florens serves as "a shocking lesson in what it is like to be the expendable Other" (117) and characterizes Florens's language as "Other English" (120).

38. Yvette Christiansë interprets the tragedy of the novel as the conflict between the "singularity" of personal bonds and "the possessive economy that attempts to name it" (*Toni Morrison*, 192)—which is to say, a conflict between interpersonal ethics and impersonal power structures.

39. Maria Rice Bellamy ("'These Careful Words'") argues that *A Mercy* stands as a prequel to *Beloved* and that both of these novels perform their narrative ethics by allowing the reader to enter into the "space of rememory." Bellamy describes this narrative space as bestowing on the reader powers of identification and fusion: "Thus, we become Florens, the lost child, and hear *my mother* speaking words of love. We become the mother speaking love to other lost children. The contemporary reader becomes the bridge across the chasm that separates mother and child and holds them in the love they could not share with each other, thus healing their tormented souls" (28; emphasis in the original). Jami Carlacio ("Narrative, Epistemology") similarly argues that the narrative installs the reader in a position of characterological identification: "As readers, we are intimately linked to Florens, identifying with her imaginatively, because we are beckoned by the command with which she begins her story ('Don't be afraid' [3]); we undertake the same epistemological journey that she does in an experience that transcends the boundaries of one life. Implied in and intertwined in this journey lies the whole of human experience" (4; qtd. from *A Mercy*). Carlacio characterizes this interpretation as inspired by Adam Zachary Newton's narrative ethics, yet Carlacio's interpretation of Morrison dispenses with the sources of power that are so important to Newton's understanding of narrative (as I discuss in Chapter 5).

40. Paula Moya (*Social Imperative*) argues that Morrison's "innovations in novelistic form are ways of reconceiving, within the minoritarian imagination, the dynamic interplay that always exists between inequality and democracy, structure and individuality, language and reference" (141). For Moya, Florens's narrative dominance represents Morrison's attempt to "redress the imbalance of power accorded to Florens and Jacob by the fictional society in which they live" (144).

41. Marc Conner ("'What Lay beneath the Names'") describes this effect as deriving from Morrison's own concern with developing "an alternative language that seeks not to master, but to harmoniously inhabit and traverse the landscape itself" (156).

42. Yvette Christiansë describes Morrison's narrative as an overcoming of a given history that serves to maintain the past's hold on the present: "For all the effort to escape the violent political order of vengeance and corrupt cruelty, people recall narratives told by parents and eventually those narratives heal into their own narrated memories, which, like dreams, are ultimately known through processes of secondary revision.... On the

one hand, this is the basis of transhistorical or transgenerational identity. On the other hand, it is possession by the past" (*Toni Morrison*, 215).

43. Attridge, *Singularity of Literature*, 21.

44. See Krook, *Ordeal of Consciousness*, for a perceptive analysis of how *The Portrait of a Lady* explicitly represents the conflict between "the life of a man," which is "moral," and the "brilliant surface" of the "mere aesthetic" (59). See Freedman, *Professions of Taste*, for the cultural history of turn-of-the-century aestheticism.

45. Teahan, "*What Maisie Knew*," 127.

46. Ibid., 137.

47. Sheila Teahan describes the relation between author and character as a zero-sum game: "The recourse to the scenic method that spells Maisie's demise as reflective center is the vehicle of James's own salvation" ("*What Maisie Knew*," 134). In the revised version of this argument about *Maisie* that appears two years later, Teahan tones down the criticism directed at James personally. See her *Rhetorical Logic* (esp. 39, 63) for examples of the softened position.

48. Dorothy Van Ghent is one of the few critics who argues for the philosophical compatibility in James of the aesthetic and moral senses (*English Novel*, 218).

49. See also Eckstein, "Unsquaring the Squared Route," for an ethical interpretation of James's narrative "squaring" of his characters (177); and Foss, "Female Innocence," for a comparison of James and Sir Claude as "controlling male subject[s] to the heroine's object," brought on by the shared "androcentric aestheticism" of character and author (254).

50. The Jamesian novelist tradition that I am arguing for might usefully be compared with Jesse Matz's characterization of James's modernist legacy. See especially his *Literary Impressionism and Modernist Aesthetics* (85–120) and *The Modern Novel*. Other important literary histories of the modern novel in Britain include Malcolm Bradbury, *The Modern British Novel*; Robert L. Caserio, *The Novel in England, 1900–1950* and *The Cambridge Companion to the Twentieth-Century English Novel*; and Steven Connor, *The English Novel in History, 1950–1995*. In *The Novel Art*, Mark McGurl explores the response of American writers to James's high art project.

51. Woolf, "On Re-reading Novels," 342.

52. Ibid., 338.

53. Lubbock, *Craft of Fiction*, 186–187; emphasis in the original.

54. Lubbock, introduction to *The Letters of Henry James*, xxii, xxviii. James's position as "master" had wide endorsement among English novelists. See also Conrad, "Henry James," 11; Ford, *Henry James*, 9; and West, *Henry James*, 104.

55. The burgeoning number of what she regards as "silly" novels led George Eliot famously to bemoan the genre's formlessness: "Every art which has its absolute *technique* is, to a certain extent, guarded from the intrusions of mere left-handed imbecility. But

in novel-writing there are no barriers for incapacity to stumble against, no external criteria to prevent a writer from mistaking foolish facility for mastery" ("Silly Novels," 324; emphasis in the original).

56. Lodge, *Language of Fiction*, 72.
57. Ibid., 68.
58. Brooke-Rose, *Invisible Author*, 1, 13.
59. Byatt, *On Histories and Stories*, 6.
60. Virginia Woolf published two volumes of her essays in *The Common Reader*: *First Series* (1925) and *Second Series* (1932).
61. Woolf, "Mr. Bennett and Mrs. Brown," 200–206, and "Modern Fiction," 159. The argument for the novel as an art is routinely positioned against the view of the novel as social document. See, e.g., Murdoch, "The Sublime and the Beautiful Revisited," 257, 260.
62. Woolf, "Narrow Bridge of Art," 13.
63. Woolf, "Modern Fiction," 160.
64. Ford, "On Impressionism," 43. For excellent discussions of James's relation to the cultural and literary history of impressionism, see Hildalgo, "(Dis)orienting the Reader"; Matz, *Literary Impressionism*; and Scholar, *Henry James*.
65. The phrase "invisibly visible" comes from Friedrich Schlegel's "Letter about the Novel" (99).
66. Ford, *Henry James*, 9.
67. Woolf, *Room of One's Own*, 71, and "Phases of Fiction," 119.
68. Rushdie, "Is Nothing Sacred?," 420.
69. Lawrence, "The Novel," 159.
70. Lawrence, "Morality and the Novel," 150.
71. Lawrence, "The Novel", 158–159.
72. Rushdie, "Is Nothing Sacred?," 420 (emphasis in the original).
73. Ibid., 416.
74. Lawrence, "Art and Morality," 147; emphasis in the original.
75. Woolf, "Mr. Bennett and Mrs. Brown," 199.
76. Ibid., 198.
77. Byatt and Sodré, *Imagining Characters*, 248. See also Murdoch, "The Sublime and the Beautiful Revisited," 257; and Conrad, "Books," 9.
78. Murdoch, "The Sublime and the Beautiful Revisited," 261.
79. Martin, "Houses of Fiction," 124; Martin's emphasis. Murdoch also provides an important line of connection with Zadie Smith's investment in "love" and "negative capability" as defining features of the novel art. See my discussion of Murdoch in Chapter 3.
80. Murdoch, "The Sublime and the Beautiful Revisited," 270.
81. Ibid., 257.

82. Lee, *Handling of Words*, 26.
83. Ibid., 27.
84. Woolf, "Art and Life," 277. Notably, Woolf was impatient with what she regarded as the amateurism of her contemporary Vernon Lee's writings on the novel as an art, bemoaning the absence in Lee's argument of the careful definition of terms and precise formulation of claims that had distinguished *The Craft of Fiction* as an act of aesthetic theory.
85. Lee, *Handling of Words*, 26.
86. Liddell, *Treatise on the Novel*, 106; emphasis in the original.
87. Ibid.
88. Ibid., 108; Liddell, *Some Principles of Fiction*, 65–66.
89. Lessing, "Small, Personal Voice," 12.
90. Jackson, "Eve's Side of It," 170.
91. Ibid.
92. Ibid.
93. Harris, "Closing Statement," 245.
94. Harris, "The Frontier," 87.
95. Harris, "Phenomenal Legacy," 46.
96. Ibid., 47.
97. Harris, "Tradition and the West Indian Novel," 36.
98. Harris, "Phenomenal Legacy," 45.
99. Harris, "Books," 21, and "Resistances to Alterities," 3.
100. Harris, "Quetzalcoatl," 194.
101. James, preface to *The Portrait of a Lady*, 46.
102. Brophy, "The Novel as a Takeover Bid," 96.
103. Ibid., 97.
104. Forster, *Aspects of the Novel*, 24.
105. Lawrence, "Why the Novel Matters," 169.

Chapter 3: Zadie Smith's *On Beauty*

1. Smith, "Zadie, Take Three."
2. See Dick and Lupton, "On Lecturing and Being Beautiful," for a powerful ideological interpretation of *On Beauty and Being Just*. Dick and Lupton note that Scarry's essay is a published version of the 1998 lecture that Scarry delivered at Yale for the Tanner Lectures on Human Values. Their focus on Smith's depiction of liberal education generates a compelling account of how the lecture as social discourse, and Scarry's essay as generated through the lecture format, performs liberal values. Through an examination of Scarry's rhetorical mode, they argue that Scarry stages her lecture as "a total experience through the simultaneous arrangement of constituent elements and the emptying out of

their specific content. All things to all people, the Tanner Lectures become a kind of rhetorical embodiment for authentic expression" (127). On Dick and Lupton's view, Smith's novelistic practice emulates the lecture mode and reproduces its liberal politics: "The fact that the listing of particular and remarkable visual details is itself an ideology becomes clearer still when we consider that this technique, rather than any more overt argument about beauty, is the thing Zadie Smith has inherited wholeheartedly from Scarry" (128). Ann Marie Adams similarly argues that Smith strives to emulate Scarry's position, as well as that this position is a liberal humanist attitude toward beauty, but unlike Dick and Lupton, who critique this politics, Adams admires the novel for its defense of liberalism: "Relying heavily on the philosophical work of Elaine Scarry, Smith demonstrates how a liberal character might begin to (re)forge a Forsterian connection between a love of beauty and 'being just'" ("A Passage to Forster," 395). Kathleen Wall also upholds this view of the novel's positive endorsement of liberalism: "The characters' inability to connect with beauty and its representative in the social world—art—is implicated in their inattention to the humanity of others and their limited view of the world, whereas their engagement with beauty opens up a space outside themselves that can reflectively include other people and other perspectives" (in "Ethics, Knowledge, and the Need for Beauty," 758).

3. Smith, *On Beauty*, xiii.

4. In "The Aesthetic Turn," Roy Sommer argues that the consideration of aesthetics is particularly urgent for black writers because the value of their work is so often equated with the representation of identity: "Critical approaches to 'black' British literature have either emphasized aspects of content, such as the treatment of racism and cultural stereotypes, or have highlighted questions of ideology and identity. . . . This focus on the cultural functions of 'black' British novels tends to neglect their formal innovations, aesthetic achievements, and narrative structures (e.g., framing devices, multiple perspectives, characterization, plot structures, meta-narrative and meta-fictional elements, narrative unreliability or irony)" (178–179). See Anjaria, "*On Beauty* and Being Postcolonial," for an interpretation of *On Beauty* that argues for the "co-existence of beauty and being postcolonial in a world that tends to see the two as irreconcilable" (32).

5. Smith, "Zadie, Take Three"; emphasis in the original.

6. See Smith's "Read Better" for the explicit contrast she makes between novelistic perspectivalism and philosophical reductionism. She contrasts the systematizing literary critic with the ethically open novel writer and reader. The critic "committed to his theory" mistakes this theory of literature for "'literature' itself, recasting his own failure of imagination as a principle of aesthetics" (21). By contrast, she claims that through the novel "both the writer and the reader must undergo an ethical expansion—allow me to call it an expansion of the heart—in order to comprehend the human otherness that fiction confronts them with" (22).

7. See Su, "Beauty and the Beastly Prime Minister," for an argument that locates Smith's aesthetic investigation in the social context of British Thatcherism. Beginning with the assumption that "even the unwieldy, multifarious notion of 'beauty' takes on particular resonances in light of the cultural, political, and economic circumstances in which it is invoked" (1085), Su argues more narrowly than I would that "*On Beauty* . . . portrays its central conflict as a consequence of Thatcherism" (1096). See Jackson, "Imagining Boston," for a counterview of the novel's defining cultural context: "But the novel is most important here as a Boston book. . . . I aim to show that the social commentary of *On Beauty* functions specifically through the enactment of place and the sense that what is meaningful in social life occurs in and through place" (856).

8. Woolf, "The Narrow Bridge of Art," 18. Anna Glab draws out one of the important points of connection between Woolf and Smith that locate their projects in the Jamesian tradition of ethical alterity I am theorizing: "Smith's words suggest that her novels not be interpreted in political, ideological, racial, feminist, or ethnic terms and not through the lens of concepts such as postcolonialism, multiculturalism, or globalization . . . but rather they should be experienced or *lived*" ("The Ethical Laboratory," 492; emphasis in the original). On my view, Smith proposes that the life of the novel and novel reading is always situated in relation to a self-consciousness about the identitarian and political construction of identity that Glab's list of terms implies.

9. Smith, "Zadie, Take Three."

10. Smith, *On Beauty*, xiii.

11. See Chapter 5 for my analysis of the ethical theory of the novel developed by Martha Nussbaum in *Love's Knowledge*. See Chapter 2 for my discussion of Iris Murdoch's place in the twentieth-century development of the Jamesian aesthetics of alterity.

12. Smith, "Love, Actually," 4. In "Fascinated to Presume," Smith locates Morrison's work in relation to the ethics and politics of otherness, and echoes some of Morrison's key ideas. "Fiction's people," Smith tells us, are ethical others: "the conflicted, the liars, the self-deceiving, the willfully blind, the abject, the unresolved, the imperfect, the evil, the unwell, the lost and divided" (8). Smith's list parallels *Playing in the Dark*'s list of "strangers" (which I discuss in Chapter 2). Smith also echoes Morrison's language of ethical "risk": "We've gotten into the habit of not experiencing the private, risky act of reading so much as performing our response to what we read, which is then translated into data points" (10).

13. Smith, "Love Actually," 6. In *Aesthetics and Ethics in Twenty-First Century British Novels*, Peter Childs and James Green note that Smith develops her notion of ethical love through Nussbaum, as well as noting the connection Smith makes with James, but they then oversimplify both Nussbaum and James by interpreting the ethics of that tradition through the lens of Scarry's philosophy. Thus they conclude that Smith's "novels reiterate

a transcendent faith in ethical living, including the practical possibility of 'the ethical alchemy of beauty' in Elaine Scarry's words" (55).

14. Smith, "Read Better," 22.

15. Ibid.

16. Smith, "*Middlemarch* and Everybody," 29.

17. James, "George Eliot's *Middlemarch*," 81. James's evaluation of *Middlemarch* is worth quoting at length because it expresses not only his own notion of aesthetic unity but also the kind of unity staged by *On Beauty*'s plot design: "We can well remember how keenly we wondered, while its earlier chapters unfolded themselves, what turn in the way of form the story would take—that of organized, moulded, balanced composition, gratifying the reader with a sense of design and construction, or a mere chain of episodes, broken into accidental lengths and unconscious influence of a plan." In deploying a highly self-conscious unified plot, *On Beauty* performs the ethical clash between the characters it brings to life and the instrumentalizing of these lives through authorial design.

18. Ibid.

19. Smith, "Zadie, Take Three."

20. As Charles Green notes in "The Droves of Academe," "Smith's real accomplishment . . . [is] that she moves incredibly deftly from character to character, inventing fictional academics, disappointed wives, ambitious street rappers, and fledgling feminists." Green concludes this sentence with an approving value judgment about Smith's ethical relation to this diverse cast of characters, a relation expressed narratively: the author treats them all "with both acid honesty and tremendous accuracy, and even love" (184).

21. In *Learning from Experience*, Paula Moya argues that "what is noteworthy about Faulkner's departure in the last section of the novel from the pattern of focalization he sets up in the first three sections is his apparent inability, or unwillingness, to view the world from the perspective of a black female servant" (190). The switch in narrative mode is also crucial for Philip Weinstein's interpretation in his *Faulkner's Subject*, but he has a more benign view than Moya of how the switch to omniscience refers back to Faulkner's personal point of view:

> Presented from without (this distinction is crucial), the black family is conceived in nostalgia, Faulkner's nostalgia. He seems to have climbed back into his own childhood to find them, and he presents them not subjectively, as figures drowning in those conflicting internal urges and sanctions of his own (which he creatively bestowed upon the Compson siblings), but instead objectively, as figures of stability, seen from a gentle distance, reminders of the warm and witty talk, of the saving routines of childhood recollected. (48)

See my "*As I Lay Dying*'s Heterogeneous Discourse" for a discussion of the perspectival functioning of the lyric mode in that novel.

22. Wayne Booth makes this claim about the stream of consciousness generally while discussing Faulkner's method in particular in his *Rhetoric of Fiction*: "Our roving visitation into the minds of sixteen characters in Faulkner's *As I Lay Dying*, seeing nothing but what those minds contain, may seem in one sense not to depend on an omniscient narrator. But this method is omniscience with teeth in it: the implied author demands our absolute faith in his powers of divination. We must never for a moment doubt that he knows everything about each of these sixteen minds or that he has chosen correctly how much to show of each" (161). My own reading of *As I Lay Dying* ("*As I Lay Dying*'s Heterogeneous Discourse") emphasizes the way the narrative mode of that novel establishes limits to authorial omniscience by referencing not an implied author but the biographical author, William Faulkner.

23. Faulkner, *The Sound and the Fury*, 165.

24. The possibility of transcendent value that beauty represents is invoked by Virginia Woolf in her discussion of *Tristram Shandy*: "For Sterne by the beauty of his style has let us pass beyond the range of personality into a world which is not altogether the world of fiction. It is above" ("Phases of Fiction," 135). But as we can see in a novel such as *The Waves*, for the novelist committed to the representation of characters' lives the novel's aesthetic beauty might gesture to some absolute notion of beauty as its own good, but that value always stands in dialectical relation to the perspectival signification of narrative modes of lyricism.

25. In *The Return of the Omniscient Narrator*, Paul Dawson does not explicitly address Smith's narrative use of point of view but gets at the narrative duality that I am describing here through his complex understanding of how Smith's omniscient narration floats between self-authority and other-orientation. For example, Dawson concludes his close reading of a passage from *White Teeth* by explaining the implicit perspectivalism of this novel's negotiation between authorial self and characterological other: "The narrative authority of this voice invokes the cultural authority of Smith—as the child of an immigrant Jamaican mother and English father—beginning the section with an editorial 'we' that establishes complicity with the implied reader's difference from the characters, and concluding with a direct address that speaks on behalf of the characters' experience" (128). See Sommer, "The Aesthetic Turn in 'Black' Literary Studies," for an alternative understanding of *On Beauty*'s omniscient narration as a nonanthropomorphic "entity." But Sommer's Boothian view of artworks as harboring implied ethical values means that the novel ("the whole narrative") takes up the ethical address that the inhuman narration lacks: "Despite the absence of an anthropomorphic narrator imposing his or her own view on the 'gentle readers,' however, some sort

of extradiegetic communication is implied by the occasional use of the unobtrusive first-person pronoun. Yet who is the implied reader, the addressee constructed by the narrative as a whole? Who is 'we'?" (187).

26. In "Two Directions for the Novel," Smith mounts her own critique of contemporary novelists who deploy what she calls "lyrical realism," which she identifies as a legacy of Balzac and Flaubert (73). She objects to this style in terms that resonate with the reading of Faulkner I have just offered. Of Joseph O'Neill's *Netherland* she writes: "Everything must be made literary. Nothing escapes. . . . Even the mini traumas of a middle-class life are given the high lyric treatment, in what feels, at its best, like a grim satire on the profound fatuity of twenty-first century bourgeois existence" (80). Smith argues that lyricism as a signifier of the literary ultimately aestheticizes the novel's realism—turns the novel into an art object—by canceling out its ethical effects: "It seems perfectly done—in a sense, that's the problem. It's so precisely the image of what we have been taught to value in fiction that it throws that image into a kind of existential crisis, as the photograph gifts a nervous breakdown to the painted portrait" (73). See David James, "In Defense of Lyrical Realism," for an explicit engagement with Smith that mounts a defense of lyrical realism as an ethical mode (esp. 71). For the relation of James's defense of lyrical realism to a larger literary tradition that he calls "solace," see his *Discrepant Solace*: "By drawing the work of form into critical contact with dramas of devastation . . . the phenomenon of discrepant solace brings together narratives that twin the aesthetic conundrum surrounding how writing consoles with the ethical one of whether consolation is desirable at all" (7).

27. Scarry, *On Beauty*, 17.

28. The politics I am suggesting seem upheld by the fact that Alexander Nehamas, in a review of *On Beauty and Being Just*, is respectfully skeptical about the persuasiveness of Scarry's argument except when it comes to his response to the beauty of her lyrical style: "The best part of Scarry's book—a really wonderful section—is her account of her coming to see the beauty of palm trees" ("Return of the Beautiful," 395).

29. If Smith's comic rendering of the academic debates she depicts suggests her own skepticism about the quality of knowledge produced in such a setting, it is Smith's novelistic project to show how truth claims produced within the academy are no better or worse than those produced within any other social discourse. Smith puts at the center of her novel the debate between two art history professors on the nature of beauty in painting, a move that clearly invites the reader to take sides. Yet the extremity of the positions and the endlessness of the argument also suggest the self-generating nature of academic disagreement. The beliefs of each professor are too entrenched for either to change the other's mind. But Smith's portrayal of the futility of agreement between rival intellectual camps does not mean that academic debate is itself meaningless. *On Beauty* shows how

the ideas formulated and the values theorized in universities become incorporated into the thoughts of other types of social subjects. A dying woman's belief in the wisdom to be found in poetry, for example, becomes a basis of discussion that leads to a new female friendship. "An unanchored sentence" from his professor father's dry lecture becomes a way for his son to describe the sudden rush of beauty he feels when he happens upon urban bootleggers setting up their DVD display (*On Beauty*, 194).

30. See Chapters 1 and 5 for my discussion of how the new ethics positions itself as an attempt to move beyond the social determinism and what is understood as the political defeatism of Foucauldianism.

31. Smith repeatedly encourages writers to be strong enough to shoulder the burden of readerly ethical evaluation. Her most recent essay on the ethical value of fiction again emphasizes the way that authorial values inform each word of the novel: "As if . . . a writer could hope to bypass the intimate judgment of the reader, which happens sentence by sentence, moment by moment. Is it this judgment we fear? It's so uncertain, so risky" ("Fascinated to Presume," 6).

32. Smith, "Zadie, Take Three."

33. In the foreword to *Changing My Mind*, Smith emphasizes how her nonfiction writing emerged in response to specific professional invitations. What she now calls "the solemn, theoretical book about writing, *Fail Better*," never gets written because, she states, other social topics simply came to interest her more (xiii–xiv). One should also note in this regard that even earlier, in the interview "Zadie, Take Three," when she discusses her plan to write a book of literary theory, Smith describes that project as itself motivated by a professional goal and an institutional context: she explains that *Fail Better* is conceived as a way of earning a higher degree that will enable faculty employment: "I'd love to be an academic. But I'd need to get a Ph.D., so that's what I'm half working on at the moment. I'm writing a book of essays that I'd like to submit to my old college. That's the plan." This self-characterization interestingly reproduces the tension between free choice and the institutional constraints that are at stake in her novelistic sense of alterity.

34. In "Read Better," Smith explicitly declares that reading "novels is a process like no other." She holds up the novel as a corrective to systematic definitions of literature and literary value. It is the novelist, on her view, who embraces perspectivalism, expressing through the novel "this is what I love, this what I believe" (21).

35. Lubbock, *Craft of Fiction*, 251.

36. As Anna Glab notes in "The Ethical Laboratory of Beauty," "in Smith's novels, the ethical dimension does not consist of Smith moralizing or proposing ethical concepts or stances. She is aware that ethical questions are an inherent part of creating characters and representing human relationships" (491).

37. The social relation that narrative establishes between author and character works

to consolidate the social positionality of each. Thus, while Smith emphasizes in later essays that a defining attribute of fiction is its investigation into "what likeness between selves might even mean, given the profound mystery of consciousness itself" ("Fascinated to Presume," 6), through the narrative act of representing a diverse social world, the novel defines identity first and foremost in terms of social alterity. Smith's examples of the "strangers" to whom she is drawn are above all social others. She wonders, "What would it be like to be Polish or Ghanaian or Irish or Bengali, to be richer or poorer, to say these prayers or hold those politics[?]" ("Fascinated to Presume," 4).

38. See Martin, "Houses of Fiction," 124. Verifying my sense of the literary history I have sketched in Chapter 2, Dominic Head argues that Ian McEwan is "Murdoch's natural heir," despite McEwan's expressed distaste for her writing (*Ian McEwan*, 8–13). As I have been arguing, the understanding of the novel as an ethics of alterity that has no single formal mode becomes the basis of connection not just between Smith and Murdoch, McEwan and Murdoch, and Smith and McEwan, but with all these novelists and Henry James.

39. Murdoch has in mind here the famous lines that Keats wrote in a letter to Richard Woodhouse on October 27, 1818: "As for the poetical Character itself, (I mean that sort of which, if I am anything, I am a Member; that sort distinguished from the wordsworthian or egotistical sublime; which is a thing per se and stands alone) it is not itself—it has no self—it is everything and nothing—It has no character—it enjoys light and shade; it lives in gusto, be it foul or fair, high or low, rich or poor, mean or elevated—It has as much delight in conceiving an Iago as an Imogen" (qtd. in Bate, *John Keats*, 260–261). For more on the ethical connection between Murdoch and Smith, see Glab, "Ethical Laboratory of Beauty."

40. See Nussbaum, *Love's Knowledge*, esp. 144–145, for the idea that the lover excludes others as much as he "lets other things be through him" (to use Murdoch's phrase). In her discussion of James's narrative technique in these pages, Nussbaum argues that the characters who lie outside or beyond the narrator's love are those who remain mysterious for the reader. The language of Keatsian negative capability (someone capable of "being in uncertainties, Mysteries, doubts, without any irritable reaching after fact & reason" [qtd. in Bate, *John Keats*, 249]) thus creeps into Nussbaum's own account of the novelistic representation of character, both as a formal distinction between characters and as a formal relation of the reader to certain characters. See Tolan, "Zadie Smith's Forsterian Ethics," for the connection between Nussbaum's ethical notion of love and how it relates to Smith's and Forster's (esp. 143–144).

41. See Bate, *John Keats*, for the background and context for Keats's introduction of the idea of negative capability as the "quality" that "went to form a Man of Achievement, especially in Literature & which Shakespeare possessed so enormously" (249). Smith's changes of mind seem not to extend to the importance of negative capability as a way

of thinking about literature's engagement with alterity. See "Speaking in Tongues" for her re-citation of Keats (144). As I argue below, her project in this essay is to argue for Obama's perspectival diversity and to claim that he thus possesses a literary sensibility rare in political leaders. In this essay she also explicitly describes her positive valuation of multiperspectivalism as in keeping with her "novelist credo" (148).

42. In *Novel Style*, Ben Masters furthers the argument I am making here through his powerful analysis of the narrative ethics of alterity Smith deploys in *NW*. Masters attends to the way Smith uses narrative to show "how the smallest formal unit can in fact enact and confer specific ways of knowing the mind of another" (141). Master usefully situates Smith's ethical project alongside those undertaken by Nicola Barker's *Darkmans* (2007) and David Mitchell's *Cloud Atlas* (2004) (see esp. 141–152).

43. Kanika Batra makes the case for Kiki's feminism in her "Kipps, Belsey, and Jegede," but her reading of *On Beauty* attends little to the complications to this feminism raised by Smith's narrative organization (see esp. 1088–1090).

44. Blackham, *Six Existentialist Thinkers*, 118.

45. Rich, "Zadie Smith's Culture Warriors."

46. Kermode, "Here She Is."

47. See Driscoll, "'Our Economic Position,'" for a critique of Smith that levels against her the same type of criticisms that Raymond Williams directed toward George Eliot (qtd. in Chapter 1). Driscoll sees class as setting the ideological limit for her representation of characterological otherness, arguing that *On Beauty* replicates "the ideological marginalization of the working-class subject" (61). Interestingly, he contrasts what he sees as Smith's political failure with Forster's success: "While Smith is valorizing [her characters' emotional] muddle for its humanist power and goodness, in Forster it [class bias] is something that his text is actively trying to move beyond" (65).

48. Forster, *Aspects of the Novel*, 24.

49. In the interview "Zadie, Take Three," Smith indicates her awareness of the tension that structures the novel's aesthetic economy as a conflict between the creation of living characters and the achievement of aesthetic form. She states that the characters in *On Beauty* are the first she has written that she could "engage at all with the idea that they were in a way real people." She implies that this autonomy and vitality is directly related to her self-conscious effort to move away from the strong philosophical and formal control she exercised over her other fictional works: "I'd think of a theme and tie up all the ends and ta-da!" I would argue that the degree to which her characters seem newly living to her is the degree to which the authorial "ta-da" becomes an aesthetic problem, which is to say, the problem posed by the novelistic aesthetics of alterity that informs her view of the novel.

50. Kermode also understands Smith's novelistic project as invested in truth-telling and wisdom claims. He rightly sees this commitment as a strong basis of connection

between Smith and Forster. Kermode notes that Forster's use of aphorism landed him in the *Oxford Dictionary of Quotations* as a source of pithy philosophical wisdom, but this same stylistic feature opened his novels up to the aesthetic flaw of preachiness. I take Kermode to be implicitly diagnosing contemporary culture's relativity and perspectivalism when he notes that "Smith's seriousness cannot be expressed in the same way [as Forster's aphorisms], not because she thinks relationships in the larger [philosophical] sense are unimportant but because they can't be separated from relationships more narrowly conceived" ("Here She Is").

51. See Fischer, "'Gimme Shelter,'" for an alternative view of the function of stereotypes in the novel. Fisher focuses on the way the characters' understanding of one another is mediated by stereotypes, and, guided by Scarry's philosophical text, concludes that Smith "urges us to reject binary paradigms and to connect across socially constructed differences so that we can see the full beauty of humanity" (107).

52. Smith, "Fail Better," par. 19.

53. Smith, *Changing My Mind*, xiii–xiv.

54. In her recent "Fascinated to Presume," Smith implicitly reinvokes her earlier views about how fiction performs its ethics of alterity when she distinguishes the felt ethical risk the novelist takes when she represents a social world of persons different from herself and the triumphalism that she detects in the lines that she quotes from Walt Whitman: "Do I contradict myself? / Very well then I contradict myself, / (I am large, I contain multitudes)." Smith poses a set of critical questions that articulate the kind of political and material considerations at issue for the novelistic aesthetics of alterity: "How can Whitman—white, gay, American—possibly contain, say, a black polysexual British girl or a nonbinary Palestinian or a Republican Baptist from Atlanta?" (4).

55. "E. M. Forster, Middle Manager" was originally written as a review of *The BBC Talks of E. M. Forster* and published in the *New York Review of Books* in 2008.

56. Pankaj Mishira's review of *Changing My Mind* gently (but tellingly for my argument) disparages Smith's need as an essay writer to rely on philosophy-speak: "A few of [Smith's] readers may still pause to wonder if the growing irrelevance of academic philosophy is as strong an influence—even on people at university campuses—as the ravages of 'late capitalism'" ("Other Voices, Other Selves").

57. For a reading of *On Beauty* that understands Smith's ethical praise of Forster as a defense of cosmopolitanism, see Moraru, "The Forster Connection": "What draws Smith to Forster and, in particular, to the 1910 classic is her precursor's relational imagination, and, behind it, his uniquely cosmopolitan mindset. The connection is just one among many setting forth the strong emphasis Forster places on disinterested ties, friendship and affective bonds, human affiliations, and generally on the other's nurturing proximity to the self no matter how far apart the two may be by location, ethno-racial background, or political

allegiance.... The Jamaican-British writer finds a generous model of worldliness and sociality that she extends to a place and time where such values seem in short supply" (134).

58. See Dick and Lupton, "On Lecturing and Being Beautiful," for an astute analysis of Smith's depiction of the social function of the lecture in *On Beauty* (see note 2). In keeping with my analysis of the difference Smith sees between Forster the novelist and Forster the lecturer, Dick and Lupton define the lecture as "a form of discourse in which aesthetic experience is routinely presented, by theorists from Adam Smith to John Stuart Mill to Jacques Derrida, as being beyond the systems that a lecturer describes" (117).

59. "Speaking in Tongues" made three different public appearances: first in 2008 as a public lecture given at the New York Public Library, then as an essay in the *New York Review of Books*, and then reprinted in *Changing My Mind*.

60. See my analysis of double consciousness as double voice in *Social Formalism* (197–220).

61. Robbins, "Pretend What You Like," 203, 199. Robbins offers an incisive analysis of how ungrounded claims for the positive nature of literary value have proliferated in an attempt to move literary studies away from the post-Foucauldian prisonhouse of power and the negativity of critique. More particularly, he argues that Judith Butler's concept of performativity, which he defines as "the self-consciously theatrical way of playing with identities and revealing their constructedness," reproduces the notion of literature's freedom "to re-imagine and recreate the social world" (199). My reading of Butler alternatively sees a connection between her theory of ethical otherness and the material restrictions integral to the construction of that identity as illuminated from within the Jamesian novel tradition.

62. Ibid.

63. Robbins's critique of gender performativity is derived from Phillips, "Keeping It Moving"; see Robbins, "Pretend What You Like," n34. See Eagleton, *Trouble with Strangers*, for a critique of poststructuralist new ethics that echoes Robbins and Phillips (esp. 305–313). Robbins, through Phillips, glosses performativity as a theory of identity as willed possibility, which can be summed up through the catch phrase "pretend what you like" (199). Eagleton develops this idea from his own perspective: ethics as "imperatives, prohibitions, promises, prescriptions and the like proves convenient for the poststructuralists.... It promises to reduce the question of ethics to the performative realm where they feel most at home" (313).

Chapter 4: J. M. Coetzee's *Elizabeth Costello*

1. Coetzee, *Waiting for the Barbarians*, 49.

2. Gilbert Yeoh argues that this novel accomplishes its ethical alterity through an "ethics of love" that governs the meaning of characterological action and formal design: *The Age of Iron*'s "implicit chiasmic form ... invites one to enact a *reversal* of the dynamics

in the novel. A crucial reversal reveals that it is not Mrs. Curren who loves Verceuil, but Verceuil who loves Mrs. Curren" (107; emphasis in the original).

3. See Attwell, *J. M. Coetzee*, for an overview of Coetzee's early oeuvre, especially as those novels depict the agency of the individual and "the conditions governing this freedom" under what Atwell calls South Africa's "colonial postcolonialism" (6).

4. In "J. M. Coetzee and the Limits of Language," Carol Clarkson describes the ethical problem at the heart of *Disgrace* in Levinasian terms as, "How does one write the other, the singular, the as-yet-untold, in language that inexorably follows tracks of the known, the familiar, the already-said?" (107). See Dekoven, "Going to the Dogs," for an interpretation of *Disgrace* as telling a "salvation narrative" in which the "possibility of hope" in a world ruled by "the seemingly terminally destructive power of global capital" is located in the "alliance" of two different kinds of subaltern others: "middle-aged women, who function for the purpose of this ethical narrative as shamanic figures, with nonhuman animals" (847). The critical record on *Disgrace* is evenly split between critics who argue that the novel dramatizes the success of David Lurie's ethical development and those who argue that Coetzee ironizes the terms of that success. See, e.g., Marais, "J. M. Coetzee's *Disgrace*," which argues that "Coetzee tasks his protagonist with the ethical obligation of developing a sympathetic imagination" but "undermines, even as it installs, the possibility of this development" (76). In *Fiction across Borders*, Shameem Black takes Marais's description of imagination's limits as his starting point but emphasizes "the ethically productive moments of failure that seem to mark Coetzee's portrayal of sympathy" (218). See Willett, "Ground Zero," for a useful overview of the various conceptions of ethical alterity that critics bring to this novel (esp. 7).

5. Adding to the sense of this novel's discursive complexity is the fact that many of the lessons were delivered by Coetzee as academic lectures. These include "What Is Realism?" (Bennington College, 1996), "The Lives of Animals" (two Princeton Tanner lectures, 1997–1998), and "The Novel in Africa" (delivered at the University of California, Berkeley's Townsend Center for the Humanities, 1999). As David Lodge notes, "Instead of delivering conventional lectures . . . he read to his audience a work of fiction, about a distinguished Australian novelist called Elizabeth Costello" ("Disturbing the Peace," par. 2). As noted in the acknowledgments to the novel, earlier versions of Lessons One through Six were all previously published. The character of Elizabeth Costello also appears in the short story "As a Woman Grows Older" (2004) and the novel *Slow Man* (2005).

6. See Chesney, "Towards an Ethics of Silence," for a reading of *Michael K* that relates the ethical achievement of alterity to the failure of narrative representation (esp. 317–318).

7. See Kompridis, "Recognition and Receptivity," for an argument that explicitly works out the ethics of alterity in regard to the personhood that should be accorded to Elizabeth Costello: "If we are to make sense of what it is Nora Helmer [from Ibsen's *A*

Doll's House] and Elizabeth Costello are demanding from their audiences, from us, we must recognize that theirs are calls for acknowledgement—calls that call in turn for some change in us we are reluctant, or that we refuse, to answer. . . . But is there not violence in the resistance to change, in its refusal?" (14).

8. In "J. M. Coetzee's Australian Realism," Elleke Boehmer explores the notion of "making up an Australia" as it pertains to Coetzee's own project. She notes how he both strives to represent his knowledge of everyday Australia but also destabilizes this authority by casting doubt on the "real" and how you can attain it. Patrick Hayes argues that what it means for Coetzee to make up Australia is for him to have "moved away from an overt concern with the politics of difference and the problem of inhabiting a radically intercultural society such as South Africa, to focus on the different, though related, moral debate over what it means to live in a cultural space dominated by the skeptical, rational, and egalitarian side of post-Enlightenment political culture" (*J. M. Coetzee and the Novel*, 223). Melinda Harvey by contrast argues that "Coetzee's late novels do not set themselves the task of summoning a sense of Australian place; in fact, they set themselves the task of testing and proving treacherous the usual methods by which a sense of place is summoned in novels" ("'In Australia You Start Zero,'" 27).

9. Coetzee, *Elizabeth Costello*, 12. See Attwell, "J. M. Coetzee and the Idea of Africa," for a critical investigation that effectively turns Costello's example of "making up" Australia into an interpretive question about Coetzee's own ethical and aesthetic success in bringing Africa to life. The terms of Attwell's argument are, significantly, in keeping with the antinomy that I am arguing is at play in the novelistic aesthetics of alterity: "Coetzee develops the idea of Africa in ways that chasten and embolden his art but at the price of rendering Africa obscure" (81). Attwell further argues that the failure of the novels to stabilize the idea of Africa as a master signifier represents Coetzee's refusal to submit to his readers' desire for a view of Africa that would "leave open the possibility of a perfectly quotidian Africa, and also a dynamic Africa in which processes of cultural translation enable us to put aside the unreconstructed myths of the past" (82).

10. In another example of the coherence of the literary tradition I am charting, Costello's ethical view of the world-making task of the novel is echoed by Zadie Smith, who describes that process from the point of view of the reader: "When it comes to reading, it's a Kierkegaardian level of commitment that we've forgotten about: intimate, painstaking, with nothing at all to do with Hegelian system-building or theoretical schools, and everything to do with our ethical reality as subjects. You have to make the map of Copenhagen yourself. You have to be open to the idea that Copenhagen might look and feel completely different to what you expect it to be. You have to throw away other people's maps" ("Read Better," 21).

11. Derek Attridge has perhaps more than any other critic established the terms for the ethical understanding of Coetzee's narrative form. As he writes in *J. M. Coetzee and*

the Ethics of Reading, what makes Coetzee's novels "singular, and singularly powerful is what they do, how they happen . . . how otherness is engaged, staged, distanced, embraced, how it is manifested in the rupturing of narrative discourse, in the lasting uncertainties of reference, in the simultaneous exhibiting and doubting of the novelist's authority" (30–31). And crucial to what they do, as Attridge elucidates it through his examples, is the solicitation of one kind of readerly response in order to turn it into another: to transform the pleasures of the reader's engagement with the storyworld (the gripping emotions triggered by storyworld action and conflict; the easy judgments or wisdom claims that the reader may abstract from storyworld events and outcomes) into an experience of alterity. Literature gains its ethical privilege (it is singularly powerful) through the way Coetzee puts the reader in the position of looking in at or upon an autonomous social world in order to confound that distanced view through acts of narrative representation that interrupt the reader's familiar emotional responses and disable confident ethical judgment (30–31). The development of Attridge's thinking about the exceptionalism of literary creativity can be traced from his early claims about the "peculiarity" of literature in *Peculiar Language* and the larger theory of creativity as the invention of the "new" that he advances in *The Singularity of Literature* (2004).

12. Alter, *Partial Magic*, xiii. See Weinberger, "Critical Desire and the Novel," for an important theorization from a Girardian perspective of a novelistic ethics particular to self-conscious novels.

13. As Coetzee writes of *Robinson Crusoe*, readers don't regard *Robinson Crusoe* "in light of a literary performance. Defoe has none of their thoughts—Robinson all" (*Stranger Shores*, 18).

14. See Wicomb, "*Slow Man* and the Real," for an example of how Barthes's critique of novelistic realism has been applied to Coetzee. Because *Slow Man* is arguably a more typical metafiction, it lends itself more readily than *Elizabeth Costello* to Wicomb's deconstructive interpretation: "*Slow Man* offers itself as prothesis, lays out on the credence table its own hermeneutic. It waves its flags; there is ultimately nothing hidden; I can only describe what-has-been-read" (23).

15. See Moses, "'King of the Amphibians,'" for a description of the variety of nonfictional speech genres that organize discourse in the storyworld (esp. 28). See Carstensen, "Shattering the Word-Mirror," for a thorough categorization of the novelistic modes at play across the novel. Whereas Carstensen argues that this multiplicity is deployed by Coetzee to represent the death of the novel as a literary form for the contemporary age, to reflect, that is to say, the loss of belief in all of its long history of representational conventions, I am arguing that this aesthetic multiplicity is in fact monolithically unified by the ethics of alterity that Coetzee credits to each mode. That Carstensen's interpretation of *Elizabeth Costello* ultimately comes back to making an ethical claim proves my point: "It

is by addressing this question of the moral and ethical value of any literary activity—by scrutinizing the writer's responsibility in the world—that *Elizabeth Costello* leaves the purely metafictional realm and re-emerges as a truly political text" (94). But I would argue as well that Carstensen, having overgeneralized about the meaninglessness represented by narrative modal variety, also overestimates the clarity of the novel's political message.

16. Michael Moses goes even further to argue that *Elizabeth Costello* depicts the variety of representational modes from the whole of literary history as available to the contemporary novelist:

> Coetzee opts to depict [fictional beings] by whatever formal devices and technical means he can bring to hand (including those that prevailed in the literary epochs before the rise of realism). Not just "real" men and women, but gods and beasts, the living and the dead, those who dwell in this world or an alternative one, can be embodied in his fiction—and their forms may be represented by any and all means at the disposal of his artistic imagination regardless of their "historical" appropriateness. (36–37)

17. In "The Human Document," Nancy Ruttenburg offers an important challenge to understanding *Elizabeth Costello* in light of the ethics of alterity (53). Ruttenburg argues on the contrary that Lesson Six, "The Problem of Evil," presents the novel's generic power as a readerly merging with fictional characters that is so involuntary as to be "instantaneous" (56), so bodily as to be a "species of incarnation" that joins characters and readers in one "flesh," and so outside the bounds of sociality that it leaves behind "the ethical law meant to govern and limit it" (63). My own reading of "The Problem of Evil" would note that the tenability of this ontological view of character is qualified by the narrative arc of Costello's meditation. Seeking to explain why she is so profoundly disturbed by Paul West's novel, her final position is to expose the act of merger as a mask worn by ethical complicity. The progress of her analysis first holds West as author responsible for bringing to life "Hitler's butcherman" (176): "Where did that energy come from? To herself she has called it satanic, but perhaps she should let go of that word now. For the energy came, in a certain sense, from West himself. It was West who invented the gibes (English gibes, not German), put them in the hangman's mouth" (177). Whatever illusion of characterological ontological autonomy and priority is created by fiction, ethical responsibility returns to a human origin. And this includes the reader. Costello's disturbing conclusion ends in self-criticism: "He [West] made her read, *excited* her to read. For that she will not easily forgive him" (179; emphasis in the original). Her aesthetic response is thus distinguishable from the readerly sympathy that Ruttenburg takes as the basis of literary "incarnation." Excitement is the aesthetic remainder of the difference between readerly and characterological persons. And it is

also what reintroduces ethics: the evil that Costello feels she experiences comes not only, as Ruttenburg puts it, from the "interpenetration of consciousness" that novels afford (63) but from her own personal sense that she "conspired" in her own ethical violation by surrendering to West's narrative power.

18. In "Double Entendre," Shaun Irlam describes this as *Elizabeth Costello*'s depiction of "the chameleon capabilities that enable the artistic imagination to negate itself in order to inhabit and give body to other characters, personae, forms of consciousness, and modes of being" (136).

19. Eckard Smuts, in "Reading Through the Gates," argues more generally for the political self-consciousness that the novel develops through and as the destabilization of generic structures, exploring "the implications for subjective authenticity of the limits imposed by the structural necessities of representation, and how Coetzee deals with the totalitarian propensities of form by embedding in his text a self-reflexive awareness of these propensities" (221).

20. The connection between this particular formulation of ethical alterity with Zadie Smith and Ian McEwan is drawn in a 2005 interview that Smith conducts with McEwan. Smith offers this characterization of her agreement with McEwan: "You say that if the terrorists [in *Saturday*] had been able to empathize properly with these others, with the very *idea* of otherness, then they couldn't have done what they did. Now that's something I do believe, and it's a belief I sort of 'push' in my fiction—that real empathy makes cruelty an impossibility" ("Zadie Smith Talks with Ian McEwan," 211; emphasis in the original).

21. In his exchange with the psychoanalyst Arabella Kurtz, Coetzee articulates the ethics of alterity as a good to be achieved in life as well as in the novel: "Yet at a deeper level dialogue requires a power of projecting oneself, via a faculty of sympathy, into the life-view and ultimately the being of the other. This projection of oneself cannot be into some imagined version of the other: it has to be into the actual being of the other, no matter how difficult and unpleasant and even boring that may be" (Coetzee and Kurtz, *The Good Story*, 52). Yet he also claims in the same exchange, "I would contend that our sympathetic identifications have a fiction-like status, and that our sympathetic intuitions can be relied on only to yield fictional truths" (134).

22. Anna Jones Abramson argues similarly that the model of ethical sympathy developed in *Elizabeth Costello* is tied to "a consistently spatialized act of inhabiting (not just imagining) the other" ("Ethics of Inhabiting," 21). Abramson's emphasis on the materialities that she believes are projected through the effort to constitute the other as a place and in a place leads to her intriguing claim that "inhabiting pushes imagination beyond familiar models of sympathy and perception by demanding a more radical sort of investment in other bodily, affective, proprioceptive, and environmental spaces. It follows that for an author, character-drawing becomes a kind of world-making" (21–22).

23. See Coetzee and Kurtz, *The Good Story*, for Coetzee's nonfictional critique of Nagel and his support of Costello's notion that through "a strenuous effort of sympathetic projection one can reach a flickering intuition of what it is like for a bat to be a bat. But this does not amount to the claim that one can have intuitions of what is it *really* like for a bat to be a bat" (136).

24. In "Sympathy with Animals and Salvation of the Soul," Jonathan Lamb powerfully argues that in Costello's model of the sympathetic imagination "the measure of the likeness is registered by passion—joy—and to talk of joy is to talk either of being like a god or like an animal." He further argues that "this extraordinary state of consciousness . . . requires something like a person (whether divine, animal, or human) to improve the noncoincidence of self-perception: So it is by persons, phantoms, and passions we find out what is our own, what belongs to us, whoever we are, and how to save our souls" (83–84).

25. James, preface to *The Ambassadors*. In reflecting retrospectively on the characterological project that he set himself in *The Ambassadors*, James describes Lambert Strether as "having imagination galore" and regards this quality as taxing his own imagination as how to best represent this "enriched" "personage": "It was immeasurable, the opportunity to 'do' a man of imagination" (310).

26. Coetzee explicitly invites the question as to whether Costello's lectures and intellectual opinions possess philosophical coherence and weight. "The Poets and the Animals" begins with John Bernard's wife Norma, an academic philosopher, eviscerating the argument that Costello makes in "The Lives of Animals," the Appleton College lecture that she has delivered the night before. But even before that, in Lesson One, John Bernard, listening to his mother answer questions for an interviewer, muses to himself that he "is still not sure what she thinks about the big questions. Not sure and, on the whole, thankful not to have to hear. For her thoughts would be, he suspects, as uninteresting as most people's. A writer, not a thinker. Writers and thinkers: chalk and cheese" (10). His mother echoes her son's view that a gift for fiction does not necessarily equate with philosophical power: as she states in her Gates Lecture, "But the fact is, if you had wanted someone to come here and discriminate for you between mortal and immortal souls, or between rights and duties, you would have called in a philosopher, not a person whose sole claim to your attention is to have written stories about made-up people" (66). Yet like the fictional radio interviewers, television producers, and literary critics in the social world of the novel, real-life literary critics find philosophical consistency in Costello's views. See Anker, "*Elizabeth Costello*, Embodiment, and the Limits of Rights," for example, on how the opinions expressed by Costello in "The Lives of Animals" have been connected to "a recent theoretical preoccupation with animality, a trend fueled in part by Derrida's late writings" (171). Significantly for my argument, Anker does not quarrel with the notion that Costello's

opinions add up to a rigorous philosophical position; she only disagrees with the kind of philosophy Costello supports: the phenomenology of Merleau-Ponty rather than the poststructuralist ethics of Derrida. In turning Coetzee's novel into a philosophical position (poststructuralist or phenomenological), literary critics in real life fulfill Coetzee's fictional depiction of the cultural need to treat as oracles writers with a talent for making up people. As John accompanies his mother on her publicity tour, he thinks of himself as serving "at her shrine, cleaning up after the turmoil of the holy day, sweeping up the petals, collecting the offerings, putting the widows' mites together, ready to bank" (*Elizabeth Costello*, 31).

For other examples of philosophical systematizations of Coetzee's ideas, see Dovey, *Novels of J. M. Coetzee* (a Lacanian reading); Pippen, "Paradoxes of Power" (a Hegelian reading); and Ryan, "A Woman Thinking" (an Arendtian reading). Anton Leist and Peter Singer, in "Coetzee and Philosophy," the introduction to their volume of essays *Coetzee and Ethics*, offer perhaps the most sophisticated understanding of Coetzee as a philosophical writer by taking on board the difference between being a philosophical writer of fiction and using fiction to uphold the ideas of a particular philosopher. Identifying Coetzee's philosophical vision as distinguished by the qualities of reflectivity, paradoxical truth-seeking, and an ethics of social relationships, List and Singer usefully explain how these qualities function as a problematic, each quality raising questions of priority, and compellingly describe how "the self-destructive excesses" of each philosophical position are contained through the fiction writer's characterological project, a project that allows "a much more differentiated grasp of the same qualities" (7–8).

For an example of interpretations that argue instead for the novel's deliberate defiance of philosophical coherence, see Carstensen, "Shattering the Word-Mirror" (esp. 89). See MacLeod, "'Do We of Necessity'" for a reading mounted through *Foe* that defends novelistic storytelling against the reductionism imposed on novels by "critical apparatus" (15). In *J. M. Coetzee*, Dominic Head similarly argues against philosophical/critical reductiveness: "Coetzee's distrust of criticism, his refusal to see it as an object deserving of respect, does not, of course, deny the presence of theoretical ideas as inspiration for his fictional motifs. But the insistence on the uniqueness of the creative process must alert us to the special ways in which such ideas are fictionalized, and make us skeptical of finding the theorists's agenda untransformed" (26–27). Cynthia Willett's reading of *Disgrace* might seem an example of Head's view, but in arguing that Julia Kristeva's "rendition of alterity ethics brings us close to the novel's vision, and yet the novel points towards a more primordial basis of ethics in the search for meaning through the human encounter with other animal species" (1), Willett does not appeal, as Head does, to the power of fictionality per se to transform theory. See Mulhall, *Wounded Animal*, for a book-length investigation of the way *Elizabeth Costello* stages the relation between philosophical and literary inquiry. Mulhall calls on an array of philosophers to adjudicate the points of contact between literature and philosophy (from Plato to Heidegger, from Aquinas to Cavell). He concludes:

> It is only a Kafkaesque realism such as Coetzee's that can hope to convey an accurate impression of the various difficulties of reality, both for literature and philosophy. And only philosophy that is both realist and modernist—committed to achieving a lucid grasp of reality, and willing to put in question any prevailing philosophical conventions concerning that enterprise that appear at present to block or subvert its progress, including the convention that philosophical realism is no more literature's business than literary realism is any concern of philosophy's—will be capable of being properly, genuinely impressed by Coetzee's achievement. (252)

27. See Klopper, "'We Are Not Made for Revelation,'" for an interpretation of how Costello's use of language in the postscript functions as an attempt to know divinity through embodiment: "In the narrative, Costello shares with Chandos the aspiration towards a language of the body, a language that connects us with things that are of the same substance as the body, brute material things, and like Chandos, suggests that this language of the body is the closest we can get to a kind of divine language that connects us with all of creation" (127).

28. Rather than interpreting this passage as a deliberate performance of paradoxical thinking in service of an imaginative experience of alterity, Anker understands the thematization of paradox through the philosophical framework of Merleau-Ponty: "Predicated on a sustained incoherence—which is to say that philosophical expatiation and analysis will only deepen such a paradox—our embodiment simultaneously subverts customary assumptions about rational knowledge and contests the fiction of the self-determining, autonomous self" (180–181). Anker thus by way of Merleau-Ponty turns Costello's account of a specific act of ethical alterity that Costello states is available to those who possess an exceptional amount of imagination into a universal truth about the human condition.

29. This notion of the imagination's capacity to perform ethical work through the disablement of reason is at issue in Marais's description of the ethical imagination that he finds operative in *Disgrace*:

> At the same time as it assigns the reader the task of completing it, the novel indicates that this cannot be done, and consequently that the task that it requires the reader to perform is not properly a task, that is, a work that the subject is able to accomplish in a world of possibility and action. In stating this paradox, the novel seeks not to render futile the reader's endeavor to say the unsayable, to imagine the unimaginable, but

> rather to inscribe the infinite distance between itself and its own reading, and thereby attempt to make of reading an event in which the reader encounters what exceeds the cognitive categories of his culture and over which he thus exercises no control. (88)

Marais goes on to characterize this readerly experience as one of embodied alterity: "The reader would be unable to exclude the otherness of what he reads from his psyche. In being unable to complete the novel, he would be invaded and possessed by that which exceeds it and the language and discourses in which it is situated" (89).

30. In "Reading in the In-Between," Reingard Nethersole credits literary language qua language with the "double meaning" that in Nethersole's quotation of Elizabeth Costello's words "'allows us to share at times the being of another'" (272). On his view, the postscript serves as a metacommentary on the novel precisely because its citationality "exposes . . . the aporiatic quality of figurality that dwells in all language and especially in creative fiction" (273). But I would note that in the phrase "especially creative fiction" Nethersole ends up privileging the novel as a literary genre of alterity, despite the fact that his aim is to argue more generally for the "triangular relation" between author, writer/writing, and the written (256). Mark Sanders develops a similar argument through the framework of Derridean linguistics to explain the act of characterological othering operative in Coetzee's Nobel Prize speech ("The Writing Business," see esp. 44). Patrick Hays also advocates for a Heideggerian-deconstructive" view of Coetzee's ethics: "True difference will bring about an interruption in the very terms used to gain knowledge of the other; sustained dialogue will therefore bring about a sustainedly unsettling 'churn of words,' in which a given pattern of thinking is placed in transformative contact with that which it excludes" (*J. M. Coetzee and the Novel*, 31).

31. For a feminist investigation of the gender politics of Coetzee's representation of Elizabeth Costello that complicates through the consideration of race the ideological terms of praise Susan bestows on Costello's novels, see Sue Kossew's "'Women's Words.'" Kossew argues that "Coetzee's women are each, in their own way, concerned to find an authentic 'women's voice' to set against patriarchal authority but their search is complicated by their own complicity in that authority [because they are all white]" (168). In "The South African Literary Establishment and the Textual Production of 'Woman,'" Josephine Dodd draws attention to the sexist depictions of women in most major South African literature and includes Coetzee in this indictment. "Why," Dodd asks, "do women's bodies have to be used as the vehicle for discussion of socio-political issues like racism or aesthetic inquiries into the nature of creativity?" (164).

In "Staging John Coetzee / Elizabeth Costello," Heather Walton investigates Coetzee's gender politics by focusing on Coetzee's live readings of sections from the novel, which dramatize how public performance and textual representation both are "iconic representations of a man *imagining* a woman, a man *becoming* a woman in the privileged space of the dramatic arena and an *author on trial* before an audience" (287; emphasis in the original). Walton concludes that Coetzee's investment in a female protagonist ultimately reflects his attempt to redress South African apartheid cultural ideologies, which she describes as a "perverse desire for purity and a fear of mixing" (290). She further argues that the instability of Coetzee's relation to Costello "demonstrates the impurity and mixture that constitute literature. The disturbed response of his audiences demonstrate [sic] not only legitimate political anxieties but archaic concerns that boundaries have been transgressed and a contagion has occurred" (291). While Susan finds in Costello's narrative modes the truth of female experience, Walton attributes to literary language more generally a truth about representation that she believes is politicized and particularized by Coetzee's South African identity. See Judie Newman's "Intertextuality, Power, and Danger" for a similar argument about the "pollution anxiety" conveyed through Coetzee's intertextuality and allusiveness. Newman's focus is on *Waiting for the Barbarians*, whose uses of allusion, she contends, "dramatize the attraction of category membership and the extent to which the desire for such rigid categorizations implicates the reader in the dirty story of Empire" (132).

32. See Spivak, "Three Women's Texts." Spivak argues that the narrative construction of *Jane Eyre* reflects the ideology of Brontë's white, bourgeois feminism.

33. Dirk Klopper interprets Costello's investment in Kafka as working toward a new and better modality of novelistic representation that would move beyond the "binary opposition between realism and allegory" ("'We Are Not Made for Revelation,'" 128).

34. Coetzee voices this view of the artist in *The Good Story*: "While we sleep, the artist is awake" (Coetzee and Kurtz, 59).

35. Chris Danta brings Kafka's notion of the sacrificial animal to bear on Costello's praise for Red Peter as narratively embedded ("'Like a Dog . . . like a Lamb,'" 728).

36. In "Coetzee in/and Afrikaans," Rita Barnard argues that Coetzee's interrogation of authorship from the character's point of view is so essential to his thinking about fiction writing that he devotes his Nobel Prize address to calling into question the "usual hierarchy" between author and character. Bernard seeks to establish a biographical basis for Coetzee's investment in the notion that authorial identity is attached to fictional others. By contrast, Nancy Ruttenburg argues that Coetzee explores on philosophical grounds "the possibility of a literary ontology," one of the features of which is "the ontological priority" of characters over readers ("Human Document," 51).

37. See Wittenberg, "Imperial Space," for an application of this politicized view of the novel's generic identity as developed out of and then applied to *Foe*. Bill Ashcroft more generally praises Coetzee for resisting "what may be the ultimate imperialism, the empire of the author's voice" ("Silence as Heterotopia," 141).

38. See Attwell, "J. M. Coetzee and the Idea of Africa," for an incisive analysis of how Egudu's representation as an "indubitably seedy figure" serves as a lightning rod for readers who desire positive portraits of African identity and those who argue that "Coetzee deconstructs the discourses of power from within" by "scrupulously . . . acknowledging the positionality of his work" (68).

39. Aarthi Vadde usefully adds to the literary history I am tracing by making the connection between Woolf's refusal in *A Room of One's Own* to provide her audience with "a nugget of pure truth to wrap up between the pages of your notebooks and keep on the mantelpiece forever" ("Guidance in Perplexity," 238; qtd. from Woolf) with Elizabeth Costello's reluctance to fulfill the cultural position of oracle and Coetzee's own comment, made one day after winning the Nobel Prize, that "the idea of writer as sage is pretty much dead today" ("Guidance in Perplexity," 233; qtd. from Coetzee).

40. As Valeria Mosca notes, the question of the relationship of Coetzee to his character is usually formulated as a critical question of authorial identification: "Is she an alter-ego of Coetzee, or a mask he wears?" ("'A Purgatory of Clichés,'" 127).

41. Thorsten Carstensen interprets Costello's loss of belief as emblematizing "the postmodern loss of metanarratives" that is anticipated by "Lord Chandos's skepticism toward rational judgments." He regards her desire to be "no more than a 'secretary of the invisible'" as a disciplined retreat from "the Hegelian narrative of modernity" ("Shattering the Word-Mirror," 92, 90). Michael Moses agrees that "Coetzee wishes us to consider seriously the merits of Lady Elizabeth's raptures" ("'King of the Amphibians,'" 31). Moses intriguingly interprets "At the Gate" as depicting Costello's "post-mortem existence in a simulacrum of a turn-of-the-century Austro-Italian border town translated to the great beyond" (33). From the philosopher's perspective represented by Michael Funk Deckard and Ralph Palm in "Irony and Belief in *Elizabeth Costello*," Costello "remains forever on one side of the gate, caught inarticulately in an opposition, unable to either articulate a belief in something or to abandon her attachment to the possibility of an abstract, ineffable alternative. She wants beliefs without belief, to convince others without reason, justification without grounds, a 'heart' without blood. Ultimately this unresolved conflict is the tragedy of *Elizabeth Costello*" (352).

42. Lodge's interpretation of the novel would understand Costello's question as reflecting Coetzee's despair over the regard for literature in our contemporary moment: "Certainly one senses in the book's implied author, as well as in its heroine, a disillusionment with the value our culture attributes to literature, a strong feeling that, in Marianne Moore's words, 'there are things that are important beyond all this fiddle,' and a kind of restiveness at being regarded as 'a writer of world importance'" ("Disturbing the Peace," par. 22).

Chapter 5: The New Ethics in the Academy

1. Jessica Berman's theory of the ethically transformative nature of the literary imagination is introduced by way of Hannah Arendt: "Hannah Arendt makes clear that this act of narration, which goes on between and among people, constitutes a 'web of human relations' in which political action takes place" (*Modernist Commitments*, 6). Berman develops Arendt's view into an ethics of alterity that privileges not just the literary imagination, but the novel's capacity for a range of autonomies that she values as achieved alterities: "By reordering, recasting, and reconfiguring events, characters, and stories, narrative functions as the site of innovation and re-creation of the world, the intersection of the aesthetic and epistemological in the creation of new 'facts' or ways of viewing them, the construction of a new narrative world as an object of knowledge and sensation, and the world of language and the imagination to figure and transform this world" (6).

2. For arguments about the origins of this ethical turn, see Buell, "In Pursuit of Ethics"; Davis and Womack, *Mapping the Ethical Turn*; Garber, Hanssen, and Walkowitz, *Turn to Ethics*; Harpham, *Shadows of Ethics*, 1–49; Marchitello, *What Happens to History*; Parker, "Introduction"; and Sanders, "Ethics and Interdisciplinarity." For the influence of Levinas on the new ethical literary theory, see Critchley, *Ethics, Politics, Subjectivity*; and Eaglestone, *Ethical Criticism*. For an attempt to move new ethics away from Levinas, see Badiou, *Ethics*, esp. 19–20. See my notes to Chapter 1 for salient applications of the new ethical criticism to the contemporary novelists I discuss in that chapter.

3. In *Giving an Account*, Judith Butler launches her inquiry into "how to pose the question of moral philosophy . . . within a contemporary social frame" by defending the notion of individual agency as against postmodern critique: "Although many contemporary critics worry that this means there is no concept of the subject that can serve as the ground of moral agency and moral accountability, that conclusion does not follow" (8).

4. The argument advanced in this chapter has been expanded and refined since the early versions published as "Fiction as Restriction" (2007) and "Aesthetics and the New Ethics" (2009).

5. Peggy Kamuf is an example of a theorist who argues for the ethical value of literature generally: "Fiction, poetry, would be experience only on the condition that we understand: experience of the other" ("'Fiction,'" 162).

6. See Altieri, "Lyrical Ethics" and "Taking Lyrics Literally," for an important counterpoint to the ethical valorization of the novel.

7. See Altieri's *Particulars of Rapture* for an alternative interpretation of Nussbaum's literary ethics (153–180). Altieri makes the case that Nussbaum is a bad reader of literary texts: her "impatience with particularity and eagerness to find wisdom in literary texts often lead her to distort probable authorial intentions to ignore the work style does, and to force concrete affective responses into thematic frameworks that she can formulate in

philosophical terms" (159). In *J. M. Coetzee*, Derek Attridge seems to have Nussbaum in mind when he argues against reading the storyworld of novels for ethical wisdom about "our daily existence and the choices it presents us with" (xi). But Attridge also allies himself with the ethics of alterity at play in both Nussbaum and Butler by characterizing such reading as objectionable because it violates the "integrity" and "singularity" of the literary work, as manifested in its irreducibility and rich particularity (7–11). In *The Singularity of Literature*, Attridge coins the term "textualterity" to describe the ethical otherness that literary works possess (11). Thus, in a pattern of logic that I am discussing in relation to new ethical readings of James and in James's own view of the novelistic imagination, Attridge argues both for readerly ethics as "inventive recreation" (31) and as "scrupulous responsiveness" (11n17).

8. Sanders, "Ethics and Interdisciplinarity," 3.

9. Ibid., 4.

10. For recent work in moral philosophy on literary value, see Appiah, *Cosmopolitanism* and *Ethics of Identity* (2005); Diamond, "Having a Rough Story" and "Henry James"; Levinson, *Aesthetics and Ethics*; McGinn, *Ethics, Evil, and Fiction*; Palmer, *Literature and Moral Understanding*; and Pippin, *Henry James*. For new ethical literary theory, see Altieri, "Lyrical Ethics" and *Particulars of Rapture*; Attridge, *Peculiar Language* and *Singularity of Literature*; Bernstein, *Foregone Conclusions*; Buell, "In Pursuit of Ethics"; Davis and Womack, *Mapping the Ethical Turn*; Gibson, *Postmodernity, Ethics and the Novel*; Glowacka and Boos, *Between Ethics and Aesthetics*; Harpham, *Shadows of Ethics*; Helgesson, *Writing in Crisis*; Huffer, "'There Is No Gomorrah'"; Miller, *Ethics of Reading* and *Literature as Conduct*; Nash, *Feminist Narrative Ethics*; Nealon, *Alterity Politics*; Newton, *Narrative Ethics*; Rainsford and Woods, *Critical Ethics*; Reynier and Ganteau, *Ethics of Alterity*; Serpell, *Seven Modes of Uncertainty*; and Spivak, *Critique of Postcolonial Reason*.

11. Nussbaum, "Professor of Parody," 37.

12. Gibson, *Postmodernity, Ethics and the Novel*, 11.

13. Harpham, "The Hunger of Martha Nussbaum," 57. For my analysis of Harpham's relation to the novelistic ethics of alterity, see my "Fiction as Restriction," esp. 191–193. For Harpham's own account of Nussbaum's relation to Butler, see "The Hunger of Martha Nussbaum," 72–73.

14. Nussbaum, *Love's Knowledge*, 192.

15. Trilling, "Manners, Morals, and the Novel," 22. Trilling's essay was written for and delivered at a 1947 conference held at Kenyon College. The immediate political context for the paper is reflected by the title of the conference, "The Heritage of the English-Speaking Peoples and Their Responsibility," and is further suggested by the first sentence of the preface that accompanies the printed collection of essays: "While all eyes are directed towards the East, near and far, the College has determined critically to review

and consider what we are as western men and a western society" (n.p.). Other papers given at the conference include "Responsibility for World Peace and Justice"; "Our Liberal Heritage: What It Is and How to Keep It"; and "The Bond of the Nation."

16. Miller, *The Novel and the Police*, x.
17. Ibid., 27.
18. Jameson, *Political Unconscious*, 221.
19. Ibid., 154. The poststructuralist new ethicists implicitly seek to move beyond the wholly negative political critique of ethics that Fredric Jameson credits to Nietzsche: "It is ethics itself which is the ideological vehicle and the legitimation of concrete structures of power and domination" (*Political Unconscious*, 114). Jameson goes on to elucidate the operation of hegemonic class power as explicitly an act of othering: the "Other" is feared not because he is evil but "rather he is evil *because* he is Other, alien, different, strange, unclean, and unfamiliar" (115; emphasis in the original).
20. Gilmore, "Book Marketplace," 70–71. See Blair, *Henry James*; Freedman, *Professions of Taste*; Jacobs, *Eye's Mind*; and Porter, *Seeing and Being*, for particularly powerful political critiques of Jamesian aestheticism.
21. Miller, *The Novel and the Police*, x.
22. Armstrong, *Desire and Domestic Fiction*, 6.
23. Armstrong, *How Novels Think*, 10.
24. Horton, "Life, Literature and Ethical Theory," 88.
25. Trilling, "Manners, Morals, and the Novel," 27; George Eliot to Charles Bray, July 5, 1859, in *The George Eliot Letters*, 3:110. The ethical good of the novelistic feeling for otherness can also be heard in Charles Dickens's recommendation that novelists bestow the "touch of feeling" upon the parlor maids and "rustics" they depict (Dickens to Frank Stone, June 1, 1857, in *Selected Letters of Charles Dickens*, 316–317).
26. Trilling, "Manners, Morals, and the Novel," 24.
27. Trilling signals out Forster's *The Longest Journey* and James's *The Princess Casamassima* as novels that accomplish the "broadening of social sympathies" (ibid., 22) through the power of their "moral realism." In *Time, Tense, and American Literature*, Cindy Weinstein notes how Trilling champions James's style on ethical grounds as against what Trilling takes to be the jingoist enthusiasm for Theodore Dreiser's style (see esp. 90–91).
28. On Trilling's view, the polemics of social-issue novels incite moral indignation at the expense of moral realism. Trilling points to Steinbeck as a novelist who fashions characters out of a political vision rather than loving friendship: the "basis of his creation is the coldest response to abstract ideas" ("Manners, Morals, and the Novel," 23).
29. Ibid., 26.
30. Miller, *The Novel and the Police*, viii.
31. Ibid.

32. James, *Portrait of a Lady*, 261.

33. Ozick, *What Henry James Knew*, 2.

34. See Critchley, *Ethics, Politics, Subjectivity*; and Marchitello, *What Happens to History*, for studies of the political theory underlying the new ethics.

35. See Flannery, "Judith Butler's Henry James," for an interpretation of Butler as influenced by James's prose style.

36. Miller, *Literature as Conduct*, 15.

37. See my *Social Formalism* for an extended analysis of the way the novelistic ethics of alterity bridges James's and Bakhtin's views of the novel. See esp. 161–196 for a fuller account of Bakhtinian alterity.

38. Spivak, "Three Women's Texts," 250–253.

39. Bakhtin, "Discourse in the Novel," 315.

40. Butler, "Values of Difficulty," 208; qtd. from her edition of James, *Washington Square*, 219.

41. See Palmer, *Literature and Moral Understanding*, for fine-tuned distinctions between fiction and other modalities of imagination. See Gallagher, "What Would Napoleon Do?," for an argument that defines fictionality in terms of the ontological distinction between imaginary characters and historical persons.

42. This is also J. Hillis Miller's position, discussed below.

43. Wayne Booth defines translation itself as something undergone by the reader through reading: "Great art can bring men of different convictions together by translating, as it were, their different vocabularies into a tangible experience that incorporates what they mean" (*Rhetoric of Fiction*, 141). His "as it were" is offered in a different spirit than Butler's but also suggests the willed and unverifiable nature of the reader's encounter with alterity.

44. Bruce Robbins connects the new ethical notion of imaginative possibility to a view of literature's distinctiveness older even than liberal humanism. He argues that "Butler's concept of 'performativity,' the self-consciously theatrical way of playing with identities and revealing their constructedness that Butler finds exemplified by drag, is of course associated with literature's freedom to re-imagine and recreate the social world" ("Pretend What You Like," 199). My difference from Robbins lies in my sense that the Jamesian notion of novelistic ethics still refers the ethico-literary imagination to "the constraints of life itself" (Robbins, "Pretend What You Like," 199) and acknowledges that the "freedom to pretend" is "systematically constrained" (199). However, I argue in this chapter that to the degree that ethical alterity is formulated as a phenomenology, theorists and critics replace the novel's sense of the cultural contingency of ethics and aesthetics with the certainty of the affective apprehension of alterity.

45. Miller, *The Novel and the Police*, x.

46. Ibid.

47. Of course, this is not Nussbaum's account of her relationship to Trilling. She locates her ideas in agreement with his and suggests that she is building upon Trilling's foundation. See, e.g., *Love's Knowledge*, 48.

48. See Robbins, "Pretend What You Like," for an incisive comparison of Nussbaum and Butler (esp. 199–203).

49. See Armstrong, *Desire and Domestic Fiction* and *How Novels Think*; and Williams, *The Country and the City*.

50. In *Fictions across Borders*, Shameem Black articulates a version of the novel's ethical alterity in which the epistemological uncertainty that is the legacy of the ideological critique of the novelist's ethical imagination should be countered by the ethical act of supporting novelists who nonetheless display the virtue of otherness through their good-faith attempt to try to represent the social other outside and beyond authorial point of view: "Though invasive imagination continues to abound in the millennial world, we need to celebrate moments in which imaginative projection surmounts the temptation to replicate familiar forms of discursive domination. As the writers throughout this study show [all novelists], although no representation is above critique, it is possible to dramatize the process of conceptualizing others without inevitably trapping them within the prisons of one's needs and desires" (254).

51. In addition to those by Adam Zachary Newton, Andrew Gibson, and J. Hillis Miller (which I discuss in this chapter), other recent studies of Jamesian ethics include Buelens, *Enacting History*; Jottkandt, *Acting Beautifully*; Larson, *Ethics and Narrative*; Pick, "Miracles of Arrangement"; and Serpell, *Seven Modes of Uncertainty*. Even though Michael Wood's key term is knowledge and not ethics, I would argue that his notion of literary knowledge as an ethics, and his working out of this notion through *What Maisie Knew* (esp. 13–36), locates his *Literature and the Taste of Knowledge* within the new ethical approach to James. As for Butler, the problem of translation is of particular concern for Wood, but on his view the problem of translation is not one of cross-cultural understanding but of the otherness that defines the difference between the semantic richness of the reading experience and the impoverished account of that experience available through interpretation. Thus Wood's theory of literary knowledge implies an ethics of otherness: "Pausing over the untranslated perceptions, settling for coarseness when we have to, but remembering the subtlety we have just betrayed, is not moral relativism but a form of patience, a way of looking the world's complexity in the face" (36).

52. James, preface to *Portrait of a Lady*, 42.

53. Narrative ethics as a kind of revenge that then calls for expatiation is at issue in many of the interpretations of McEwan's *Atonement*.

54. Nussbaum, *Love's Knowledge*, 238.

55. Ibid., 180.
56. Nussbaum, *Poetic Justice*, 22.
57. Barthes, *S/Z*, 5.
58. Gibson, *Postmodernity, Ethics and the Novel*, 162.
59. In *Love's Knowledge*, Nussbaum also formulates citation as an ethical problem for the critic. Her sense of the ethical singularity represented by the literary text leads her to say of *The Golden Bowl* that "any pretense that we could paraphrase this scene without losing its moral quality would belie the argument I am about to make. I presuppose, then, the quotation of Book Fifth, Chapter III of *The Golden Bowl*. Indeed, honoring its 'chain of relation and responsibility,' I presuppose the quotation of the entire novel. What follows is a commentary" (149).
60. Coetzee, *Waiting for the Barbarians*, 49.
61. See Booth, *Rhetoric of Fiction*. Booth's pedagogic view can be summed up in his assertion that "in short, the author's judgment is always present, always evident to anyone who knows how to look for it" (20). The brief of *Rhetoric* is to train the reader to see the implied ethical values that Booth believes are manifested by a given novelist's narrative choices.
62. See Spivak's *Critique of Postcolonial Reason*, 174–197, for an interpretation of *Foe* that establishes a hierarchy of characterological silence keyed to degrees of political marginalization: "Yet it is Friday rather than Susan who is the unemphatic agent of withholding in the text. For every territorial space that is value coded by colonialism *and* every command of metropolitan anticolonialism for the native to yield his 'voice,' there is a space of withholding, marked by a secret that may not be a secret but cannot be unlocked" (190; emphasis in the original).
63. Wood, *Literature*, also uses the term "taste" as a synesthesia to express the readerly experience of coming to embodied knowledge through literature.
64. As a critic of Levinas, Alain Badiou emphasizes what most literary theorists and critics suppress: the religious nature of Levinasian thought. Badiou argues that Levinas rejects classical Greek ethics as rule-bound because he believes that "ethical action presumes an initial theoretical mastery of experience, which ensures that the action is in conformity with the rationality of being." Badiou notes that Levinas does not do without law but instead, by nominating God as the ultimate other, replaces the law of reason with the law of spirit: "According to Jewish ethics, in Levinas's sense, everything is grounded in the immediacy of an opening to the Other which disarms the reflexive subject. The 'thou' prevails over the 'I.' Such is the only meaning of *the* Law" (*Ethics*, 19 ; emphasis in the original).
65. Further evidence of the common ground shared by liberal humanists and poststructural ethical theorists can be found in Wayne Booth's notion of "coduction," first put forward in *Company We Keep*. Booth similarly posits the shared steps of reading as the

common ground for understanding and community (see 381). In "Why Ethical Criticism," Booth provides a brief summary of his position: "It is from such disagreements that the most productive literary criticism can emerge. When undertaken seriously, neither side is likely to feel fully victorious. Both sides will have learned something overlooked, either about the work itself or about the world of ethical values in which we all live. And both sides, whether in reading the work or discussing it, are *undergoing* the ethical growth that serious encounters with such conflict can produce" (27; emphasis added).

66. "Leap in the dark" is a phrase popularized by William James, who ends his *Will to Believe* with a quotation from James Fitzjames Stephen that includes this figure (31).

67. The quotations from Woolf and Harris are referenced in Chapter 2.

Coda: Henry James in the Clinician's Office

1. Charon, "Gifts of Perception."
2. Charon, *Narrative Medicine*, viii.
3. "The Novelization of the Body" begins: "We are contained by the spaces and times given us, chosen by us, or that simply, randomly, befall us. Like the water jug or the sonnet form, containers simultaneously confine and give shape. The freedom we achieve during and beyond our lives is, perhaps, not unrelated to the containers that hold us and from which we free ourselves. How we live in and become free from what contains us—our mother's uterus, for example, or the town we grew up in—influences the attained freedom" (33).
4. Significantly for the Jamesian ethics of alterity as an aesthetics of alterity, and with strong similarities to Elizabeth Costello's varying interpretations of Kafka's narrative ethics, Charon is not consistent in her description of the narrative functioning of James's ethical effects. What is consistent is the value of ethical otherness that she ascribes to these effects. For example, the visibility of character as an ethical good in her reading of "The Bench of Desolation" contrasts with her account of *The Wings of the Dove* and *What Maisie Knew*, in which the ethicality of Jamesian narrative is expressed through and as "the expendable characters like Milly and Maisie [who] function in their own narrative worlds as entities who achieve their plenitude by disappearing" ("Narrative Lights," 51).
5. Charon developed this view of the ethical particularity of medical notation in 2011, ultimately calling it the "novelization of the body":

> What I mean by the "novelization of the body" is the exposure of the body's plot, form, voice, temporality, and governing images. We have within our bodies themselves a means toward the deepest and most exposing telling of the self, if only the signs are recognized and the story is told. We have here the means to listen to the

accounts given by bodies about those whose homes they are, whether by the gestures of the foot massage or the movements of the dance or the redness deep within the inner ear of my patient with an earache. In clinical practice, we have a duty to equip ourselves with the skills to not tamper with that which is uttered but rather to support its utterance in any way we can. ("Novelization," 47)

Whereas in her earlier formulation the discourse of notation brought the individual body into visibility as a singular being, now the body tells its own story. As I have been arguing, Charon's thinking wavers between crediting the writer/clinician with bringing the patient into ethical embodiment and regarding the body as an autonomous other who tells its own story, to which the doctor-writer should openly and transparently attend but at the same time respond in a bodily way that communicates care and self-subordination.

6. In *Gender Trouble*, Judith Butler influentially attacks mind/body dualism through a radically constructivist theory of gender that theorizes all gender markers as performative: "Acts, gestures, and desire produce the effect of an internal core of substance, but produce this *on the surface* of the body, through the play of signifying absences that suggest, but never reveal, the organizing principle of identity as a cause" (136; emphasis in the original).

7. Famously, Walter Benjamin holds the storyteller up as a nonreified alternative to the novelist. The storyteller weaves his stories into the everyday life of a community; the novelist reflects reification under capitalism through the single individual he privileges as a protagonist and also through his mode of production (writing in solitude, creating a mass-produced commodity whose readers he will never know). See "The Storyteller," esp. 364–365.

8. In "Literary Concepts for Medical Readers," Charon details the detriments of practicing medicine without a knowledge of literature, describing doctors who fail to seek narrative training as those "who cannot follow a narrative thread; who cannot adopt an alien perspective; who become unreliable narrators of other people's stories; who are deaf to voice and image; and who do not always include in their regard human motives, yearnings, symbols and the fellowship born of a common language" (30).

9. See Segalovitz, "William Faulkner," for a far-reaching account of how ethical alterity, as an implicit value of close reading, developed out of Anglo-American New Criticism. In *Novel Sounds*, Florence Dore provocatively argues that the New Critical ideas that led to Faulkner's canonization fail to describe what Dore sees as an alternative to close reading: what she calls "the electric music" paradigm of reading at play in novels like *The Town*, which for this reason escaped canonization by the New Critics.

10. "To put it crudely: Levinas's enterprise serves to remind us, with extraordinary insistence, that every effort to turn ethics into the principle of thought and action is essentially religious. We might say that Levinas is the coherent and inventive thinker of an assumption that no academic exercise of veiling or abstraction can obscure: distanced from its Greek usage (according to which it is clearly subordinated to the theoretical), and taken in general, ethics is a category of pious discourse" (Badiou, *Ethics*, 23).

Bibliography

Abrams, M. H. *The Mirror and the Lamp: Romantic Theory and the Critical Tradition*. Oxford: Oxford University Press, 1953.
Abramson, Anna Jones. "The Ethics of Inhabiting in J. M. Coetzee's *Elizabeth Costello*." *Otherness: Essays and Studies* 4 (2014): 21–50.
Adams, Ann Marie. "Mr. McEwan and Mrs. Woolf: How a Saturday in February Follows 'This Moment of June.'" *Contemporary Literature* 53 (2012): 548–572.
———. "A Passage to Forster: Zadie Smith's Attempt to 'Only Connect' to *Howards End*." *Critique* 52 (2011): 377–399.
Alber, Jan, and Rüdiger Heinze, eds. *Unnatural Narratives—Unnatural Narratology*. Berlin: Walter de Gruyter, 2011.
Alden, Natasha. "Words of War, War of Words: *Atonement* and the Question of Plagiarism." In *Ian McEwan*, edited by Sebastian Groes, 57–69. London: Bloomsbury, 2009.
Alter, Robert. *Partial Magic*. Oakland: University of California Press, 1975.
Altieri, Charles. "Lyrical Ethics and Literary Experience." In *Mapping the Ethical Turn*, edited by Todd F. Davis and Kenneth Womack, 30–58. Charlottesville: University Press of Virginia, 2001.
———. *The Particulars of Rapture: An Aesthetics of the Affects*. Ithaca, NY: Cornell University Press, 2003.
———. "Taking Lyrics Literally: Teaching Poetry in a Prose Culture." *New Literary History* 32 (2001): 259–281.
Anker, Elizabeth Susan. "*Elizabeth Costello*, Embodiment, and the Limits of Rights." *New Literary History* 42 (2011): 169–192.
Anjaria, Ulka. "*On Beauty* and Being Postcolonial." In *Zadie Smith: Critical Essays*, edited by Tracy L. Walters, 31–55. New York: Peter Lang, 2008.
Appiah, Kwame Anthony. *Cosmopolitanism: Ethics in a World of Strangers*. New York: Norton, 2006.
———. *The Ethics of Identity*. Princeton, NJ: Princeton University Press, 2005.

Argyos, Ellen. *"Without Any Check of Proud Reserve": Sympathy and Its Limits in George Eliot's Novels*. New York: Peter Lang, 2000.
Armstrong, Nancy. *Desire and Domestic Fiction: A Political History of the Novel*. New York: Oxford, 1987.
Armstrong, Nancy. *How Novels Think: The Limits of British Individualism from 1719-1900*. New York: Columbia University Press, 2005.
Ashcroft, Bill. "Silence as Heterotopia in Coetzee's Fiction." In *Strong Opinions: J. M. Coetzee and the Authority of Contemporary Fiction*, edited by Chris Danta, Sue Kossew, and Julian Murphet, 141–157. New York: Continuum International, 2011.
Attridge, Derek. *J. M. Coetzee and the Ethics of Reading: Literature in the Event*. Chicago: University of Chicago Press, 2004.
———. *Peculiar Language: Literature as Difference from the Renaissance to James Joyce*. Ithaca, NY: Cornell University Press, 1988.
———. *The Singularity of Literature*. New York: Routledge, 2004.
Attwell, David. "J. M. Coetzee and the Idea of Africa." *Journal of Literary Studies* 25 (2009): 67–83.
———. *J. M. Coetzee: South Africa and the Politics of Writing*. Berkeley: University of California Press, 1993.
Avelar, Idelber. *The Letter of Violence: Essays on Narrative, Ethics, and Politics*. London: Palgrave, 2004.
Babb, Valerie. "'E Pluribus Unum?' The American Origins Narrative in Toni Morrison's *A Mercy*." *MELUS* 36 (2011): 147–164.
Badiou, Alain. *Ethics: An Essay on the Understanding of Evil*. 1994. Translated by Peter Hallward. New York: Verso, 2001.
Bakhtin, M. M. "Discourse in the Novel." 1934–1935. Reprinted in *The Dialogic Imagination: Four Essays by M. M. Bakhtin*, translated by Caryl Emerson and edited by Michael Holquist, 259–422. Austin: University of Texas Press, 1981.
Balliro, Matthew. *The New Sincerity in American Literature*. Kingston: University of Rhode Island Press, 2018.
Banta, Martha. "The Quality of Experience in *What Maisie Knew*." *New England Quarterly* 42 (1969): 483–510.
Barnard, Rita. "Coetzee in/as Afrikaans." *Journal of Literary Studies* 25 (2009): 84–105.
Barth, John. "Life-Story." In *Lost in the Fun House*, 116–129. New York: Anchor, 1963.
Barthes, Roland. *S/Z: An Essay*. 1970. Translated by Richard Miller. New York: Hill and Wang, 1975.
Bate, W. Jackson. *John Keats*. Cambridge, MA: Harvard University Press, 1963.
Batra, Kanika. "Kipps, Belsey, and Jegede: Cosmopolitanism, Transnationalism, and Black Studies in Zadie Smith's *On Beauty*." *Callalloo* 33 (2010): 1079–1092.

Baudrillard, Jean, and Marc Guillaume. *Radical Alterity*. 1994. Translated by Ames Hodges. Los Angeles: Semiotext(e), 2008.

Bell, Millicent. *Meaning in Henry James*. Cambridge, MA: Harvard University Press, 1991.

Bellamy, Maria Rice. "'These Careful Words . . . Will Talk to Themselves': Textual Remains and Reader Responsibility in Toni Morrison's *A Mercy*." In *Contested Boundaries: New Critical Essays on the Fiction of Toni Morrison*, edited by Maxine L. Montgomery, 14–32. Newcastle, UK: Cambridge Scholars, 2013.

Belluck, Pam. "For Better Social Skills, Scientists Recommend a Little Chekhov." *New York Times*, October 3, 2013. https://well.blogs.nytimes.com/2013/10/03/i-know-how-youre-feeling-i-read-chekhov/.

Benjamin, Walter. "The Storyteller: Reflections on the Works of Nikolai Leskov." 1936. Reprinted in *The Novel: An Anthology of Criticism and Theory, 1900–2000*, edited by Dorothy J. Hale, 361–378. Malden, MA: Blackwell, 2006.

Bennett, Alice. *Contemporary Fictions of Attention: Reading and Distraction in the Twenty-First Century*. London: Bloomsbury, 2018.

Berkeley, George. *Siris: A Chain of Philosophical Reflections and Inquiries Concerning the Virtues of Tar Water, and Divers Other Subjects Connected Together and Arising One from Another*. Emended and rev. ed. London: Printed for W. Innys, C. Hitch; Holbourn: Printed for C. Davis, 1744.

Berman, Jessica. *Modernist Commitments: Ethics, Politics, and Transnational Modernism*. New York: Columbia University Press, 2011.

Bernstein, Michael André. *Foregone Conclusions: Against Apocalyptic History*. Oakland: University of California Press, 1994.

Bersani, Leo. *A Future for Astyanax: Character and Desire in Literature*. New York: Columbia University Press, 1984.

Bewley, Marius. *The Complex Fate: Hawthorne, Henry James and Some Other American Writers*. New York: Gordian Press, 1967.

Black, Shameem. *Fiction across Borders: Imagining the Lives of Others in Late Twentieth-Century Novels*. New York: Columbia University Press, 2010.

Blackham, H. J. *Six Existentialist Thinkers*. New York: Routledge, 1983.

Blair, Sara. *Henry James and the Writing of Race and Nation*. Cambridge: Cambridge University Press, 1996.

Boehmer, Elleke. "J. M. Coetzee's Australian Realism." In *Postcolonial Poetics: Genre and Form*, edited by Patrick Crowley and Jane Hiddleston, 202–216. Liverpool, UK: Liverpool University Press, 2011.

Booth, Naomi. "Restricted View: The Problem of Perspective in the Novels of Ian McEwan." *Textual Practice* 29 (2015): 845–868.

Booth, Wayne. *The Company We Keep: An Ethics of Fiction.* Oakland: University of California Press, 1988.
———. *The Rhetoric of Fiction.* 1961. Chicago: University of Chicago Press, 1983.
———. "Why Ethical Criticism Can Never Be Simple." In *Mapping the Ethical Turn*, edited by Todd F. Davis and Kenneth Womack, 16–29. Charlottesville: University Press of Virginia, 2001.
Bradbury, Malcolm. *The Modern British Novel.* New York: Penguin, 1993.
Brooke-Rose, Christine. *Invisible Author: Last Essays.* Columbus: Ohio State University Press, 2002.
Brooks, Peter. *Henry James Goes to Paris.* Princeton, NJ: Princeton University Press, 2007.
Brophy, Brigid. "The Novel as a Takeover Bid." 1963. Reprinted in *Don't Never Forget: Collected Views and Reviews*, 93–100. New York: Jonathan Cape, 1966.
Brown, Christopher. "The Rhetoric of Closure in *What Maisie Knew*." *Style* 20 (1986): 58–65.
Buelens, Gert, ed. *Enacting History in Henry James: Narrative, Power, and Ethics.* Cambridge: Cambridge University Press, 1997.
Buell, Lawrence. "In Pursuit of Ethics." *PMLA* 114 (1999): 7–19.
Butler, Judith. *Gender Trouble: Feminism and the Subversion of Identity.* New York: Routledge, 1990.
———. *Giving an Account of Oneself.* New York: Fordham University Press, 2005.
———. "Values of Difficulty." In *Just Being Difficult? Academic Writing in the Public Arena*, edited by Jonathan Culler and Kevin Lamb, 199–215. Stanford, CA: Stanford University Press, 2003.
Byatt, A. S. *On Histories and Stories: Selected Essays.* Cambridge, MA: Harvard University Press, 2001.
Byatt, A. S., and Ignês Sodré. *Imagining Characters: Six Conversations about Women Writers.* Edited by Rebecca Swift. London: Chatto and Windus, 1995.
Carlacio, Jami. "Narrative Epistemology: Storytelling as Agency in *A Mercy*." In *Toni Morrison: Paradise, Love, A Mercy*, edited by Lucille P. Fultz, 129–146. New York: Continuum, 2012.
Carstensen, Thorsten. "Shattering the Word-Mirror in *Elizabeth Costello*: J. M. Coetzee's Deconstructive Experiment." *Journal of Commonwealth Literature* 42 (2007): 79–96.
Caserio, Robert L. *The Cambridge Companion to the Twentieth-Century English Novel.* Cambridge: Cambridge University Press, 2009.
———. *The Novel in England, 1900–1950: History and Theory.* Boston: Twayne, 1999.
Charon, Rita. "The Gifts of Perception." Interview by Alexander Kafka. *Chronicle of Higher Education*, October 12, 2018.

———. "Literary Concepts for Medical Readers: Frame, Time, Plot, Desire." In *Teaching Literature and Medicine*, edited by Anne Hawkins and Marilyn Chandler McEntyre, 29–41. New York: MLA Press, 2000.

———. "Narrative Lights on Clinical Acts: What We, Like Maisie, Know." *Partial Answers: Journal of Literature and the History of Ideas* 4 (2006): 41–58.

———. *Narrative Medicine: Honoring the Stories of Illness*. Oxford: Oxford University Press, 2006.

———. "The Novelization of the Body, or, How Medicine and Stories Need One Another." *Narrative* 19 (2011): 33–50.

———. "The Perilous Fate of the Teller, or What Bench? What Desolation?" *Literature and Medicine* 25 (2006): 412–438.

———. "Why Storytelling Matters in Fields beyond the Humanities." Interview by Alexander C. Kafka, *Chronicle of Higher Education*. October 4, 2018. https://www.chronicle.com/article/Why-Storytelling-Matters-in/244729.

Chase, Richard. *The American Novel and Its Tradition*. Baltimore: Johns Hopkins University Press, 1957.

Chen, Fu-Jen, and Su-Lin Yu. "The Parallax Gap in Gish Jen's *The Love Wife*: The Imaginary Relationship between First-World and Third-World Women." *Critique* 51 (2010): 394–415.

Chesney, Duncan McColl. "Towards an Ethics of Silence: Michael K." *Criticism* 46 (2007): 307–325.

Childs, Peter, and James Green. *Aesthetics and Ethics in Twenty-First Century British Novels: Zadie Smith, Nadeem Aslam, Hari Kunzru, and David Mitchell*. London: Bloomsbury, 2013.

Christiansë, Yvette. *Toni Morrison: An Ethical Poetics*. New York: Fordham University Press, 2013.

Clarkson, Carol. "J. M. Coetzee and the Limits of Language." *Journal of Literary Studies* 25 (2009): 106–124.

Coetzee, J. M. *Age of Iron*. New York: Penguin, 1990.

———. *Disgrace*. New York: Penguin, 1999.

———. *Elizabeth Costello*. New York: Penguin, 2003.

———. *Stranger Shores: Literary Essays, 1986–1999*. New York: Penguin, 2001.

———. *Waiting for the Barbarians*. New York: Penguin, 1980.

Coetzee, J. M., and Arabella Kurtz. *The Good Story: Exchanges on Truth, Fiction, and Psychotherapy*. New York: Penguin, 2015.

Coleridge, Samuel Taylor. *Table Talk*. 1835. In *The Table Talk and Omniana of Samuel Taylor Coleridge*, 33–321. New York: Oxford University Press, 1917.

Conner, Marc C. "'What Lay beneath the Names': The Language and Landscapes of *A Mercy*." In *Toni Morrison: Paradise, Love, A Mercy*, edited by Lucille P. Fultz, 147–165. New York: Continuum, 2012.

Connor, Steven. *The English Novel in History, 1950–1995*. New York: Routledge, 1996.

Conrad, Joseph. "Books." 1905. Reprinted in *Notes on Life and Letters*, 3–10. Garden City, NY: Doubleday, 1921.

———. "Henry James: An Appreciation." 1905. Reprinted in *Notes on Life and Letters*, 11–19. New York: Doubleday, 1921.

Cormack, Alistair. "Postmodernism and the Ethics of Fiction in *Atonement*." In *Ian McEwan*, edited by Sebastian Groes, 70–82. London: Bloomsbury, 2009.

Cornell, Drucilla. *The Philosophy of the Limit*. New York: Routledge, 1992.

Cowell, Alan. "Eyebrows Are Raised over Passages in a Best Seller by Ian McEwan." *New York Times*, November 28, 2006. https://www.nytimes.com/2006/11/28/books/28aton.html.

Critchley, Simon. *The Ethics of Deconstruction: Derrida and Levinas*. 2nd ed. Edinburgh: Edinburgh University Press, 1992.

———. *Ethics, Politics, Subjectivity: Essays on Derrida, Levinas and Contemporary French Thought*. New York: Verso, 1999.

Cross, Samuel. "The Ethics of Tact in *The Wings of the Dove*." *Novel: A Forum on Fiction* 43 (2010): 401–423.

Culler, Jonathan. *Theory of the Lyric*. Cambridge, MA: Harvard University Press, 2017.

Currie, Gregory. "Does Great Literature Make Us Better People?" *New York Times*, June 1, 2013. https://opinionator.blogs.nytimes.com/2013/06/01/does-great-literature-make-us-better/.

Danta, Chris. "'Like a Dog . . . like a Lamb': Becoming Sacrificial Animal in Kafka and Coetzee." *New Literary History* 38 (2007): 721–737.

Davis, Todd F., and Kenneth Womack, eds. *Mapping the Ethical Turn: A Reader in Ethics, Culture, and Literary Theory*. Charlottesville: University Press of Virginia, 2001.

Dawson, Paul. *The Return of the Omniscient Narrator: Authorship and Authority in Twenty-First Century Fiction*. Columbus: Ohio State University Press, 2013.

Deckard, Michael Funk, and Ralph Palm. "Irony and Belief in *Elizabeth Costello*." In *J. M. Coetzee and Ethics: Philosophical Perspectives on Literature*, edited by Anton Leist and Peter Singer, 337–356. New York: Columbia University Press, 2010.

Dekoven, Marianne. "Going to the Dogs in *Disgrace*." *ELH* 76 (2009): 847–875.

Deo, Veena. "Studies in M(othering): Unpacking the 'Wicked Thing' in Toni Morrison's *A Mercy* and *Beloved*." In *Toni Morrison on Mothers and Motherhood*, edited by Lee Baxter and Martha Satz, 69–87. Ontario: Demeter, 2017.

Derrida, Jacques. *Adieu: To Emmanuel Levinas*. 1997. Translated by Pascale-Anne Brault and Michael Naas. Stanford, CA: Stanford University Press, 1999.

———. *The Animal That Therefore I Am*. 2002. Translated by David Wills. Edited by Marie-Louse Mallet. New York: Fordham University Press, 2008.

———. *Ethics, Institutions, and the Right to Philosophy*. Translated and edited by Peter Pericles Trifonas. Lanham, MD: Rowman and Littlefield, 2002.

———. *The Gift of Death*. 1999. Reprint, *The Gift of Death and Literature in Secret*, 2nd ed. Translated by David Wills. Chicago: University of Chicago Press, 2008.

Diamond, Cora. "Having a Rough Story about What Moral Philosophy Is." *New Literary History* 15 (1983): 155–169.

———. "Henry James, Moral Philosophers, Moralism." *Henry James Review* 18 (1997): 243–257.

DiBattista, Maria. *Novel Characters: A Genealogy*. Hoboken, NJ: Blackwell, 2010.

Dick, Alexander, and Christina Lupton. "On Lecturing and Being Beautiful: Zadie Smith, Elaine Scarry, and the Liberal Aesthetic." *ESC* 39 (2013): 115–137.

Dickens, Charles. *Selected Letters of Charles Dickens*. Edited by David Paroissien. New York: Macmillan, 1985.

Dobrogoszcz, Tomasz. *Family and Relationships in Ian McEwan's Fiction: Between Fantasy and Desire*. Lanham, MD: Lexington Books, 2018.

Dodd, Josephine. "The South African Literary Establishment and the Textual Production of 'Woman': J. M. Coetzee and Lewis Nkosi." *Current Writing: Text and Reception in Southern Africa* 2 (1990): 117–129.

Dore, Florence. *Novel Sounds: Southern Fiction in the Age of Rock and Roll*. New York: Columbia University Press, 2018.

Dovey, Teresa. *The Novels of J. M. Coetzee: Lacanian Allegories*. Johannesburg: Ad Donker, 1988.

Driscoll, Lawrence. "'Our Economic Position': Middle-Class Consciousness in Zadie Smith, and Will Self." In *Evading Class in Contemporary British Culture*, 61–96. New York: Palgrave, 2009.

Dyer, Geoff. "Who's Afraid of Influence?" Review of *Atonement*, by Ian McEwan. *The Guardian*, September 21, 2001. https://www.theguardian.com/books/2001/sep/22/fiction.ianmcewan.

Eaglestone, Robert. *Ethical Criticism: Reading after Levinas*. Edinburgh: Edinburgh University Press, 1997.

Eagleton, Terry. *The English Novel: An Introduction*. Hoboken, NJ: Blackwell, 2005.

———. *Trouble with Strangers: A Study of Ethics*. Hoboken, NJ: Blackwell, 2009.

Eckstein, Barbara. "Unsquaring the Squared Route of *What Maisie Knew*." *Henry James Review* 9 (1988): 177–187.

Elias, Amy J. "Postmodern Metafiction." In *The Cambridge Companion to American Fiction after 1945*, edited by John Duvall, 15–29. Cambridge: Cambridge University Press, 2012.

Eliot, George. *The George Eliot Letters*. Edited by Gordon S. Haight. Vol. 3. New Haven, CT: Yale University Press, 1954.

———. *Middlemarch*. 1874. New York: Norton, 2000.

———. "Silly Novels by Lady Novelists." 1856. Reprinted in *Essays of George Eliot*, edited by Thomas Pinney, 324. New York: Columbia University Press, 1963.

Ermarth, Elizabeth Deeds. *Realism and Consensus in the English Novel: Time, Space, and Narrative*. 1983. Edinburgh: Edinburgh University Press, 1988.

Faulkner, William. *As I Lay Dying*. 1930. New York: Vintage, 1985.

———. *Faulkner in the University: Class Conferences at the University of Virginia, 1957–1958*. Edited by Frederick L. Gwynn and Joseph L. Blotner. New York: Vintage, 1959.

———. *The Sound and the Fury*. 1929. Reprinted in *The Sound and the Fury (A Norton Critical Edition)*, 2nd ed., edited by David Minter, 3–209. New York: Norton, 1994.

Felski, Rita. Introduction to "Character," special issue, *New Literary History* 42 (2011): v–ix.

Figlerowicz, Marta. *Flat Protagonists: A Theory of Novel Character*. Oxford: Oxford University Press, 2016.

Finney, Brian. "Briony's Stand against Oblivion: The Making of Fiction in Ian McEwan's *Atonement*." *Journal of Modern Literature* 27 (2004): 68–82.

Fisher, Susan Alice. "'Gimme Shelter': Zadie Smith's *On Beauty*." In *Zadie Smith: Critical Essays*, edited by Tracy L. Walters, 107–121. New York: Peter Lang, 2008.

Fitzgerald, Jonathan D. *Not Your Mother's Morals: How the New Sincerity Is Changing Pop Culture for the Better*. New York: Rosetta Books, 2013.

Flannery, Denis. "Judith Butler's Henry James." *Henry James Review* 32 (2011): 12–19.

Ford, Ford Madox. *Henry James: A Critical Study*. 1913. London: Octagon Books, 1964.

———. "On Impressionism." 1913. In *Critical Writings of Ford Madox Ford*, ed. Frank MacShane, 33–55. Lincoln: University of Nebraska Press, 1964.

Forster, E. M. *Aspects of the Novel*. 1927. New York: Harcourt Brace, 1954.

Foss, Chris. "Female Innocence as Other in *The Portrait of a Lady* and *What Maisie Knew*: Reassessing Feminist Recuperation of Henry James." *Essays in Literature* 22 (1995): 253–268.

Fowles, John. *The French Lieutenant's Woman*. 1969. New York: Back Bay Books, 2010.

Franklin, R. W. "Narrative Management in *As I Lay Dying*." *Modern Fiction Studies* 13 (1967): 57–65.

Franzen, Jonathan. "Perchance to Dream." *Harpers Magazine*, April 1996.

———. "A Rooting Interest." *New Yorker*, February 5, 2012. https://www.newyorker.com/magazine/2012/02/13/a-rooting-interest.

Freedman, Jonathan. *Professions of Taste: Henry James, British Aestheticism, and Commodity Culture*. Stanford, CA: Stanford University Press, 1990.

Fulmer, Constance M. *George Eliot's Moral Aesthetic: Compelling Contradictions*. New York: Routledge, 2018.

Gallagher, Catherine. *Nobody's Story: The Vanishing Acts of Women Writers in the Market Place, 1670–1820*. Oxford: Oxford University Press, 1994.

———. "What Would Napoleon Do? Historical, Fictional, and Counterfactual Characters." *New Literary History* 42 (2011): 315–336.

Garber, Marjorie, Beatrice Hanssen, and Rebecca L. Walkowitz, eds. *The Turn to Ethics*. New York: Routledge, 2000.

Gargano, James W. "*What Maisie Knew*: The Evolution of a 'Moral Sense.'" *Nineteenth-Century Fiction* 16 (1961): 33–46.

Genette, Gérard. *Narrative Discourse: An Essay in Method*. 1972. Translated by Jane E. Lewin. Ithaca, NY: Cornell University Press, 1980.

Gibson, Andrew. *Postmodernity, Ethics and the Novel: From Leavis to Levinas*. New York: Routledge, 1999.

Gilbert, W. S. *A Sensation Novel in Three Volumes*. 1912. Cambridge, UK: Chadwyck-Healey, 1997.

Gilmore, Michael T. "The Book Marketplace." In *The Columbia History of the American Novel*, edited by Emory Elliott, 46–71. New York: Columbia University Press, 1991.

Glab, Anna. "The Ethical Laboratory of Beauty in Zadie Smith's *On Beauty*." *Tulsa Studies in Women's Literature* 35 (2016): 491–512.

Glowacka, Dorota, and Stephen Boos. *Between Ethics and Aesthetics: Crossing the Boundaries*. Albany: SUNY Press, 2002.

Green, Charles. "The Droves of Academe." *Missouri Review* 31 (2008): 177–188.

Greiner, Rae. *Sympathetic Realism and the Victorian Novel*. Baltimore: Johns Hopkins University Press, 2012.

Griffen, Susan, and Alan Nadel, eds. *The Men Who Knew Too Much: Henry James and Alfred Hitchcock*. Oxford: Oxford University Press, 2012.

Groes, Sebastian, ed. *Ian McEwan*. London: Bloomsbury, 2009.

Habegger, Alfred. *Henry James and the "Woman Business."* Cambridge: Cambridge University Press, 1989.

Hale, Dorothy. "Aesthetics and the New Ethics: Theorizing the Novel in the Twenty-First Century." *PMLA* 124 (2009): 896–905.

———. "The Art of English Fiction in the Twentieth Century." In *The Cambridge*

Companion to the Twentieth-Century English Novel, edited by Robert L. Caserio, 10–22. Cambridge: Cambridge University Press, 2009.

———. "*As I Lay Dying*'s Heterogeneous Discourse." *Novel: A Forum on Fiction* 23 (1989): 5–23.

———. "Fiction as Restriction: Self-Binding in New Ethical Theories of the Novel." *Narrative* 15 (2007): 187–206.

———. *The Novel: An Anthology of Criticism and Theory 1900–2000*. Malden, MA: Blackwell, 2006.

———. "*On Beauty* as Beautiful? The Problem of Novelistic Aesthetics by Way of Zadie Smith." *Contemporary Literature* 53 (2012): 814–844.

———. "The Place of the Novel in Reparative Reading." *Studies in the Novel* 1 (2019): 104–109.

———. *Social Formalism: The Novel in Theory from Henry James to the Present*. Stanford, CA: Stanford University Press, 1998.

Hanson, Ellis. "Screwing with Children in Henry James." *GLQ* 9 (2003): 367–391.

Harpham, Geoffrey Galt. "The Hunger of Martha Nussbaum." *Representations* 77 (2002): 52–81.

———. *Shadows of Ethics: Criticism and the Just Society*. Durham, NC: Duke University Press, 1999.

Harris, Wilson. "Books—A Long View." In *Tradition, the Writer and Society*, 21–27. London: New Beacon, 1967.

———. "Closing Statement: Apprenticeship to the Furies." In *Comparing Postcolonial Literatures: Dislocations*, edited by Ashok Bery and Patricia Murray, 240–251. New York: Macmillan, 2000.

———. "The Frontier on Which *Heart of Darkness* Stands." *Research in African Literatures* 12 (1981): 86–93.

———. "The Phenomenal Legacy." 1970. Reprinted in *Explorations: A Selection of Talks and Articles, 1966–81*, edited by Hera Maes-Jelinek, 43–48. Sydney: Dangaroo Press, 1981.

———. "Quetzalcoatl and the Smoking Mirror: Reflections on Originality and Tradition." In *Selected Essays of Wilson Harris: The Unfinished Genesis of the Imagination*, edited by A. J. M. Bundy, 184–195. New York: Routledge, 1999.

———. "Resistances to Alterities." In *Resisting Alterities: Wilson Harris and Other Avatars of Otherness*, edited by Marco Fazzini, 3–7. Amsterdam: Rodolpi, 2004.

———. "Tradition and the West Indian Novel." In *Tradition, the Writer and Society: Critical Essays*, 28–47. London: New Beacon, 1967.

Harvey, Melinda. "'In Australia You Start Zero': The Escape from Place in J. M. Coetzee's Late Novels." In *Strong Opinions: J. M. Coetzee and the Authority of Contemporary*

Fiction, edited by Chris Danta, Sue Kossew, and Julian Murphet, 19–34. London: Continuum, 2011.

Hayes, Patrick. *J. M. Coetzee and the Novel: Writing and Politics after Beckett*. New York: Oxford University Press, 2010.

Head, Dominic. *Ian McEwan*. Manchester, UK: Manchester University Press, 2007.

———. *J. M. Coetzee*. Cambridge: Cambridge University Press, 1997.

Helgesson, Stefan. *Writing in Crisis: Ethics and History in Gordimer, Ndebele and Coetzee*. Durban: University of KwaZulu-Natal Press, 2004.

Herbrechter, Stefan. *Lawrence Durrell: Postmodernism and the Ethics of Alterity*. Amsterdam: Rodopi, 1999.

Hildalgo, Monica. "(Dis)orienting the Reader: Literary Impressionism and the Case of Herman Bang." PhD diss., University of California, Berkeley, 2015.

Himmelfarb, Gertrude. "Manners into Morals: What the Victorians Knew." *American Scholar* 57 (1988): 223–232.

Hollander, Rachel. *Narrative Hospitality in Late Victorian Fiction: Novel Ethics*. New York: Routledge, 2012.

Horton, John. "Life, Literature and Ethical Theory: Martha Nussbaum on the Role of the Literary Imagination in Ethical Thought." In *Literature and the Political Imagination*, edited by John Horton and Andrea T. Baumeister, 70–97. New York: Routledge, 1996.

Huffer, Lynne. "'There Is No Gomorrah': Narrative Ethics in Feminist and Queer Theory." *Differences* 12.3 (2001): 1–32.

Hughes, Robert. *Ethics, Aesthetics, and the Beyond of Language*. Albany: SUNY Press, 2010.

Hurst, Mary Jane. *The Voice of the Child in American Literature: Linguistic Approaches to Fictional Child Language*. Lexington: University Press of Kentucky, 1990.

Irigaray, Luce. *To Be Two*. 1994. Translated by Monique M. Rhodes and Marco F. Cocito-Monoc. New York: Routledge, 2001.

Irlam, Shaun. "Double Entendre: Listening for Angels." *Journal of Literary Studies* 25 (2009): 125–139.

Jackson, Laura (Riding). *Anarchism Is Not Enough*. 1928. Edited by Lisa Samuels. Berkeley: University of California Press, 2001.

———. "Eve's Side of It." 1935. Reprinted in *The Word "Woman" and Other Related Writings*, edited by Elizabeth Friedmann and Alan J. Clark, 157–170. New York: Persea Books, 1993.

Jackson, Regine. "Imagining Boston: Haitian Immigrants and Place in Zadie Smith's *On Beauty*." *Journal of American Studies* 46 (2012): 855–873.

Jacobs, Karen. *The Eye's Mind: Literary Modernism and Visual Culture*. Ithaca, NY: Cornell University Press, 2001.

James, David. "In Defense of Lyrical Realism." *Diacritics* 45 (2017): 68–91.

———. *Discrepant Solace: Contemporary Literature and the Work of Consolation.* Oxford: Oxford University Press, 2019.

James, Henry. "The Art of Fiction." In *The Future of the Novel: Essays on the Art of Fiction*, edited by Leon Edel, 3–27. New York: Vintage, 1956.

———. *The Art of the Novel.* 1909. Edited by R. P. Blackmur. New York: Scribner's, 1934.

———. "George Eliot's *Middlemarch*." In *The Future of the Novel: Essays on the Art of Fiction*, edited by Leon Edel, 80–89. New York: Vintage, 1956.

———. *The Portrait of a Lady.* 1881. Edited by Michael Gorra. New York: Norton, 2018.

———. Preface to *The Ambassadors*. In *The Art of the Novel*, 307–326.

———. Preface to *The American*. In *The Art of the Novel*, 20–39.

———. Preface to *The Portrait of a Lady*. In *The Art of the Novel*, 40–58.

———. Review of *Life of George Eliot*, by J. W. Cross. *Atlantic Monthly*, May 1885. Reprinted in Henry James, *Partial Portraits*, 37–62. Ann Arbor: University of Michigan Press, 1970.

———. Review of *Middlemarch*, by George Eliot. *Galaxy*, March 1873.

———. *A Small Boy and Others.* 1913. In *Henry James: Autobiography*, edited by Frederick W. Dupee, 3–238. New York: Criterion Books, 1956.

———. *Washington Square.* 1880. New York: Penguin, 1979.

———. *What Maisie Knew.* Oxford: Oxford University Press, 2008.

James, William. *Psychology: Briefer Course.* 1892. New York: Collier, 1962.

———. *The Will to Believe.* 1896. Reprinted in *The Will To Believe and Other Essays in Popular Philosophy*. Mineola, NY: Dover, 1956.

Jameson, Fredric. *The Antinomies of Realism.* New York: Verso, 2013.

———. *The Political Unconscious: Narrative as a Socially Symbolic Act.* Ithaca, NY: Cornell University Press, 1981.

Jen, Gish. *The Love Wife.* New York: Vintage, 2004.

———. *Tiger Writing: Art, Culture, and the Interdependent Self.* Cambridge, MA: Harvard University Press, 2013.

Johnson, Barbara. "Apostrophe, Animation, and Abortion." In *A World of Difference*, 184–199. Baltimore: Johns Hopkins University Press, 1987.

Johnson, Kendall. "The Scarlet Feather: Racial Phantasmagoria in *What Maisie Knew*." *Henry James Review* 22 (2001): 128–146.

Jottkandt, Sigi. *Acting Beautifully: Henry James and the Ethical Aesthetic.* Albany: SUNY Press, 2005.

Kamuf, Peggy. "'Fiction' and the Experience of the Other." In *The Question of Literature: The Place of the Literary in Contemporary Theory*, edited by Elizabeth Beaumont Bissell, 156–173. Manchester, UK: Manchester University Press, 2002.

Kaston, Carren Osna. "Houses of Fiction in *What Maisie Knew*." *Criticism: A Quarterly for Literature and the Arts* 18 (1976): 27–42.

Keen, Suzanne. *Empathy and the Novel*. Oxford: Oxford University Press, 2007.

Kelly, Adam. "Dialectic of Sincerity: Lionel Trilling and David Foster Wallace." *Post-45*, October 17, 2014. http://post45.research.yale.edu/2014/10/dialectic-of-sincerity-lionel-trilling-and-david-foster-wallace/.

———. "The New Sincerity." In *Postmodern/Postwar—and After: Rethinking American Literature*, edited by Jason Gladstone, Andrew Hoberek, and Daniel Worden, 197–208. Iowa City: University of Iowa Press, 2016.

Kermode, Frank. "Here She Is: *On Beauty* by Zadie Smith." Review of *On Beauty*, by Zadie Smith. *London Review of Books*, October 6, 2005. https://www.lrb.co.uk/the-paper/v27/n19/frank-kermode/here-she-is.

Kidd, David Comer, and Emanuele Castano. "Reading Fiction Improves Theory of Mind." *Science* 342 (2013): 377–380.

King, Martin Luther, Jr. "Beyond Vietnam." In *Black Protest: History, Documents, and Analyses, 1619 to the Present*, 2nd ed., edited by Joanne Grant, 418–425. Greenwich, CT: Fawcett, 1974.

Kingsolver, Barbara. "Dave Eggers's New Novel Follows a Family into the Alaskan Wild." *New York Times*, July 21, 2016. https://www.nytimes.com/2016/07/24/books/review/dave-eggers-heroes-of-the-frontier.html.

Kitzinger, Chloë. "Illusion and Instrument: Problems of Mimetic Characterization in Dostoevsky and Tolstoy." PhD diss., University of California, Berkeley, 2016.

Klopper, Dirk. "'We Are Not Made for Revelation.' Letters to Francis Bacon in the Postscript to J. M. Coetzee's *Elizabeth Costello*." *English in Africa* 35.2 (2008): 119–132.

Kompridis, Nikolas. "Recognition and Receptivity: Forms of Normative Response in the Lives of the Animals We Are." *New Literary History* 44 (2013): 1–24.

Kossew, Sue. "'Women's Words': A Reading of J. M. Coetzee's Women Narrators." In *Critical Essays on J. M. Coetzee*, edited by Sue Kossew, 166–179. New York: G. K. Hall, 1998.

Kristeva, Julia. *Desire in Language: A Semiotic Approach to Literature and Art*. 1977. Edited by Leon S. Roudiez. Translated by Thomas Gora, Alice Jardine, and Leon S. Roudiez. New York: Columbia University Press, 1980.

Krook, Dorothea. *The Ordeal of Consciousness in Henry James*. Cambridge: Cambridge University Press, 1967.

Ksiezopolska, Irena. "Turning Tables: Enchantment, Entrapment, and Empowerment in McEwan's *Sweet Tooth*." *Critique* 56.4 (2015): 415–434.

Lacan, Jacques. "Aggressiveness in Psychoanalysis." 1966. In *Écrits*, 8–29.

———. *Écrits: A Selection*. 1966. Translated by Alan Sheridan. New York: W. W. Norton, 1977.

———. "Introduction and Reply to Jean Hyppolite's Presentation of Freud's *Verneinung*." 1975. In *The Seminar of Jacques Lacan*: bk. 1, *Freud's Papers on Technique 1953–1954*, edited by Jacques-Alain Miller and translated by John Forrester, 52–61. New York: Cambridge University Press, 1988.

Lamb, Jonathan. "Sympathy with Animals and Salvation of the Soul." *Eighteenth Century* 52 (2011): 69–85.

Larson, Jil. *Ethics and Narrative in the English Novel, 1880–1914*. Cambridge: Cambridge University Press, 2001.

Lawrence, D. H. "Art and Morality." 1925. In *Study of Thomas Hardy and Other Essays*, 143–148.

———. "Morality and the Novel." 1925. In *Study of Thomas Hardy and Other Essays*, 149–154.

———. "The Novel." 1925. In *Study of Thomas Hardy and Other Essays*, 155–166.

———. *Study of Thomas Hardy and Other Essays*. 1925. Edited by Bruce Steele. London: Grafton Books, 1986.

———. "Why the Novel Matters." In *Study of Thomas Hardy and Other Essays*, 167–172.

Leavis, F. R. *The Great Tradition: George Eliot, Henry James, Joseph Conrad*. New York: NYU Press, 1964.

———. "What Maisie Knew: A Disagreement by F. R. Leavis." In *The Complex Fate: Hawthorne, Henry James and Some Other American Writers*, edited by Marius Bewley, 111–131. New York: Gordian Press, 1967.

Lee, Vernon. *The Handling of Words and Other Studies in Literary Psychology*. London: Bodley Head, 1923.

Leist, Anton, and Peter Singer. Introduction to *J. M. Coetzee and Ethics: Philosophical Perspectives on Literature*, edited by Anton Leist and Peter Singer, 1–15. New York: Columbia University Press, 2010.

Lessing, Doris. "The Small, Personal Voice." In *A Small Personal Voice: Essays, Reviews, Interviews*, edited by Paul Schlueter, 3–21. New York: Knopf, 1974.

Levinas, Emmanuel. *Alterity and Transcendence*. 1995. Translated by Michael B. Smith. New York: Columbia University Press, 1999.

———. *Ethics and Infinity*. 1982. Translated by Richard A. Cohen. Pittsburgh: Duquesne University Press, 1985.

———. *Otherwise than Being: Or Beyond Essence*. 1974. Translated by Alphonso Lingis. Pittsburgh: Duquesne University Press, 1981.

———. *Totality and Infinity: An Essay on Exteriority*. 1961. Translated by Alphonso Lingis. Pittsburgh: Duquesne University Press, 1969.

Levinson, Jerrold, ed. *Aesthetics and Ethics: Essays at the Intersection*. Cambridge: Cambridge University Press, 1998.

Levithan, David. *Every Day*. New York: Knopf, 2012.

Levy, Ariel. "Elizabeth Strout's Long Homecoming." *New Yorker*, May 1, 2017.

Liddell, Robert. *Some Principles of Fiction*. London: Jonathan Cape, 1953.

———. *A Treatise on the Novel*. London: Jonathan Cape, 1947.

Lodge, David. "Disturbing the Peace." Review of *Elizabeth Costello*, by J. M. Coetzee. *New York Review of Books*, November 20, 2003. https://www.nybooks.com/articles/2003/11/20/disturbing-the-peace/.

———. *The Language of Fiction: Essays in Criticism and Verbal Analysis of the English Novel*. New York: Columbia University Press, 1966.

Lubbock, Percy. *The Craft of Fiction*. 1921. New York: Peter Smith, 1931.

———. Introduction to *The Letters of Henry James*, 1:xiii–xxxi. Edited by Percy Lubbock. 2 vols. New York: Scribner's, 1920.

Lukács, Georg. *The Theory of the Novel: A Historico-Philosophical Essay on the Forms of Great Epic Literature*. 1920. Translated by Anna Bostok. Cambridge, MA: MIT Press, 1971.

MacLeod, Lewis. "'Do We of Necessity Become Puppets in a Story?' or Narrating the World: On Speech, Silence, and Discourse in J. M. Coetzee's *Foe*." *Modern Fiction Studies* 52 (2006): 1–17.

Marais, Mike. "J. M. Coetzee's *Disgrace* and the Task of the Imagination." *Journal of Modern Literature* 29 (2006): 75–93.

Marchitello, Howard, ed. *What Happens to History: The Renewal of Ethics in Contemporary Thought*. New York: Routledge, 2001.

Martin, Priscilla. "Houses of Fiction: Iris Murdoch and Henry James." In *Iris Murdoch: A Reassessment*, edited by Anne Rowe, 124–135. New York: Palgrave, 2007.

Masters, Ben. *Novel Style: Ethics and Excess in English Fiction since the 1960s*. Oxford: Oxford University Press, 2017.

Matz, Jesse. *Literary Impressionism and Modernist Aesthetics*. Cambridge: Cambridge University Press, 2001.

———. *The Modern Novel: A Short Introduction*. New York: Wiley-Blackwell, 2004.

McCall, Dan. "What Maisie Saw." *Henry James Review* 16 (1995): 48–52.

McEwan, Ian. "Nihilism, the Novel and Political Creativity." Speech, Jerusalem, February 22, 2011. ABC Religion and Ethics. https://www.abc.net.au/religion/nihilism-the-novel-and-political-creativity/10101686.

———. *Sweet Tooth*. New York: Doubleday, 2012.

McGilligan, Patrick. *Alfred Hitchcock: A Life in Darkness and Light*. New York: Regan Books, 2003.

McGinn, Colin. *Ethics, Evil, and Fiction*. Oxford: Clarendon Press, 1997.

McGurl, Mark. *The Novel Art: Elevations of American Fiction after Henry James*. Princeton, NJ: Princeton University Press, 2001.

Michaels, Walter Benn. "Jim Crow Henry James?" *Henry James Review* 16 (1995): 286–291.

———. *The Shape of the Signifier: 1967 to the End of History*. Princeton, NJ: Princeton University Press, 2004.

Miller, D. A. *The Novel and the Police*. Berkeley: University of California Press, 1988.

Miller, J. Hillis. *The Ethics of Reading: Kant, de Man, Eliot, Trollope, James, and Benjamin*. New York: Columbia University Press, 1987.

———. *Literature as Conduct: Speech Acts in Henry James*. New York: Fordham University Press, 2005.

Mishira, Pankaj. "Other Voices, Other Selves." Review of *Changing My Mind: Occasional Essays*, by Zadie Smith. *New York Times*, January 14, 2010. https://www.nytimes.com/2010/01/17/books/review/Mishra-t.html.

Mitchell, Juliet. "*What Maisie Knew*: Portrait of the Artist as a Young Girl." In *The Air of Reality: New Essays on Henry James*, edited by John Goode, 168–189. London: Methuen, 1972.

Mitchell, Lee Clark. "Ethics, Aesthetics, and the Case of Late James." *Raritan* 22 (2003): 71–89.

Moore, Caroline. Review of *A Mercy*. *The Telegraph*, November 14, 2008.

Moraru, Christian. "The Forster Connection or, Cosmopolitanism Redux: Zadie Smith's *On Beauty*, *Howards End*, and the Schlegels." *The Comparatist* 35 (2011): 133–149.

More, Henry. 1642. *Psychodia Platonica*. Cambridge: Printed by Roger Daniel, printer to the Universitie [*sic*]. Early English Books Online.

Morrison, Toni. *A Mercy*. New York: Knopf, 2008.

———. *The Origin of Others*. Cambridge, MA: Harvard University Press, 2017.

———. *Playing in the Dark: Whiteness and the Literary Imagination*. New York: Random House, 1992.

Mosca, Valeria. "'A Purgatory of Clichés': Elizabeth Costello and the Impossible Paradise for Writers." *Other Modernities: Journal of Literature and Culture* 7 (2012): 127–139.

Moses, Michael Valdez. "'King of the Amphibians': *Elizabeth Costello* and Coetzee's Metamorphoric Fictions." *Journal of Literary Studies* 25 (2009): 25–38.

Moya, Paula M. L. *Learning from Experience: Minorities, Identities, Multicultural Struggles*. Berkeley: University of California Press, 2002.

———. *The Social Imperative: Race, Close Reading and Contemporary Literary Criticism*. Stanford, CA: Stanford University Press, 2015.

Mulhall, Stephen. *The Wounded Animal: J. M. Coetzee and the Difficulty of Reality in Literature and Philosophy*. Princeton, NJ: Princeton University Press, 2009.

Murdoch, Iris. "The Sublime and the Beautiful Revisited." *Yale Review* 49.2 (1959): 247–271.

Nash, Katherine Saunders. *Feminist Narrative Ethics: Tacit Persuasion in Modernist Form*. Columbus: Ohio State University Press, 2014.

Nealon, Jeffrey T. *Alterity Politics: Ethics and Performative Subjectivity*. Durham, NC: Duke University Press, 1998.

Nehamas, Alexander. "The Return of the Beautiful: Morality, Pleasure and the Value of Uncertainty." *Journal of Aesthetics and Art Criticism* 58.4 (2000): 393–403.

Nethersole, Reingard. "Reading in the In-between: Pre-scripting the 'Postscript' to *Elizabeth Costello*." *Journal of Literary Studies* 21 (2007): 254–276.

Newman, Judie. "Intertextuality, Power, and Danger: *Waiting for the Barbarians* as a Dirty Story." In *Critical Essays on J. M. Coetzee*, edited by Sue Kossew, 126–138. New York: G. K. Hall, 1998.

Newton, Adam Zachary. *Narrative Ethics*. Cambridge, MA: Harvard University Press, 1995.

Niedzviecki, Hal. "Winning the Appropriation Prize." *Write* (Spring 2017).

Norris, Frank. "The True Reward of the Novelist." In *The Responsibilities of the Novelist*, 13–22. New York: Doubleday, 1903.

Nunning, Ansgar. "'The Extension of Our Sympathies': George Eliot's Aesthetic Theory and Narrative Technique as a Key to the Affective, Cognitive and Social Value of Literature." In *Values of Literature*, edited by Hanna Meretoja, Saija Isomaa, Pirjo Lyytikäinen, and Kristina Malmo, 117–136. Amsterdam: Rodopi, 2015.

Nussbaum, Martha. *Love's Knowledge: Essays on Philosophy and Literature*. Oxford: Oxford University Press, 1990.

———. *Poetic Justice: The Literary Imagination and Public Life*. Boston: Beacon Press, 1995.

———. "The Professor of Parody." *New Republic*, February 22, 1999, 37–45.

O'Hara, David K. "Briony's Being-For: Metafictional Narrative Ethics in Ian McEwan's *Atonement*." *Critique* 52 (2011): 74–100.

Ozick, Cynthia. *What Henry James Knew and Other Essays on Writers*. London: Jonathan Cape, 1993.

Öztürk, Riza. *Evolutionary Aesthetics of Human Ethics in Hardy's Tragic Narratives*. Newcastle, UK: Cambridge Scholars, 2011.

Palmer, Alan. *Fictional Minds*. Lincoln: University of Nebraska Press, 2004.

Palmer, Frank. *Literature and Moral Understanding: A Philosophical Essay on Ethics, Aesthetics, Education, and Culture*. Oxford: Clarendon Press, 1992.

Parker, David. "Introduction: The Turn to Ethics in the 1990s." In *Renegotiating Ethics in Literature, Philosophy, and Theory*, edited by Jane Adamson, Richard Freadman, and David Parker, 1–20. Cambridge: Cambridge University Press, 1998.

Pastoor, Charles Cornelius. "Authorial Atonement in Ian McEwan's *Atonement* and *Sweet Tooth*." *Christianity and Literature* 68 (2019): 297–310.

Phelan, James. *Living to Tell about It: A Rhetoric and Ethics of Character*. Ithaca, NY: Cornell University Press, 2004.

Phillips, Adam. "Keeping It Moving: Commentary on Judith Butler." Reprinted in *The Psychic Life of Power: Theories in Subjection*, by Judith Butler, 151–159. Stanford, CA: Stanford University Press, 1997.

Phillips, Michelle H. "The 'Partagé Child' and the Emergence of the Modernist Novel in *What Maisie Knew*." *Henry James Review* 31 (2010): 95–110.

Pick, Anat. "Miracles of Arrangement: Structures of Multiplicity and the Birth of Justice in Henry James's *The Golden Bowl*." *Henry James Review* 21 (2000): 115–132.

Pilkington, John. *The Heart of Yoknapatawpha*. Jackson: University Press of Mississippi, 1981.

Pippin, Robert B. *Henry James and Modern Moral Life*. Cambridge: Cambridge University Press, 2000.

———. "On Maisie Knowing Her Own Mind." In *A Companion to Henry James*, edited by Greg W. Zacharias, 121–138. New York: Wiley-Blackwell, 2008.

———. "The Paradoxes of Power in the Early Novels of J. M. Coetzee." In *J. M. Coetzee and Ethics: Philosophical Perspectives on Literature*, edited by Anton Leist and Peter Singer, 19–41. New York: Columbia University Press, 2010.

Pirandello, Luigi. *Six Characters in Search of an Author and Other Plays*. New York: Penguin, 1995.

Plato. *The Parmenides of Plato*. Translated by A. E. Taylor. Oxford: Clarendon Press, 1934.

Poirier, Richard. *The Comic Sense of Henry James: A Study of the Early Novels*. Oxford: Oxford University Press, 1960.

Porter, Carolyn. *Seeing and Being: The Plight of the Participant Observer in Emerson, James, Adams, and Faulkner*. Middletown, CT: Wesleyan University Press, 1981.

Proust, Marcel. *In Search of Lost Time*. Vol. 1, *Swann's Way*. 1913. Translated by C. K. Scott Moncrieff and Terence Kilmartin. New York: Vintage, 1989.

Rainsford, Dominic, and Tim Woods, eds. *Critical Ethics: Text, Theory and Responsibility*. New York: Macmillan, 1999.

Review of *What Maisie Knew*, by Henry James. *Literary World: A Monthly Review of Current Literature*, December 2, 1897, 454.

Reynier, Christine, and Jean-Michel Ganteau, eds. *Ethics of Alterity, Confrontation and Responsibility in 19th- to 21st-Century British Literature*. Montpellier: Presses universitaires de la Méditerranée, 2013.

Rhys, Jean. *Good Morning, Midnight*. Harmondsworth, UK: Penguin, 1984.

Rich, Frank. "Zadie Smith's Culture Warriors." *New York Times*, September 18, 2005.

https://www.nytimes.com/2005/09/18/books/review/zadie-smiths-culture-war riors.html.

Robbe-Grillet, Alain. "On Several Obsolete Notions." 1963. In *For a New Novel*, translated by Richard Howard, 25–47. Evanston, IL: Northwestern University Press, 1965.

Robbins, Bruce. "Pretend What You Like: Literature under Construction." In *The Question of Literature: The Place of the Literary in Contemporary Theory*, edited by Elizabeth Beaumont Bissell, 190–206. Manchester, UK: Manchester University Press, 2002.

Robinson, Marilynne. "The Art of Fiction, No. 198." Interview by Sarah Fay, *Paris Review*, September/October 2008. https://www.theparisreview.org/interviews/5863/marilynne-robinson-the-art-of-fiction-no-198-marilynne-robinson.

———. "A Conversation with Marilynne Robinson." *Willow Springs* (2006): 77–95.

———. "An Interview with Thomas Schaub." *Contemporary Literature* 35 (1994): 231–251.

———. "Marilynne Robinson on Democracy, Reading, and Religion in America." Interview by Joe Fassler, *The Atlantic*, May 16, 2012. https://www.theatlantic.com/entertainment/archive/2012/05/marilynne-robinson-on-democracy-reading-and-religion-in-america/257211/.

Robinson, Richard. "The Modernism of Ian McEwan's *Atonement*." *Modern Fiction Studies* 56 (2010): 473–495.

Rospide, Maylis, and Sandrine Sorlin, eds. *The Ethics and Poetics of Alterity: New Perspectives on Genre Literature*. Newcastle, UK: Cambridge Scholars, 2015.

Ross, Stephen. "Modernist Ethics, Critique, and Utopia." In Reynier and Ganteau, *Ethics of Alterity*, 49–63.

Rushdie, Salman. "Is Nothing Sacred?" 1990. In *Imaginary Homelands: Essays and Criticism 1981–1991*, 415–429. New York: Penguin, 1991.

Russo, Richard. "Horseman." In *Trajectory*, 3–38. New York: Knopf, 2017.

Ruttenburg, Nancy. "The Human Document." *Journal of Literary Studies* 25 (2009): 51–66.

Ryan, Judith. "The Vanishing Subject: Empirical Psychology and the Modern Novel." *PMLA* 95 (1980): 857–869.

Sanders, Mark. "Ethics and Interdisciplinarity in Philosophy and Literary Theory." *diacritics* 32.3 (2002): 3–16.

———. "The Writing Business: 'He and His Man,' Coetzee and Defoe." *Journal of Literary Studies* 25 (2009): 39–50.

Sartre, Jean-Paul. "Why Write?" 1947. In *"What Is Literature?" and Other Essays*, 58–65. Cambridge, MA: Harvard University Press, 1988.

Scarry, Elaine. *On Beauty and Being Just*. Princeton, NJ: Princeton University Press, 1999.

Schlegel, Friedrich. "Letter about the Novel, 1799–1800." In *Dialogue on Poetry and Literary Aphorisms*, translated by Ernst Behler and Roman Struc, 99–116. University Park: Penn State University Press, 1968.

Scholar, John. *Henry James and the Art of Impressions*. Oxford: Oxford University Press, 2020.

Sears, Sally. *The Negative Imagination: Form and Perspective in the Novels of Henry James*. Ithaca, NY: Cornell University Press, 1968.

Sedgwick, Eve. "Paranoid Reading and Reparative Reading, or, You're So Paranoid, You Probably Think This Essay Is about You." In *Touching Feeling: Affect, Pedagogy, Performativity*, 123–151. Durham, NC: Duke University Press, 2003.

———. "Queer Performativity: Henry James's *The Art of the Novel*." *GLQ: Journal of Lesbian and Gay Studies* 1 (1993): 1–16.

Schuessler, Jennifer. "Editor Resigns over an Article Defending 'Cultural Appropriation.'" *New York Times*, May 11, 2017. https://www.nytimes.com/2017/05/11/arts/editor-resigns-over-article-defending-cultural-appropriation.html.

Segalovitz, Yael. "William Faulkner, Cleanth Brooks, and the Living-Dead Reader of New Critical Theory." *Arizona Quarterly* 75 (2019): 49–83.

Serpell, C. Namwali. *Seven Modes of Uncertainty*. Cambridge, MA: Harvard University Press, 2014.

Shklovsky, Victor. "Art as Technique." 1917. In *Russian Formalist Criticism: Four Essays*, translated by Lee T. Lemon and Marion J. Reis, 3–24. Lincoln: University of Nebraska Press, 1965.

Silverman, Kaja. "Too Early / Too Late: Subjectivity and the Primal Scene in Henry James." *Novel: A Forum on Fiction* 21 (1988): 147–173.

Smallwood, Christine. "Back Talk: Toni Morrison." *The Nation*, December 8, 2008.

Smith, Alena. *The New Sincerity*. New York: Dramatists Play Service, 2015.

Smith, Zadie. *Changing My Mind: Occasional Essays*. New York: Penguin, 2009.

———. "E. M. Forster, Middle Manager." In *Changing My Mind*, 14–28.

———. "Fail Better." *The Guardian*, January 13, 2007.

———. "Fascinated to Presume: In Defense of Fiction." *New York Review of Books*, October 24, 2019, 4–10.

———. Introduction to *The Book of Other People*, vii–ix. Edited by Zadie Smith. New York: Penguin, 2007.

———. "Love, Actually." *The Guardian*, October 31, 2003, 4–6.

———. "*Middlemarch* and Everybody." In *Changing My Mind*, 29–41.

———. *On Beauty*. New York: Penguin, 2005.

———. "Read Better." *The Guardian*, January 20, 2007, 21–22.

———. "Speaking in Tongues." 2008. Reprinted in *Changing My Mind*, 132–148.

———. "Two Directions for the Novel." Reprinted in *Changing My Mind*, 72–96.

———. "Zadie, Take Three." Interview by Jessica Murphy Moo, *The Atlantic*, July 15, 2010. https://www.theatlantic.com/magazine/archive/2005/10/zadie-take-three/304294/.

Smith, Zadie, and Ian McEwan. "Zadie Smith Talks with Ian McEwan." In *The Believers Book of Writers Talking to Writers*, edited by Vendela Vida, 207–239. San Francisco: Believer Books, 2005.

Smuts, Eckard. "Reading through the Gates: Structure, Desire and Subjectivity in J. M. Coetzee's *Elizabeth Costello*." *English in Africa* 36 (2009): 63–77.

Sokolowski, Jeanne. "The Limits of Hospitality in Gish Jen's *The Love Wife*." *Journal of Transnational American Studies* 4 (2012). https://escholarship.org/uc/item/6v8636jz.

Sommer, Roy. "The Aesthetic Turn in 'Black' Literary Studies: Zadie Smith's *On Beauty* and the Case for an Intercultural Narratology." In *"Black" British Aesthetics Today*, edited by R. Victoria Arana, 176–192. Newcastle, UK: Cambridge Scholars, 2007.

Spivak, Gayatri Chakravorty. *A Critique of Postcolonial Reason: Toward a History of the Vanishing Present*. Cambridge, MA: Harvard University Press, 1999.

———. "Ethics and Politics in Tagore, Coetzee, and Certain Scenes of Teaching." *diacritics* 32.3–4 (2002): 17–31.

———. "Three Women's Texts and a Critique of Imperialism." *Critical Inquiry* 12 (1985): 243–261.

Stanley, Thomas. *The History of Philosophy*. Vol. 3. London: Printed for Humphrey Moseley and Thomas Dring, 1660.

Stevens, Hugh. "Queer Henry *In the Cage*." In *The Cambridge Companion to Henry James*, edited by Jonathan Freedman, 120–138. Cambridge: Cambridge University Press, 1998.

Strehle, Susan. "'I Am a Thing Apart': Toni Morrison, *A Mercy*, and American Exceptionalism." *Critique* 54 (2013): 109–123.

Strout, Elizabeth. "Elizabeth Strout's Long Homecoming." Interview by Ariel Levy, *New Yorker*, May 1, 2017. https://www.newyorker.com/magazine/2017/05/01/elizabeth-strouts-long-homecoming.

Su, John. "Beauty and the Beastly Prime Minister." *ELH* 81 (2014): 1083–1110.

Tanner, Tony. *Henry James: The Writer and His Work*. Amherst: University of Massachusetts Press, 1985.

Teahan, Sheila. *The Rhetorical Logic of Henry James*. Baton Rouge: Louisiana State University Press, 1995.

———. "*What Maisie Knew* and the Improper Third Person." *Studies in American Fiction* 21 (1993): 127–140.

Thackeray, William Makepeace. *Early and Late Papers*. Boston: Ticknor and Fields, 1867.

Tolan, Fiona. "Zadie Smith's Forsterian Ethics: *White Teeth, The Autograph Man, On Beauty*." *Critique* 54 (2013): 135–146.

Trilling, Lionel. "Manners, Morals, and the Novel." *Kenyon Review* 10 (1948): 11–27.

Trollope, Anthony. *An Autobiography*. Vol. 2. Edinburgh: Blackwood and Sons, 1883.

Truffaut, Francois, with Helen G. Scott. *Hitchcock: A Definitive Study of Alfred Hitchcock*. New York: Simon and Schuster, 1984.

Tucker, Irene. "What Maisie Promised: Realism, Liberalism and the Ends of Contract." *Yale Journal of Criticism* 11 (1998): 335–364.

Utell, Janine. "*On Chesil Beach* and Fordian Technique: Intertextuality, Intimacy, Ethical Reading." *Journal of Modern Literature* 39 (2016): 89–104.

Vadde, Aarthi. "Guidance in Perplexity: Recasting Postcolonial Politics in J. M. Coetzee's *Elizabeth Costello*." *Ariel* 41.3–4 (2011): 231–247.

Van Ghent, Dorothy. *The English Novel: Form and Function*. New York: Harper, 1961.

Walker, Laura Savu. "'A Balance of Power': The Covert Authorship of Ian McEwan's Double Agents in *Sweet Tooth*." *Modern Fiction Studies* 61 (2015): 493–514.

Wall, Kathleen. "Ethics, Knowledge, and the Need for Beauty: Zadie Smith's *On Beauty* and Ian McEwan's *Saturday*." *University of Toronto Quarterly* 77 (2008): 757–788.

Wallace, David Foster. "*E Unibus Pluram*: Television and U.S. Fiction." 1993. Reprinted in *A Supposedly Fun Thing I'll Never Do Again: Essays and Arguments*, 21–82. Boston: Little, Brown, 1997.

Walters, Margaret. "'Keeping the Place Tidy for the Young Female Mind': *The Awkward Age*." In *The Air of Reality: New Essays on Henry James*, edited by John Goode, 190–208. London: Methuen, 1972.

Walton, Heather. "Staging John Coetzee / Elizabeth Costello." *Literature and Theology* 22 (2008): 280–294.

Ward, J. A. *The Imagination of Disaster: Evil in the Fiction of Henry James*. Lincoln: University of Nebraska Press, 1961.

Weinberger, Christopher. "Critical Desire and the Novel: Ethics of Self-Consciousness in Cervantes and Nabokov." *Narrative* 20 (2012): 277–300.

Weinstein, Cindy. *Time, Tense, and American Literature: When Is Now?* Cambridge: Cambridge University Press, 2015.

Weinstein, Philip M. *Faulkner's Subject: A Cosmos No One Owns*. Cambridge: Cambridge University Press, 1992.

West, Rebecca. *Henry James*. New York: Henry Holt, 1916.

Westover, Jeff. "Handing Over Power in James's *What Maisie Knew*." *Style* 28 (1994): 201–218.

Wicomb, Zoë. "*Slow Man* and the Real: A Lesson in Reading and Writing." *Journal of Literary Studies* 25 (2009): 7–24.

Widiss, Benjamin. *Obscure Invitations: The Persistence of the Author in Twentieth-Century American Literature.* Stanford: Stanford University Press, 2011.

Willett, Cynthia. "Ground Zero for a Post-moral Ethics in J. M. Coetzee's *Disgrace* and Julia Kristeva's Melancholic." *Continental Philosophy Review* 45 (2012): 1–22.

Williams, Raymond. *The Country and the City.* Oxford: Oxford University Press, 1973.

Wittenberg, Hermann. "Imperial Space and the Discourse of the Novel." *Journal of Literary Studies* 13 (1997): 127–150.

Woloch, Alex. *The One vs. the Many: Minor Characters and the Space of the Protagonist in the Novel.* Princeton, NJ: Princeton University Press, 2003.

Wood, Gaby. "The Return of Zadie Smith." *The Telegraph*, August 25, 2012. https://www.telegraph.co.uk/culture/books/9495181/The-return-of-Zadie-Smith.html.

Wood, James. *How Fiction Works.* New York: Farrar, Straus and Giroux, 2008.

Wood, Michael. *Literature and the Taste of Knowledge.* Cambridge: Cambridge University Press, 2005.

Woolf, Virginia. "Art and Life." 1909. Reprinted in *The Essays of Virginia Woolf*, 1:277–280.

———. *The Essays of Virginia Woolf.* Edited by Andrew McNeillie. 4 vols. London: Hogarth Press, 1994.

———. *Granite and Rainbow: Essays by Virginia Woolf.* New York: Harcourt Brace Jovanovich, 1958.

———. "Modern Fiction." 1925. Reprinted in The *Essays of Virginia Woolf*, 4:157–164.

———. "Mr. Bennett and Mrs. Brown." 1924. Reprinted in *The Virginia Woolf Reader*, edited by Mitchell A. Leaska, 192–212. New York: Harcourt Brace Jovanovich, 1984.

———. "The Narrow Bridge of Art." 1927. Reprinted in *Granite and Rainbow*, 11–23.

———. "On Re-reading Novels." Reprinted in *The Essays of Virginia Woolf*, 3:336–346.

———. "Phases of Fiction." 1929. Reprinted in *Granite and Rainbow*, 93–145.

———. *A Room of One's Own.* New York: Harcourt, Brace, 1929.

———. "Women and Fiction." Reprinted in *The Novel: An Anthology of Criticism and Theory, 1900–2000*, edited by Dorothy J. Hale, 579–585. Malden, MA: Blackwell, 2006.

Wyatt, Jean. "Failed Messages, Maternal Loss, and Narrative Form in Toni Morrison's *A Mercy*." *Modern Fiction Studies* 58 (2012): 128–151.

Yeazell, Ruth Bernard. *Language and Knowledge in the Late Novels of Henry James.* Chicago: University of Chicago Press, 1976.

Yeoh, Gilbert. "Love and Indifference in J. M. Coetzee's *Age of Iron*." *Journal of Commonwealth Literature* 38.3 (2003): 107–134.

Young, Kay. *Imagining Minds: The Neuro-Aesthetics of Austen, Eliot, and Hardy*. Columbus: Ohio State University Press, 2010.

Zalewski, Daniel. "The Background Hum: Ian McEwan's Art of Unease." *New Yorker*, February 23, 2009. https://www.newyorker.com/magazine/2009/02/23/the-background-hum.

Zunshine, Lisa. *Why We Read Fiction: Theory of Mind and the Novel*. Columbus: Ohio State University Press, 2006.

Zwinger, Lynda. "Bodies That Don't Matter: The Queering of 'Henry James.'" *Modern Fiction Studies* 41 (1995): 558–680.

———. *Telling in Henry James: The Web of Experience and the Forms of Reality*. London: Bloomsbury, 2015.

Index

Abrams, M. H., 242n49
Abramson, Anna Jones, 269n22
abstraction, xvi, 3, 5, 49, 51, 54, 104, 106, 135, 145, 167, 168, 193, 198, 199, 204, 215, 275n41, 278n28, 284n10
Adams, Ann Marie, 238n18, 255n2
aesthetic functionalism, 191
aesthetic value, ix, 16, 25, 65, 70–71, 84, 103, 177, 182. *See also specific novelists and scholars*
affect, encountering. *See* emotional/affective experience
African American identity, 52, 129, 255n4
Africanist presence, 38, 52, 53, 73
African tradition, 164–169
agency, 2–3, 15, 16, 38, 101, 117, 130, 131, 173, 182, 188, 191, 193, 202, 245n61, 265n3, 276n3; and James's *What Maisie Knew*, 52, 53, 57, 58, 59, 80, 246–247n5. *See also* freedom
alienation, 6, 54, 75, 81, 128, 142, 147, 169
allegory, 41, 49, 92, 140, 141, 206, 207, 274n33
allusion, 274n31
Alter, Robert, 139
alterity: characterological, 91, 99, 108, 119, 193, 195; ethics of, as a term, reason for using, 5; novelistic aesthetics of, significance of, xi, xiii, xiv, 9, 10–11, 19, 83, 134, 175, 217; resistance to, driver of, 94; as a term,

popular usage of, expansion of, 5–8, 237–238n17. *See also* otherness; *specific novelists and scholars*
Althusser, Louis, 203–204
Altieri, Charles, 276–277n7
altruism, x, 54, 91, 112, 194, 247n7
ambiguity, 57, 74, 81, 161, 185, 186, 201, 205
analogy, 35, 37, 72, 208
Andrews, Lucilla, 243n53
Anglo-American academy: J. Hillis Miller on, 209; powerful force within, 218, 234n5; pursuit undertaken by, xvii, 38, 85, 173, 175; quality of knowledge produced within, Smith addressing, 101, 259–260n29. *See also* literary studies; *specific scholars*
Anglo-American literary tradition, ix, x, xi, xii, xiii, xvi, 2, 4–5, 10, 25, 27–28, 47, 82, 85, 98, 139, 141, 228–229. *See also specific literary movements, literary terms, and individual authors*
Anglo-American New Criticism, 228, 283n9
Anglo-Protestant tradition, 238n17
animal alterity, 144–149, 153, 161–62
Anjara, Ulka, 255n4
Anker, Elizabeth Susan, 270–272n26, 272n28
anthropocentricism, 236n7
anthropomorphism, 258n25
anticolonialism, 281n62
antifiction, 208–209

309

anti-instrumentality, 176
antirealism, xiv, xv
anxiety, 37, 184–185, 188, 191, 195, 198, 200, 201, 205, 214, 217, 274n31
aphorisms, 120–123, 262–263n50
apprehension, xvi, 6, 9, 12, 30, 63, 64, 79, 89, 97, 101, 105, 106, 109, 111, 112, 118, 120, 122, 151, 152, 174, 189, 190, 191, 199, 206–207, 211, 279n44
appropriation, 11–13, 20, 66, 248n15
Arendt, Hannah, 276n1
Aristotle, 107, 176; Aristotelians, xviii
Armstrong, Nancy, 177, 191
art of the novel: as autonomous art, 84, 89, 250n31; as cannibal art, 2, 38, 97, 139, 167–168, 232n5; developing a theory of, problems unique to, xi, 82, 85, 86–87, 253n61; as high art, xi, xii, 25, 48, 55, 75, 85, 102–103, 177, 218; James's theory of, xiii, 26–27, 47, 48–49, 169, 177, 217; as living art, 15, 17, 27, 48–49, 77, 83, 86, 95, 160, 165, 234n4, 262n49; pursuit of, criticism directed at, 81, 98, 180–181, 194, 196, 225; twentieth-century conception of, ix, xi, xiii, 3–4, 4–5, 18, 25, 27, 98, 217. See also specific novelists, scholars, and literary traditions
Ashcroft, Bill, 274n37
Asian American identity, 19–20, 24
Attridge, Derek, 80, 82, 181, 266–267n11, 277n7
Attwell, David, 266n9, 275n38
Austen, Jane, 84, 88
Austin, J. L., 192, 205
autonomy: and Adorno, 232n6; of art, 84, 89; Berman on, 276n1; body, 283n5; Butler on, 187; of character, xiv, 2, 14, 15, 18, 22, 23, 49, 72, 81, 98, 120, 138, 183; and Charon, 221; and Coetzee, 138, 156, 163–164, 267n11, 268n17, 272n28; and Faulkner, 22, 103; of the fictional world, 156; and Franzen, 39–40, 40–41, 44, 246n65; and humanism, 57; and James, 30, 31, 49, 55, 57, 59, 63, 72, 183, 190, 249n31, 250n31; and Jen, 19, 23; J. Hillis Miller on, 203, 208; and Kafka, 160, 161, 162; and Lee, 91; and Levithan, 245n60; and Liddell, 91–92; limits on, 215–216; of literary text, 192, 193; and McEwan, 34; and Morrison, 50, 51, 72; and Newton, 198; range of, capacity for, 276n1; and Smith, 98, 109, 111, 120, 262n49; of the social world, 191, 267n11; and Thackeray, 50; and Trollope, 50; and Woolf, 23. See also freedom; independence; living art
avowal of disavowal, 181, 189, 198

Badiou, Alain, 228, 281n64, 284n10
Baker, Houston, 129
Bakhtin, M. M.: on empathy and subjectivity, 231–232n2; and notions of heteroglossia and dialogism, 182, 185
Balzac, 3, 259n26
Banta, Martha, 248–249n23
Banville, John, 8
Barker, Nicola, 262n42
Barnard, Rita, 274n36
Barth, John, 4, 141
Barthes, Roland, xiii, 175, 176; on empathy and subjectivity, 231–232n2; on realism, 141; on subjectivity, 3; S/Z, 3; on textual dissemination, 203
Batra, Kanika, 262n43
beauty: as bodily 116; notions of 41, 70, 71, 84, 98–99, 103, 117, 258n24; questions on, 96; and social positionally 103–106
Beckett, Samuel, xiv
beliefs, relativized view of, issue of, 124, 170–171, 275n41
Bellamy, Maria Rice, 251n39
Benjamin, Walter, 227, 283n7

Bennett, Arnold, 87
Berman, Jessica, 232n6, 236n8, 276n1
Bernstein, Michael André, 181
Besant, Walter, 26, 168
Bewley, Marius, 249nn25–26
bias, 94, 95, 167, 170, 216, 262n47
bildungsroman, 59, 141, 248n21
binary paradigms, rejecting/moving beyond, 263n51, 274n33
binding, 39–40, 43, 162, 179, 183, 184, 187, 189, 190, 199, 203, 210. *See also* self-binding
biracial identity, 129–130
Black, Shameem, 239n28, 265n4, 280n50
Blackham, H. J., 115
black identity, 52, 102, 113, 117–18, 129, 255n4
blind spots, 62, 80, 94, 100, 105, 118, 205, 256n12
bodies, novelization of, 282–283n5
bodily action, 166, 205, 207–208
bodily knowledge, 190, 205, 207, 221, 222, 224
bodily relation. *See* embodiment
Boehmer, Elleke, 266n8
book clubs, 86
Booth, Naomi, 244n59, 245n61
Booth, Wayne, 102, 210, 279n43, 281–282n65; *The Rhetoric of Fiction*, 248n18, 258n22, 281n61
Borges, Jorge Luis, 140
boundaries, 194, 196, 198, 201, 274n31
Bradbury, Malcolm, 86
bridges/bridging, 142, 145–146, 149, 150, 155, 165, 166, 167, 179, 225–226, 251n39
British literary tradition, 23, 84, 86, 87, 89, 93, 120, 178, 232n5, 238n18, 255n4
Brontë, Charlotte, 24, 159, 274n32
Brooke-Rose, Christine, 85–86
Brophy, Brigid, 87, 95
Brown, Christopher, 249n29
Butler, Judith: and agency, 276n3; and Bakhtin, 182, 185; and Foucault, 222; *Gender Trouble*, 283n6; and Gibson, 200, 201, 202; *Giving an Account of Oneself*, 222, 276n3; influence of, 181; and James, 181, 182–185, 185–186, 187, 189, 191, 195, 198, 206, 212, 222, 264n61, 279n44; and J. Hillis Miller, 206, 207; and Levinas, 184, 222; and Newton, 197, 198; and the notion of evanescence, 46; and Nussbaum, 174, 176, 189, 201, 277n7; and performativity, 264n61, 279n44; on reading and affect, 182–188; "Values of Difficulty," 182, 188
Byatt, A. S., 86, 87, 90

cannibal art, 2, 38, 84, 97, 139, 167–168, 232n5
capitalism, 3, 6, 43, 177, 181, 225, 263n56, 283n7
care, xii, 10, 40, 45, 56–57, 58, 59, 60, 61–62, 64, 66, 73, 77, 100, 162, 163, 170, 178, 179, 188, 228, 283n5
Carlacio, Jami, 251n39
Carstensen, Thorsten, 267–268n15, 275n41
Castano, Emanuele, 231nn1–2
Cavell, Stanley, 192, 198
certainty, troubling of, 9, 161, 187, 188, 190, 214. *See also* negative capability; uncertainty
Cervantes, Miguel de, 139
change: call for, 223, 266n7; capacity for, 39, 107, 123–124; possibility of, 187, 188, 233; resistance to, 159, 266n7; social, 94, 128, 132, 148, 188; textural, experts in, 211
character: author's relation to, 19, 26, 28, 31, 32, 37, 39, 48, 53, 55–56, 63, 65, 70, 73, 117, 125, 136, 196, 220; autonomy of, xiv, 2, 14, 15, 18, 22, 23, 49, 72, 81, 98, 120, 138, 183; determinative for, 11; fictional, 47, 163, 216; independence of, 16, 17, 32, 34, 91; as novel form, 9, 11, 19, 43–45, 54, 63, 90, 111, 162, 193, 199;

as other, 6, 12, 13, 19, 22, 25, 27, 29–30, 51, 52, 78, 82, 142; personhood of, xii, 5, 10, 55, 102, 155; reader's relation to, 40, 41, 50, 143, 174, 190; return to/revival of, 2–3, 8, 25, 174, 234n5. *See also specific novelists and scholars*
Charon, Rita, 218–229, 282–283nn3–5, 283n8; *Narrative Medicine*, 226–228
Childs, Peter, 256–257n13
Christiansë, Yvette, 251n38, 251–252n42
citationality, 63, 97, 98, 104, 105, 115, 118, 140, 141, 166, 206, 273n30, 281n59
civil rights, 131
Clarkson, Carol, 265n4
class: and ideology, 262n47; and point of view, 116; and positionality, 113; and the unconscious, 247n6
class bias, 262n47
class difference, 30, 78, 116
class identity, 197
class power, 278n19
class stratification, 225
clinical medicine, interdisciplinary field involving, 218–228, 229
close reading, 76, 85, 227–228, 283n9
co-creation, 39–40, 204, 246n65
"coduction," 281n65
Coetzee, J. M.: acclaimed work of, 137; *Age of Iron*, 135–136, 137, 138, 140, 264–265n2; Attridge on, 82, 266–267n11; *The Childhood of Jesus*, 140; and Defoe, 267n13; *Disgrace*, 136–137, 138, 140, 210, 211–214, 265n4, 271n26, 272–273n29; *Foe*, 140, 281n62; and formalism, 138; *The Good Story*, 274n34; lectures delivered by, 265n5; "The Lives of Animals," 265n5; and Nagel, 270n23; "The Novel in Africa," 265n5; and the novelistic aesthetics of alterity, 163, 170; and plot, 171; and the return to ethics, 1–2; *Slow Man*, 140, 265n5, 267n14; and social value, 172; Spivak on, 211–14; on sympathy, 269n21; *Waiting for the Barbarians*, 135, 137, 138, 209, 274n31; "What is Realism," 265n5; "As a Woman Grows Older," 265n5. *See also Elizabeth Costello* (Coetzee)
collectivism, 79, 92, 138
colonialism, 94, 166, 167, 212, 265n3, 281n62
comedy, 18, 57, 58, 66, 68, 75, 239n28, 243n53, 259n29
commodification, 38
common ground, 215, 281–282n65
communal identity, 155
Conner, Marc, 251n41
Conrad, Joseph, 90, 250n35
consciousness: Eliot and, 12, 239n23; Faulkner and, 21–22, 101, 102, 103, 258n22; and James, 29, 32, 36, 54, 59, 62, 109–110, 180, 221, 250n32; Lamb on, 270n24; McEwan on, 31–32, 33; Morrison and, 50, 51, 52, 78; Newton and, 197; and point of view, 95; Robbe-Grillet on, 236n7; Ruttenburg and, 269n17; Smith and, 29, 107, 110, 114, 117, 261n37; William James and, 6, 250n32
contamination, 54, 73, 102
contemporary writers, return to ethics for, 1–2. *See also specific writers*
contextualization, 109, 118, 119–120, 133
contingency, 94, 97, 106, 109, 122, 131, 133, 185, 193, 213, 219, 226, 279n44
Cormack, Alistair, 243n53
corruption, 29, 43, 54, 55, 56, 60, 62, 69, 72, 80–81, 109, 233n7, 251n42
counterfocalization, 212–213, 214
creative writing workshop, imperative of, 101, 118–119, 217
cultural appropriation, 11–13
cultural beauty, representing, 117–118
cultural bias, 167–168, 275n38
cultural difference, accomplishment of, 174

cultural embodiment, 164–165
cultural identity, 12, 166
cultural preference, issue with, 168
cultural prestige, ix, xi
Cunningham, Michael, 8
curiosity, 32, 33, 34, 234n5, 249n31
Currie, Gregory, 231n1

Danta, Chris, 274n35
Dawson, Paul, 258n25
Deckard, Michael Funk, 275n41
deconstruction, 3, 4, 5, 137, 192, 203, 211, 237n17, 245n61, 267n14, 275n38
Defoe, Daniel, 140, 267n13
Dekoven, Marianne, 265n4
dependency, 61, 63, 163–164
Derrida, Jacques, 174, 192, 205, 237n17, 264n58, 270–271n26
description: and Coetzee's *Elizabeth Costello*, 144; and individuation, 156; and James's *What Maisie Knew*, 52, 74–75; power invested in, 44–45
design: conflict between alterity and, 119; James and, 71, 72, 73, 77, 81, 82, 257n17; Lawrence on, 89; and Smith, 257n17
determinative forces, 33, 186, 210
developmental model: and Coetzee's *Disgrace*, 265n4; and James's *What Maisie Knew*, 56, 57–59, 60, 248n17, 248–249nn23–24; and Smith's "Speaking in Tongues," 131, 133
dialogism, 182, 185
dialogue: as autonomy effect, 45; breaking out of first-person narration into, 21, 241n39; deeper level of, Coetzee on, 269n21; sustained, 273n30
Díaz, Junot, xvii
DiBattista, Maria, 235n5
Dick, Alexander, 254–255n2, 264n58
Dickens, Charles, xii, 3, 31–32, 38, 48, 84, 178, 185, 188, 278n25; *David Copperfield*, 180; *Oliver Twist*, 43, 44

Diderot, Denis, 139
disavowal, 43, 177, 180, 181, 189, 198
divinity, 15, 33, 89, 91–92, 93, 151, 152, 153–154, 155, 157, 158, 163, 164, 214, 272n27. *See also* spiritualism
Dobrogoszcz, Tomasz, 243n53, 245n61
Dodd, Josephine, 273n31
domination/oppression, 38, 94, 117, 120, 136, 167, 195, 197, 198, 201, 208, 212, 213, 266n8, 278n19, 280n50. *See also* hegemony
Donne, John, 214, 228
Dore, Florence, 283n9
Dostoevsky, Fyodor, 50
doubled identity, 129
dramas/plays, 18, 41, 127–128
Dreiser, Theodore, 278n27
Driscoll, Lawrence, 262n47
duality, contribution of, 160
Du Bois, W. E. B., 129
Dyer, Geoff, 238n18

Eagleton, Terry, 232n5, 264n63
Egan, Jennifer, xvii
Eggers, Dave, 7
eighteenth-century literary tradition, 141
Eliot, George: and Dickens, 3, 48; and emotional response, 178; and Franzen, 38, 246n67; James and, xii, 100, 117, 232–233nn7–8, 239n22, 257n17; lament of, on form, 84, 252–253n55; McEwan on, 31–32; *Middlemarch*, 12, 100, 117, 233n8, 239n22, 246n68, 257n17; and perspectivalism, 12, 90, 239nn22–23; and Smith, 117, 120, 246n68; Williams on, 239n23; on women as novel writers, 24; Woolf on, 24
Eliot, T. S., 228
Elizabeth Costello (Coetzee): acknowledgments to, 265n5; and the aesthetics of alterity, xiv–xv, 139, 266n9; and the African novel, 164–169; alterity project in, 142, 155, 167, 269n18; chapter

314 Index

structure in, 139, 159–160, 210; characters in, role of, 143–144; comparison of poets and novelists in, 150–156; connection between traditions forged in, xiv–xv, 139; discursive complexity of, 137, 265n5, 266–267n11; and the ethical aesthetic, 156–164; ethics or aesthetics, question of, addressing, 170–171, 275nn40–42; exploration of imagination and emplacement in, 143–149; and formalism, 138; interpretations of Kafka's "A Report to the Academy" in, 160–163, 274n35, 282n4; and Lesson Eight: "At the Gate," 170–171, 275n41; and Lesson One: "Realism," 156–159, 163–164, 165–166, 270n25; and Lesson Six: "The Problem of Evil," 148, 268–269n17; and Lesson Two: "The Novel in Africa," 164–169, 275n38; and the "The Lives of Animals" lessons, 144–149, 150–151, 270n26; modal variety in, 38, 140–141, 267–268nn15–16; moving from Lesson One through Lesson Eight in, 140, 141, 159–160; and narrative techniques, 142, 156–169, 273–275nn31–39; notion of form in, 143; overarching narrative structure in, 141; philosophical problematic presented in, 142, 143–156, 159–160, 269–273nn19–30; postscript in, 141, 273n30; questions on, 140, 142–143; staging of disagreement in, view on, 138–139; theme in, xiv–xv, 137; unifying concern in, 138
embeddedness, 66, 69, 101, 121, 137, 155, 161–162, 163, 164, 168, 196, 212, 215, 269n19, 274n35
embodiment, 5, 7, 18, 29–30, 30–31, 33, 35, 50, 97, 108, 142, 145, 146, 147–148, 150–156, 163, 164–169, 193, 199, 209, 210, 211, 221–224, 226, 242n50, 244–245n60, 255n2, 268n16, 272–273nn27–29, 281n63, 283n5. *See also* emplacement
Emerson, Ralph Waldo, 129
emotional/affective experience, xv–xvi, 5, 6, 10, 13, 39, 41, 43, 45, 73, 110, 157, 161, 174, 177, 178–179, 183, 184, 186, 187, 190, 198, 199, 200, 214, 267n11. *See also specific feelings/ emotions*
emotional binding, 187
emotional intensity, mental state of. *See* apprehension
emotional knowledge, 199
emotional relation, 91
emotional stance, 35, 36
emotional training, 179
emotional work, 111
empathy, x, 119, 125, 219, 231–232nn1–2, 269n20
emplacement, 145–149, 150–151, 165, 224, 269nn21–22. *See also* bodily relations; embodiment
English literary tradition. *See* British literary tradition
epistemology, xv, xvi, 36, 73, 93, 106, 178, 185, 187, 190, 191, 193, 201, 205, 207, 209, 214, 246n2, 251n39, 276n1, 280n50
epistles, 140
Ermarth, Elizabeth Deeds, 36
estrangement, 41, 51, 52, 53, 111, 189, 214
ethical action, 9, 148, 203, 206, 224
ethical good, x, 11, 13, 20, 22, 32–33, 37, 63, 73, 98, 111, 123, 129, 132, 133, 136, 144, 156, 159, 162, 178, 181, 229, 278n25, 282n4
ethical imagination, 13, 32, 70, 146–50, 154, 211, 272n29, 280n50
ethical relation, 15, 24, 28, 47, 49, 61, 66, 68–69, 102, 161, 194–195, 210, 219, 225, 257n20
ethical risk, 50, 62, 82, 98, 122, 188, 194, 198, 226–227, 256n12, 263n54
ethical value: absolute, x, 193, 200, 219,

227; age-old conversation about, addressing, ix–x; explicit pursuit of, x, xiii, 1–2; implied/inherent, ix, x, xiii, 25, 70, 173, 193, 227, 258n25, 281n61. *See also specific novelists and scholars*
Eugenides, Jeffrey, 8
European tradition, xv, 141, 166–167, 235n5

Faulkner, William: *Absalom, Absalom!* 8; *As I Lay Dying*, 21–22, 78, 250n37, 258n22; Jen and, 15–17, 21–22; on morality, xii; Morrison and, xvi, 8, 50, 78, 250nn36–37; and New Critical reception, 283n9; renewed appreciation for, 2; Smith and, 113–114; *The Sound and the Fury*, 78, 101–103, 250nn36–37
Felski, Rita, 234n5
feminism, 23, 92, 113, 158, 159, 262n43, 273n31, 274n32
fictionality, 133, 185–187, 236n10, 271–272n26. *See also* character: fictional
Fielding, Henry, 19
Figlerowicz, Marta, 235n5
figurality/figuration, 189, 273n30
film, as a medium, compared to the novel, 38, 40, 41–42, 243n55
first-person narration: Barth and, 4; breaking out of, into dialogue, 21, 241n39; and Gibson, 200; and James, 46, 196, 206, 242n47; J. Hillis Miller on, 206; Kafka's, interpretations of, 160–163, 274n35; McEwan and, 33–34, 243n53; in Morrison's *A Mercy*, 78; Proust and, xv; Robinson on, 242n47; and Smith's *On Beauty*, 259n25
Fisher, Susan Alice, 263n51
Flaubert, Gustave, 50, 259n26
Ford, Ford Maddox, 87–88
formalism, xiii, 138, 194–195, 210, 215, 217, 224, 235n5
formlessness, xi, 24, 168, 169, 252–253n55

Forster, E. M., 87; *Aspects of the Novel*, 119; BBC lectures, 125, 126, 263n55; *Howards End*, 8, 98, 118; *The Longest Journey*, 278n27; renewed appreciation for, 2; and Smith, xvi, 8, 113, 119, 124–126, 252n2, 262n47, 262–263n50, 263–264nn57–58; and Trilling, 179, 278n27
Foucault, Michel: Butler and, 222; D. A. Miller and, 37, 38, 42, 179; and functionalism, 189; and James, 221; power model of, 43; shift from the critique of, 210, 211; Smith and, 105, 106
Fowles, John, xiv
Fox, Paula, 41
Franzen, Jonathan: on commodification of the novel, 38; D. A. Miller and, 38, 42, 44; on the novel and film, 243n55; and novel reading, 37, 38–42, 245–246n65, 246n67; on novel writing, 38–39, 140; phenomenological view of, 39, 41, 42; and the return to ethics, 1–2
freedom: Faulkner on, 15–17; ideological, 245n61; James and, 48, 55, 191, 250n33; Jen on, 14–15, 16–17, 19; Lee on, 91; McEwan on, 31–32; D. A. Miller on, 45; Murdoch on, 90; narrative effects of, 18; restriction of, 120, 216. *See also* character; agency; autonomy; individualism
free indirect discourse, xvi, 45, 120, 121, 250n34

Gallagher, Catherine, 236–237n12
Galsworthy, John, 87
Gargano, James, 249n24
Gates, Henry Louis, xiii, 129
gender: and Coetzee's *Elizabeth Costello*, 142, 158, 170; and McEwan's *Sweet Tooth*, 33–34; narrative limits posed by, 102; and Smith's *On Beauty*, 116; and Woolf's "Women and Fiction," 24

gender difference, 19, 30, 77, 78
gender markers, 283n6
gender roles, 225
Genette, Gérard, xiii, xvi
geopoliticization, 166
Gibson, Andrew: and Butler, 200, 201, 202; and James, 192–93, 200–202; and J. Hillis Miller, 208; and Newton, 199–201; and Nussbaum, 176, 200, 201–202; philosophical framework of, 192; *Postmodernity, Ethics and the Novel*, 199–202
Gilbert, W. S., 18, 239n29
Gilmore, Michael, 177
Glab, Anna, 256n8, 260n36
globalization, 130
godlike/godliness. *See* divinity
goodness, capacity for, 156. *See also* ethical good; social good
Gordimer, Nadine, xvii
Greek ethics, 281n64
Green, Charles, 257n20
Green, James, 256–257n13

Hagedorn, Jessica, xvii
Hale, Dorothy, *Social Formalism*, xii, xiii, xiv
Hansen, Ellis, 248n14
Harpham, Geoffrey Galt, 181
Harris, Wilson, 87, 92, 93–94, 95, 215, 216
Harvey, Melinda, 266n8
Hayes, Patrick, 266n8, 273n30
Head, Dominic, 236n8, 261n38, 271n26
Heath, Shirley Brice, 38–39, 42
hegemony: and Coetzee's *Elizabeth Costello*, 145, 158, 166, 167; ideological, 5, 38, 169, 179; Jameson on, 278n19; and James's *What Maisie Knew*, 74, 75, 169; morality and, xii; and Morrison's *A Mercy*, 78; as narrative, view on, 216; and poststructuralism, 191; and race, 129; and Smith's "Speaking in Tongues," 129; Spivak on, 213, 215. *See also* domination/oppression
heterogeneity, 10, 94, 126, 127, 129, 130, 139, 174, 181, 182
heteroglossia, 182, 185, 236n10
heteronormativity, 214
hierarchical power, 145, 146, 219, 249n31
Hofmannsthal, Hugo von, 141
Hollinghurst, Alan, 8
Homer, 49–50
homogeneity, 21
Horton, John, 177–178
humanism: and autonomy, 57; in Coetzee's *Elizabeth Costello*, 158, 159, 160; Harris on, 93; and James's *What Maisie Knew*, 53, 56, 57, 59, 77, 248nn18–19; and Lee, 111; and McEwan, 32–33, 36; and Morrison, 48, 77, 79; and Murdoch, 111–112; and Nussbaum, 32, 33, 111–112; and poststructuralism, 2–3, 5, 19, 174, 189, 244n57, 281n65; and relationality, 90; and Smith's *On Beauty*, 111–112, 115, 254–255n2; and Trilling, 111–112, 179; virtues in, 32–33
human rights, 92, 190
Hurston, Zora Neale, xvi, 233n13

identification, 41, 54, 66, 67, 81, 111, 122, 125, 127, 128, 130, 147, 183, 216, 251n39, 269n21, 275n40
identity: aesthetic, emergence of, 103–104; authorial, 87, 111, 112, 220, 274n31, 274n36; barrier to realization of, 53; biracial, 129–130; black, 52, 129, 255n4; class, 19, 128, 197; Coetzee and, 161, 274n36, 275n38; communal, 155; co-optation of, 115; cultural, 12, 166; disinstantiation of, 130, 133; doubled, 129; and embodiment, 7, 166; gender, 34, 116, 142, 158; ideological, 169; James on, 63, 109–110; literary,

171–172; lived, 164; mimetic reproduction of, 128–129; Morrison's use of narrative as marker of, 78; and particularity, 12; patient, 227; and performativity, 162, 234n5, 264n61, 264n63, 279n44, 283n6; politics of, 22–23, 24; readerly, 110–111; and self-consciousness, 256n8; selfhood and, 234n5; Smith and, 107, 109–110, 110–111, 112, 115, 122, 129, 131, 261n37; theories of, 264n61, 264n63; writing as an expression of, 167. *See also* social identity

idiom, 21, 92, 190, 241nn40–41

imagination: altruism and, 194; and boundaries, 194; capacity for, combined with narrative resources, 156, 163; constraints on, 279n44; embodied act of, 146, 166; and emplacement, 146, 148, 150, 224, 269n22; ethical, 13, 32, 40, 70; excessive, 149, 150, 270n25, 272n28; experience of, offered by novels, significance of, 174; failure of, 19; Franzen and, 40–41; freedom of, 134, 188, 194, 264n61, 279n44; Harris on, 93, 94; and James, 46, 54, 70, 71, 193–194; Lee on, 91; liberal, 177, 180; limits of, 158; McEwan and, 32, 33; metaphorical, 189; moral, 176, 177, 189; Morrison on, 47, 50–52, 78; Newton on, 195–196, 198; and paradox, 152–153, 154, 155, 272nn28–29; and possibility, 71, 279n44, 280n50; power of, 49; readerly, 211; and responsibility, 13, 15; and self-transformation, 9–10; Smith and, 127, 128, 129; Spivak on, 213, 214; texture of, expert on, 211; transformative nature of, 49, 93, 276n1; Woolf and, 22, 93. *See also* sympathetic imagination

imperialism, 176, 183, 274n31, 274n37
incorruptibility, 71
independence, 15, 16–17, 34, 41, 55, 57, 58–59, 72, 90–91, 92, 98. *See also* autonomy; freedom

indeterminacy, 178, 182, 188, 207, 209, 214

individualism, 5, 6, 20, 32, 48, 79, 92, 164, 174, 177, 219

individuality, 2, 3, 13, 19, 122, 228
individual power, 43
individuation, 156
inhabiting, 7, 14, 32, 132, 151, 157, 158, 163, 189, 244n56, 245n60, 251n41, 266n8, 269n18, 269n22

instrumentalization, 34, 54, 55, 57, 62, 65, 66, 72, 73, 81, 106, 116, 120, 127, 130, 166, 191, 208, 215, 250n31, 257n17

integrity, 3, 70, 203, 249n31, 277n7
intellectual work, 111
interiority, 13, 18, 30–31, 41, 44, 51, 102, 103, 156, 189

interior monologue, 8, 101, 103, 240–241n39

Internet, 86
intersubjectivity, 6, 196, 216
intertextuality, 98, 245n61, 274n31
intimacy, 1, 13, 17, 35, 36, 48, 50, 62, 78, 79, 91, 102, 115, 135, 143, 162, 227, 251n39, 260n31, 266n10

intrinsic model of ethical nature, 56, 60–61, 63, 71, 249nn24–25

intuition, 67, 269n21, 270n23
Irlam, Shaun, 269n18
irony, 2, 35, 45, 53, 54, 71, 115, 116, 184, 212, 213, 249n29

Jackson, Laura (Riding), 87, 92–93
Jackson, Regine, 256n7
James, David, 259n26
James, Henry: and aesthetics of alterity, 49; and the African tradition, 164, 167, 168–169; "Altar of the Dead," 37; *The Ambassadors*, 36; *The American*, 243n52; "The Art of Fiction," 25–26, 32, 86; *The Art of the Novel*, 25; "The Aspern Papers,"

196, 197, 206; autobiography of, 37; "The Beast in the Jungle," 37; "The Bench of Desolation," 220–221, 223, 282n4; biographical details, 52; and Butler, 181, 182–185, 185–186, 187, 189, 191, 195, 198, 206, 212, 222, 264n61, 279n44; "In the Cage," 196; and Charon, 219–221, 222, 223, 224–226, 228–229, 282n4; "Daisy Miller," 37; developing upon the tradition of, xiii, 8, 28, 30, 47–48, 109–110, 139, 174, 175, 181, 195, 215, 218, 228–229; and Eliot, xii, 100, 117, 232–233nn7–8, 239n22, 246n68, 257n17; endorsement of, as "the master," 83–84, 88, 252n54; *The Europeans*, 246n3; and Gibson, 192, 199–202; *The Golden Bowl*, 201, 225, 281n59; on his artistic success, 29; Jameson on, 6, 176–177; and J. Hillis Miller, 192, 202–203, 204, 206–208, 210; legacy of, 83, 252n50; Lubbock on, 83–84, 86–87; master lesson provided by, xviii, 210; McEwan and, 28, 31–32, 33, 36–37, 238n18, 242n48, 243n53, 261n38; on morality, xii, 232–233n7; morality of, critics on, 80–82, 252nn47–48; Morrison and, xvi, 47, 48, 52, 72–73; and Murdoch, 90, 261n38; and Newton, 192, 193–199; on novel writing, 72–73; and Nussbaum, 32, 159, 176, 177, 178, 180, 181, 195, 197, 281n59; and particularity, 84, 184; *The Portrait of a Lady*, 98, 180, 182, 206–207; poststructuralism and, 81, 181, 190, 192; and prefaces to the New York Edition, analysis of, 27, 36, 83–84, 85, 168, 217; preface to *Portrait of a Lady*, 249–250n31; preface to *The Ambassadors*, 46, 180, 270n25; preface to *The American*, 29, 30–31, 242n50, 243n52; *The Princess Casamassima*, 278n27; "The Real Thing," 195–197; renewed appreciation for, 2, 181–182; Smith and, 28, 29–30, 99–101, 108, 109–110, 117, 246n68, 256n13, 261n38; and social value, xiii, 82, 181–182; and Spivak, 213; theory and practice of novel writing, xiii, 26–27, 47, 48–49, 169, 177, 217; and Trilling, 32, 176, 177, 179, 278n27; *Turn of the Screw*, 60, 249n26; *Washington Square*, 182–185, 185–186, 187, 212, 222; and William James, 6, 250n32; *The Wings of the Dove*, 218, 282n4; works refashioned after, 8. See also *What Maisie Knew* (James)

James, William, 6, 250n32, 282n66

Jameson, Fredric: on character, 234n5; on hegemony, 278n19; on individualism, 6; and James, 6; on James, 176–177; and Marxism, 235n5; and political critique, 177, 278n19; *The Political Unconscious*, 176–177

Jen, Gish: biographical details, 25; and Faulkner, 15–17, 21–22; Levithan and, 20; *The Love Wife*, 21, 22, 240–241nn38–41; on novel reading, 20–21; and the return to ethics, 1–2; *Tiger Writing*, 14–15, 16–17, 19–21, 25, 245n64; and the trope of laughter, 16, 239n28; and Woolf, 23, 24

Jewish ethics, 281n64

Johnson, Barbara, 129

Joyce, James: and Charon, 228; McEwan on, 31–32; on morality, xii; *Ulysses*, 21, 84, 241n39

judgment: Attridge on, 267n11; Booth and, 281n61; Butler on, 183, 184, 186, 187, 198; Coetzee and, 157, 275n41; D. A. Miller and, 45; Franzen and, 40; James and, 57–58, 59, 75, 81, 82, 183, 184, 186; J. Hillis Miller on, 206–207, 208, 209; legal, 174; Lessing and, 92; Nussbaum and, 188, 197; Smith and, 106, 117, 121–122, 123, 124–125, 133, 257n20,

260n31; Spivak and, 215; and uncertainty, 185, 207; Woolf and, 87

Kael, Pauline, 130
Kafka, Franz, 140, 170, 272n26; "A Report to an Academy" interpretations, 160–163, 274n35, 282n4
Kamuf, Peggy, 276n5
Kaston, Carren Osna, 248n19
Keats, John, 90, 112, 113, 126, 261nn39–41
Kermode, Frank, 118–119, 262–263n50
Kidd, David Comer, 231nn1–2
King, Martin Luther, Jr., 213
Kingsolver, Barbara, 6, 7
Klay, Phil, xvii
Klopper, Dirk, 272n27, 274n33
Kompridis, Nikolas, 266–267n7
Kossew, Sue, 273n31
Kristeva, Julia, 246n3, 271n26
Ksiezopolska, Irena, 245n61
Kurtz, Arabella, 269n21

Laird, Nick, 97
Lamb, Jonathan, 270n24
language: and Bakhtin, 182, 185, 236n10; of the body, aspiration toward, 272n27; common, Charon on, 283n8; and crossing cultural barriers, 182; in Faulkner's *The Sound and the Fury*, 101, 102–103; and figurality, 189, 273n30; foreign, 246n3; homogeneity of, 21; James and, 30, 64, 65–66, 67, 68, 69–70; and James's *What Maisie Knew*, 57, 74–75, 250n37; in Morrison's *A Mercy*, 250nn36–37, 251n41; and Newton, 197; object of, 177; parroting, 69–70; power of, 49, 103; in Smith's *On Beauty*, 97, 121, 123; and tonal modulation/shifts, 45, 103, 121; visual, 40. *See also specific aspects of language*
laughter, trope of, 16, 239n28
Lawrence, D. H., 87, 88–89, 90, 95

Leavis, F. R., 243n53
lecture, as genre, 125–126, 254–255n2, 264n58, 265n5
Lee, Vernon, 87; *The Handling of Words*, 91; and humanism, 111–112; Woolf on, 91, 254n84
Leist, Anton, 271n26
Lessing, Doris, 92
Levinas, Emmanuel: and affective encounter, 198; and Butler, 184, 222; and Charon, 219, 221, 228; and Gibson, 192, 202; and James's *What Maisie Knew*, 55–56; and Newton, 192, 193; and notions of alterity, 6, 237n17; and particularity, 6; phenomenological view of, 6, 174, 199; religious philosophy of, 215, 281n64, 284n10; and singularity, 6, 204, 265n4; and Spivak, 216
Lévi-Strauss, Claude, 167
Levithan, David: *Every Day*, 13–14, 239n25, 244–245n60; and Jen, 20; and social value, 14
Lewis, Wyndham, 92
libel laws, protection against, 237n12
liberal humanism. *See* humanism
Liddell, Robert, 87, 91–92
likeness, 145, 147, 148, 151–152, 154, 155, 157, 163, 167, 261n37, 270n24
limitlessness, 23, 225, 226, 232n5
literary history, performance of, 141, 267–268nn15–16
literary knowledge, theory of, 280n51
literary power, 38, 192
literary studies: Charon on, 218; regrounding, as an academic discipline, xvii, 210–217, 218; Robbins on, 264n61. *See also* reading; *specific scholars*
literary value, ethical defense of, significance of, x, xi, xvii, 173, 181, 217, 228. *See also specific novelists and scholars*
living art, 86, 95; as living character, 17, 27, 48, 49, 160

Lodge, David, 85, 265n5, 275n42
love: authorial, 253n79; Barth and, 4; being in, symptom of, 95; beyond, 191; Gibson and, 200, 201; intellectual and emotional work as, 111; James and, 266n8; Lee and, 91; Liddell and, 92; McEwan and, 32–33, 35, 245n61; Murdoch and, 90, 112; Newton and, 198; Nussbaum and, 33, 112, 178, 188, 195, 261n40; Rushdie and, 89; Smith and, 112–113, 115, 125; Trilling and, 179; Trollope on, 17
love relations, 18
Lubbock, Percy, 95, 210; *The Craft of Fiction*, 83–84, 85, 91, 254n84; on point of view, 108; Woolf in comparison to, 86–87
Lupton, Christina, 254–255n2, 264n58
lyricism, use of, 21, 102–103, 104, 123, 241nn39–40, 250n37, 259n26, 259n28

Man, Paul de, 206
Marais, Mike, 265n4, 272–273n29
Martin, Priscilla, 90
Marxism, 189, 235n5
masculinity, 170. *See also* gender
Masters, Ben, 262n42
materiality, continued privileging of, as an issue, xiii
Matz, Jesse, 252n50
McCall, Dan, 248n17
McEwan, Ian: and the aesthetics of alterity, 34–35; *Atonement*, 8, 33, 238n18, 243n53, 244nn57–58, 280n53; biographical details, 31; on characterological freedom, 31–32; *On Chesil Beach*, 244n57; on empathy, 269n20; and humanism, 32–33, 36, 244n57; James and, 28, 31–32, 33, 36–37, 238n18, 242n48, 243n53, 261n38; *Machines Like Me*, 243n53; and Murdoch, 261n38; on the novel and film, 243n55; *Nutshell*, 243n53; and the return to ethics, 1–2; Smith and, 32, 33, 243n55, 261n38, 269n20; *Sweet Tooth*, 33–36, 37, 243n53, 244nn58–59, 245n61
meaning-making, 200, 204–205, 211
media: new, 40, 42, 86; topic of attention in, significance of, 11
medical notation/reporting, 223–224
Melville, Herman, 50
Merleau-Ponty, Maurice, 271n26, 272n28
meta-ethical emotion, 191
metafiction, xiv, xv, 4, 33–34, 140, 143, 163, 166, 169, 186, 267n14, 268n15
metanarrative, 139–140, 275n41
metaphor, 72, 189, 220
metaphysics, 110, 118, 158, 177, 180, 189, 191, 203
metarepresentation, 53
Michaels, Walter Benn, 239n24, 247n6
Mill, John Stuart, 264n58
Miller, D. A.: and agency, 38; and Foucault, 37, 38, 42, 179; and Franzen, 38, 42, 44; *The Novel and the Police*, 42; and novel reading, 37, 38, 42–45; Sedgwick on, 38; social value and, 43–44, 45, 176
Miller, J. Hillis: and Butler, 206, 207; and Charon, 221, 222; contribution of, 209–210; *The Ethics of Reading*, 203; and Gibson, 208; influence of, 181; and James, 35, 192, 202, 221; *Literature as Conduct*, 202–203, 203–209; and Newton, 208; philosophical framework of, 192; and Spivak, 211
mimicry, 4, 34, 48, 67, 111, 128–129, 130, 158
minor characters, 25, 114
Mishira, Pankaj, 263n56
Mitchell, David, xvii, 262n42
Mitchell, S., 150–151, 151–152
modal variety, 38, 140–141, 142, 162, 229, 267–268nn15–16
modernism: basis of, 83, 84; challenge to, presented by poststructuralism, 2–4; and disembodiment, 168;

implied ethical value in, ix, x;
intensifying and complexifying,
x; and morality, xii, 232n6; and
narrative form, ix, xi; novelistic
aesthetics developed out of, 215;
and postmodernism, ix, 3, 4, 16,
88–89, 101; realism and, 272n26;
renewed appreciation for, 2; return
to, 8
monologue, 78, 160–161, 170, 241n41,
250nn36–37. *See also* interior
monologue
Moore, Caroline, 250n37
Moore, Marianne, 275n42
moral good, xii
moral ideal, 249n25
moral imagination, 176, 177, 189
morality: of James, critics on, 80–82,
252nn47–48; James on, xii, 232–
233n7; and modernism, xii, 232n6;
and Smith, 123
moral judgments, 124–125, 215
moral philosophy, 175, 176, 276n3
moral realism, 278nn27–28
Moraru, Christian, 263–264n57
Morrison, Toni: and aesthetics of
alterity, 47–48; on Africanist
presence, 38, 52, 53, 73; *Beloved*,
251n39; and Charon, 226–227;
on ethical becoming, 50–51; and
Faulkner, xvi, 8, 50, 78, 250nn36–37;
and humanism, 48, 77, 79; on
imagination, 47, 50–52, 78; and
James, xvi, 47, 48, 52, 72–73; on
James's *What Maisie Knew*, 38, 48,
49, 50, 52–53, 54, 62–63, 73, 75, 77,
80, 169, 247n6; *Jazz*, 8; *A Mercy*,
8, 77–78, 79, 250–251nn36–42;
on novel reading, 47, 50; on novel
writing, 72–73; *The Origin of Others*,
77–78, 79; other works admired
by, 49–50; phenomenological view
of, 73; *Playing in the Dark*, 47, 48,
49–50, 51, 52, 54, 77, 256n12; on
racism, 48; and the return to ethics,
1–2; Smith and, 256n12; *Sula*, 8; and
Woolf, xvi, 8
Mosca, Valeria, 275n40
Moses, Michael, 268n16, 275n41
Moya, Paula, 251n40, 257n21
Mulhall, Stephen, 272n26
multiculturalism, 21
multiperspectivalism, 21, 78, 90, 94, 114,
127, 130, 132, 240n38, 262n41
murder (narrative), 54
Murdoch, Iris, 87; on authorial love and
negative capability, 90, 253n79; and
humanism, 111–112; and James,
90, 261n38; and Keats, 261n39; on
love, 90, 112; and McEwan, 261n38;
as novelist and scholar, 86; and
perspectivalism, 90; and Smith, xvi,
99–100, 112, 113, 261n38

Nabokov, Vladimir, 139
Nagel, Thomas, 147, 270n23
Naipaul, V. S., 87
narration. *See* first-person narration;
second-person narration; third-
person narration
narrative: amplification of, 66, 67; as
defining the art of the novel, 11, 15,
24; as ethical other, 5, 9; as ethics of
alterity, defined, xiii, 9; as structure
13, 16, 18
narrative medicine, 218–228, 229
narratology, 202, 234–235n5
necessary ethics, ix, 10
negative capability, 36, 90, 92, 93,
113, 126–128, 132, 171, 253n79,
261nn40–41
Nehamas, Alexander, 258n28
Nethersole, Reingard, 273n30
neurological studies, x
new ethics, meaning of, ix–x
New Literary History, 234n5
Newman, Judie, 274n31
new media, 40, 42, 86
Newton, Adam Zachary: and Butler, 197,
198; and Gibson, 199–201; influence

of, 181; and James, 192–98; and
J. Hillis Miller, 208; *Narrative Ethics*,
193–199, 251n39; and Nussbaum,
197, 198; philosophical framework
of, 192
Niedzviecki, Hal, 11–12, 12–13
Nietzsche, 278n19
nineteenth-century literature, xii, xv, 4,
31–32, 44, 83, 86, 120, 177, 210, 235
nonanthropomorphism, 142
Norris, Frank, 242n50
Nussbaum, Martha: Altieri on, 276–
277n7; on the art of the novel, 178;
and Butler, 174, 176, 189, 201,
277n7; and citationality, 281n59; and
Coetzee, 159; and Dickens, 180, 185,
188; on the emotional experience
of life, 179–180; and Gibson, 176,
200, 201–202; and humanism, 32,
33, 111–112; and James, 32, 159,
176, 177, 178, 180, 181, 195, 197,
281n59; and literary value, 177–178;
Love's Knowledge, 99, 112, 176, 178,
180, 261n40, 281n59; and Newton,
197; and particularity, 178, 276n7;
Poetic Justice, 176, 189; on reading
and affect, 179–180, 188–189; Smith
and, 99, 100, 112, 256n13; and social
value, 175; and Trilling, 178, 189,
280n47; and the value of feeling, 178

Oates, Joyce Carol, 8
Obama, Barack, 126–127, 128–129,
130–131, 132, 133, 262n41
objectification, 44, 98, 215, 229, 235n5,
236n10
objectivity, 9, 43, 44, 46, 84, 87–88, 89,
91, 109, 175, 205, 207, 257n21
O'Brien, Flann, xiv
O'Hara, David K., 244n57
Okri, Ben, 166
omnipresence, 163
omniscient narration: in Faulkner's *As I
Lay Dying*, 22, 258n22; in Faulkner's
The Sound and the Fury, 101–102,
257n21; and Gibson, 200; and the
implied reader, 258–259n25; in
Morrison's *A Mercy*, 78; in Smith's
On Beauty, 120, 121, 258–259n25; in
Smith's *White Teeth*, 258n25
On Beauty (Smith), 262n43;
acknowledgments to, 96, 98; and
aesthetics of alterity, 28, 97, 98,
99, 100, 106, 113–123, 257n17,
258–259n25; character omission
in, 103–104; early reviews of, 117,
118–119; epigraphs in, 98; and the
ethical aesthetic, 109–110; and
Faulkner's *The Sound and the Fury*,
101–103; homage to novelists in, xvi,
8, 98, 112; philosophical expressions
informing, 96, 97–98, 104–107,
255n2; questions on, 96, 114, 117,
119, 123; and Scarry's philosophical
project, 96, 97, 104–105, 115,
254–255n2; and significance of the
title, 96, 97–98; and social context,
97, 256n7
O'Neill, Joseph, 259n26
ontology, xiv, 5, 15, 18, 22, 38, 72,
112–113, 142, 160, 163, 200, 209,
237n12, 240n32, 268n17, 274n36
openness, 32, 73, 80, 125, 129, 132, 177,
188, 191, 195, 200, 201, 202, 245n61,
266n10
orality, 164, 165, 166, 167, 168
Orange, Tommy, xvii
otherness: encounter with, investigation
of, 6; ethics of, significance of, ix, xii;
as family of ideas, 6–7; honoring,
question of, 9; inherent capacity
for, 87; social, domestic and global
dimensions of, novels addressing
ethics of, xvii; term for, popular
usage of, 237n17. *See also* alterity;
specific novelists and scholars
outsiderness, 78
Ozick, Cynthia, 8, 181

Palm, Ralph, 275n41

paradox, 87, 109, 124, 152–153, 154, 155, 166, 272nn28–29
partiality, 133
particularity: and the art of the novel, 4; assumption involving, 174; and Attridge, 277n7; capacity for, 13; and Charon, 221–222, 228, 282–283n5; and Coetzee, 274n31; and identity, 12; and James, 87, 184; and Kafka, 162; and Levinas, 6; and McEwan, 245n61; and Nussbaum, 178, 188, 276n7; retaining, 99; and Smith, 97, 255n2; and Spivak, 215; valuing, 228
Pastoor, Charles Cornelius, 244n58
patience, 280n51
patriarchy, 23, 158, 159, 273n31
performativity, 162, 234n5, 264n61, 264n63, 279n44, 283n6
personalization, 102, 103, 119–120, 146
personhood: Butler on, 184, 187, 222; Charon on, 219, 220, 222; and Coetzee, 135, 138, 141, 142, 156, 165, 214; D. A. Miller on, 45; and Faulkner, 102; Felski on, 234n5; humanism and, 57; and James, xii, 28, 30, 32, 36, 53, 55, 57, 62, 65, 72–73, 75, 77, 82, 183, 184, 187, 191, 193, 208, 213, 220, 249–250n31; Jen on, 14–15, 19; and J. Hillis Miller, 208, 222; and Levinas, 6; and McEwan, 32, 35; as mediated, understanding of, 5; Morrison and, 47, 48, 51, 72–73; Murdoch on, 112; Newton on, 194–195, 196, 197; and positionality of the reader, 10; Proust on, xv; and realism, 141; and Robinson, 233n1; significance of, xii, 229; and Smith, 115, 129, 130; and Spivak, 213, 214; Woolf and, 22, 23
perspectivalism: and Charon, 229, 283n8; and Coetzee, 150, 163, 167, 169; Eliot and, 12, 90, 239nn22–23; and James, 169, 177, 223, 242n47; and Morrison, 78; and Murdoch, 90; paradox of, 109; relativized, 89; and Smith, 100, 105, 108, 109, 110–111, 117–119, 122, 255n6, 258n25, 260n34, 262n41; Woolf and, 103. *See also* character; multiperspectivalism; point of view; positionality
perspective system, 36
phenomenology, 279n44; and Coetzee, 271n26; and Franzen, 39, 41, 42; Gibson and, 199–200; and James, 73; and Levinas, 6, 174, 199; of literary reading, 175, 192, 200; and Morrison, 73; paradigm, 9–10; of reader response, 39, 173–174; and Scarry, 97, 104, 105; and the self, engagement with, ix-x, 5–6; and Smith, 106–107; and Spivak, 213
Phillips, Michelle, 249n29
pious discourse, 133, 228, 229, 284n10
Pippin, Robert, 59
Pirandello, Luigi, 18, 240n32
place, 138, 165, 266nn8–9, 269n22. *See also* emplacement; social context
plays/dramas, 18, 41, 127–128
plot: Charon on, 220, 282n5; and Coetzee's *Elizabeth Costello*, 139, 171; determinative for, 11; and Eliot, 239n23; formulaic, 22, 23; and Forster, 120; and James's *Washington Square*, 184; and James's *What Maisie Knew*, 52, 53, 71, 76, 77; in Levithan's *Every Day*, 13, 244–245n60; and McEwan's *Sweet Tooth*, 35; Robinson on, 242n47; and Smith's *On Beauty*, 98, 119, 120, 257n17; Woolf on, 22, 23
pluralism, 26–27, 32, 126, 129, 130, 131, 132, 261n38
poetry, 105, 111, 150–152, 153, 228, 242n49, 260n29
point of view: and Charon, 221, 223; in Coetzee's *Disgrace*, 212; and Coetzee's *Elizabeth Costello*, 142, 150, 154, 155, 156, 163, 170, 274n36; Faulkner and, 257n21; Jackson on, 92–93; James and, xii, 6, 36–37, 95, 177, 190–191, 219; in James's

Washington Square, 183, 184; and James's *What Maisie Knew*, 54, 62, 63, 66, 74–75, 76, 82, 99, 238n18; Lubbock on, 108; and McEwan's *Sweet Tooth*, 245n61; Morrison and, 51; in Morrison's *A Mercy*, 78, 99; Smith and, 108, 109, 110, 111; and Smith's *On Beauty*, 98, 106, 114–115, 116, 117, 118, 119, 122. *See also* first-person narration; interior monologue; perspectivalism; second-person narration; stream of consciousness; third-person narration

Poirier, Richard, 250n33
political action, 173, 276n1
political critique, 37, 42
political good, 80, 98, 124, 129, 144
political power, 31, 177, 222. *See also* power
political risk, 106, 122
political theory, tendency toward, issue with, 175–81
politicization, 5, 11, 31, 95, 99, 102, 117–118, 189–190, 212, 234n5, 274n31
positionality: Althusser on, 203–204; Bakhtin and, 185; class, 113; in Coetzee's *Elizabeth Costello*, 142, 157, 170, 275n38; in Faulkner's *The Sound and the Fury*, 102, 103; functional, 216; Gibson and, 201, 202; in James's *Washington Square*, 183; limited, 113, 184; Morrison and, 51; in Morrison's *A Mercy*, 78, 79; and Newton, 200; of the novelist, 95; of the reader, 10, 117, 214; in Smith's *On Beauty*, 113, 115, 117, 118, 120, 121, 122, 123, 261n37. *See also* perspectivalism; social positionality
possibility, 9, 46, 56, 70, 71–72, 89, 99, 131, 142, 157, 174, 175, 178, 185, 187, 188, 189, 190, 192, 214, 279n44, 280n50
postcolonialism, 94, 255n4, 265n3

post-Foucauldianism, 176, 177, 191
post-Marxism, 42, 177
postmodernism: and Coetzee, 140, 141, 275n41; modernism and, ix, 3, 4, 16, 88–89, 101; and narrative, 37–38; sense of, 137; shift away from, 2; world of, cultural distance in, sign of, 181
poststructuralism: challenge to modernism presented by, 2–4; and Coetzee, 271n26; emphasis of, on the ethics of fiction, 185; engagement with, and the self, x; humanism and, 2–3, 5, 19, 174, 189, 244n57, 281n65; and James, 81, 181, 190, 192, 218; and notions of alterity, 237n17; on novels of character, 2–3; and social value, 173; and unverifiability, 191
Pound, Ezra, 83
power: affective, 177; of alterity, 187; authorial, 16, 31, 192–193, 198, 244n58; circulation of, 216; class, 278n19; colonizing, 166; of emotion, 112; ethical, 224, 225; of fiction, 111; godlike/divine, 15, 91–92, 157; hierarchical, 145, 146, 219, 249n31; ideological, 45; individual, 43; institutional, 219; knowledge as, 219; of language, 49, 103; literary, 38, 192; narrative, claims about, 215–216, 219; Nietzsche on, 278n19; ontological, 38; political, 177, 222. *See also* social power
power relations, 15, 16, 17–18, 19, 31, 77, 78, 89, 97, 127, 128, 130, 133, 147, 198, 208, 223, 249n31. *See also* hegemony
power structure, 73, 251n38
projection, 34, 41, 72, 89, 91, 126, 133, 148, 250n31, 269n21, 270n23, 280n50
Propp, Vladimir, 235n5
Proust, Marcel, xv–xvi, 168
pseudomaterial properties, attending to, xiii

psychoanalytic context, 41, 238n17
public good, xii
public policy, issue with, 176, 277–278n15
Pynchon, Thomas, xiv, 141

questioning, significance of, 171

race: and hegemony, 129; and Morrison, 77, 78; narrative limits posed by, 102
racial othering, 52–53, 73, 74–77
racism: and cultural bias, 167–168; treatment of, emphasizing, issue involving, 255n4; and the unconscious, 48, 52, 53, 54, 73, 74, 76, 77, 247n6
rationality, 113, 180, 281n64. *See also* reason, disablement of; paradox
readerly affect, 41, 187, 212. *See also* emotional/affective experience
readerly competence, 11, 211
readerly responsibility, 203–204, 206, 207, 208, 281n59
readerly self, 173
reader response: to Coetzee's novels, 135, 267n11; to James's *What Maisie Knew*, 55; Morrison on, 50, 256n12; phenomenological models of, 39, 173–174; and positionality, 10, 117; Smith on, 110, 260n31
reading: Butler on, and affect, 182–188; Coetzee and, 157, 159; competent, 11, 211; and D. A. Miller, 37, 38, 42–45; decline in, 38; Dickens and, 180; endpoint of, 25; ethical value of, studies involving, issue with, x, 231nn1–2; felt efficacy of, 174; and Franzen, 37, 38–42, 245–246n65, 246n67; guidance on, issues surrounding, 190; inherent value in, 25, 173; Jen on, 20–21; J. Hillis Miller on, 203, 204–205; justifications for, xi; Morrison on, 47, 50; Nussbaum on, and affect, 179–180, 188–189; by ordinary readers, Byatt on, 86; questions on, 216; right way of, 191–192; shared steps of, benefit of, 281–282n65; Smith and, 110–111, 117, 255n6, 256n8, 260n34, 266n10; training in, importance of, xvii, 210, 211, 212, 281n61; as a writer, Morrison on, 47, 50. *See also* literary studies; *specific scholars*
realism: and allegory, 92, 274n33; and Coetzee, 140, 141, 272n26, 274n33; and James, 36; and Kafka, 162, 274n33; legacy of, 259n26; lyrical, 259n26; on a metalevel, 186; and modernism, 272n26; and narration, 3, 236n10; perspective system of, 36; protocols of, 232n5; and secularism, 93; Trilling on, 278nn27–28
reason, disablement of, 152–153, 154, 272n29; tool of hegemony, 191; transgressive nature of, 205; truth beyond, 113, 190, 205. *See also* paradox
reception theory, 199–200
reductionism, 223, 255n6, 271n26
Reed, Ishmael, xiv
reflectivity, 7, 78, 106, 197, 252n47, 255n2, 271n26
reflector-narrator, 200–201, 208, 212–213
relationality, 88–89, 90, 92–93, 95. *See also* power relations
relativity, 89, 90, 95, 97, 129, 130, 133, 169, 170–171
religious philosophy, 93, 214, 215, 281n64
reportage, practice of, xv, 67
respect, 32, 33, 90, 133, 174, 191, 197, 226, 233n1, 245n60, 271n26
revenge, 34, 197, 201, 280n53
Rich, Frank, 117, 118
Richardson, Samuel, 19, 140
Ricoeur, Paul, 244n57
Robbe-Grillet, Alain, 2–3, 42–43, 141, 175, 235–236n7

326   Index

Robbins, Bruce, 133–134, 264n61, 279n44
Robinson, Marilynne, 1–2, 6–7, 234n4; *Gilead*, 233n1, 242n47
Robinson, Richard, 238n18
Romanticism, 109–110, 220
Ross, Stephen, 232n6
Roth, Philip, xv
Rushdie, Salman, 87, 88, 89, 90
Russian tradition, xv
Russo, Richard, "Horseman," 1, 7–8
Ruttenburg, Nancy, 268–269n17, 274n36
Ryan, Judith, 250n32

sacredness, 193, 214, 215
sacrifice, 54, 57, 63, 81, 113, 274n35
salvation narrative, 265n4
Sanders, Mark, 175–176, 181, 273n30
Sartre, Jean-Paul, 10, 245–246n65
Scarry, Elaine: *On Beauty and Being Just*, 96, 97, 98, 104–105, 254–255n2, 256–257n13, 259n28, 263n51; biographical details, 97–98; lecture delivered by, 254–255n2
Schama, Simon, 98
secondary revision, 251–252n42
secondary schools, teaching the novel in, 13, 239n25
second-person narration, 78
secularism, 92, 93, 106, 129, 214, 215
secular transcendence, 88, 89
Sedgwick, Eve, 30, 38, 243n52
seduction, 24, 54, 90
self: and the capacity for change, 123; communal, 164; and encounters with other states of being, notion of, 5–6; engagement with philosophies of, ix–x; imagining, as other, 146; individualistic, 164; investigation of, 236n8; negotiation between other and, 258n25; outside and beyond, 95; plurality of, 129, 132; questioning of, 202; readerly, 173; social, 164
self-abnegation, 90, 92
self-apprehension, 223, 224
self-awareness, 175, 199
self-binding, 183, 190, 195, 197, 214
self-consciousness, xiv, 4, 9, 13–14, 27, 33, 84, 89, 92, 108–109, 110, 124, 138, 139–140, 141, 158, 164, 171, 173, 182, 185, 187, 191–192, 197–198, 199, 200, 201, 207, 210, 214, 236n10, 238n18, 244n57, 256n8, 257n17, 262n49, 264n61, 269n19, 279n44
self-contingency, 130
self-criticism, 268n17
self-discipline: novelist, 89, 90; readerly act of, xvii, 210
self-expression, 21, 109, 130, 220, 235n5, 241n40
selfhood, 166, 209, 223, 234n5
self-identification, 132
self-knowledge, 7
self-obliteration, 110
self-perception, 270n24
self-positioning, 214
self-recognition, 130
self-reflection, 79, 87, 123
self-restriction, xviii, 63, 113, 165, 179, 189, 194, 210–217, 220, 224, 225, 232n5, 281n62. *See also* binding
self-sacrifice, 57–58, 113
selfsame, 126, 130, 155
self-subjection, 46
self-subordination, 174, 224, 249n31, 283n5
self-transformation, 9–10, 50
self-translation, 185
sensibility: Eggers and, 7; Forster and, 126; James and, 26, 28, 30, 36, 66, 68, 69; Lodge and, 85; Newton and, 196, 197; Proust and, xv, xvi; Romantic, 110; Smith and, 29, 110, 262n41; Spivak on, 214
sexism, 23–24, 273n31
sexuality, 30
Shakespeare, 127–128, 132, 261n41
Shaw, George Bernard, 127, 128
Shelley, Mary, 50, 159

Shklovsky, Victor, 171
silence, 66, 167, 183, 281n62
Singer, Peter, 271n26
singularity: and Attridge, 277n7; and Charon, 219, 221–222, 223, 228; and Christiansë, 251n38; Clarkson on, 265n4; in Coetzee's *Elizabeth Costello*, 144, 161; in James's *What Maisie Knew*, 55–56; and J. Hillis Miller, 204; and Levinas, 6, 204, 265n4; and McEwan, 243n53; and Newton, 194; and Nussbaum, 281n59; in Smith's *On Beauty*, 115; and Spivak, 215; and Woolf, 22, 23
situatedness, xii, 4, 21, 36, 39, 48, 77, 101, 103, 118, 256n8, 262n42, 273n29
Smith, Adam, 264n58
Smith, Zadie, 1; biographical details, xvi, 97–98, 130, 233n13, 258n25, 260n33; *The Book of Other People*, 28, 98; challenge for, and questions, 101; *Changing My Mind*, xvi, 123–124, 223, 260n33, 263n56, 264n59; and Charon, 220; and Eliot, 117, 120, 246n68; "E. M. Forster: Middle Manager," 124, 125–126, 133, 263n55; "Fail Better," 28–29, 30, 106–107, 107–108, 108–109, 110, 123; "Fascinated to Presume," 28, 123, 256n12, 260n31, 263n54; Faulkner and, 113–114; and Forster, 113, 119, 124–126, 262n47, 262–263n50, 263–264nn57–58; Glab on, 260n36; Green on, 257n20; and James, 28, 29–30, 99–101, 108, 109–110, 117, 246n68, 256n13, 261n38; and Keats, 113, 261–262n41; lecture delivered by, 264n59; on love, 112–113, 115, 125; "Love, Actually," 99, 106–107, 123, 124–125; and McEwan, 32, 33, 243n55, 261n38, 269n20; "*Middlemarch* and Everybody," 239n22; and Morrison, 256n12; and Murdoch, xvi, 99–100, 112, 113, 261n38; and Nussbaum, 99, 100, 112, 256n13; *NW*, 262n42; "Read Better," 99–100, 106–107, 123, 255n6, 260n34; and the return to ethics, 2; and Scarry's *On Beauty and Being Just*, 96, 256–257n13, 263n51; on Shakespeare, 127–128, 132; on Shaw, 127, 128; on social value, 107, 111; "Speaking in Tongues," 126–132, 133, 262n41, 264n59; "Two Directions for the Novel," 259n26; and the unwritten *Fail Better*, 107, 123, 260n33; *White Teeth*, 258n25; and Woolf, 97, 256n8; on the world-making task of the novel, 266n10; "Zadie, Take Three" interview, 260n33, 262n49. *See also On Beauty* (Smith)
Smuts, Eckard, 269n19
social action, 10, 126
social change, 94, 148, 188
social constraint, 189, 190
social context, 97, 109, 256n7. *See also* place
social determination model, transition involving, 131–132
social discourse, 105, 107, 168, 182, 254n2, 259–260n29
social diversity, 13, 14, 20, 90, 112, 127–128, 130, 131, 133
social domination, ideological modes of, visibility of, 38
social formalism, xiii, 217
social good, xii, 10, 12, 20, 98, 174, 215
social identity, xvii, 20, 21, 33, 103, 109, 133, 157, 184, 187, 193, 217, 223
social justice, 112, 144, 146
social pluralism, 126, 129, 130, 131
social policy, issue with, 179, 278n28
social positionality, 21, 97, 106, 117, 118, 122, 128, 146, 177, 185, 189, 190, 203, 241n41, 260–261n37
social power, 3, 9, 43, 44, 53, 80, 129, 131, 146, 148, 214, 216
social reform, 39, 148, 176, 190
social relations, xiii, 18, 41, 63, 65, 81,

109, 135, 224, 236n9, 260–261n37, 271n26
social relativity, 130, 133
social revolution, harnessing fiction for, 92, 93
social transformation, harnessing fiction for, 92–93, 216
social value: Coetzee and, 172, 275n42; cultural view of the novel and, xi, xvii; D. A. Miller and, 43–44, 45, 176; defining feature of, 82; and James, xiii, 82, 181–182; and Lessing, 92; and Levithan, 14; and modernism, ix; new ethical theorists on, 181–182, 185; Nussbaum and, 175; poststructuralists and, 173; Smith on, 107, 111
social world, 39, 40, 44, 45, 134, 156, 215, 218, 246n65
sociological studies, recent findings of, skepticism toward, x
Sommer, Roy, 255n4, 258–259n25
speech act theory, 192, 205, 209
spiritualism, 42, 87, 88, 92, 93, 94, 99, 215, 216, 228. *See also* divinity
Spivak, Gayatri: and Brontë, 159, 274n32; and Coetzee's *Disgrace*, 210, 211–214; and Coetzee's *Elizabeth Costello*, 159; and Coetzee's *Foe*, 281n62; on counterfocalization, 212–214; "Ethics and Politics in Tagore, Coetzee, and Certain Scenes of Teaching," 211–215; on identification, 183; influence of, 181; and James, 213; and J. Hillis Miller, 211; and Levinas, 216
Steinbeck, John, 278n28
stereotypes: engaging in, 122, 255n4, 263n51; resistance to, 22–23
Sterne, Laurence, 139, 258n24
storytelling, notions of, 164, 168, 227, 283n7
storyworld, 44, 101, 109. *See also* autonomy; social world
Stowe, Harriett Beecher, xii, 38
stream of consciousness: Booth on, 102,

258n22; in Faulkner's *The Sound and the Fury*, 101, 102
Strehle, Susan, 250–251n37
Strout, Elizabeth, 6, 7
Su, John, 256n7
subaltern restriction, 152
subaltern subjects, 5, 24, 129, 146, 148, 158, 212, 213, 214, 265n4
subjectification, xii, 28, 30, 49, 77, 190–191, 204
subjectivity: Barthes on, 3, 232n2; and capitalism, 177; and Coetzee, 269n19; doubleness of, 216; and functionalism, 189, 216; James and, 62, 63, 65, 66, 72, 77, 204, 208; Jen on, 20, 22; J. Hillis Miller on, 208, 209, 211; and Kafka, 162; limits of, 12, 232n2; of literary text, 193, 215; and love, 112–113; restriction of, 216; retaining, 87–88, 99; and Smith, 122, 128. *See also* bias
surprise, capacity to, 33–34, 235n5
syllogisms, 144–145
symbolism, 52, 87, 92, 140, 235n5
sympathetic imagination, 142, 145–148, 149, 150–151, 153, 154, 165, 265n4, 269nn21–22, 270nn23–24
sympathy, xv, 12, 32, 45, 67, 93, 117, 145, 178, 183, 212, 246n67, 265n4, 268n17, 269n22, 278n27

Tanner, Tony, 248n19, 249n25
Tanner Lectures on Human Values, 254–255n2
Teahan, Sheila, 81–82, 252n47
textuality, 3, 13, 142, 195, 196, 197, 199, 204, 273–274n31
"textualterity," 277n7
textural change, experts in, 211
Thackeray, William Makepeace, 17, 19, 48, 50, 52
Thatcherism, 256n7
theme: and Coetzee, xiv–xv, 137; determinative for, 11; and James, 37, 71; Smith on, 262n49

third-person narration: in Coetzee's *Disgrace*, 212; and the doubleness of subjectivity, 216; and Gibson, 200; and James, 46, 196; J. Hillis Miller on, 208; in Morrison's *A Mercy*, 78; Robinson on, 234n4. *See also* free indirect discourse; omniscient narration; reflector-narrator; subjectivity
tolerance, 112, 113
Tolstoy, Leo, 228
tonality and vocabulary. *See* language
translation, 33, 64, 183, 184, 185, 186, 197, 215, 239n23, 241n40, 256n12, 266n9, 275n41, 279n43, 280n51
transmutation, creative act of, 72–73
Trilling, Lionel: and Forster, 179, 278n27; and humanism, 32, 111–112, 179; and James, 32, 176, 177, 179, 278n27; and love, 178–179; and moral realism, 278nn27–28; and Nussbaum, 178, 189, 280n47; social value and, 277–278n15; and Steinbeck, 278n28
Trollope, Anthony, 17, 19, 48, 50
truth claims, 11, 105, 120–121, 122, 133, 186, 259n29
truth telling, 92, 106, 132, 262n50
Tucker, Irene, 246–247n5

uncertainty, 75, 80, 113, 126, 127, 128, 132, 185, 191, 205, 214, 261n40, 267n11, 280n50
unconsciousness: apprehension of, 6; ideology and, 79, 173; power of, 49; racism and, 48, 52, 53, 54, 73, 74, 76, 77, 247n6
unverifiability, 186, 191, 207–208, 215, 279n43
Updike, John, 244n56
Utell, Janine, 244n57

Vadde, Aarthi, 275n39
Van Ghent, Dorothy, 252n48
variety, value of, xvii, 111, 178, 179, 182, 246n3

Victorian novel, 42, 43, 44
visual epistemology, 36
visual language, 40
vocabulary and tonality. *See* language
voice, in the African tradition, 164, 165; authoritative, 121, 258n25; Bakhtin and, 182, 185; Charon on, 283n8; and Coetzee, 162, 165, 214, 273n31, 274n37, 281n62; D. A. Miller on, 45; Gibson on, 201; homogenized, 21; and imperialism, 274n37; and James, 55, 182, 201; J. Hillis Miller on, 206; and Kafka, 162; of the playwright, 128; Robinson on, 233n1, 242n47; Smith on Obama and, 129, 130, 131, 132; and Smith's *On Beauty*, 121, 122
vulnerability, 73, 93, 163, 188–189, 191

Walker, Laura Savu, 245n61
Wall, Kathleen, 252n2
Wallace, David Foster, 2
Walters, Margaret, 247–248n14
Walton, Heather, 273–274n31
Wang, Qi, 245n64
Watt, Ian, 6
Weinstein, Cindy, 278n27
Weinstein, Philip, 257n21
Wells, H. G., 87
West, Paul, 268–269n17
Western tradition, 164, 165, 166, 167, 168, 225
Wharton, Edith, 8
What Maisie Knew (James), 182, 238n18; and the aesthetics of alterity, 62–70, 99, 244n56, 249n29, 250n34, 282n4; alterity project in, 54, 62, 249n31; idea for, source of, 70; Morrison on, 38, 48, 49, 50, 52–53, 54, 62–63, 73, 75, 77, 80, 169, 247n6; philosophical frameworks and competing models of ethicality in, 55–61, 82, 247–248n14, 248nn17–19, 248n21, 248–249nn23–26; preface to, 62–64, 65, 70–72, 73, 80, 82, 249n31; questions on, 56, 65, 73–74,

77; racial othering in, 52–53, 73, 74–77; readerly condemnation of, 55; reviewers of, criticism by, 80–82, 252n47; theory of literary knowledge applied to, 280n51
Whitman, Walt, 263n54
Wicomb, Zoë, 267n14
Willett, Cynthia, 271–272n26
Williams, Raymond, 86, 239n23, 262n47
Williams, William Carlos, 228
wisdom, 45, 121–122, 228, 260n29, 262–263n50, 267n11, 276–277n7
Wolfowitz, Paul, 211
Woloch, Alex, 234–235n5
women: as novel writers, Woolf on, 23–24; stereotyping, resistance to, 22–23; subaltern status of, 24, 157–58
Wood, Gaby, 233n13
Wood, James, 244n56
Wood, Michael, 280n51
Woolf, Virginia: on Austen, 88; *The Common Reader*, 86, 253n60; in comparison to Lubbock, 86–87; description of the novel, 2, 38, 97, 139, 167; Harris and, 93, 94, 215, 216; Jen and, 23, 24; on Lee, 91, 254n84; *To the Lighthouse*, 84; on Lubbock's *The Craft of Fiction*, 83, 254n84; and McEwan, 8, 31–32, 238n18; "Modern Fiction," 87; on morality, xii; Morrison and, xvi, 8; "Mr. Bennett and Mrs. Brown," 22–23, 87; *Mrs. Dalloway*, 8, 24, 84; on novel's generic purpose, 86–87; and perspectivalism, 103; on relationality, 90; renewed appreciation for, 2; on reportage, xv; *A Room of One's Own*, 275n39; Smith and, 97, 256n8; *The Waves*, 21, 23, 241n39, 258n24; "Women and Fiction," 23–24. *See also* cannibal art; character
Write (Canadian magazine), 11, 13
writer's block, 38
writing: James on, 72–73; justifications for, xi; Morrison on, 72–73; Smith on, 101, 108, 110. *See also* art of the novel; *specific novelists*
Wyatt, Jean, 250n36

Yeoh, Gilbert, 264–265n2

Zalewski, Daniel, 242n48
Žižek, Slavoj, 240n38

Christine Hong, *A Violent Peace: Race, U.S. Militarism, and Cultures of Democratization in Cold War Asia and the Pacific*

Sarah Brouillette, *UNESCO and the Fate of the Literary*

Sophie Seita, *Provisional Avant-Gardes: Little Magazine Communities from Dada to Digital*

Guy Davidson, *Categorically Famous: Literary Celebrity and Sexual Liberation in 1960s America*

Joseph Jonghyun Jeon, *Vicious Circuits: Korea's IMF Cinema and the End of the American Century*

Lytle Shaw, *Narrowcast: Poetry and Audio Research*

Stephen Schryer, *Maximum Feasible Participation: American Literature and the War on Poverty*

Margaret Ronda, *Remainders: American Poetry at Nature's End*

Jasper Bernes, *The Work of Art in the Age of Deindustrialization*

Annie McClanahan, *Dead Pledges: Debt, Crisis, and Twenty-First-Century Culture*

Amy Hungerford, *Making Literature Now*

J. D. Connor, *The Studios After the Studios: Neoclassical Hollywood (1970–2010)*

Michael Trask, *Camp Sites: Sex, Politics, and Academic Style in Postwar America*

Loren Glass, *Counterculture Colophon: Grove Press, the "Evergreen Review," and the Incorporation of the Avant-Garde*

Michael Szalay, *Hip Figures: A Literary History of the Democratic Party*

Jared Gardner, *Projections: Comics and the History of Twenty-First-Century Storytelling*

Jerome Christensen, *America's Corporate Art: The Studio Authorship of Hollywood Motion Pictures*

The authorized representative in the EU for product safety and compliance is:
Mare Nostrum Group
B.V Doelen 72
4831 GR Breda
The Netherlands

www.ingramcontent.com/pod-product-compliance
Lightning Source LLC
Chambersburg PA
CBHW030604230426
43661CB00053B/1843